# ∼ *Antecedent Control* ∼

# ~ *Antecedent Control* ~
## Innovative Approaches
## to Behavioral Support

*edited by*

**James K. Luiselli, Ed.D.**

*and*

**Michael J. Cameron, M.A.**

*The May Institute, Inc.*
*Norwood, Massachusetts*

·P A U L·H·
BROOKES
PUBLISHING Cº

Baltimore • London • Toronto • Sydney

**Paul H. Brookes Publishing Co.**
Post Office Box 10624
Baltimore, Maryland 21285-0624

www.pbrookes.com

Typeset by PRO-Image Corporation, York, Pennsylvania.
Manufactured in the United States of America by
Versa Press, East Peoria, Illinois.

The case studies appearing in Chapter 12 represent actual people and circumstances and are published with the individuals' written permission. Names have been changed to protect identities. The other case studies described in this book are composites based on the authors' experiences; these case studies do not represent the lives or experiences of specific individuals, and no implications should be inferred.

The copyright for the software program depicted in Chapter 6 is held by Raymond G. Romanczyk.

**Library of Congress Cataloging-in-Publication Data**

Antecedent control : innovative approaches to behavioral support /
    edited by James K. Luiselli and Michael J. Cameron.
        p.        cm.
    Includes bibliographical references and index.
    ISBN 1-55766-334-3
    1. Mentally handicapped—Behavior modification.   2. Autistic
children—Behavior modification.   3. Behavioral assessment.
I. Luiselli, James K.   II. Cameron, Michael J., 1957–        .
RC451.4.M57A58      1998
616.85'8806—dc21                                                        98-19004
                                                                              CIP

British Library Cataloguing in Publication data are available from the British Library.

# ~ *Contents* ~

v

# ～ *Contributors* ～

## Editors

**James K. Luiselli, Ed.D.**
Director
The May Center for Applied
  Research
The May Institute, Inc.
220 Norwood Park South, Suite 204
Norwood, Massachusetts 02062

**Michael J. Cameron, M.A.**
Assistant Director
The May Center for Applied
  Research
The May Institute, Inc.
220 Norwood Park South, Suite 204
Norwood, Massachusetts 02062

## Contributors

**Jennifer M. Asmus, Ph.D.**
Clinical Director Biobehavioral
  Inpatient Service
University Hospital
The University of Iowa
100 Hawkins Drive
Psychology Department
Room 349 HS
Iowa City, Iowa 52242

**Philip K. Axtell, B.S.**
Research Specialist
Commonwealth Institute for Child
  and Family Studies
Medical College of Virginia
Virginia Commonwealth University
Box 980506
Richmond, Virginia 23298
Adolescent Counselor
WOODS Program
Virginia Baptist Children's Home
  and Family Services
Roanoke, Virginia

**Wendy K. Berg, M.A.**
Senior Research Assistant
University Hospital School
The University of Iowa
100 Hawkins Drive
Room 251
Iowa City, Iowa 52242

**Jane I. Carlson, M.A.**
Department of Psychology
State University of New York at
  Stony Brook
Stony Brook, New York 11794
Developmental Disabilities Institute
99 Hollywood Drive
Smithtown, New York 11787

**Edward G. Carr, Ph.D.**
Professor
Department of Psychology
State University of New York at
  Stony Brook
Stony Brook, New York 11794

**Cynthia M. Carter, M.A.**
Educational Therapist and
  Researcher
Department of Educational
  Psychology
University of California at Santa
  Barbara
Santa Barbara, California 93106

**Linda J. Cooper, Ed.S., Ph.D.**
Assistant Research Scientist
Department of Pediatrics-2525JCP
The University of Iowa Hospitals
  and Clinics
200 Hawkins Drive
Iowa City, Iowa 52242

**Anthony J. Cuvo, Ph.D.**
Professor
Rehabilitation Institute
Southern Illinois University at
    Carbondale
Mailcode 4609
Carbondale, Illinois 62901

**Paula K. Davis, Ph.D.**
Associate Professor
Rehabilitation Institute
Southern Illinois University at
    Carbondale
Mailcode 4609
Carbondale, Illinois 62901

**Glen Dunlap, Ph.D.**
Professor
University of South Florida
13301 Bruce B. Downs Boulevard
Tampa, Florida 33612

**Cynthia R. Ellis, M.D.**
Assistant Professor of Pediatrics and
    Psychiatry
Commonwealth Institute for Child
    and Family Studies
Medical College of Virginia
Virginia Commonwealth University
Box 980506
Richmond, Virginia 23298

**Jay W. Harding, Ed.S.**
Program Associate
University Hospital School
The University of Iowa
100 Hawkins Drive
Iowa City, Iowa 52242

**Craig H. Kennedy, Ph.D.**
Associate Professor
Department of Special Education
Peabody College of Vanderbilt
    University
Post Office Box 328
Nashville, Tennessee 37203

**Lee Kern, Ph.D.**
Assistant Professor
University of Pennsylvania
3405 Civic Center Boulevard
Philadelphia, Pennsylvania 19104

**Lynn Kern Koegel, Ph.D.**
Clinical Director
Autism Research and Training
    Center
C/C/S Psychology Clinic
Graduate School of Education
University of California at Santa
    Barbara
Santa Barbara, California 93106

**Robert L. Koegel, Ph.D.**
Professor and Director
Autism Research and Training
    Center
C/C/S Psychology Clinic
Graduate School of Education
University of California at Santa
    Barbara
Santa Barbara, California 93106

**Nancy A. Langdon, M.A.**
Doctoral Student
Department of Psychology
State University of New York at
    Stony Brook
Stony Brook, New York 11794

**Darlene Magito-McLaughlin, M.A.**
Doctoral Student
Department of Psychology
State University of New York at
    Stony Brook
Stony Brook, New York 11794

**Melissa Maguire, M.A.**
Vice President
Joseph P. Kennedy Foundation
305 Whitney Street
Leominster, Massachusetts 01453

**Russell W. Maguire, Ph.D.**
Clinical Psychologist
Greater Lawrence Educational
    Collaborative
14 Pemberton Way
Lawrence, Massachusetts 01840

**Amy L. Matthews, Ph.D.**
Postdoctoral Fellow
Children's Health Council
700 Sand Hill Road
Palo Alto, California 94042

**Jennifer J. McComas, Ph.D.**
Assistant Professor
Department of Psychology
Queens College/CUNY
65-30 Kissena Boulevard
Flushing, New York 11367

**Kim A. Meyer, Ph.D.**
Assistant Professor
Department of Psychology
East Carolina University
Greenville, North Carolina 32213

**Raymond G. Miltenberger, Ph.D.**
Professor of Psychology
Department of Psychology
115 Minard Hall
North Dakota State University
Fargo, North Dakota 58105

**Freddy A. Paniagua, Ph.D.**
Professor
Department of Psychiatry and
  Behavioral Sciences
University of Texas Medical Branch
Galveston, Texas 77555

**Patrick R. Progar, Ph.D.**
Case Manager
Children's Seashore House
3405 Civic Center Boulevard
Philadelphia, Pennsylvania 19104

**Raymond G. Romanczyk, Ph.D.**
Professor of Clinical Psychology
Psychology Department
State University of New York at
  Binghamton
Post Office Box 6000
Binghamton, New York 13902

**Muriel D. Saunders, Ph.D.**
Assistant Research Professor
Schiefelbusch Institute for Life Span
  Studies
2601 Gabriel
Parsons, Kansas 67357

**Richard R. Saunders, Ph.D.**
Senior Scientist
Schiefelbusch Institute for Life Span
  Studies
2601 Gabriel
Parsons, Kansas 67357

**Jeff Sigafoos, Ph.D.**
Associate Professor
Fred and Eleanor Schonell Special
  Education Research Centre
The University of Queensland
Brisbane, Queensland 4072
AUSTRALIA

**Nirbhay N. Singh, Ph.D.**
Professor of Psychiatry and
  Pediatrics
Medical College of Virginia
Virginia Commonwealth University
515 North 10th Street
Richmond, Virginia 23219

**Carole M. Van Camp, B.S.**
Children's Seashore House
3405 Civic Center Boulevard
Philadelphia, Pennsylvania 19104

**Timothy R. Vollmer, Ph.D.**
Associate Professor of Behavioral
  Psychology
University of Pennsylvania School of
  Medicine
3405 Civic Center Boulevard
Philadelphia, Pennsylvania 19104

**David P. Wacker, Ph.D.**
Professor of Pediatrics and Special
  Education
University Hospital School
The University of Iowa
100 Hawkins Drive
Room 251
Iowa City, Iowa 52242

**Scott C. Yarbrough, M.A.**
Doctoral Student
Department of Psychology
State University of New York at
  Stony Brook
Stony Brook, New York 11794

# ~ *Preface* ~

Like most of our colleagues, we emerged from graduate school training and clinical supervision in applied behavior analysis with a solid grounding in operant conditioning methodology. We learned a great deal about schedules of reinforcement, the influence of consequences on behavior, and multiple approaches toward "contingency management." In interventions for challenging behaviors, techniques such as differential reinforcement of other behavior, time out, and overcorrection were popular; and they were employed frequently in educational and habilitative settings. Much of our work incorporated these and similar consequence-based strategies, often with good results and positive reactions from journal editors.

The field of applied behavior analysis has changed in many ways since our earlier schooling and experiences. A very significant outcome has been the realization of the importance of antecedent control from both theoretical and clinical perspectives. In fact, there has been an increasing trend in research reports concerning antecedent control and its relevance to the understanding and intervention for challenging behaviors. This focus encompasses methods to prevent the occurrence of problem responses, to promote replacement skills, and to enhance the effectiveness of positive reinforcement. In addition, new conceptualizations regarding the emergence and maintenance of challenging behaviors have developed from the study of antecedent variables such as establishing operations and their interactions with personal learning histories. This orientation does not undermine the critical role of consequence events because, after all, antecedent control is established through the pairing of stimulus events with reinforcement and punishment contingencies. Instead, it emphasizes the selection, manipulation, and management of antecedent conditions as an alternative to more "traditional" methods of behavioral intervention.

This book addresses the topic of antecedent control in the education of, habilitation of, and intervention for people with developmental disabilities. We view the chapters as a presentation and synthesis of theoretical, conceptual, methodological, and evaluative issues composing contemporary knowledge of antecedent control, behavior

xi

disorders, and therapeutic decision making. Each author selected for this volume brings the unique perspective of a clinician, educator, or researcher who has embraced the concepts of antecedent control in his or her work with children, adolescents, and adults who have developmental disabilities and challenging behaviors.

We are indebted to the staff of Paul H. Brookes Publishing Company who assisted us so diligently from conception of the book through its completion. To the authors, we offer our gratitude for preparing informative chapters that are both timely and comprehensive. Both of us were privileged to know and work with professionals who taught us the intricacies of stimulus control; and for that we thank the late David Marholin, II, Warren Steinman, and Paul Touchette (JKL), and the late Larry Stoddard (MJC). Finally, this book is dedicated to our wives and children who always teach us the most about human behavior and keep us focused on the joy of living and the pleasure that comes from contributing to the welfare of others. Thanks for always being there.

*To Dr. Tracy Evans Luiselli and Gabrielle Anna Luiselli*
*JKL*

*To Susan A. Ainsleigh and Joshua Cameron*
*MJC*

# ～ *Antecedent Control* ～

# ~ *I* ~
## *Introduction*

# ~ *1* ~

# *Two Perspectives on Antecedent Control*
## Molecular and Molar

Edward G. Carr, Jane I. Carlson, Nancy A. Langdon,
Darlene Magito-McLaughlin, and Scott C. Yarbrough

From the beginning of behavior analysis, basic research in the discipline was always concerned with the theoretical and empirical study of antecedent variables (Skinner, 1938). Stimulus control issues remained a dominant theme in the operant conditioning literature for decades (Mostofsky, 1965), continuing with such present-day topics as stimulus equivalence (Sidman, 1990). In contrast, the applied behavior analysis literature, particularly that portion concerned with challenging behavior, has tended historically to emphasize the role of response consequences, in terms of both the theoretical analysis of the functional variables maintaining challenging behavior (Carr, 1977) and the intervention strategies designed to eliminate such behavior (Axelrod & Apsche, 1983). In the late 1990s, however, there has been an accelerating interest in the role of antecedent variables in understanding challenging behavior and in planning for its remediation (Carr, Reeve, & Magito-McLaughlin, 1996). This interest is transforming how we think about challenging behavior and, therefore, what constitutes meaningful intervention.

## DEFINING TWO APPROACHES TO ANTECEDENT CONTROL

The published literature can be conceptualized as embodying two different approaches to antecedent control: a *molecular approach* that is

Preparation of this chapter was supported in part by Grant No. H133G200098 from the U.S. Department of Education.

microanalytic in nature and a *molar approach* that is macroanalytic in nature. The former has a long and distinctive history in the research literature, but the latter has only begun to fully emerge in the late 1990s. These two approaches generally differ in terms of where they take place and what they involve.

The molecular approach often (but not always) takes place in controlled settings in which there is an attempt to simulate aspects of the natural environment. These settings may include university-based laboratories, special tutorial rooms, hospital wards, and clinics. A premium is placed on rigor, control, and the precise specification of critical stimulus parameters that are relevant to the control of challenging behavior. In contrast, the molar approach takes place in natural settings such as the home, integrated school, workplace, and community. A premium is placed on normalization, community integration, and enhancing global aspects of lifestyle.

The molecular approach is concerned with the impact of discrete antecedent stimuli such as task demands, the sequelae of negative feedback, types of prompts, presence of preferred reinforcers that are temporarily inaccessible, and a host of other easily operationalized and temporally distinct stimulus variables. The molar approach is concerned with broad, continuous variables involving social, biological, and physical contexts (Carr, 1994). Examples of these variables include friendship patterns and family support (social context), physical illness and physiological deprivation states (biological context), and architectural arrangement of living spaces (physical context). Many of these variables (e.g., friendship patterns) are not easily operationalized, yet their potential for strengthening repertoires of positive behavior is considerable (Hurley-Geffner, 1995). A comparison of these two approaches, molecular and molar, constitutes the substantive focus of this chapter.

## DIFFERING PURPOSES OF ASSESSMENT AND INTERVENTION

### Assessment

This section contrasts the purposes of assessment using both the molecular and molar approach.

***Molecular Approach*** The purpose of molecular assessment is to identify the discrete antecedent stimuli that trigger (i.e., are discriminative for) challenging behavior. The identification of such stimuli often provides critical information with respect to what function (i.e., purpose) the challenging behavior may serve. This information, in turn, can later be used in intervention planning. In illustration, consider a young girl with autism who bangs her head and bites her hands until she bleeds. The key question in antecedent molecular assessment is as follows: What stimuli trigger self-injury? The purpose of the assessment is fulfilled when one establishes, for example, that self-injury occurs frequently when the girl is given nonpreferred task demands (e.g., her mother says, "Clean your room") and rarely when given preferred demands (e.g., her mother says, "Let's bake a cake") or no demands. Furthermore, this information becomes especially important when it is demonstrated that self-injury in the presence of the antecedent demands causes her mother to withdraw the nonpreferred task (e.g., "Okay, you're too upset now. We'll finish cleaning up later"). In this instance, the pattern of responding suggests that specific antecedent stimuli (nonpreferred task demands) are aversive and, perhaps, that self-injury serves an escape or avoidance function, permitting the child to get out of having to complete the task.

Molecular assessment has the related purpose of identifying antecedent stimuli at a level of specificity sufficient for effective intervention planning. Thus, in the illustration given, it would be important to know the specific trigger for challenging behavior. That is, it may not simply be the presentation of the nonpreferred task per se that is critical. Rather, it may be the negative feedback associated with poor task performance (e.g., "No, you need to clean up better than that") that triggers challenging behavior, or it may be physical prompting (e.g., "Here, I'll hold your hand, and we'll make the bed together"), or it may be how quickly or slowly the task is paced (e.g., "Come on, you can clean faster than that") that determines the level of challenging behavior. The different critical features just described each lead to different intervention considerations. Antecedent assessment that results in this level of specificity has fulfilled its intervention planning purpose.

Finally, a less researched but equally important purpose of molecular assessment is to identify discrete antecedent stimuli that reliably evoke specific, constructive behaviors (Cooper, Wacker, Sasso, Reimers, & Donn, 1990). Especially critical is the identification of those antecedents that control positive behaviors that can potentially compete with, and ultimately replace, challenging behavior.

**Molar Approach**  The purpose of molar assessment is to identify broad contextual variables that effectively support constructive, adaptive behaviors that can contribute to a normalized and satisfying lifestyle in the community. Of greatest concern is the contextual assessment (Stark & Faulkner, 1996) of living environments (e.g., community residences versus institutions), social relationships (e.g., participation in a friendship network versus isolation), educational placement (e.g., integrated versus segregated classrooms), workplace (e.g., supported employment versus sheltered workshops), and leisure situations (e.g., self-selected activities versus externally imposed routines).

A key purpose served by molar assessment is the elucidation of variables that promote a good fit among characteristics of the individual for whom services are being provided, the people responsible for implementing those services, and properties of the system in which the intervention will occur (Albin, Lucyshyn, Horner, & Flannery, 1996). Consistent with the constructive, prosocial orientation of molar assessment, it is first critical to determine an individual's strengths and competencies. As an example, a man diagnosed as having mental retardation and being unable to speak may nonetheless have some facility for sign language. He also may engage in stereotypies involving sifting sand and lining up objects in neat rows. If he were to be placed in a greenhouse work situation with staff who understood basic sign language, then these behavior characteristics would be capitalized on to enhance goodness-of-fit. Specifically, his communicative attempts would be understood by others and theirs by him. Furthermore, his preexisting behavioral stereotypies could be marshaled to perfect skills such as filling pots with earth and seeds and aligning the finished products in neat rows for transport and sale. In contrast, if he were to be placed with nonsigning staff in a fast-food restaurant, he would (communicatively) neither understand nor be understood, and his stereotypies might well interfere with his performing tasks such as picking up trash and cleaning the floor. The former situation, a good fit, would support constructive work relationships and satisfactory work performance. The latter situation, a bad fit, could easily engender frustration and subsequent challenging behavior. The significant difference between these two outcomes underlines the importance of conducting a molar assessment to assess the communicative competencies of the man with disabilities and those of his co-workers as well as to assess the behavior characteristics of this man and the work demands of the situation in which he must perform.

### Intervention

The following sections demonstrate that there are clear differences between the purposes of intervention at the molecular and molar levels.

*Molecular Approach*   The purpose of intervention at the molecular level is to prevent or reduce challenging behaviors as well as to increase the level of competing positive behaviors through manipulation of specific antecedent stimuli identified during assessment. Reduction of challenging behavior per se constitutes the main focus of intervention. The prevention purpose is served when the intervention agent eliminates the offending stimulus. For example, if physical prompting evokes aggression, then that type of prompt may be eliminated as an instructional tool for a particular individual. The programmed absence of physical prompts may effectively prevent future episodes of aggression during the learning situation. The reduction purpose is served when features of the offending stimulus are altered or the method of presentation is changed to bring about a decrease in the rate of an ongoing challenging behavior. Thus, if nonpreferred demands evoke aggression, then gradually fading in the frequency of those demands during the instructional situation or, perhaps, changing the rate at which they are presented could produce a progressive decline in the frequency of aggressive behavior. Finally, the purpose of increasing the level of competing positive behaviors is served when those stimuli identified through assessment as controlling constructive behaviors are systematically introduced into the problem situation. Thus, if jokes and funny stories that regularly evoke smiling and laughing (but not self-injury) are introduced into a demand situation that regularly evokes self-injury, one may find that the introduction of the humorous stimuli evokes competing nonchallenging behaviors (laughter) that apparently compete with self-injury, producing a decline in the frequency of that behavior (Carr, Newsom, & Binkoff, 1976).

**Molar Approach**    The purpose of intervention using a molar approach is to introduce the individual into those living environments, social networks, educational sites, jobsites, and leisure settings that have been identified as supporting a normalized and satisfying lifestyle in the community. Although reduction of challenging behavior often may occur as a consequence of this strategy, it constitutes a secondary purpose. The main purpose is the attainment of a normalized, satisfying lifestyle—that is, an improvement in quality of life.

Because placing an individual in integrated community settings is, by itself, no guarantee of success, the second purpose of a molar approach is to use the assessment data on goodness-of-fit to alter various contexts in ways that make enhancement of constructive and satisfying lifestyles more probable. First, if an individual's behavioral repertoire is inadequate for him or her to take full advantage of opportunities afforded by broad contexts, then molar interventions must be designed to teach generalized behavioral repertoires that are relevant to a variety of home, school, job, social, and leisure situations as needed. Second, if the people with whom the individual must interact (e.g., parents, teachers, co-workers, classmates, potential friends) have behavioral repertoires that are inadequate for supporting community living opportunities, then molar interventions are designed to educate, train, or replace relevant people. Third, if the social, physical, or bio-logical dimensions of community contexts diminish the effectiveness of the individual in allowing him or her to take advantage of im-proved lifestyle opportunities, or the ability of others to support the individual in attaining these goals, then molar interventions are de-signed to alter the system itself. Such alterations may include changes in scheduling, curriculum, personnel allocation, linkages among var-ious components of the service delivery system, and even altering the stated goals (philosophy) of the system (Emerson, McGill, & Mansell, 1994). The purpose of the three strategies just described is to enhance goodness-of-fit between the individual and the community situation in which he or she must function. This enhancement helps achieve the primary goal of attaining a normalized and satisfying lifestyle for the individual involved as well as the secondary goal of minimizing the sorts of chronic frustrations that are often the source of serious challenging behavior.

## DIFFERING METHODS AND RESULTS OF ASSESSMENT AND INTERVENTION

### Assessment

Clear differences also exist with respect to the methods and results associated with the molecular and molar approaches. The following sections describe some of the major differences.

**Molecular Approach**  Three methods are commonly used to address the purpose of identifying trigger stimuli for challenging be-havior: interview, description, and functional analysis (Carr et al., 1994). These three methods are often used sequentially.

Molecular antecedent assessment typically begins with an inter-view of key informants (e.g., teachers, parents). Informants are asked to identify the circumstances that predict the occurrence and nonoc-currence of challenging behavior. In illustration, a teacher may note that a child becomes aggressive when given a difficult vocabulary task but not at other times. Thus, "vocabulary task" is identified as a pos-sible trigger for challenging behavior. At this point, the assessment continues via direct observation (descriptive phase). The information derived from the interview is used to guide when and where the de-scriptive observations will be made—in this case, during periods when vocabulary tasks are given in the classroom versus periods when those tasks are absent. Observations typically involve the use of data collection forms organized around events that precede and follow challenging behavior (O'Neill, Horner, Albin, Storey, & Sprague, 1990).

One outcome is that the assessment yields comparative data on the level of challenging behavior in the presence versus absence of the trigger stimuli (e.g., vocabulary tasks). It is important to note that direct observation affords an objective opportunity to validate (or disconfirm) the more subjective information on trigger stimuli gathered during the interview.

Descriptive observation often yields more detailed information about trigger stimuli than that typically obtained through interview alone, thereby helping to address another purpose of molecular assessment, namely, identifying triggers for challenging behavior at a level of specificity useful for effective intervention planning. Two common methods of detailed assessment involve the use of A-B-C data sheets (Carr et al., 1994; Gardner & Sovner, 1994; O'Neill et al., 1990) and formal data recording (Lalli, Browder, Mace, & Brown, 1993; Lerman & Iwata, 1993).

A-B-C data sheets provide a direct observational record of specific antecedent trigger stimuli (A), the behaviors evoked by these stimuli (B), and the environmental consequences that follow the behavior (C). With respect to the central topic of interest here—namely, antecedents—the observer first notes the occurrence of the challenging behavior on the sheet. Then, the observer notes the stimuli that immediately preceded the behavior. With this simple methodology, it is frequently possible to observe specific dimensions of trigger stimuli not mentioned during the interview. Using the previous illustration, it may be that "vocabulary tasks," per se, are not the critical factor. Rather, when tasks evoke incorrect responding, negative feedback is given. Following such feedback, aggression occurs. Thus, it is the negative feedback—and not the tasks—that constitutes the trigger stimulus for aggression. The absence of such feedback following incorrect responding does not result in aggressive behavior. Careful, systematic observation in task situations can yield information on a host of specific triggers such as type of aversive demands, gestural prompts, physical prompts, negative feedback, and generalized conditioned aversive stimuli (Carr & Carlson, 1993; Kemp & Carr, 1995). In contrast to A-B-C data sheets, formal data recording involves the documentation of the exact temporal relationships between antecedents and behavior, often through the use of time-sampling methodologies. Meticulous formal recording also permits identification of specific stimulus triggers for challenging behavior. With these procedures, one can identify, for example, how antecedents are temporally related to type of task (e.g., personal care, daily living, vocational, academic), task structure (e.g., one-to-one versus group), play structure (e.g., teacher–child, child–child), and the precise level of challenging behavior associated with the various antecedents that are not documented by A-B-C assessment alone (Lalli et al., 1993).

Another reason that direct observation (description) is necessary is that, sometimes, the trigger stimuli for challenging behavior have been eliminated by caregivers who have learned that certain situations reliably evoke problems. Because these triggers are no longer present, informants may not identify them during an interview. Only when direct observations are made over a long enough period of time during which the trigger stimuli are inadvertently reintroduced does it become apparent that certain antecedents, not mentioned during the interview, are significant determinants of challenging behavior. These "child effects" (Carr, Taylor, & Robinson, 1991; McConnachie & Carr, 1997; Taylor & Carr, 1992a, 1992b) virtually necessitate direct observation as part of molecular assessment. In illustration, the teacher may present a vocabulary task and a motor task to a child. The former task is followed reliably by severe punching of the teacher; the latter, by cheerful compliance. Over time, the teacher may drop the vocabulary task from the curriculum and retain the motor task because, in operant terms, the former task is associated with the teacher's instructional efforts being punished and the latter task is associated with the teacher's instructional efforts being reinforced. If, at the time of the interview, the vocabulary task has not been part of the curriculum for many months, the teacher may not mention it as a trigger. Nonetheless, if during direct observation a substitute teacher is seen to present the task with disastrous results, then the vocabulary task will be identified as a significant trigger for aggressive behavior.

There are three results obtained from descriptive molecular assessment. First, both general and specific triggers for challenging behavior are identified. Second, the level and type of challenging behavior (e.g., aggression, self-injury, tantrums, property destruction) evoked by various triggers are documented. Finally, and more speculatively, tentative hypotheses concerning the function of challenging behavior are derived from the database. In illustration, a replicable correlation between presence versus absence of negative feedback and subsequent aggression leads to the hypothesis that the aggressive behavior may be escape motivated. Of course, this hypothesis is considerably strengthened if direct observation also shows that the teacher, for example, withdraws the negative feedback (consequence) in the face of aggressive behavior. An escape hypothesis, however, might well be formulated even in the absence of corroborating data involving consequences. Likewise, self-injurious behavior that occurs following initiation of independent (nonsocial) activity but is absent following the initiation of one-to-one activity between parent and child, or teacher and child, would typically generate the hypothesis that self-injury is likely an attention-seeking behavior. Hypothesis generation resulting from molecular assessment often leads directly to intervention planning, although it may sometimes be followed by additional experimental analyses.

Functional (experimental) analysis involves systematic manipulation of specific trigger stimuli to see whether they influence challenging behavior. In other words, functional analysis constitutes a formal experiment, in contrast to passive direct observation. Thus, if interview and direct observation suggested a strong positive association between the presence of difficult demands and aggressive behavior, one could confirm that a causal relationship existed between these two variables by manipulating the level of demands (Carr & Durand, 1985; Carr & Newsom, 1985; Carr, Newsom, & Binkoff, 1976, 1980). Thus, one might systematically introduce difficult demands for a few days, then switch to easy demands for a few more days, and then switch back to difficult demands, and so forth. By alternating between easy and difficult demands a number of times, one might observe a pattern in which aggressive behavior increased and decreased as difficult and easy demands, respectively, were introduced. This pattern would constitute a clear demonstration that there was a causal link between some aspect of the difficult demand situation and the level of aggressive behavior.

Although it is true that the combination of interview and direct observation (description) is frequently sufficient for effective intervention planning (Carr et al., 1994), there are instances in which successful intervention outcomes subsequently are not obtained. These instances constitute the main incentive, from the standpoint of clinical application, for following the interview and descriptive phases of molecular assessment with a formal functional analysis. In illustration, following interview and description, one may hypothesize that aggression is an escape-motivated behavior occurring in response to difficult demands. However, the intervention constructed from this hypothesis fails. At this point, it is customary to repeat the interview and descriptive phases in an attempt to look more closely at the demand situation. One might find, at this time, that not only are difficult demands present during episodes of aggressive behavior but so are negative feedback and physical prompts. Thus, there is a perfect confound, at the descriptive level, among three stimulus variables: presence of difficult demands, negative feedback, and physical prompts. Careful direct observation, by itself, may not be able to disentangle the unique contribution made by each of the three antecedent variables to the instigation of aggressive behavior. The only way to be certain about how each antecedent influences aggression would be to manipulate each systematically—that is, to carry out a functional analysis (experiment). Thus, the presence of several highly correlated trigger stimuli during direct observation and/or the failure to obtain good outcomes following an intervention that is based on the interview and descriptive data alone generally serve to cue the assessor that a full-fledged functional analysis is in order.

Often more than one functional analysis may have to be conducted (Carr, 1994). For example, the first analysis may demonstrate that the behavior problem is linked to the trigger stimuli (demands) due to escape rather than attention variables. However, the trigger stimuli may have many dimensions (e.g., varying in duration, quality). Therefore, an additional analysis is carried out to tease apart and identify what aspect of the demand situation is critical. This strategy is clearly evident in a study by Dunlap, Kern-Dunlap, Clarke, and Robbins (1991), in which it was demonstrated that the difference between gross versus fine motor tasks was the significant factor influencing the display of challenging behavior. In summary, then, molecular assessment may take the form of a sequentially refined series of functional analyses that results in the gradual and progressive identification of specific trigger stimuli whose demonstrated influence on challenging behavior become a critical consideration in intervention planning.

Finally, as noted previously, an additional purpose of molecular assessment is to identify triggers for appropriate behavior. In principle, one could apply the interview, descriptive, and functional analysis procedures already outlined in order to identify specific stimuli in the physical and social environment that reliably evoke appropriate behavior. In actuality, there is very little systematic literature that focuses on the identification of triggers for appropriate behavior within the context of dealing with challenging behavior. A study by Cooper et al. (1990), however, made clear why this type of assessment might be important. The authors used functional analysis procedures to identify, on a case-by-case basis, how the presence of specific tasks and toys could evoke high levels of appropriate behavior such as reading, following directions, making eye contact with the speaker, working on assigned tasks, and asking relevant questions. The enhancement of appropriate behavior achieved under certain stimulus conditions was correlated with decreases in a variety of aggressive and destructive behaviors. This demonstration suggests that gathering information about trigger stimuli for appropriate behavior could prove fruitful for the subsequent design of situations that are correlated with minimal levels of challenging behavior.

**Molar Approach** The purpose of the molar approach to assessment is to identify contexts that support adaptive behavior in key domains related to living arrangements, social relationships, education, work, and leisure. The focus is not on identifying triggers for challenging behavior, as in the case of molecular assessment.

One aspect of context that is critical, and therefore must be assessed first, pertains to the individual's needs and competencies. Needs are roughly synonymous with reinforcers. Thus, a primary question concerns what it is that an individual wants in different situations (i.e., what stimuli function as reinforcers?). This question can be answered indirectly by soliciting judgments from key informants (e.g., Newton, Ard, & Horner, 1993) or directly by measuring approach responses to a variety of potential reinforcers (e.g., Fisher et al., 1992). A combination of interview, direct observation, and experimental manipulation provides information on the individual's material and social needs (reinforcers). Additional assessment, however, is required to determine whether the individual's competencies are adequate for satisfying his or her needs. In illustration, one may find that playing on swings constitutes a powerful reinforcer for a young boy with autism. Nonetheless, this need may not be met if the boy cannot communicate his desire to play on the swings to his mother or teacher. There is a gap between his needs and his competencies. Competency assessment is a well-developed area offering many protocols to identify skills relevant to daily living, social relationships, education, work, and leisure (Ford et al., 1989; Snell, 1993).

An individual's needs, as well as competencies to meet those needs, constitute only one aspect of context that needs to be assessed within a molar approach. Another aspect relates to assessing the performance requirements within the person's home, social, education, work, and leisure environments. These performance requirements are partially determined by the behavior characteristics of the service providers, family members, friends, and co-workers who interact with the individual with disabilities, and partially by the structure and organization of the systems that define the various environments in which he or she must function. Consider again the young boy with autism who enjoys playing on the swings. If his school day is structured so that only minimal time is allotted for playground activities, then the school environment itself mitigates against the boy's gaining access to a strongly preferred reinforcer (i.e., the environment is organized in such a way as to fail to meet the boy's needs). Thus, whether the boy has good communication skills (i.e., can request playground time) is irrelevant because opportunities are lacking for gaining access to the desired activity. In a related situation, teachers may demand high levels of academic performance prior to permitting adequate access to playground activity. If the child fails to meet his teacher's high standards, then the teacher may declare that he has not "earned" more than a minimal amount of playground time. In this case, strict performance requirements sharply reduce the number of opportunities available for gaining access to playground activities, including the swings. Assessment of provider characteristics, as well as the structure and organization of systems, is emerging as an important topic in the published literature. A framework for developing methods to assess these molar variables is implicit in discussions of environmental design (Brown, 1991; McGill, Emerson, & Mansell, 1994; Sailor, 1996), structuring support services (Albin et al., 1996; Hedeen, Ayres, Meyer, & Waite, 1996), and selection of goals for community living (Ford et al., 1989).

The results of the molar assessment just outlined permit measurement of the degree of discrepancy between an individual's needs and competencies, on the one hand, and performance requirements set by service providers (support people) and organizational structures, on the other hand. If the gap between the two is great, then the likelihood is low that an individual will have his or her needs met. In lay language, we would say that the individual is likely to be frustrated a lot of the time, a situation that facilitates the display of serious challenging behavior. In behavioral terms, we would say that much socially appropriate behavior would likely be on extinction, which in turn could produce "bursts" of undesirable aggressive and self-injurious behaviors—behaviors that may occasionally be effective in generating greater access to the desired reinforcer. Hence, when goodness-of-fit between people and their environments is low, challenging behavior can be expected to be high (Schalock & Jensen, 1986). Molar assessment identifies necessary, positive contextual features, thereby permitting, as shall be seen shortly, the design of constructive approaches that enhance competencies and/or the restructuring of performance requirements with a view to preempting future occurrences of challenging behavior through the use of multicomponent, proactive intervention strategies.

## Intervention

Finally, we examine the major differences between the methods and results associated with the molecular and molar approaches.

**Molecular Approach** The assessment information on trigger stimuli for challenging behavior can be used to design antecedent intervention strategies that address the dual purposes of preventing and reducing challenging behavior. One strategy is simply to eliminate the offending stimulus altogether. For example, if instructional demands have been identified as a trigger stimulus for challenging behavior, then one can produce an immediate reduction in aggression (Carr et al., 1980), self-injury (Carr et al., 1976), and tantrums (Carr & Newsom, 1985) by eliminating the demands. If difficult demands evoke challenging behavior but easy demands do not, then a switch from difficult to easy demands can produce an abrupt decrease in challenging behavior (Carr & Durand, 1985; Horner, Day, Sprague, O'Brien, & Heathfield, 1991). These outcomes would be especially important if one were dealing with a crisis situation in which there was a need to produce an immediate decrease in the level of some dangerous challenging behavior. In the long run, however, educational considerations require that demands, easy or difficult, need to be retained. Such considerations lead to two other antecedent-based approaches for dealing with serious challenging behavior: fading and stimulus modification.

*Fading* is a procedure that addresses both the prevention and reduction goals. To illustrate, consider a situation in which self-care demands (e.g., "Comb your hair," "Put on your shoes") have been identified as a trigger for self-injury in an escape paradigm. That is, the individual is able to bring about the withdrawal of these demands by a parent or teacher simply by engaging in self-injury. In this case, one strategy is to initially withdraw the offending trigger stimuli (i.e., self-care demands) thereby temporarily preventing any new occurrences of challenging behavior. Then, one gradually reintroduces the trigger stimuli over a period of time, eventually reaching the same rate of instructions that was present prior to intervention. This gradual fading in of the instructional stimuli (triggers) can be an effective means for reducing self-injury to low levels, provided that steps are taken to ensure that the individual is also not permitted to escape from the demands following occasional episodes of self-injury (Zarcone, Iwata, Smith, Mazaleski, & Lerman, 1994).

*Stimulus modification* is a procedure in which certain features of the trigger stimulus class are altered so that the level of challenging behavior is greatly reduced. In illustration, consider a task involving multistep assembly. One may find that certain variants of this task (e.g., repetitive assembly of pens) are correlated with high levels of challenging behavior. Other variants of this task that are associated with potent reinforcing outcomes (e.g., a five-step task to make peanut butter and jelly sandwiches), however, are correlated with low levels of challenging behavior (Dunlap, Foster-Johnson, Clarke, Kern, & Childs, 1995). By modifying the nature of the multistep task from making pens to making sandwiches, one can provide practice at mastering the generic task (multistep assembly) without simultaneously evoking challenging behavior. Likewise, a physical prompt may be identified as an antecedent for challenging behavior, whereas a gestural prompt is not. By modifying the nature of the prompt (from physical to gestural), one could reduce challenging behavior. Finally, loud reprimands may be correlated with subsequent challenging behavior, whereas soft reprimands are not. By altering the voice volume of the reprimand given (i.e., from loud to soft), one may be able to produce lower levels of challenging behavior (O'Leary, Kaufman, Kass, & Drabman, 1970). In each example, assessment information concerning stimulus parameters that do or do not trigger challenging behavior is used to modify antecedents to reduce or eliminate such behavior.

Another molecular intervention procedure relies on assessment information gathered on the triggers for appropriate behavior. This procedure involves the systematic introduction of triggers for appropriate behavior, with the result that the level of appropriate behavior is greatly increased and "crowds out" challenging behavior. The mechanism underlying this effect is likely a combination of topographical incompatibility (e.g., an individual cannot simultaneously draw pictures using both hands and slap his or her face) and functional incompatibility (e.g., an individual who can get attention from others by asking for it verbally may no longer need to bang his or her head to get attention). In the Cooper et al. (1990) study described previously, certain tasks and toys triggered a variety of appropriate behaviors. Thus, the systematic introduction of such antecedent stimuli could be used to produce high levels of appropriate behavior, with a concomitant decrease in challenging behavior. In actuality, one might conceptualize the entire educational enterprise as involving, among other things, the creation of a vast array of triggers for appropriate behavior. In the Cooper et al. study, such triggers already existed and only needed to be identified so that they could be subsequently integrated into an intervention plan. Even if such triggers do not currently exist, however, they can be created through teaching efforts. There is indeed a large body of literature demonstrating how antecedent stimuli can be established as triggers for appropriate behavior in the domains of language, social skills, motor skills, and activities for daily living (Koegel & Koegel, 1995; Smith, 1990). Multiplying the numbers of such triggers constitutes one step toward the elimination of challenging behavior at the level of molecular intervention.

Triggers for appropriate behavior can also be created even in instances in which specific antecedent stimuli currently evoke challenging behavior. Thus, one may find that negative feedback following poor task performance (e.g., "No, that's wrong!") evokes aggression from a particular individual. One common intervention, at the molecular level, is to prompt the individual to request a break from the difficult task or to request assistance in completing the task. In doing so, the intervention agent is converting a trigger stimulus for aggressive behavior (i.e., "No, that's wrong!" initially evokes aggression) to a trigger stimulus for appropriate behavior (i.e., "No, that's wrong!" now evokes a request for a break or assistance). As negative feedback becomes increasingly effective (through training) as a trigger stimulus for appropriate behavior, aggressive behavior decreases to a low level (e.g., Carr & Durand, 1985). In summary, the systematic introduction of triggers for appropriate behaviors is made possible by 1) identifying preexisting triggers for such behavior, 2) creating new triggers, and 3) providing instruction that results in converting triggers for challenging behavior into triggers for appropriate behavior. Irrespective of the strategy used for identifying and introducing triggers for appropriate behaviors, systematic introduction of triggers for appropriate behavior can contribute to the reduction of challenging behavior.

**Molar Approach**   The assessment information on goodness-of-fit typically suggests several avenues of intervention. As noted previously, when a person displays high levels of challenging behavior, there is typically a discrepancy between the person's needs and competencies and performance requirements set by service providers (support people) and organizational structures. Because multiple aspects of context need to be altered to minimize this discrepancy, molar intervention is always multicomponent in nature.

One aspect of the context for challenging behavior that must be altered relates to the person's needs and competencies. In illustration, consider a man with mental retardation who lives in a group home. Reinforcer assessment indicates that attention is a powerful need (reinforcer) for him. Competency assessment indicates that the man has poor functional communication skills. When he wants attention from another person, he simply pulls that person's hair or shoves him or her. The gap between the man's need for attention, on the one hand, and the communicative skills necessary for obtaining attention, on the other hand, is great. Reducing this discrepancy might involve teaching the man communication skills (Carr & Durand, 1985) to replace the challenging behavior (e.g., prompting him to greet others verbally, "How are you doing today?"). It is likely that the man prefers the company of some people (e.g., staff, other residents) to others, that he prefers some types of attention (e.g., conversation, social activities) to others, and that he prefers attention more during some periods of the day (e.g., dinner time, television time) than others (e.g., wake-up time). Therefore, many different kinds of communicative skills will need to be taught so that the man can make his various needs known. In other words, addressing even this one aspect of context (pertaining to the discrepancy between needs and competencies) requires a multicomponent intervention. The synthesis of many specific interventions into a totally integrated, functional package is an important hallmark of the molar approach.

The performance requirements set by service providers are another aspect of context that may have to be altered. Service providers and, more generally, support people do not enter the life of a person with disabilities free from specific attitudes and values. These features of the interpersonal context may affect what standards of behavior are set for people with disabilities and which approaches to intervention are deemed appropriate (Albin et al., 1996; Emerson, Hastings, & McGill, 1994). To continue with the previous example of the man living in a group home, the staff may feel that adults should be independent and, therefore, that repeated bids for attention are a mark of immaturity. Hence, they believe that requests for attention should not be honored too frequently. In addition, staff may believe that they, and not the person with disabilities, are in charge. Hence, they, and only they, will determine where, when, how, and from whom attention is given. These values help promote staff behavior that undermines the effectiveness of the man's communicative skills, thereby contributing to a context that facilitates challenging behavior. Staff values and behavior need to be changed as part of a multicomponent intervention. Hence, staff need to be educated as to the merits of honoring bids for attention as well as sharing control. Ignoring or responding minimally to a person's bids for attention is not the same thing as promoting independence. Staff can be taught how to help the man to become more independent in important areas of his life (e.g., self-care) while at the same time recognizing and promoting the human need to socialize with others. Likewise, staff can be taught how to share control by teaching the man to make choices (Dunlap et al., 1994; Sigafoos & Dempsey, 1992) regarding where, when, how, and with whom he wishes to interact. Staff can be educated so that they embrace a value system that emphasizes personal choice and assertiveness over passivity and gratuitous obedience to authority. The change in staff values and subsequent behavior produces a new context that helps minimize the necessity for displaying challenging behavior. Should staff prove resistant to such changes, further education may be necessary, and in rare cases, staff may need to be reassigned. Likewise, the individual with disabilities could be relocated to a setting in which staff values and behavior produce a better fit with the individual's needs.

The structure and organization of the living environment itself is a final aspect of context that may contribute to increasing the level of challenging behavior. Continuing with the example, molar assessment may indicate that the daily group home routine is dominated by isolated activities such as listening to tapes alone in one's bedroom, watching television by oneself, and taking solo walks in the vicinity of the group home. Excessive programming of such routines limits opportunity for social interaction and attention. Molar intervention might therefore involve transforming each routine to maximize social interaction, for example, by emphasizing group singing in response to music tapes, discussion "clubs" based on recently viewed television programs, and conversational walks taken by two or more residents who choose to be with one another. Likewise, molar assessment may indicate that the physical structure of the house lacks common areas that invite social interaction and group activity (Thompson, Robinson, Dietrich, Farris, & Sinclair, 1996). Therefore, molar intervention might involve creating a game area, a gym area, and a hobby area, each of which entices people who have shared interests and, therefore, a reason to communicate (i.e., pay attention to one another). Finally, certain biological variables are known to alter reinforcer effectiveness for a given individual (Bailey & Pyles, 1989; Carr & Smith, 1995). Thus, molar assessment may indicate that when the man is ill, he becomes more "needy" (i.e., he exhibits more attention-seeking behaviors). If so, molar intervention might involve the proactive strategy of changing staff schedules and duties to permit one or more staff members to spend more time with the man when he is ill. By increasing the overall level of attention available, staff may be able to prevent escalations of challenging behavior associated with physical illness. In summary, altering the organization of the living environment to address social, physical, and biological variables represents another aspect of multicomponent intervention at the molar level.

The main intended result of molar intervention is to produce an improvement in the individual's quality of life—that is, to ensure that his or her basic needs are met and that he or she has the same opportunities as everyone else to achieve goals in home, community, school, and work settings (Schalock, 1996). These positive results are theoretically attainable by enhancing the goodness-of-fit between the individual and his or her environment. Quality of life is itself a multidimensional construct (Hughes, Hwang, Kim, Eisenman, & Killian, 1995) that refers to improvements in social relationships (e.g., friendship formation), personal satisfaction (e.g., self-confidence, happiness), employment (e.g., productivity, job prestige, good job match), self-determination (e.g., personal control and autonomy, independence), recreation and leisure (e.g., adequate opportunities, good quality of activities), community adjustment (e.g., domestic skills, survival skills), community integration (e.g., mobility, opportunities for participation in community activities), and a host of other normalized activities and opportunities. There is a rapidly growing body of literature that demonstrates how molar interventions can be used to improve quality of life (e.g., Dennis, Williams, Giangreco, & Cloninger, 1993; Risley, 1996; Sands, Kozleski, & Goodwin, 1991; Schalock, 1990, 1996). This same literature demonstrates that an important side effect of molar intervention is a reduction in the level of challenging behavior (e.g., Belcher, 1994; Felce & Repp, 1992; Horner, Close, et al., 1996).

Because the molar approach has only begun to receive intensive systematic investigation in the late 1990s, it is not clear what parameters of the approach are critical for producing enhancement in quality of life. The fact, however, that a focus on quality-of-life issues, rather than on challenging behavior, may nonetheless produce a decrease in the level of challenging behavior is an intriguing finding that justifies the attention being paid to the molar approach.

## MECHANISMS OF EFFECTIVENESS: THE NEED FOR INTEGRATION

This chapter discusses the molecular and molar approaches to antecedent control separately in order to highlight the unique contributions that each makes to the assessment of and intervention for serious challenging behavior. In practice, it is necessary to integrate these two approaches to maximize effectiveness.

### Discriminative Stimulus Effects

*Discriminative stimuli* derive their control over a given response class from the fact that their presence predicts that specific reinforcing consequences will occur when behaviors from the response class are emitted. This predictiveness, in turn, is due to a history in which emission of members of the response class have been systematically and reliably followed by specific reinforcers over a period of time. One virtue of the molecular approach is that, through careful analysis, the discriminative stimuli for challenging behavior are identified. As noted previously, this assessment outcome opens up the possibility of minimizing challenging behavior by redesigning the environment so as to 1) eliminate the discriminative stimulus, 2) withdraw it and gradually reintroduce it, or 3) alter its constituent parameters so that it no longer evokes challenging behavior. Of course, another option would be to rearrange the environment so that the antecedent stimuli are no longer predictive of reinforcing outcomes. Thus, if a discriminative stimulus for challenging behavior (e.g., demands) predicts negative reinforcement (e.g., cessation of demands) after the challenging behavior (e.g., aggression) is emitted, then one could weaken the discriminative properties of the stimulus by ensuring that challenging behavior no longer resulted in negative reinforcement in the presence of the stimuli. This effect could be achieved by means of *escape extinction,* a procedure in which challenging behavior no longer produces cessation of demands (Carr et al., 1980) or by programming the cessation of demands independently of the challenging behavior itself, a procedure referred to as *noncontingent reinforcement* (Gaylord-Ross, Weeks, & Lipner, 1980). In either case, the antecedent stimulus (e.g., demands) no longer predicts negative reinforcement (e.g., cessation of demands) after the challenging behavior (e.g., aggression) is emitted. Therefore, the antecedent stimulus eventually fails to evoke the challenging behavior.

At the molecular level it is also possible, as indicated previously, to identify and create discriminative stimuli for appropriate behavior. Educational efforts typically involve transforming previously neutral stimuli (e.g., the sight of an apple may initially fail to evoke the verbal response, "I want apple") into discriminative stimuli (e.g., the sight of the apple comes to evoke the verbal response, "I want apple"). This outcome is achieved by making antecedent stimuli (e.g., sight of the apple) predictive of reinforcement (e.g., obtaining the apple) following emission of an appropriate response (e.g., asking for the apple). Through education, one can create large numbers of discriminative stimuli for appropriate behavior, effectively reducing the proportion of discriminative stimuli for challenging behavior present in the environment. The sole reliance on molecular intervention to achieve this effect can be an arduous and time-consuming strategy. A useful complementary strategy would be to identify environments that already contain large numbers of discriminative stimuli for appropriate behavior. Functionally, molar interventions that focus on goodness-of-fit may in fact succeed largely because they identify environments that are already rich in discriminative stimuli for appropriate behavior. These stimuli trigger various prosocial, adaptive responses. The concept of engagement (McGill et al., 1994; Risley, 1996) in the molar intervention literature is related to this issue. Specifically, the notion is that when an individual is constructively engaged in meaningful activities throughout the day, reduction of challenging behavior will occur as a side effect of engagement (Allen, 1994). In behavioral jargon, engagement occurs when the environment contains many stimuli that are discriminative for prosocial behavior. The preceding analysis suggests the following intervention strategy: 1) Begin by choosing environments that already contain large numbers of discriminative stimuli for prosocial behavior (molar strategy); 2) minimize the presence of discriminative stimuli for challenging behavior (molecular approach); and 3) create, when necessary, new discriminative stimuli for prosocial behavior (molecular strategy). By strategically integrating the molar and molecular approaches, the probability of maximizing intervention effectiveness is increased.

## Setting Event Effects

*Setting events* (Bijou & Baer, 1961) include those variables that alter ongoing stimulus–response relationships. Consider a discriminative stimulus such as a task demand. On some days, the person with disabilities is physically ill and responds to the task demand by becoming aggressive, so the task is withdrawn. On other days, the person is well and responds to the same demand with cheerful compliance, so the task is completed. In this case, physical illness is considered to be a setting event because it clearly alters the response (i.e., aggression versus compliance) that is made to the stimulus (i.e., the task demand). Some setting events appear to affect behavior by altering reinforcer effectiveness. Thus, in the example given, physical illness may act as an establishing operation (Michael, 1982) to make the task demand more aversive than usual. Thus, the negative reinforcement (due to task termination) associated with escape-motivated aggression is enhanced, thereby promoting an increase in the level of that challenging behavior.

Regardless of the specific processes accounting for setting event effects, the concept itself is a critical bridge between the molecular and molar approaches, and plausibly represents the key to their successful integration. The literature on setting events has many characteristics of the molar approach, including 1) a concern for broad, continuous variables involving biological (e.g., illness), social (e.g., friendship patterns), and physical (e.g., how the home setting is structured) factors; 2) a focus on natural settings (e.g., home, workplace), and normalized routines (e.g., the sequencing of social activities within the community); 3) an interest in assessing goodness-of-fit (e.g., measuring an individual's need to be alone against the level of crowding characteristic of dinner, television, and bedtime routines in a home); and 4) intervention strategies that include, among other tactics, reorganizing systems to accommodate the needs of the individual, thereby enhancing goodness-of-fit (e.g., rescheduling or canceling activities to accommodate a person when he or she is ill). The literature on setting events also has many characteristics of the molecular approach, including 1) empirical analysis of how such events influence challenging behavior; 2) a concern with challenging behavior per se, both in assessment and intervention; 3) assessment procedures that rely on systematic direct observation and/or functional analysis; and 4) interventions that stress the elimination or mitigation of specific setting events as a means of reducing challenging behavior.

It is clear from the discussion thus far that setting events can play a role at both the molecular and molar level. The amount of research on setting events is accelerating in the late 1990s. One example from the published literature demonstrates how these variables connect the molecular with the molar as well as the positive outcomes that accrue from such integration. Horner, Vaughn, Day, and Ard (1996) worked with a number of individuals in home and community settings. On days on which certain setting events (e.g., physical illness, schedule changes, loss of anticipated reinforcers) had occurred, the individuals responded to discrete antecedents (e.g., staff demands) with serious challenging behavior. (Challenging behavior, however, was much lower on days when the setting events had not occurred.) Intervention included a variety of strategies such as 1) eliminating the setting event, 2) withholding the discriminative stimuli, and 3) introducing new setting events. These strategies, which had both molecular and molar features, produced decreases in challenging behavior. The last strategy, introducing new setting events (described by the authors as "neutralizing routines"), is of special interest. In illustration, if a girl had just had a fight on the playground (setting event) and immediately returned to her classroom, she would be very likely to respond to academic demands (discriminative stimuli) with aggression (challenging behavior). The authors would deal with this situation by introducing a neutralizing routine (setting event) that involves relaxation training. The relaxation routine could, of course, be conceptualized as a setting event for nonchallenging behavior in regard to the discriminative stimulus; and, in fact, it resulted in low levels of challenging behavior being emitted in response to that stimulus.

The critical message here is that the field would do well to assess setting events associated with nonchallenging (i.e., constructive, prosocial) behavior as well as those events associated with challenging behavior. In essence, a major focus of the molar approach can be conceptualized as the identification of setting events for prosocial behavior. Thus, the process of enhancing goodness-of-fit can be viewed, functionally, as identifying and/or altering contexts (setting events) so that the discriminative stimuli for challenging behavior become less likely to evoke challenging behaviors, and the discriminative stimuli for prosocial behaviors become more likely to evoke prosocial behaviors.

## CONCLUSIONS

Molecular and molar approaches can each make a contribution to resolving assessment and intervention issues. Arguably, the major research priority for the field in the next generation is to analyze these two approaches so that global strategies involving the enhancement of goodness-of-fit can be related to key concepts involving discriminative stimuli and setting events. By developing assessment and intervention protocols relevant to these antecedent variables, we will accelerate the movement of applied research from controlled, laboratory conditions into the complex world of the community. This movement, successfully implemented, would be the ultimate justification for the past 30 years of applied behavior analysis research.

## REFERENCES

Albin, R.W., Lucyshyn, J.M., Horner, R.H., & Flannery, K.B. (1996). Contextual fit for behavior support plans: A model for "goodness of fit." In L.K. Koegel, R.L. Koegel, & G. Dunlap (Eds.), *Positive behavioral support: Including people with difficult behavior in the community* (pp. 81–98). Baltimore: Paul H. Brookes Publishing Co.

Allen, D. (1994). Towards meaningful daytime activity. In E. Emerson, P. McGill, & J. Mansell (Eds.), *Severe learning disabilities and challenging behaviours* (pp. 157–178). London: Chapman & Hall.

Axelrod, S., & Apsche, J. (Eds.). (1983). *The effects of punishment on human behavior.* New York: Academic Press.

Bailey, J.S., & Pyles, D.A.M. (1989). Behavioral diagnostics. In E. Cipani (Ed.), The treatment of severe behavior disorders (pp. 85–107). *Monographs of the American Association on Mental Retardation, 12.*

Belcher, T. (1994). Movement to the community: Reduction of behavioral difficulties. *Mental Retardation, 32,* 89–90.

Bijou, S.W., & Baer, D.M. (1961). *Child development: A systematic and empirical theory.* Englewood Cliffs, NJ: Prentice-Hall.

Brown, F. (1991). Creative daily scheduling: A nonintrusive approach to challenging behaviors in community residences. *Journal of The Association for Persons with Severe Handicaps, 16,* 75–84.

Carr, E.G. (1977). The motivation of self-injurious behavior: A review of some hypotheses. *Psychological Bulletin, 84,* 800–816.

Carr, E.G. (1994). Emerging themes in the functional analysis of problem behavior. *Journal of Applied Behavior Analysis, 27,* 393–399.

Carr, E.G., & Carlson, J.I. (1993). Reduction of severe behavior problems in the community using a multicomponent treatment approach. *Journal of Applied Behavior Analysis, 26,* 157–172.

Carr, E.G., & Durand, V.M. (1985). Reducing behavior problems through functional communication training. *Journal of Applied Behavior Analysis, 18,* 111–126.

Carr, E.G., Levin, L., McConnachie, G., Carlson, J.I., Kemp, D.C., & Smith, C.E. (1994). *Communication-based intervention for problem behavior. A user's guide for producing positive change.* Baltimore: Paul H. Brookes Publishing Co.

Carr, E.G., & Newsom, C.D. (1985). Demand-related tantrums: Conceptualization and treatment. *Behavior Modification, 9,* 403–426.

Carr, E.G., Newsom, C.D., & Binkoff, J.A. (1976). Stimulus control of self-destructive behavior in a psychotic child. *Journal of Abnormal Child Psychology, 4,* 139–153.

Carr, E.G., Newsom, C.D., & Binkoff, J.A. (1980). Escape as a factor in the aggressive behavior of two retarded children. *Journal of Applied Behavior Analysis, 13,* 101–117.

Carr, E.G., Reeve, C.E., & Magito-McLaughlin, D. (1996). Contextual influences on problem behavior in people with developmental disabilities. In L.K. Koegel, R.L. Koegel, & G. Dunlap (Eds.), *Positive behavioral support: Including people with difficult behavior in the community* (pp. 403–423). Baltimore: Paul H. Brookes Publishing Co.

Carr, E.G., & Smith, C.E. (1995). Biological setting events for self-injury. *Mental Retardation and Developmental Disabilities Research Reviews, 1,* 94–98.

Carr, E.G., Taylor, J.C., & Robinson, S. (1991). The effects of severe behavior problems in children on the teaching behavior of adults. *Journal of Applied Behavior Analysis, 24,* 523–535.

Cooper, L.J., Wacker, D.P., Sasso, G.M., Reimers, T.M., & Donn, L.K. (1990). Using parents as therapists to evaluate appropriate behavior of their children: Application to a tertiary diagnostic clinic. *Journal of Applied Behavior Analysis, 23,* 285–296.

Dennis, R.E., Williams, W., Giangreco, M.F., & Cloninger, C.J. (1993). Quality of life as a context for planning and evaluation of services for people with disabilities. *Exceptional Children, 59,* 499–512.

Dunlap, G., dePerczel, M., Clarke, S., Wilson, D., Wright, S., White, R., & Gomez, A. (1994). Choice making and proactive behavioral support for students with emotional and behavioral challenges. *Journal of Applied Behavior Analysis, 27,* 505–518.

Dunlap, G., Foster-Johnson, L., Clarke, S., Kern, L., & Childs, K.E. (1995). Modifying activities to produce functional outcomes: Effects on the problem behaviors of students with disabilities. *Journal of The Association for Persons with Severe Handicaps, 20,* 248–258.

Dunlap, G., Kern-Dunlap, L., Clarke, S., & Robbins, F.R. (1991). Functional assessment, curricular revisions, and severe problem behavior. *Journal of Applied Behavior Analysis, 24,* 387–397.

Emerson, E., Hastings, R., & McGill, P. (1994). Values, attitudes, and service ideology. In E. Emerson, P. McGill, & J. Mansell (Eds.), *Severe learning disabilities and challenging behaviours* (pp. 209–231). London: Chapman & Hall.

Emerson, E., McGill, P., & Mansell, J. (Eds.). (1994). *Severe learning disabilities and challenging behaviours.* London: Chapman & Hall.

Felce, D., & Repp, A. (1992). The behavioral and social ecology of community houses. *Research in Developmental Disabilities, 13,* 27–42.

Fisher, W., Piazza, C.C., Bowman, L.G., Hagopian, L.P., Owens, J.C., & Slevin, I. (1992). A comparison of two approaches for identifying reinforcers for persons with severe and profound disabilities. *Journal of Applied Behavior Analysis, 25,* 491–498.

Ford, A., Schnorr, R., Meyer, L., Davern, L., Black, J., & Dempsey, P. (1989). *The Syracuse community-referenced curriculum guide for students with moderate and severe disabilities.* Baltimore: Paul H. Brookes Publishing Co.

Gardner, W.I., & Sovner, R. (1994). *Self-injurious behaviors.* Willow Street, PA: Vida Publishing.

Gaylord-Ross, R., Weeks, M., & Lipner, C. (1980). An analysis of antecedent, response, and consequence events in the treatment of self-injurious behavior. *Education and Training of the Mentally Retarded, 15,* 35–42.

Hedeen, D.L., Ayres, B.J., Meyer, L.H., & Waite, J. (1996). Quality inclusive schooling for students with severe behavioral challenges. In D.H Lehr & F. Brown (Eds.), *People with disabilities who challenge the system* (pp. 127–171). Baltimore: Paul H. Brookes Publishing Co.

Horner, R.H., Close, D.W., Fredericks, H.D.B., O'Neill, R.E., Albin, R.W., Sprague, J.R., Kennedy, C.H., Flannery, K.B., & Heathfield, L.T. (1996). Supported living for people with profound disabilities and severe problem behaviors. In D.H. Lehr & F. Brown (Eds.), *People with disabilities who challenge the system* (pp. 209–240). Baltimore: Paul H. Brookes Publishing Co.

Horner, R.H., Day, H.M., Sprague, J.R., O'Brien, M., & Heathfield, L.T. (1991). Interspersed requests: A nonaversive procedure for decreasing aggression and self-injury during instruction. *Journal of Applied Behavior Analysis, 24,* 265–278.

Horner, R.H., Vaughn, B.J., Day, H.M., & Ard, W.R., Jr. (1996). The relationship between setting events and problem behavior: Expanding our understanding of behavioral support. In L.K. Koegel, R.L. Koegel, & G. Dunlap (Eds.), *Positive behavioral support: Including people with difficult behavior in the community* (pp. 381–402). Baltimore: Paul H. Brookes Publishing Co.

Hughes, C., Hwang, B., Kim, J.H., Eisenman, L.T., & Killian, D.J. (1995). Quality of life in applied research: A review and analysis of empirical measures. *American Journal on Mental Retardation, 99,* 623–641.

Hurley-Geffner, C.M. (1995). Friendships between children with and without developmental disabilities. In R.L. Koegel & L.K. Koegel (Eds.), *Teaching children with autism: Strategies for initiating positive interactions and improving opportunities* (pp. 105–125). Baltimore: Paul H. Brookes Publishing Co.

Kemp, D.C., & Carr, E.G. (1995). Reduction of severe problem behavior in community employment using an hypothesis-driven multicomponent intervention approach. *Journal of The Association for Persons with Severe Handicaps, 20,* 229–247.

Koegel, R.L., & Koegel, L.K. (1995). *Teaching children with autism: Strategies for initiating positive interactions and improving opportunities.* Baltimore: Paul H. Brookes Publishing Co.

Lalli, J.S., Browder, D.M., Mace, F.C., & Brown, D.K. (1993). Teacher use of descriptive analysis data to implement interventions to decrease students' problem behaviors. *Journal of Applied Behavior Analysis, 26,* 227–238.

Lerman, D.C., & Iwata, B.A. (1993). Descriptive and experimental analyses of variables maintaining self-injurious behavior. *Journal of Applied Behavior Analysis, 26,* 293–319.

McConnachie, G., & Carr, E.G. (1997). The effects of child behavior problems on the maintenance of intervention fidelity. *Behavior Modification, 21,* 123–158.

McGill, P., Emerson, E., & Mansell, J. (1994). Individually designed residential provision for people with seriously challenging behaviours. In E. Emerson,

P. McGill, & J. Mansell (Eds.), *Severe learning disabilities and challenging behaviours* (pp. 119–156). London: Chapman & Hall.

Michael, J. (1982). Distinguishing between discriminative and motivational functions of stimuli. *Journal of the Experimental Analysis of Behavior, 37,* 149–155.

Mostofsky, D.I. (1965). *Stimulus generalization.* Stanford, CA: Stanford University Press.

Newton, T.S., Ard, W.R., & Horner, R.H. (1993). Validating predicted activity preferences of individuals with severe disabilities. *Journal of Applied Behavior Analysis, 26,* 239–245.

O'Leary, K.D., Kaufman, K.F., Kass, R.E., & Drabman, R.S. (1970). The effects of loud and soft reprimands on the behavior of disruptive students. *Exceptional Children, 37,* 145–155.

O'Neill, R.E., Horner, R.H., Albin, R.W., Storey, K., & Sprague, J.R. (1990). *Functional analysis of problem behavior: A practical assessment guide.* Sycamore, IL: Sycamore Press.

Risley, T. (1996). Get a life!: Positive behavioral intervention for challenging behavior through life arrangement and life coaching. In L.K. Koegel, R.L. Koegel, & G. Dunlap (Eds.), *Positive behavioral support: Including people with difficult behavior in the community* (pp. 425–437). Baltimore: Paul H. Brookes Publishing Co.

Sailor, W. (1996). New structures and systems change for comprehensive positive behavioral support. In L.K. Koegel, R.L. Koegel, & G. Dunlap (Eds.), *Positive behavioral support: Including people with difficult behavior in the community* (pp. 163–206). Baltimore: Paul H. Brookes Publishing Co.

Sands, D.J., Kozleski, E.B., & Goodwin, L.D. (1991). Whose needs are we meeting? Results of a consumer satisfaction survey of persons with developmental disabilities in Colorado. *Research in Developmental Disabilities, 12,* 297–314.

Schalock, R.L. (Ed.). (1990). *Quality of life. Vol. 1. Conceptualization and measurement.* Washington, DC: American Association on Mental Retardation.

Schalock, R.L. (Ed.). (1996). *Quality of life: Perspectives and issues.* Washington, DC: American Association on Mental Retardation.

Schalock, R.L., & Jensen, C.M. (1986). Assessing the goodness-of-fit between persons and their environments. *Journal of The Association for Persons with Severe Handicaps, 11,* 103–109.

Sidman, M. (1990). Equivalence relations: Where do they come from? In D.E. Blackman & H. Lejeune (Eds.), *Behavior analysis in theory and practice: Contributions and controversies* (pp. 93–114). Hillsdale, NJ: Lawrence Erlbaum Associates.

Sigafoos, J., & Dempsey, R. (1992). Assessing choice making among children with multiple disabilities. *Journal of Applied Behavior Analysis, 25,* 747–755.

Skinner, B.F. (1938). *The behavior of organisms.* New York: Appleton-Century-Crofts.

Smith, M.D. (1990). *Autism and life in the community: Successful interventions for behavioral challenges.* Baltimore: Paul H. Brookes Publishing Co.

Snell, M.E. (Ed.). (1993). *Instruction of students with disabilities* (4th ed.). New York: Merrill.

Stark, J., & Faulkner, E. (1996). Quality of life across the life span. In R.L. Schalock (Ed.), *Quality of life. Vol. 1. Conceptualization and measurement* (pp. 23–32). Washington, DC: American Association on Mental Retardation.

Taylor, J.C., & Carr, E.G. (1992a). Severe problem behaviors related to social interaction. I: Attention seeking and social avoidance. *Behavior Modification, 16,* 305–335.

Taylor, J.C., & Carr, E.G. (1992b). Severe problem behaviors related to social interaction: II. A systems analysis. *Behavior Modification, 16,* 336–371.

Thompson, T., Robinson, J., Dietrich, M., Farris, M., & Sinclair, V. (1996). Interdependence of architectural features and program variables in community residences for people with mental retardation. *American Journal of Mental Retardation, 101,* 315–327.

Zarcone, J.R., Iwata, B.A., Smith, R.G., Mazaleski, J.L., & Lerman, D.C. (1994). Reemergence and extinction of self-injurious escape behavior during stimulus (instructional) fading. *Journal of Applied Behavior Analysis, 27,* 307–316.

# ~ 2 ~

# Intervention Conceptualization and Formulation

## James K. Luiselli

Mary, a 23-year-old woman with mental retardation, was referred to the author by the supervisor of her community residence. Staff at the home had been working with her for many months to overcome behavior challenges that she presented during her morning routine and had requested consultation to assist with program development. Mary engaged in extremely disruptive and agitated behaviors when she was instructed to take her shower in the morning before getting dressed and having breakfast. Staff reported that Mary "tantrummed" excessively when prompted to enter the bathroom and resisted their efforts to help her with the routine. Numerous behavioral interventions had been attempted, including various methods of positive reinforcement for compliance, use of a "task card" to sequence the component steps required for showering, and time-out contingent on challenging behaviors. None of these approaches was successful, and Mary continued to experience agitation in the morning. Furthermore, other residents in the home were being affected deleteriously, and staff remained frustrated.

A functional assessment of Mary's behavior indicated that although she occasionally was noncompliant in response to staff requests, the severe outbursts were restricted exclusively to the morning showering routine. She participated successfully in a community-based vocational training program each weekday; enjoyed leisure activities; and although she did not possess extensive verbal language, she had good receptive skills. One suggestion to address the problem was to shift the response requirement imposed on Mary from the morning to the evening. This suggestion was made because it seemed that she was "rushed" in the morning, needed extra time to wake up, and was less energetic earlier in the day. Put simply, would it be acceptable to staff if Mary took her shower in the evening, before her bedtime, instead of the next morning?

Staff agreed to evaluate this "program" of revised activity scheduling, and within 2 days the agitation and challenging behaviors during showering were eliminated. Mary took her shower in the evening without resistance, did not require staff assistance, and enjoyed the "new" procedure of laying out her clothing for the next day before retiring at night. Five months after introducing the schedule change, she continued to maintain performance. Staff, of course, were delighted with the change in Mary's behavior and with the positive results that were obtained so rapidly and with so little effort.

Not all behavioral support plans for people with developmental disabilities are as simple or as effective as the intervention used with Mary. This description, however, is an example of how positive outcomes can result when the functional influences on challenging behaviors are conceived and when procedures are formulated from an antecedent control perspective. In Mary's case, it appeared that there were one or more features of the morning routine that contributed to her noncompliance and agitation. By rearranging the context of the "showering demand," it was possible to resolve her behavior difficulties.

This chapter discusses the conceptualization and formulation of behavioral support plans from an antecedent control orientation. The objectives of the chapter are to present a rationale for the intervention for challenging behaviors using antecedent control approaches, a framework to assist with the design of antecedent manipulations, and guidelines for the process of intervention formulation.

## INTERVENTION CONCEPTUALIZATION

A first step in understanding antecedent control approaches toward challenging behaviors is to ask the question, What advantages do these approaches have over other methods of intervention? As discussed frequently in this book, antecedent control approaches allow for an analysis of the "pros and cons" of consequence-based procedures. A second focus is on the types of conditions and situations that influence the occurrence of challenging and alternative behaviors.

### Situational Context of Challenging Behaviors

People frequently display challenging behaviors within very restrictive contexts—take, for example, a child with developmental disabilities who engages in extremely aggressive and self-injurious behaviors when he visits a clinic for routine medical monitoring or has a specific procedure performed (e.g., having blood drawn to document medication levels). Outside of this context, the child never demonstrates such behaviors. It seems clear that the "aversiveness" that characterizes the child's medical care is a unique "provoking stimulus" that sets the occasion for agitation and distress. Therefore, it is logical to address this child's difficulty by changing the negative features of this antecedent condition. That is, the unique situational specificity associated with the challenging behaviors leads logically to an antecedent control manipulation.

## Applying Consequences in
## Interventions for Seriously Challenging Behaviors

Many people with developmental disabilities exhibit challenging behaviors such as aggression, property destruction, tantrum outbursts, and the like. These and similar behaviors pose physical threats to the person, peers, staff, and family members as well as to the inanimate environment. There is a history in the field of applied behavior analysis of treating such problems with response-contingent procedures (e.g., overcorrection, manual restraint, guided compliance, various time-out strategies) (Matson & Taras, 1989). An inherent restriction with these approaches, however, is that they require physical contact with the person, manipulation of extremities, and immobilization of movement. With people who are large in stature, who actively resist intervention, and/or who possess great strength, it is not uncommon for two or more staff members to implement the consequence-based procedure. Another rationale for antecedent control intervention, then, is to establish clinical control by avoiding physical confrontations with individuals who engage in seriously challenging behaviors. Rather than having staff wait for a particular behavior to occur so that a "negative" (and purportedly punishing) consequence can be imposed, an alternative conceptualization would be to alter the probability of that behavior occurring so that the physical difficulties are not encountered.

## Limitations of and Restrictions
## on Positive Reinforcement Procedures

Any program that addresses challenging behaviors should include one or more methods of positive reinforcement. It is well established that development of positively oriented intervention strategies is a preferred approach toward behavior deceleration (O'Brien & Repp, 1990) and that it is ethically indefensible to provide intervention in the absence of procedures to increase skills and competencies. These considerations notwithstanding, positive reinforcement procedures have limitations, or may be restricted, under particular conditions. One concern is that it may be difficult to identify stimuli that serve as functional reinforcers for some individuals. Similarly, many behavior-deceleration support plans do not incorporate empirically derived reinforcement (Piazza, Fisher, Hagopian, Bowman, & O'Toole, 1996) but, instead, rely on arbitrarily selected stimuli. Finally, there are people who display challenging behaviors at excessively high frequencies, thereby precluding the delivery of reinforcers for alternative responses or for the absence of responding during predetermined intervals (e.g., a differential reinforcement of other behavior schedule). Again, these considerations are not intended to undermine the critical importance of positive reinforcement in the intervention for challenging behaviors but, instead, underscore the need for alternative interventions in many cases. From an antecedent control perspective, the most relevant issue would be how to enhance the effectiveness of reinforcement that is incorporated in a behavioral support plan.

## Practicality of Implementation

The experiences of many clinicians and psychologists are that efforts to reduce challenging behaviors frequently fail because the intervention procedures are either too complex or too time-intensive to support effective implementation. One reason to favor antecedent control approaches is that on many occasions they can be more practical than multicomponent, contingency management programs that typically are designed for the person with a disability. Because many antecedent interventions rely on already-existing behavior–environment relationships, positive intervention effects can be achieved by substituting or rearranging these conditions in contrast to shaping, strengthening, and maintaining "new behavior." Mary's activity-scheduling intervention illustrates how a desirable outcome can be achieved efficiently by capitalizing on conditions that support adaptive behavior instead of trying to change responding in another context.

## Permanency of Behavior Change

The altering of antecedent conditions in the intervention for challenging behaviors also can produce permanent effects. It is widely known that consequence-based behavior-reduction procedures usually are only effective as long as they are in effect. Frequently, there is a deterioration in behavior when procedures are discontinued, applied inconsistently, or "faded-out" too rapidly. In contrast, a behavioral support plan that is linked to a modification of antecedent conditions can induce meaningful changes that persist in the absence of additional procedures.

## ESTABLISHING OPERATIONS

The conceptualization of intervention from an antecedent control perspective is enhanced by an understanding of establishing operations (EOs). As defined by Michael, an EO "is an environmental event, operation, or stimulus condition that affects an organism by momentarily altering a) the reinforcing effectiveness of other events and b) the frequency of occurrence of that part of the organism's repertoire to those events as consequences" (1993, p. 192). That is, an EO has two functions. First, it has a *reinforcer-enhancing* function because it alters the "potency" of particular consequences that have been identified as "reinforcement." And second, it has an *evocative* function because it "momentarily increases the frequency of the types of behavior that have been previously reinforced" (p. 192). Michael used the example of food reinforcement to illustrate these two functions. The influence of food as a reinforcer, for example, can be enhanced through food deprivation, which in turn, "evokes any behavior that has been followed by reinforcement" (p. 192).

The concept of an EO should be distinguished from that of a discriminative stimulus ($S^D$). An $S^D$ is a stimulus condition that has been correlated with the differential availability of reinforcement when particular behaviors are exhibited. EOs, in contrast, are tied more closely to *motivative variables* in that they, "are related to the differential *reinforcer effectiveness* of environmental events" (Michael, 1993, p. 193). Schlinger (1993) noted that both EOs and $S^D$s alter the momentary frequency of behavior but are different because the former influence the effectiveness of consequences.

On an applied level, there are several variables that can be influential as EOs. The physical status of the individual, or *biological variables*, would include factors such as the presence of acute or ongoing illness, hunger, sleep, and the effects of medications to name just a few. *Environmental variables* would encompass group arrangements, activity schedules, ambient conditions, and inanimate characteristics of the person's surroundings. Finally, the frequency and quality of social interactions, instructional demands, and personal features of significant others represent *interpersonal* variables that would be relevant. As categories of EOs, these variables could be assessed to determine their controlling effects on a person's behavior and could be manipulated in different ways for therapeutic purposes.

EOs also function preceding or concurrent with responding (Gewirtz, 1972). A *preceding event* would be one that is removed in time and proximity from the setting in which a challenging behavior is evinced. Such a condition would be a child who experienced a confrontive interaction with his parents in the morning before he arrived at his school program. The negative exchange at home might set the occasion for similar difficulties with teachers or peers in the classroom later that day.

When an EO functions concurrently, it is linked more contemporaneously to the context of the challenging behavior. Imagine, as an example, a child who engages in disruptive behaviors to avoid or to escape instructional activities in his classroom. The presentation of these activities by the teacher might function as an EO that sets the occasion for challenging behaviors. In this example, each time the child encounters activity "demands" within the context of his classroom, the relative effectiveness of escape and avoidance behaviors are enhanced, and they are evoked by the immediacy of the situation.

The preceding discussion illustrates the interrelationships that exist among various dimensions of EOs. In effect, biological, environmental, and interpersonal variables can have a reinforcer effectiveness or evocative function that occurs preceding or concurrent with behaviors. The complexity of such interactions among these dimensions, and their intervention implications, were elucidated in a study by Kennedy and Meyer (1996). The challenging behaviors (self-injury, hitting, throwing objects) of three students with mental retardation requiring limited to pervasive supports were recorded during functional analysis sessions, and the results indicated that their responding was influenced primarily by negative reinforcement in the form of escape from task demands. For all three students, however, occurrences of escape-motivated behaviors were greater when particular extraneous events were present. For one student, allergy symptoms were correlated with increased rates of challenging behaviors. For the two other students, responding was more frequent under "demand" conditions when they had had reduced hours of sleep the night before. These results are useful because they point out the possible role of biological variables as EOs and emphasize how the presence or absence of such influences can alter behavior–reinforcer relationships.

## INTERVENTION FORMULATION

Intervention formulation from the perspective of antecedent control begins with an assessment of $S^D$ and EO functions. The primary objective is to identify biological, environmental, and interpersonal variables that are associated with the *presence* and *absence* of challenging behaviors. The intent is to conduct a *functional assessment and analysis* of antecedent control.

Other chapters discuss in detail the implementation of data collection and functional assessment methodologies. Briefly, there are three approaches toward functional assessment and analysis: indirect, descriptive, and experimental-analogue (Iwata, Vollmer, & Zarcone, 1990). *Indirect* methods include informant surveys, rating checklists, and interview formats that ask significant others to identify subjectively the conditions associated with the occurrence and nonoccurrence of challenging behaviors. Figure 1 is an example of a screening instrument used by the author when interviewing service providers during the initial phases of clinical consultation. The structured interview seeks to elicit information concerning multiple antecedent influences on a person's behavior as a first step toward a more comprehensive functional assessment. Although based on subjective impressions from informants, the information can lead to initial impressions regarding controlling variables and may reveal certain interactive effects. For example, suspected relationships between "medication" and "time of day" might suggest a pharmacological side effect that is apparent in late afternoon (e.g., sedative effects from a neuroleptic drug that take hold during the period of 2:00 P.M.–5:00 P.M.). Or, the presence of particular staff during certain activities, but not others, could be influential (Touchette, MacDonald, & Langer, 1985).

The second type of functional assessment is *descriptive* methods in which data are recorded to provide more objective and empirical measures of behavior. Figure 2 shows a Detailed Behavior Recording Form that was used to assess the conditions under which "aggressive" behavior was exhibited by a 16-year-old boy with autism. The behavior defined on the form occurred at a relatively low frequency (e.g., 1–2 times weekly) but was very intense and posed physical harm to staff at his residential school. The purpose of the recording form was to document each behavior incident in such a way that antecedent influences could be isolated and their functional control over his responding could be understood better.

Finally, *experimental-analogue* methods of functional assessment consist of the direct manipulation of possible controlling variables. When evaluating the role of antecedent control over responding, one or more challenging behaviors would be recorded while particular conditions are introduced and removed. During such manipulations, consequence events would not be altered but, instead, would remain constant. Smith, Iwata, Goh, and Shore (1995), for example, examined the effects of different instructional variables (antecedents) on escape-

Name:_____          Date of interview:_____

Informant:_____          Interviewer:_____

Target behavior (#   ): _____

Instructions: The information gathered during this interview seeks to identify conditions that might be associated with occurrences of the target behavior. Please indicate the "level" of the target behavior per listed influence. If levels 2 or 3 are endorsed, then explain the purported relationship. Score "N/A" if the conditions are not applicable.

| Variable | Level of target behavior | | |
| --- | --- | --- | --- |
| | No relationship (1) | Possibly related (2) | Definitely related (3) |
| **Biological** | | | |
| Hunger | | | |
| Thirst | | | |
| Sleep | | | |
| Medication | | | |
| Activity level | | | |
| Exercise | | | |
| Other | | | |
| **Environmental** | | | |
| Time of day | | | |
| Indoors/outdoors | | | |
| Climate/season | | | |
| Home setting | | | |
| School setting | | | |
| Work setting | | | |
| Activity schedule | | | |
| Other | | | |
| **Interpersonal** | | | |
| Instructional activities | | | |
| Vocational activities | | | |
| Self-care activities | | | |
| Social interaction with staff | | | |
| Social interaction with peers | | | |
| Social interaction with family | | | |
| Time alone | | | |
| Other | | | |

Figure 1.   Interview Screening Form.

Individual's name: _____

Target behavior: <u>Aggression (striking another person with hands or feet)</u>

Instructions: This recording form should be used to document the occurrence of aggression. Each time the behavior is observed, enter relevant information in the spaces provided.

Today's date: _____

Staff or individual involved: _____

Time of occurrence: _____

Duration of incident: _____

Location (setting) where incident occurred: _____
_____

Ongoing activity at time of incident: _____
_____

Brief description of incident: _____
_____
_____

Additional information: _____

Figure 2.   Detailed Behavior Recording Form.

motivated self-injurious behaviors of nine adults with mental retardation requiring pervasive supports. Variables such as the novelty of tasks, the duration of instructional sessions, and the rate of task presentation were shown to influence the frequency of self-injury of the participants (i.e., they served as EOs for the behaviors that were maintained by escape). In this research, the antecedent variables were manipulated in such a way that their functional control over responding was demonstrated experimentally.

Once information and data are gathered, the next step in intervention formulation is to develop one or more behavior "hypotheses"

(Repp & Karsh, 1993). This process entails a thorough analysis of those antecedent conditions which appear to be implicated as either a $S^D$ or EO for the challenging behavior. The purported controlling effects of these conditions then are described so that intervention guidelines can be "matched" accordingly. Figure 3 represents an Antecedent Control Intervention Planning Form that can be used to document purported functional influences and respective intervention strategies. Several antecedent control methods and manipulations—such as eliminating conditions that are associated with challenging behaviors, introducing conditions that preempt challenging behaviors, introducing a transfer-of-stimulus control paradigm, and altering reinforcer effectiveness—can be incorporated in clinical decision making.

## Eliminate Conditions that Are
## Associated with Challenging Behaviors

Although practitioners sometimes view the elimination of conditions that appear to provoke or set the occasion for challenging behaviors as "giving up" on an individual because difficult situations simply are "avoided," the methodology actually represents a *substitutability* of stimulus control functions. That is, the objective is not to overlook critical areas of education or habilitation but, instead, to select alternative contexts to address learning objectives.

Kennedy and Itkonen (1993) described two studies that illustrate this therapeutic approach. In one study, the challenging behaviors of a 22-year-old woman with mental retardation requiring limited supports were targeted. Behaviors such as arguing, grabbing objects, self-hitting, and hitting others occurred frequently at school on days that she awoke late in the morning. By waking up late, she resisted staff prompting, missed breakfast, and required assistance with getting dressed. A setting event intervention was designed to overcome these situations by allowing the woman to turn off her alarm clock by herself and to select a preferred breakfast and clothing if she woke up within 5 minutes of the alarm. The woman's challenging behaviors were reduced to near-zero levels when this intervention was in place.

In the second study, a 20-year-old woman who had mental retardation requiring pervasive supports, cerebral palsy, and vision impairment displayed screaming, dropping to the floor, clothes-tearing, and hitting behaviors when she arrived at her school. The challenging behavior occurred following a prolonged transportation route that required her bus to make numerous stops. The setting event intervention entailed changing the transportation route from using city streets (associated with frequent stops) to the highway. The woman's challenging behaviors were essentially eliminated with this manipulation.

Individual's name: _____

Form completed by: _____

Target behavior (#  ): _____

List antecedent conditions that affect the occurrence of the target behavior:

1.

2.

3.

4.

Describe intervention approaches that will be incorporated in the behavioral support plan:

1. Elimination of provoking conditions:

2. Introduction of preemptive procedures:

3. Use of a transfer-of-stimulus control intervention:

4. Program procedures to alter reinforcer effectiveness:

Figure 3.   Antecedent Control Intervention Planning Form.

As demonstrated by Kennedy and Itkonen (1993), the elimination and substitution of specific antecedent conditions can be instrumental in achieving therapeutic goals without sacrificing other learning objectives. The participants in the studies learned to complete a morning routine and to travel successfully on a vehicle, performance goals that were not terminated but, instead, were accomplished in an alternative context.

## Introduce Conditions that Preempt Challenging Behaviors

Another approach toward intervention formulation is to arrange antecedent conditions in such a way that they preempt the occurrence of challenging behaviors. Operationally, these strategies function to set the occasion for responses that are incompatible with challenging behaviors, for example, by promoting "replacement" skills or physical alternatives.

Luiselli (1994) evaluated the use of noncontingent sensory reinforcement as a preemptive strategy with a 10-year-old girl who had posttraumatic neurological impairment. She exhibited "compulsive-like" object-grabbing and object-mouthing within her classroom, and these behaviors interfered seriously with her learning. Functional assessment suggested that the behaviors were reinforced by sensory pleasurable consequences in the forms of tactile and oral stimulation. A behavioral support plan was designed that allowed the girl to chew on an acceptable oral stimulus. The frequency of object-grabbing and object-mouthing behaviors decreased significantly following introduction of noncontingent access to pleasurable sensory stimulation.

The use of *skill-building* as a preemptive strategy was demonstrated by Cameron, Ainsleigh, and Bird (1992) with a 20-year-old man with Down syndrome who displayed aggressive and noncompliant behaviors during his evening bathing routine. Typically, a supervising staff person gave him a bar of soap and would use graduated physical assistance to prompt washing responses. Under these conditions, the man frequently resisted instruction and hit the staff person. A program was developed that included the presentation of liquid soap on the man's hands and body while requesting him to "get the soap off." This intervention virtually eliminated the aggressive and noncompliant behaviors as well as established desirable performance of the bathing routine. In this case, the provision of an alternative stimulus, liquid soap, appeared to reduce the performance "demand" of holding and manipulating a bar of soap and, in turn, eliminated aggression and noncompliance as covariant behaviors.

## Introduce a Transfer-of-Stimulus Control Paradigm

The procedures of eliminating conditions that set the occasion for challenging behaviors or preempting such responding may not be warranted clinically in certain situations. For example, it might be demonstrated that a child engages in disruptive behaviors when his teacher presents him with instructional requests. Although this antecedent condition is identified, it would not be advisable to terminate all instruction with the student. Similarly, the introduction of stimuli that immediately provoke alternative behaviors may not be possible in some cases. An intervention option in these situations is to find an already existing source of positive stimulus control and then "fade" or transfer this control to more acceptable "terminal" stimuli.

Zarcone et al. (1993) described the use of *instructional fading* in a transfer-of-stimulus control paradigm with three adults who had mental retardation requiring pervasive supports and escape-motivated self-injurious behaviors. These people participated in individualized sessions daily during which learning trials were presented every 30 seconds. During baseline, self-injurious responses resulted in a termination of the learning trial. Two intervention conditions were evaluated subsequently. During escape-extinction, learning trials continued to be presented similar to baseline except that self-injury did not terminate trials. The second intervention condition also included the identical escape-extinction procedure but incorporated instructional fading. Instructions were eliminated from the initial intervention session and then were introduced gradually at a frequency of one per session if a participant's self-injury was at or less than .50 responses per minute during the previous session. The instructional fading component plus escape-extinction proved to be more effective than escape-extinction alone in that the combined approach was not associated with an extinction "burst" phenomenon. Self-injury decreased rapidly at the onset of intervention for all participants.

The instructional fading procedure reported by Zarcone et al. (1993) was based on the frequency of trainer-presented learning trials as the source of stimulus control. In another example of this methodology, Luiselli, Teitelbaum, and Robinson (1983) evaluated a transfer-of-stimulus control intervention that was not focused on an alteration of procedure but, instead, was focused on the people who implemented it. The participant was a 10-year-old girl with mental retardation who displayed disruptive behaviors (getting out of seat, throwing objects, hitting) during speech therapy sessions but not in the presence of her classroom teacher. The teacher's classroom program consisted of positive social reinforcement and a contingent reprimand to which the child had responded very well. When the same procedures were used by the speech therapist during her sessions, however, similar intervention effects were not achieved, and challenging behaviors persisted at high rates. A stimulus fading strategy then was evaluated that consisted of having the classroom teacher (the "controlling stimulus") present with the therapist during several sessions. The teacher initially conducted the speech sessions and applied her customary intervention procedures while the therapist simply sat in the room without interacting with the child. In a series of eight fading steps, the therapist gradually sat closer to the child, initiated training with her, and applied intervention procedures while the teacher moved out of the room. After eight sessions of fading, the child's behavior was brought under effective clinical control by the speech therapist, and the positive results were maintained through a 45-week follow-up evaluation. In this study, the stimulus control already established by the teacher was transferred to the therapist.

## Alter Reinforcer Effectiveness

As noted previously, reinforcer effectiveness can be enhanced through the antecedent manipulation of EOs. Conditions of deprivation and satiation represent the most obvious examples in this regard. Thus, if an instructional program with a child includes edible reinforcement as a primary source of motivation, teaching sessions likely would be more effective if they preceded, rather than followed, lunch in the school day. Social variables also can be addressed similarly. For example, a child who demonstrated challenging behaviors that were maintained by contingent social attention might be exposed to frequent and noncontingent adult socialization for brief periods preceding activities in which the behaviors were most prevalent. This procedure would have the purpose of inducing "social satiation" so that the motivation to seek adult attention is lessened in another context. Also, as discussed by Lerman and Iwata (1996), such a manipulation could be used to enhance the effectiveness of specific intervention procedures. Thus, exposing a person to continuous social attention could serve as an EO that improves the application of extinction (withholding attention) under later conditions. As seen in these examples, therapeutic objectives can be based on increasing the effectiveness of reinforcement or attenuating reinforcement effects on challenging behaviors.

## SUMMARY

Not all challenging behaviors are influenced by antecedent conditions nor can they be altered systematically for therapeutic purposes. This fact notwithstanding, antecedent control approaches have been underutilized in the design of behavioral support plans for people with developmental disabilities. This chapter has focused on the conceptualization of intervention from an antecedent control perspective and suggested guidelines for intervention formulation. In contrast to consequence-based procedures, antecedent control methods may be preferable because 1) many challenging behaviors are highly situation-specific; 2) some behaviors are so physically imposing that they warrant alternative strategies; 3) positive reinforcement may be difficult to identify, is applied inconsistently, or is severely restricted given high-rate responding; 4) they are more practical for service providers; and 5) permanent behavior change can be achieved.

Functional assessment and analysis of antecedent control conditions is the initial step in intervention formulation. When challenging behaviors seem to be associated with one or more antecedent conditions, intervention procedures can be contemplated that include manipulating, altering, or attenuating EOs or $S^D$s. Possible strategies are to eliminate conditions that set the occasion for challenging behaviors, to promote alternative and incompatible responses, to transfer sources of stimulus control, and to enhance or reduce the effects from reinforcement contingencies. By incorporating antecedent control methods toward the intervention for challenging behaviors, educators, therapists, and clinicians will establish more robust and comprehensive approaches to improve the lives of people with developmental disabilities.

## REFERENCES

Cameron, M.J., Ainsleigh, S.A., & Bird, F.L. (1992). The acquisition of stimulus control of compliance and participation during an ADL routine. *Behavioral Residential Treatment, 7,* 327–340.

Gewirtz, J.L. (1972). Some contextual determinants of stimulus potency. In R.D. Parke (Ed.), *Recent developments in social learning theory* (pp. 7–33). New York: Academic Press.

Iwata, B.A., Vollmer, T.R., & Zarcone, J.R. (1990). The experimental (functional) analysis of behavior disorders: Methodology, applications, and limitations. In A.C. Repp & N.N. Singh (Eds.), *Perspectives on nonaversive and aversive interventions with developmentally disabled persons* (pp. 301–330). Sycamore, IL: Sycamore Publishing.

Kennedy, C.H., & Itkonen, T. (1993). Effects of setting events on the problem behaviors of students with severe disabilities. *Journal of Applied Behavior Analysis, 26,* 321–327.

Kennedy, C.H., & Meyer, K.A. (1996). Sleep deprivation, allergy symptoms, and negatively reinforced problem behavior. *Journal of Applied Behavior Analysis, 29,* 133–135.

Lerman, D.C., & Iwata, B.A. (1996). Developing a technology for the use of operant extinction in clinical settings: An examination of basic and applied research. *Journal of Applied Behavior Analysis, 29,* 345–382.

Luiselli, J.K. (1994). Effects of noncontingent sensory reinforcement on stereotypic behaviors in a child with post-traumatic neurological impairment. *Journal of Behavior Therapy & Experimental Psychiatry, 25,* 325–330.

Luiselli, J.K., Teitelbaum, M., & Robinson, M. (1983). Use of a fading procedure to overcome treatment specificity in child behavior management. *Behavioral Engineering, 9,* 1–5.

Matson, J.L., & Taras, M. (1989). A 20-year review of punishment and alternative methods to treat problem behaviors in developmentally delayed persons. *Research in Developmental Disabilities, 10,* 85–104.

Michael, J. (1993). Establishing operations. *The Behavior Analyst, 16,* 191–206.

O'Brien, S., & Repp, A.C. (1990). A review of 30 years of research on the use of differential reinforcement to reduce inappropriate responding. *Behavior Modification, 14,* 20–38.

Piazza, C.C., Fisher, W.W., Hagopian, L.P., Bowman, L.G., & O'Toole, L. (1996). Using a choice assessment to predict reinforcer effectiveness. *Journal of Applied Behavior Analysis, 29,* 1–9.

Repp, A.C., & Karsh, K. (1993). Hypothesis-based interventions for tantrum behaviors of persons with developmental disabilities in school settings. *Journal of Applied Behavior Analysis, 27,* 21–31.

Schlinger, H.D. (1993). Establishing operations: Another step toward a functional taxonomy of environmental events. *Behavior Analyst, 16,* 207–209.

Smith, R.G., Iwata, B.A., Goh, H., & Shore, B.A. (1995). Analysis of establishing operations for self-injury maintained by escape. *Journal of Applied Behavior Analysis, 28,* 515–535.

Touchette, P.E., MacDonald, R.E., & Langer, S.N. (1985). A scatter plot for identifying stimulus control of problem behavior. *Journal of Applied Behavior Analysis, 18,* 343–351.

Zarcone, J.R., Iwata, B.A., Vollmer, T.A., Jagtiani, S., Smith, R.G., & Mazaleski, J.L. (1993). Extinction of self-injurious escape behavior with and without instructional fading. *Journal of Applied Behavior Analysis, 26,* 353–360.

# ~ *II* ~

## *Issues of Assessment*

# ～ *3* ～

# *Methods for Assessing Antecedent Influences on Challenging Behaviors*

## Raymond G. Miltenberger

Behavior analysts widely accept that the functional approach is recommended practice for the assessment of and intervention for challenging behaviors in individuals with developmental disabilities (Iwata, Vollmer, & Zarcone, 1990; Iwata Vollmer, Zarcone, & Rodgers, 1993; Lennox & Miltenberger, 1989). By identifying the controlling variables that are functionally related to the occurrence of the challenging behavior, the behavior analyst can develop functional interventions that address the controlling variables (e.g., Iwata et al., 1993). Functional interventions have been shown to be effective across a number of studies (e.g., Arndorfer, Miltenberger, Rortvedt, Woster, & Gaffaney, 1994; Carr & Carlson, 1993; Kemp & Carr, 1995). Researchers have also demonstrated that functional interventions are more effective than interventions that are not based on the results of a functional assessment (e.g., Iwata, Pace, Cowdery, & Miltenberger, 1994; Repp, Felce, & Barton, 1988).

There are a number of steps involved in the functional approach to assessment and intervention (see Miltenberger, in press):

1. Conduct a functional assessment of the contingencies of reinforcement for the challenging behavior.
2. Develop a hypothesis about the antecedents and consequences that are functionally related to the occurrence of the challenging behavior based on the functional assessment results.
3. Develop functional interventions that manipulate relevant antecedents and/or consequences based on the hypothesis derived from the functional assessment results.

4. Evaluate intervention to determine its effect on the challenging behavior.

The purpose of this chapter is to describe methods for conducting a functional assessment with an emphasis on identifying the antecedents to a challenging behavior. Following a discussion of the contingencies of reinforcement maintaining challenging behaviors, the chapter describes the application of three different functional assessment approaches and the advantages and disadvantages of each approach.

## CONTINGENCIES OF REINFORCEMENT MAINTAINING CHALLENGING BEHAVIORS

To understand why a challenging behavior is occurring, one must identify the contingencies of reinforcement maintaining the challenging behavior (Skinner, 1953). The contingencies of reinforcement include the antecedents and consequences that are functionally related to the occurrence of the behavior.

### Challenging Behavior(s)

Challenging behavior(s) must be identified and defined so that they can be recorded during the functional assessment. Different dimensions of the challenging behavior that can be recorded include the frequency, duration, magnitude, and latency. With event recording, one or more of these dimensions is recorded each time the behavior occurs. Interval or time sample recording involves recording the occurrence or nonoccurrence of the behavior during continuous (interval) or noncontinuous intervals of time (time sample) to produce an estimate of the occurrence of the behavior (Miltenberger, 1997).

In addition to recording the occurrence of the challenging behavior, the amount of response effort involved in the behavior should be noted. Response effort for the challenging behavior is important, especially in relation to functionally equivalent alternative behaviors. When the response effort is greater for one behavior, the behavior is less likely to occur than a concurrent operant that requires less response effort (Friman & Poling, 1995; Horner & Day, 1991; Horner, Sprague, O'Brien, & Heathfield, 1990; Mace & Roberts, 1993).

### Antecedents

Antecedents are events that precede the occurrence of the challenging behavior. There are two classes of antecedent events that can influence the occurrence of the challenging behavior: discriminative stimuli ($S^D$s) and establishing operations (EOs) (Miltenberger, in press; Smith & Iwata, 1997).

*Discriminative Stimuli* An S$^D$ is an antecedent that is present when the occurrence of the behavior is followed by a reinforcing consequence (Skinner, 1953). As a result, the behavior is more likely to occur when the S$^D$ is present in the future, and the S$^D$ is said to exert stimulus control over the behavior. For example, if an individual engages in self-injury and a particular staff member typically reinforces the behavior with attention, that staff person is an S$^D$ for the self-injury, and the behavior will be more likely to occur in the presence of that staff person.

*Establishing Operations* An EO is an antecedent that increases the potency of a reinforcer at a particular time and increases the probability of occurrence of any behavior that has resulted in that reinforcer (Michael, 1982). Whereas the S$^D$ is present immediately prior to the occurrence of the challenging behavior, the onset of an EO may be more distal to the occurrence of the behavior, and the effects of the EO may persist over time. Events that may function as an EO are termed "setting events" or "ecological variables" (O'Neill et al., 1997). For example, after a person eats salty foods, water becomes a more potent reinforcer, and the behavior of getting a drink of water is more probable. Water will continue to be a potent reinforcer until the person drinks water (or other liquid). When a person with self-injury that is maintained by attention has not received attention over a long period, attention becomes a more powerful reinforcer, and self-injury is more likely to occur (Vollmer & Iwata, 1991; Vollmer, Iwata, Zarcone, Smith, & Mazaleski, 1993). In this case, the presence of a person who has provided attention for the self-injury in the past would be an S$^D$ for the behavior. The individual is not likely to engage in the self-injurious behavior unless the EO and the S$^D$ are both present. The EO provides the "motivation" for the behavior, and the S$^D$ provides the "opportunity" for the behavior to pay off at that time. It is important to identify the S$^D$(s) and the EO for a challenging behavior during the functional assessment because the presence of the S$^D$ and EO predicts the occurrence of the challenging behavior. In addition, one approach to intervention is to manipulate the S$^D$s and EOs to alter the probability of the challenging behavior (Miltenberger, 1997). To identify the EO for a challenging behavior, you must first identify the reinforcer for the behavior.

## Consequences

A challenging behavior is maintained by its immediate consequences through the process of positive or negative reinforcement (Skinner, 1953). Challenging behaviors are strengthened when they result in the presentation of reinforcing stimuli (positive reinforcement) or the termination or avoidance of aversive stimuli (negative reinforcement). Reinforcement may involve socially mediated consequences (e.g., attention from others, escape from a teaching interaction) or automatic consequences of the behavior itself (e.g., self-stimulation, relief from painful stimulation; Iwata et al., 1993). The reinforcing consequences of a challenging behavior must be identified through a functional assessment so that functional interventions can be developed. In addition to the manipulation of antecedent events, functional interventions involve the elimination of the reinforcer for the challenging behavior in an extinction procedure or the delivery of the reinforcer for alternative behaviors in a differential reinforcement procedure (Miltenberger, 1997).

### Alternative Behavior

In addition to information on the challenging behavior, antecedents, and consequences, a functional assessment also should identify functionally equivalent alternative behaviors in the individual's repertoire (Carr, 1988). Knowledge of alternative behaviors is important because these behaviors may be involved in differential reinforcement procedures; aspects to assess include availability, effort, efficiency, and functional equivalence (Mace & Roberts, 1993; O'Neill et al., 1997). An alternative behavior will be most likely to occur if it is in the individual's repertoire (availability), if it requires less response effort than the challenging behavior, if it results in reinforcing consequences immediately and consistently (efficiency), and if it results in the same reinforcing consequences as the challenging behavior (functional equivalence).

A thorough functional assessment will provide information on all aspects of the contingencies of reinforcement described in the previous paragraphs. This information is then used in the development of functional interventions (Carr, McConnachie, Levin, & Kemp, 1993; Durand, 1990). The rest of this chapter focuses on methods for conducting a functional assessment with an emphasis on the assessment of antecedent events.

## FUNCTIONAL ASSESSMENT METHODS

Conducting a functional assessment is an important first step in the development of intervention for challenging behaviors. There are three general approaches to conducting a functional assessment: indirect assessment, direct observation in the natural environment, and experimental manipulations or functional analyses (Iwata et al., 1990;

Lennox & Miltenberger, 1989). In more basic terms, the three ways to conduct a functional assessment are to *ask, observe,* and *test.*

## Indirect Assessment (Ask)

Indirect assessment involves the use of behavioral interviews, questionnaires, and/or rating scales to obtain information from informants who know the individual well (Iwata et al., 1990; Lennox & Miltenberger, 1989). In essence, you ask significant others (e.g., parents, teachers, staff) for information about the contingencies of reinforcement maintaining the challenging behavior using a structured interview format or available rating scales or questionnaires.

**Behavioral Interviews** The behavioral interview is typically the first step in the functional assessment process. Researchers have identified a number of important types of questions to ask in a behavioral interview to generate the information needed to understand the contingencies of reinforcement related to the challenging behavior (Iwata, Wong, Riordan, Dorsey, & Lau, 1982; Miltenberger & Fuqua, 1985; O'Neill et al., 1997). The Functional Assessment Interview (FAI), developed by O'Neill et al. (1997), includes questions that ask the informant (who should have direct contact with the person exhibiting the challenging behavior) to describe the challenging behaviors, distal antecedents (ecological variables or setting events), immediate antecedents, consequences, alternative behaviors, and other categories of information. The FAI is structured so that it can be used as an interview guide or as a questionnaire, through which the informant provides objective statements of events rather than opinion, inference, or interpretation. The information from the FAI is used to develop hypotheses or summary statements about the distal and proximal antecedents and immediate consequences related to the occurrence of the challenging behavior (O'Neill et al., 1997).

*Setting Events* One set of questions on the FAI asks about a number of possible setting events (distal antecedents) such as medications taken by the person, medical or physical conditions, sleep patterns, eating routines and diet, predictability of daily activities, the opportunity for choices, and the pattern of staff support. Information on these antecedents is important because each has the potential to function as an EO to influence challenging behaviors exhibited by the individual (e.g., O'Neill et al., 1997). For example, sleep deprivation can increase the aversiveness of tasks and can increase the probability of escape-related behaviors (e.g., Kennedy & Itkonen, 1993; Kennedy & Meyer, 1996; O'Reilly, 1995). An individual who takes the medication lithium may experience a side effect of increased thirst. Challenging behaviors related to this EO may become more probable, such as stealing beverages from housemates (e.g., Gourash, 1986). Lack of choice or predictability may increase the aversiveness of demand situations and result in an increased likelihood of escape-related challenging behaviors (e.g., Dunlap et al., 1993; Dunlap, Kern-Dunlap, Clarke, & Robbins, 1991; Flannery, O'Neill, & Horner, 1995).

Infrequent staff contact due to inadequate staffing patterns results in a relative state of deprivation, which may be an EO for challenging behaviors maintained by attention (Vollmer et al., 1993). A variety of medical problems may influence the probability of challenging behaviors (e.g., Gardner & Whalen, 1996). O'Reilly (1997) showed that the presence of otitis media in a young child made escape-related behavior more likely. One individual with profound mental retardation with whom I am familiar was more likely to engage in aggressive behavior in demand situations when he had not had a bowel movement for a few days. Presumably, the unpleasantness of constipation increased the aversiveness of some tasks and increased the likelihood of behavior reinforced by escape from those tasks. These are just a few examples of the ways in which antecedent conditions can influence challenging behaviors. The important point is that these antecedents must be identified through the functional assessment process so that interventions can be developed to address the antecedents.

*Proximal Antecedents*   The FAI asks a number of questions about proximal antecedents such as time of day, settings, people, and activities most and least likely to predict the occurrence of the challenging behavior (O'Neill et al., 1997). Each of these immediate antecedents may function as an $S^D$ (or in some cases, as an EO) that exerts stimulus control over the behavior. Again, it is important to identify the immediate antecedents that are functionally related to the challenging behavior so that they can be addressed in treatment. The most basic question to ask the informant is, "What happens immediately before the challenging behavior occurs or as the challenging behavior is occurring?" Following this open-ended question, follow-up questions can be asked until there is clear, objective information on the immediate antecedents that predict the occurrence of the challenging behavior.

**Rating Scales and Questionnaires**   Researchers have developed a number of rating scales and questionnaires to gather information about the antecedents and consequences that may be functionally related to the occurrence of challenging behaviors. These tools include the Motivation Assessment Scale (MAS; Durand & Crimmins, 1988), the Functional Analysis Screening Tool (FAST; Iwata & DeLeon,

1995), and the Setting Events Checklist (Gardner, Cole, Davidson, & Karan, 1986).

The MAS has 16 questions each answered on a seven-point scale from "never" to "always." The MAS is designed to assess four different functions of challenging behaviors: attention, escape, tangible, and self-stimulation. Some of the MAS questions ask about antecedent events that may bear a relationship to each of the four classes of reinforcing consequences; for example, "Does the behavior occur following a request to perform a difficult task?" is a question that asks about a possible antecedent to behavior maintained by escape. "Does the behavior occur when you stop attending to the person?" asks about a possible antecedent to behavior maintained by attention. "Would this behavior occur . . . if no one was around?" asks about a possible antecedent to behavior maintained by automatic reinforcement (self-stimulation). "Does this behavior occur when you take away a favorite toy, food, or activity?" asks about a possible antecedent to behavior maintained by tangible reinforcement.

The FAST has 27 statements to which the informant responds "yes" or "no." The FAST is designed to assess three possible social functions of challenging behaviors (attention, access to activities, and escape) and two nonsocial or automatic functions (sensory stimulation and pain attenuation). Similar to the MAS, the FAST has a number of statements about antecedent events that may bear a relationship to these five possible functions of challenging behaviors. Examples of items from the FAST include the following: "The behavior rarely occurs when you give the person lots of attention." "The behavior often occurs when you inform the person that he or she cannot have a certain item or cannot engage in a particular activity." "The behavior often occurs when the immediate environment is very noisy or crowded." "The behavior occurs frequently when the person is alone or unoccupied."

The Setting Events Checklist lists 16 events that may be possible antecedents to a challenging behavior. The rater, who has direct contact with the individual who exhibits the challenging behavior, identifies when the events occurred (i.e., on the same day as the challenging behavior, the morning of the behavior, or the evening before the behavior). This checklist is designed to assess more distal antecedents to the challenging behavior. The items from the Setting Events Checklist are listed in Table 1.

**Advantages and Disadvantages of Indirect Assessment** The main advantage of indirect functional assessment methods is that they are relatively quick and easy to conduct, and a number of interview/

Table 1. Items from the Setting Events Checklist

| |
| --- |
| Was informed of something unusually disappointing |
| Was refused some requested object or activity |
| Fought, argued, or had other negative interactions |
| Was disciplined/reprimanded (behavior or disciplinary action was atypical) |
| Was hurried or rushed more than usual |
| Sleep pattern (including duration) was unusual |
| Was under the care of someone new/favorite caretaker was absent |
| Experienced other major changes in living environment |
| Learned about visit/vacation with family/friends (will or will not occur) |
| Visitors arrived/failed to arrive |
| Medications were changed/missed |
| Had menstrual period |
| Appeared excessively tired/lethargic |
| Appeared excessively agitated |
| Appeared to be in a bad mood |
| Appeared or complained of being ill |

From Gardner, W.I., Cole, C.L., Davidson, D.P., & Karan, O.C. (1986). Reducing aggression in individuals with developmental disabilities: An expanded stimulus control, assessment, and intervention model. *Education and Training in Mental Retardation, 21,* 7; reprinted by permission.

Note: On the actual checklist, events are checked if they happened in the evening before, or the morning of, the day on which the challenging behavior occurred. Checked items are briefly described.

questionnaire formats and rating scales are available to aid in the process (Iwata et al., 1990; Lennox & Miltenberger, 1989). These instruments can provide a wide range of information from a number of sources about a variety of possibly relevant variables. This information can be used to develop hypotheses about the contingencies of reinforcement that maintain the challenging behavior, which forms the basis for the development of hypothesis-based interventions. Information from indirect assessments also can be used to guide subsequent direct observations. Although paraprofessionals can take an active part in providing functional assessment information, an individual must have training in behavior analysis to develop hypotheses or functional interventions based on the information.

The major disadvantage of indirect assessment is that the information is based on the informants' retrospective recall of events related to the challenging behavior (Miltenberger, in press). The informants' recall may be inaccurate or only partially accurate because of forgetting, bias, or their limited contact with the relevant events. These limitations can be minimized when a number of different informants independently provide congruent information and the information is consistent with the results of direct observations. Regardless of whether information from multiple sources is congruent, indirect assessment results do not demonstrate a functional relationship between the challenging behavior and hypothesized antecedents and consequences. Another limitation of indirect assessment is the equivocal reliability and validity data available for rating scales (Arndorfer et al., 1994; Crawford, Brockel, Schauss, & Miltenberger, 1992; Zarcone, Rodgers, Iwata, Rourke, & Dorsey, 1991). Rating scales are best used in conjunction with other functional assessment procedures. For example, after reviewing the results of the Setting Events Checklist, the behavior analyst can ask specific follow-up questions in an interview to gather more information on specific items marked on the checklist.

## Direct Observation in the Natural Environment (Observe)

With direct assessment procedures, which are often referred to as A-B-C recording (Miltenberger, in press), an individual observes and records the challenging behavior and the antecedents and consequences as they occur (Arndorfer et al., 1994; Bijou, Peterson, & Ault, 1968). Whereas indirect assessment relies on the informant's recall, direct assessment requires the observer to be present when the behavior occurs in order to observe the antecedents and consequences and to record them immediately. Therefore, it is important to know the times of day when the behavior is most likely to occur so that observations can be planned at those times. A scatter plot, used to determine when the behavior occurs, is often completed prior to A-B-C recording procedures (Touchette, MacDonald, & Langer, 1985).

*Scatter Plot*  With scatter plot recording, the observer simply records the occurrence of the challenging behavior during half-hour intervals of time. Using a datasheet consisting of a grid, with boxes corresponding to each half hour of the day across a number of weeks, the observer indicates in each box whether the behavior did not occur (by leaving the box empty), occurred one time (by putting a diagonal slash mark in the box), or occurred more than one time (by darkening the whole box). Over a number of days, the temporal pattern in the behavior becomes clear on the scatter plot. The observer can then plan antecedent-behavior-consequence (A-B-C) observations at the times that the scatter plot indicates that the behavior occurs the most. An example of a completed scatter plot is shown in Figure 1. According to the pattern indicated in this scatter plot, the challenging behavior is most likely to occur between 3:00 P.M. and 4:00 P.M. each day. Therefore, A-B-C observations would be scheduled to occur at that time of day.

*A-B-C Recording*  An observer, such as a significant other in the individual's life (e.g., teacher, parent, staff member) or a consultant with expertise in behavior analysis, conducts A-B-C recording. The

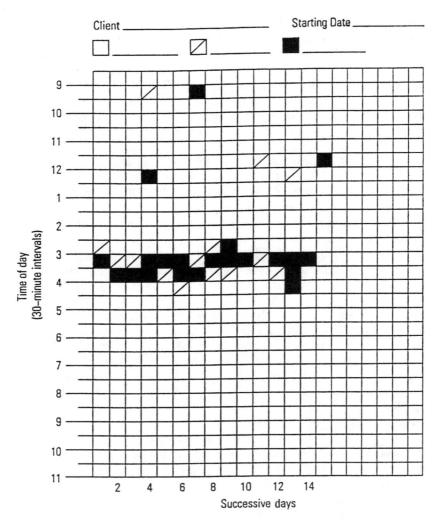

Figure 1. This completed scatter plot shows the time of occurrence of the challenging be-havior across 15 days of observation. (Key: Empty squares indicate that the behavior did not occur, slashed squares indicate that the behavior occurred one time, and darkened squares indicate that the behavior occurred two or more times in the interval.) (From Miltenberger, R.G. [1997]. *Behavior modification: Principles and procedures* [p. 295]. Pacific Grove, CA: Brooks/Cole; reprinted by permission.)

observer, who must be present in the natural environment (e.g., home, school, work) as the behavior occurs, can use one of three A-B-C re-cording methods: descriptive, checklist, or interval recording (Milten-berger, 1997, in press).

*Descriptive Method* To conduct descriptive A-B-C recording, the observer writes down a description of the events that immediately preceded the challenging behavior, notes the behavior itself, and records the immediate consequences. This recording is typically done on a datasheet with three columns—one for antecedents, behavior, and consequences. Carr et al. (1994) suggested the use of index cards for A-B-C recording. To conduct the recording correctly, the observer must write down objective descriptions of the A-B-Cs without interpretation, inferences, or opinions about the events. Before observers can successfully conduct A-B-C recordings, they should be instructed to describe events objectively and to focus on events occurring in close temporal relationship to the challenging behavior (e.g., Lennox & Miltenberger, 1989).

After the observer records the A-B-Cs of the challenging behavior across a number of occasions, the resulting descriptions can be evaluated to identify the antecedents and consequences that occur most frequently in relationship to the behavior. A hypothesis is then developed about the particular antecedents and consequences that appear to be functionally related to the behavior. At this point, hypothesis-based interventions may be developed, especially if the results of A-B-C recording are consistent with information derived from interviews or other indirect assessment procedures.

*Checklist Method* In the checklist method for conducting A-B-C recording, the observer also records the A-B-Cs as they occur in the natural environment but, instead, records on a checklist with columns for the challenging behaviors and columns for specific antecedents and consequences that are relevant for the particular individual (Miltenberger, 1997; O'Neill et al., 1997). The specific antecedents, behaviors, and consequences listed on the checklist are chosen based on information from prior indirect assessments or descriptive A-B-C recording. When a challenging behavior occurs, the observer puts a checkmark in the column that corresponds to the behavior. He or she then puts a checkmark in the columns that correspond to the particular antecedent that was observed to precede the behavior and the particular consequence that was observed to follow the behavior. If an antecedent or consequence occurs that is not on the checklist, the observer writes the event in a blank column so that it can be recorded again if it reoccurs. Across a number of observations, patterns will emerge as one or more antecedents and consequences on the checklist get scored more frequently. From these patterns, hypotheses can be developed about which events appear to be functionally related to the challenging behavior. Figure 2 shows an example of an A-B-C checklist with some hypothetical data.

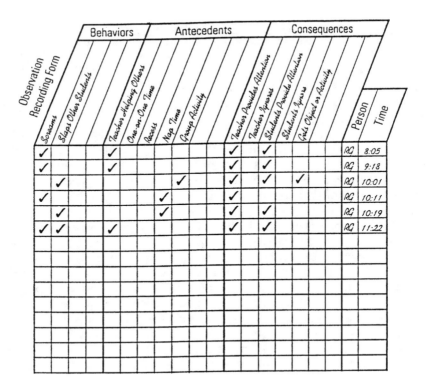

Figure 2.   This A-B-C checklist shows data collected on six occurrences of the challenging behavior. Note that the checklist has columns for a number of different challenging behaviors followed by columns for a number of antecedents and consequences. The observer checks the relevant columns each time the challenging behavior occurs. (From Miltenberger, R.G. [1997]. *Behavior modification: Principles and procedures* [p. 298]. Pacific Grove, CA: Brooks/Cole; reprinted by permission.)

*Interval Recording Method*   A third method for conducting A-B-C observations is interval recording (Mace & Lalli, 1991). Similar to the checklist method, the antecedents, challenging behaviors, and consequences relevant for a particular individual are identified in advance based on prior indirect assessment or descriptive A-B-C recording. In consecutive intervals of time (e.g., 6-, 10-, or 15-second intervals) throughout the observation period, these A-B-Cs are recorded as to whether they occur (e.g., Mace & Lalli, 1991; Rortvedt & Miltenberger, 1994). The interval method produces information on the temporal relationships among the antecedents, behavior, and consequences within the observation period. To conduct interval A-B-C recording, the observer must have some method for cueing the observation intervals (e.g., an audiotape) as he or she observes the individual in the natural environment.

**Linking Indirect Assessment and Direct Observation**  As suggested previously, A-B-C assessments are sometimes linked to indirect assessments when interview or rating scale information is used to identify the specific antecedents and consequences included in checklist or interval A-B-C recording (Miltenberger, 1997; O'Neill et al., 1997). Indirect assessment can also be linked to direct observation of a specific setting event that has been suggested to influence the challenging behavior. In such cases, an observer will record the occurrence of the putative antecedent event while also recording each occurrence of the challenging behavior to determine whether the challenging behavior is more probable given the occurrence of the antecedent event. For example, if staff report that aggressive behavior is more common when the individual's allergies are severe, the staff can record signs of increased allergy activity and record aggressive behavior to see if aggressive behavior increases on days when the allergies are worse. If parents report that their child is more likely to engage in noncompliant behavior following an evening of interrupted sleep, the parents can record sleep problems and noncompliance to see if noncompliance increases during the day following a night of interrupted sleep. In cases such as these, direct observation is used to confirm or rule out the relationship between the setting event and the challenging behavior reported in an indirect assessment.

**Advantages and Disadvantages of Direct Assessment**  The advantage of direct assessment over indirect assessment is that the observer is present to observe and record the distal setting events or the immediate antecedents and consequences of the behavior as they occur in the natural environment. Direct observation should improve the accuracy of recording because the observer does not have to rely on recall. Another advantage of direct observation assessment is that, with proper instruction, it can be carried out by individuals such as parents, teachers, or staff members who are already in the individual's natural environment. This can reduce the amount of professional time and money involved in the assessment. Finally, direct observation can confirm or refute the information provided in interviews or rating scales (Miltenberger, in press).

A disadvantage of direct assessment is the professional time and resources required to instruct individuals to record accurately. Another limitation is that some individuals in the natural environment may not have the time, interest, or ability to carry out the recording. In addition, because A-B-C assessments are typically used to record immediate antecedents and consequences, distal antecedents or setting events may be overlooked. If distal antecedents are suspected to influence the challenging behavior, direct observation of these specific antecedents should be initiated. Furthermore, the A-B-C recording must be interpreted by an individual with training in behavior analysis to develop hypotheses and hypothesis-based interventions or to determine if further assessment is needed. Finally, the results of direct assessment cannot demonstrate a functional relationship among the antecedents and consequences and the challenging behavior because no variables are manipulated (Iwata et al., 1990; Iwata et al., 1993).

## Experimental Manipulations/Functional Analyses (Test)

A functional analysis involves experimental manipulation of antecedents and/or consequences to demonstrate a functional relationship among one or more of the antecedents and consequences and the occurrence of the challenging behavior (Iwata et al., 1990; Lennox & Miltenberger, 1989). A functional analysis can be used by itself to identify controlling variables, or it can be used following a functional assessment to confirm the results of the functional assessment (Miltenberger, in press). Because Chapter 4 discusses functional analysis procedures in detail, this chapter provides only an overview.

There are essentially three steps involved in conducting a functional analysis: 1) objective measurement of the challenging behavior under controlled circumstances, 2) demonstration of a change in the level of the challenging behavior following the manipulation of antecedent and/or consequence events, and 3) replication (Miltenberger, in press). The functional analysis is actually a brief experiment carried out to identify the controlling variables for the challenging behavior.

Two different experimental designs are typically used in conducting a functional analysis: an alternating treatments design and a reversal, or ABAB, design. Iwata, Dorsey, Slifer, Bauman, and Richman (1982) used an alternating treatments design when they conducted a functional analysis of self-injury. The participants were exposed to four different experimental conditions, which were alternated rapidly each day across a number of days. In each experimental condition, Iwata, Dorsey, et al. manipulated a specific EO and reinforcer for the self-injurious behavior. If the rate of self-injury was highest in one condition relative to the others, the authors concluded that the antecedents and consequences manipulated in that condition were functionally related to the self-injury. Durand and Carr (1987) used a reversal design in which they evaluated the influence of two antecedent conditions—low attention and increased task difficulty—on stereotypic behavior. Following baseline, each condition was conducted for a number of consecutive sessions and then replicated a number of times. For all participants, the challenging behavior occurred most frequently in the increased task difficulty condition, demonstrating a functional relationship between task difficulty and the challenging behavior. Numerous studies have demonstrated the value of functional analysis procedures for identifying the antecedents and consequences that are functionally related to the challenging behavior and for developing functional treatments for the challenging behavior (Arndorfer & Miltenberger, 1993; Mace, Lalli, & Lalli, 1991).

**Advantages and Disadvantages of Functional Analysis**  The major advantage of a functional analysis is the experimental demonstration of a functional relationship among antecedents and/or consequences and the challenging behavior (Iwata et al., 1990; Lennox & Miltenberger, 1989). In essence, the functional analysis provides the best proof that particular events function as controlling variables for the challenging behavior. Other functional assessment methods provide only correlational information about potential controlling variables. Functional analysis results, however, can strengthen the confidence in the findings from other functional assessment procedures when the results are congruent (Miltenberger, 1997).

The disadvantages include the time, effort, and professional resources involved in developing and conducting a functional analysis. Time and behavioral expertise are required by the behavior analyst to arrange the experimental conditions in advance, to conduct the experimental conditions or to teach significant others to conduct the conditions, and to ensure the integrity of the conditions (Lennox & Miltenberger, 1989).

## SUMMARY

Understanding the contingencies of reinforcement controlling challenging behaviors is essential for the development of effective interventions. A thorough understanding of the antecedents and consequences allows the behavior analyst to predict the occurrence of the behavior and to identify the positively or negatively reinforcing outcome of the behavior. The antecedents are important in the context of a reinforcement contingency when they function as EOs that alter the value of the reinforcer or as $S^D$s that have stimulus control over the challenging behavior because the behavior has been reinforced in the past when similar stimuli were present (Smith & Iwata, 1997).

Three functional assessment procedures can be used to identify the antecedents and consequences of the challenging behavior: indirect assessment, direct observation, and functional analysis. Indirect assessments gather information from significant others through interviews and rating scales and result in hypotheses about controlling variables. Direct observation produces information on the antecedents and consequences that is likely to be more objective and, perhaps more accurate, because recording takes place as the challenging behavior occurs in the natural environment. When direct and indirect assessment information is consistent, firm hypotheses can be developed about the controlling variables, which leads to the development of hypothesis-based interventions. Functional analysis, involving experimental manipulation of antecedents and/or consequences, can be conducted to confirm functional assessment results. Only the functional analysis demonstrates a functional relationship among the antecedents and consequences and the challenging behavior.

## REFERENCES

Arndorfer, R.E., & Miltenberger, R.G. (1993). Functional assessment and treatment of challenging behavior: A review with implications for early childhood. *Topics in Early Childhood Special Education, 13,* 82–105.

Arndorfer, R., Miltenberger, R., Rortvedt, A., Woster, S., & Gaffaney, T. (1994). Home based descriptive and experimental analysis of problem behavior in children. *Topics in Early Childhood Special Education, 14,* 64–87.

Bijou, S.W., Peterson, R.F., & Ault, M.H. (1968). A method to integrate descriptive and experimental field studies at the level of data and empirical concepts. *Journal of Applied Behavior Analysis, 1,* 175–191.

Carr, E.G. (1988). Functional equivalence as a mechanism of response generalization. In R.H. Horner, G. Dunlap, & R.L. Koegel (Eds.), *Generalization and maintenance: Life-style changes in applied settings* (pp. 221–241). Baltimore: Paul H. Brookes Publishing Co.

Carr, E.G., & Carlson, J.I. (1993). Reduction of severe behavior problems in the community using a multicomponent treatment approach. *Journal of Applied Behavior Analysis, 26,* 157–172.

Carr, E.G., Levin, L., McConnachie, G., Carlson, J.I., Kemp, D.C., & Smith, C.E. (1994). *Communication-based intervention for problem behavior: A user's guide for producing positive change.* Baltimore: Paul H. Brookes Publishing Co.

Carr, E.G., McConnachie, G., Levin, L., & Kemp, D.C. (1993). Communication-based treatment of severe behavior problems. In R. Van Houten & S. Axelrod (Eds.), *Behavior analysis and treatment* (pp. 231–267). New York: Plenum.

Crawford, J., Brockel, B., Schauss, S., & Miltenberger, R.G. (1992). A comparison of methods for the functional assessment of stereotypic behavior. *Journal of The Association for Persons with Severe Handicaps, 17,* 77–86.

Dunlap, G., dePerczel, M., Clarke, S., Wilson, D., Wright, S., White, R., & Gomez, A. (1993). Choice making to promote adaptive behavior for students with emotional and behavioral challenges. *Journal of Applied Behavior Analysis, 27,* 505–518.

Dunlap, G., Kern-Dunlap, L., Clarke, S., & Robbins, F.R. (1991). Functional assessment, curricular revision, and severe behavior problems. *Journal of Applied Behavior Analysis, 24,* 387–397.

Durand, V.M. (1990). *Severe behavior problems: A functional communication training approach.* New York: Guilford Press.

Durand, V.M., & Carr, E.G. (1987). Social influences on "self-stimulatory" behavior: Analysis and treatment application. *Journal of Applied Behavior Analysis, 20,* 199–132.

Durand, V.M., & Crimmins, D.B. (1988). Identifying the variables maintaining
self-injurious behavior. *Journal of Autism and Developmental Disorders, 18,*
99–117.

Flannery, K.B., O'Neill, R.B., & Horner, R.H. (1995). Including predictability
in functional assessment and individual program development. *Education
and Treatment of Children, 18,* 499–509.

Friman, P.C., & Poling, A. (1995). Making life easier with effort: Basic findings
and applied research on response effort. *Journal of Applied Behavior Analysis,
28,* 583–590.

Gardner, W.I., Cole, C.L., Davidson, D.P., & Karan, O.C. (1986). Reducing aggression in individuals with developmental disabilities: An expanded stimulus control, assessment, and intervention model. *Education and Training in
Mental Retardation, 21,* 3–12.

Gardner, W.I., & Whalen, J.P. (1996). A multimodal behavior analytic model
for evaluating the effects of medical problems on nonspecific behavioral
symptoms in persons with developmental disabilities. *Behavioral Interventions, 11,* 147–161.

Gourash, L.F. (1986). Assessing and managing medical factors. In R.P. Barrett
(Ed.), *Severe behavior disorders in the mentally retarded: Nondrug approaches to
treatment* (pp. 157–205). New York: Plenum.

Horner, R.H., & Day, H.M. (1991). The effects of response efficiency on functionally equivalent competing behaviors. *Journal of Applied Behavior Analysis,
24,* 719–732.

Horner, R.H., Sprague, J.R., O'Brien, M., & Heathfield, L.T. (1990). The role of
response efficiency in the reduction of problem behavior through functional
equivalence training: A case study. *Journal of The Association for Persons with
Severe Handicaps, 15,* 91–97.

Iwata, B.A., & DeLeon, I.G. (1995). *The functional analysis screening tool (FAST).*
Unpublished manuscript, University of Florida, Gainesville.

Iwata, B.A., Dorsey, M.F., Slifer, K.J., Bauman, K.E., & Richman, G.S. (1982).
Toward a functional analysis of self-injury. *Analysis and Intervention in Developmental Disabilities, 2,* 3–20.

Iwata, B.A., Pace, G., Cowdery, G., & Miltenberger, R.G. (1994). What makes
extinction work: An analysis of procedural form and function. *Journal of
Applied Behavior Analysis, 27,* 131–144.

Iwata, B.A., Vollmer, T.R., & Zarcone, J.R. (1990). The experimental (functional)
analysis of behavior disorders: Methodology, applications, and limitations.
In A. Repp & N. Singh (Eds.), *Perspectives on the use of nonaversive and aversive interventions for persons with developmental disabilities* (pp. 301–330). Sycamore, IL: Sycamore Publishing.

Iwata, B.A., Vollmer, T.R., Zarcone, J.R., & Rodgers, T.A. (1993). Treatment
classification and selection based on behavioral function. In R. Van Houten
& S. Axelrod (Eds.), *Behavior analysis and treatment* (pp. 101–168). New York:
Plenum.

Iwata, B.A., Wong, S.E., Riordan, M.M., Dorsey, M.F., & Lau, M.M. (1982).
Assessment and training of clinical interviewing skills: Analogue analysis
and field replication. *Journal of Applied Behavior Analysis, 15,* 191–204.

Kemp, D.C., & Carr, E.G. (1995). Reduction of severe problem behavior in
community employment using an hypothesis driven multicomponent in-

tervention approach. *Journal of The Association for Persons with Severe Handicaps, 20,* 229–247.

Kennedy, C.H., & Itkonen, T. (1993). Effects of setting events on the problem behaviors of students with severe disabilities. *Journal of Applied Behavior Analysis, 26,* 321–327.

Kennedy, C.H., & Meyer, K.A. (1996). Sleep deprivation, allergy symptoms, and negatively reinforced problem behavior. *Journal of Applied Behavior Analysis, 29,* 133–135.

Lennox, D.B., & Miltenberger, R.G. (1989). Conducting a functional assessment of problem behavior in applied settings. *Journal of The Association for Persons with Severe Handicaps, 14,* 304–311.

Mace, F.C., & Lalli, J.S. (1991). Linking descriptive and experimental analysis in the treatment of bizarre speech. *Journal of Applied Behavior Analysis, 24,* 553–562.

Mace, F.C., Lalli, J.S., & Lalli, E.P. (1991). Functional analysis and treatment of aberrant behavior. *Research in Developmental Disabilities, 12,* 155–180.

Mace, F.C., & Roberts, M.L. (1993). Factors affecting selection of behavioral interventions. In J. Reichle & D.P. Wacker (Eds.), *Communication and language intervention series: Vol. 3. Communicative alternatives to challenging behavior: Integrating functional assessment and intervention strategies* (pp. 113–133). Baltimore: Paul H. Brookes Publishing Co.

Michael, J.L. (1982). Distinguishing between discriminative and motivational functions of stimuli. *Journal of the Experimental Analysis of Behavior, 37,* 149–155.

Miltenberger, R.G. (1997). *Behavior modification: Principles and procedures.* Pacific Grove, CA: Brooks/Cole.

Miltenberger, R.G. (in press). Understanding problem behaviors through functional assessment. In N. Weissler & R. Hanson (Eds.), *Challenging behaviors in persons with mental health disorders and developmental disabilities.* Washington, DC: American Association on Mental Retardation.

Miltenberger, R.G., & Fuqua, R.W. (1985). Evaluation of a training manual for the acquisition of behavioral assessment interviewing skills. *Journal of Applied Behavior Analysis, 18,* 323–328.

O'Neill, R.E., Horner, R.H., Albin, R.W., Sprague, J.R., Storey, K., & Newton, J.S. (1997). *Functional assessment and program development for problem behavior: A practical handbook.* Pacific Grove, CA: Brooks/Cole.

O'Reilly, M.F. (1995). Functional analysis and treatment of escape maintained aggression correlated with sleep deprivation. *Journal of Applied Behavior Analysis, 28,* 225–226.

O'Reilly, M.F. (1997). Functional analysis of episodic self-injury associated with otitis media. *Journal of Applied Behavior Analysis, 30,* 165–167.

Repp, A.C., Felce, D., & Barton, L.E. (1988). Basing the treatment of stereotypic and self-injurious behaviors on hypotheses of their causes. *Journal of Applied Behavior Analysis, 21,* 281–289.

Rortvedt, A.K., & Miltenberger, R.G. (1994). Analysis of a high probability instructional sequence and time out in the treatment of child noncompliance. *Journal of Applied Behavior Analysis, 27,* 327–330.

Skinner, B.F. (1953). *Science and human behavior.* New York: Macmillan.

Smith, R.G., & Iwata, B.A. (1997). Antecedent influences on behavior disorders. *Journal of Applied Behavior Analysis, 30,* 342–375.

Touchette, P.E., MacDonald, R.F., & Langer, S.N. (1985). A scatter plot for identifying stimulus control of problem behavior. *Journal of Applied Behavior
Analysis, 18,* 343–351.

Vollmer, T.R., & Iwata, B.A. (1991). Establishing operations and reinforcement
effects. *Journal of Applied Behavior Analysis, 24,* 279–291.

Vollmer, T.R., Iwata, B.A., Zarcone, J.R., Smith, R.G., & Mazaleski, J.L. (1993).
The role of attention in the treatment of attention-maintained self-injurious
behavior: Noncontingent reinforcement and differential reinforcement of
other behavior. *Journal of Applied Behavior Analysis, 26,* 9–21.

Zarcone, J.R., Rodgers, T.A., Iwata, B.A., Rourke, D.A., & Dorsey, M.F. (1991).
Reliability analysis of the Motivation Assessment Scale: A failure to repli-
cate. *Research in Developmental Disabilities, 12,* 349–360.

# ~ *4* ~

# *Experimental Analysis of Antecedent Influences on Challenging Behaviors*

David P. Wacker, Wendy K. Berg,
Jennifer M. Asmus, Jay W. Harding, and Linda J. Cooper

The fact that antecedent variables can influence occurrences of challenging behavior is unquestioned by operant researchers, but the development of experimental analysis procedures for identifying functional relationships between antecedents and responses has lagged behind that of response–reinforcer relationships (Halle & Spradlin, 1993). This is as it should be (as noted by Iwata, 1994), because the most direct, parsimonious description of ongoing responding specifies the response–reinforcer relationship. Experimental (functional) analyses of response–reinforcer relationships (Iwata, Dorsey, Slifer, Bauman, & Richman, 1994) permit clinicians to treat challenging behavior directly via the disruption of the identified response–reinforcer relationship (e.g., extinction) and the scheduling of identified reinforcers for alternative behavior (differential reinforcement of alternative behavior). Thus, functional analyses, when conducted in carefully controlled analogues, offer a methodology for both specifying the reason (mechanism) for existing target behavior and matching clinical intervention to the results of assessment. The robustness (Derby et al., 1992) and application (Arndorfer & Miltenberger, 1993; Sasso et al., 1992) of these procedures, as well as the use of this methodology for increasing our understanding of why challenging behavior occurs, have been noteworthy. Thus, the use of a functional analysis provides not only a set of very useful clinical assessment tools but also an analytical model for studying various dimensions of reinforcement within socially relevant contexts (Wacker, 1996).

Use of this analytical approach to identify functional relationships is in sharp contrast to the demographic approach that preceded it. A demographic approach provides correlations among variables such as level of functioning or diagnosis and the existence of various types of challenging behavior. This latter approach is useful for describing who is most likely to engage in challenging behavior but not for indicating why it occurs. Therefore, the implications of demographic assessment for intervention are quite limited.

As we begin the process of studying antecedent–response relationships, we need to be careful to avoid establishing a literature that is filled with interesting correlational relationships that do not further our understanding of why behavior occurs. We must use an analytical model to study antecedent–response relationships that is tied directly to underlying mechanisms of operant behavior. Otherwise, we may end up with only a rather extensive series of descriptive, correlational relationships that contribute little to our overall knowledge of challenging behavior. Just as the previous demographic approaches led to few definitive conclusions, a listing of antecedent–response relationships could result in a similar outcome: that various antecedent events are related to various types of challenging behavior some of the time or for some individuals.

A functional approach for assessing response–reinforcer relationships has clinical utility because it provides a direct analysis of the response–reinforcer relationship for a given individual. The results of this analysis permit the clinician to select from a wide array of intervention options, depending on various pragmatic aspects of the context within which intervention will take place. If reinforcement can be discontinued for the target response, then extinction paired with a dense schedule of reinforcement for an alternative behavior might constitute intervention. In situations in which reinforcement cannot be prevented, various dimensions of reinforcement (e.g., quantity) can be manipulated within a concurrent operants paradigm to bias responding in favor of desired behavior (Peck et al., 1996). Our point here is that an analytical model of assessment provides for a wide array of potential interventions—any of which may be successful—because all are based directly on the identified response–reinforcer relationship. If the clinical goal of assessment is to develop an effective intervention, then the best model of assessment is a functional analysis.

## APPLYING EXPERIMENTAL
## ANALYSIS PROCEDURES TO ANTECEDENTS

We must base antecedent analyses on our acquired knowledge of response–reinforcer relationships because the influence that antecedent variables have on subsequent behavior is derived from their association with reinforcement (Halle & Spradlin, 1993). Antecedent variables come to control or alter responding because they are paired with reinforcers or punishers or because they alter the value of reinforcement that is currently available. In Figure 1, we provide a working schematic of some of these relationships.

We have restricted this schematic to reinforcement delivered within a discrete trial situation (and have not included, for example, the evoking properties of aversive stimuli). Our assessment question pertains to identifying which, if any, of these antecedent variables are currently influencing the display of problematic behavior.

The examples in this chapter focus primarily on challenging behaviors that are socially mediated, and a likely response–reinforcer relationship typically has been identified via an *a priori* functional analysis. The occurrence of behavior is quite variable, however, even under consistently delivered schedules of reinforcement. This variability is sufficient to cause us to question if unknown antecedent variables are influencing behavior. It is within this context that we believe that antecedent analyses may prove to be most useful. Variability in the results of a functional analysis, even under tightly controlled contingent conditions, can serve as a guideline for conducting subsequent analyses of antecedent variables. This variability in responding may occur intermittently across sessions, in clusters (as a cycle of variable

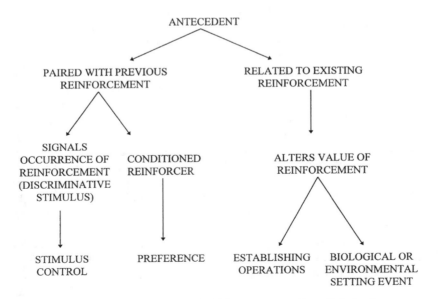

Figure 1.   Schematic of possible antecedent influences on problematic behavior.

responding), or as episodic events in which occasional displays of be-havior occur infrequently or on an apparently random basis. In situ-ations involving a high degree of variability, then, the search becomes one of attempting to identify the sources of variation. One alternative is to continue to provide the existing schedule of reinforcement across distinct antecedent conditions and to identify whether changes in an-tecedent conditions are related to changes in behavior (based, for ex-ample, on hypotheses generated from schematics such as the one in Figure 1; see also Carr & Smith, 1995).

The left side of Figure 1 provides two examples of antecedent stimuli that may occasion a response because of their historic pairing with reinforcement. In the far left case, the stimulus is discriminative for reinforcement, and, in the second case, the stimulus has become a conditioned reinforcer (i.e., is a preferred stimulus). Thus, providing a child with a colored marker for drawing may be a discriminative stimulus ($S^D$) because drawing has been associated with positive at-tention from the parent. Alternatively, the marker itself might be a conditioned reinforcer because the child enjoys drawing, prefers the color of the marker, and so forth. Either of these situations (i.e., $S^D$ or conditioned reinforcer) may cause variability in responding. For ex-ample, if pens and pencils are used in some demand situations, the presentation of a slightly different pen across trials might occasion either resistance or compliance, depending on its historic association with reinforcement.

On the right side of Figure 1, two antecedent conditions are pre-sented that cause momentary alterations in responding. In this case, the antecedent variables influence, on a momentary basis, the value or effects of existing reinforcement. Relative to establishing operations (EOs) (Michael, 1982), the most frequently studied variable has been states of deprivation or satiation (Vollmer & Iwata, 1991). For example, if the child has experienced satiation with drawing, a request to draw, even with a preferred marker, may result in avoidance responding. At all other times, the child complies with this request. Relative to bio-logical states, an individual may resist all requests to comply, even to "preferred" requests, when a specific biological condition is in place (e.g., menses, Carr & Smith, 1995). In this case, the biological setting event may increase the child's motivation to avoid requests, and the presentation of a request is now aversive. Alternatively, the setting event may simply decrease motivation (i.e., the value of a reinforcer to comply). At other times, when the biological setting event is not present, the child complies to requests because the request is not aver-sive or the value of existing reinforcement is sufficient to motivate responding. *Setting events* (Kantor, 1980; Wahler & Fox, 1981) are broad contextual variables (Bijou & Baer, 1961) that result in different chains of responding than are typical when the setting event is not present. Setting events can be tied to both biological (Carr & Smith, 1995) and environmental (Kennedy & Itkonen, 1993) variables.

## CONDUCTING EXPERIMENTAL ANALYSES OF ANTECEDENT VARIABLES

When it is determined that an analysis of antecedent variables is warranted, specific hypotheses regarding the antecedent–response relationship are needed. This is the value of basing assessments on schematics, such as the one in Figure 1. It may also be fruitful to link information collected from a descriptive assessment (Mace & Lalli, 1991), such as an antecedent-behavior-consequence (A-B-C) observation or interview (Bijou, Petersen, Harris, Allen, & Johnston, 1969), to the selection of antecedent variables to manipulate. Otherwise, assessment may prove to be inefficient because the number of potential antecedent influences on behavior is extensive. The alternative is to link assessment conditions directly to a conceptual analysis. This latter approach was used by Iwata et al. (1994) to develop the functional analysis methodology. The potential reinforcers maintaining challenging behavior were identified based on the conceptual analysis of Carr (1977). The assessment provides for direct analyses of each possible class of maintaining variable (positive and negative reinforcement) plus a "control" condition. Evaluating patterns of behavior across multiple presentations of each of these conditions permits the clinician to identify probable reinforcers.

### Methodological Approaches to Assessment

There are two basic approaches to conducting an antecedent analysis: during extinction and during ongoing reinforcement (see Figure 2). As

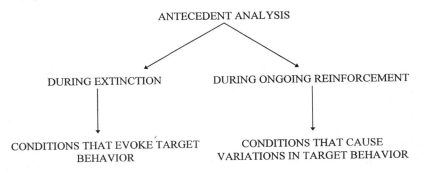

ANTECEDENT ANALYSIS

DURING EXTINCTION        DURING ONGOING REINFORCEMENT

CONDITIONS THAT EVOKE TARGET
BEHAVIOR

CONDITIONS THAT CAUSE
VARIATIONS IN TARGET BEHAVIOR

Figure 2.   Approaches to conducting experimental analyses of antecedent variables.

shown on the left side of Figure 2, the examiner can evaluate changes of behavior that occur with changes in antecedents (e.g., presence or absence of preferred items or demands; changes in level or degree of demands, attention, or other variables) under extinction conditions (Carr & Durand, 1985; Cooper, Wacker, Sasso, Reimers, & Donn, 1990; Dunlap, Kern-Dunlap, Clarke, & Robbins, 1991). In this type of assessment, the clinician is attempting to identify the historic relationship between the presence or absence of a given antecedent variable with responding. If changes in responding occur across changes in the antecedent condition, then it can be inferred that the response has been reinforced historically in the presence of that antecedent stimulus. Thus, the assessment is an analysis of existing stimulus control.

Antecedent assessment often constitutes the baseline in applied situations, such as when a child is being evaluated in a classroom setting (Cooper et al., 1992). It is seldom possible to control the schedule of reinforcement, as required by a functional analysis, but assessors often can control the presentation of antecedents (e.g., presentation of a particular type of demand, presence of a person). What is critical is that changes in reinforcement do not correlate with changes in antecedent conditions, or results will be confounded. The authors have found it best to eliminate reinforcement by telling the teacher, for example, to ignore *all* behavior during the assessment interval.

This approach to antecedent assessment has proven to be remarkably useful for identifying antecedent–response relationships that often lead to effective intervention. A variety of both antecedent- (e.g., fading) and consequence-based (e.g., functional communication training) interventions have been matched to the results of these types of assessments (Carr & Durand, 1985; Cooper et al., 1992; Dunlap et al., 1991; Durand & Carr, 1992).

As of 1998, this approach to the experimental analysis of antecedents constitutes the most systematic and clinically useful model of antecedent analysis. It is sometimes referred to as a *structural analysis* (Axelrod, 1987) because it emphasizes the structural features of the environment. Of importance is that designated antecedent variables, which function as evoking or discriminative stimuli, can be identified, manipulated systematically within a single-case design, and shown to have a functional relationship to challenging behavior.

On the right side of Figure 2, a different approach to antecedent analysis is provided. Rather than focusing on stimulus control, these assessments focus on the conditions that influence the child's responsiveness to existing reinforcement. Although this approach, of course, can be used to study stimulus control (Halle & Holt, 1991; Shore, Iwata, Lerman, & Shirley, 1994), it has been used most often to study variables such as EOs. An excellent example of this approach was provided by Vollmer and Iwata (1991), who evaluated the reinforcing effects of edibles on adaptive behavior during conditions conducted immediately before and immediately after meals. The results clearly showed that edibles were more effective as reinforcers prior to meals, presumably because of food deprivation (an EO). Similar results have been reported for negative reinforcers (Smith, Iwata, Goh, & Shore, 1995), and a similar methodology has been used to study biological variables (Carr & Smith, 1995).

## APPLICATIONS OF ANTECEDENT ANALYSIS

The following sections provide brief summaries of existing research or case examples that analyze various antecedent variables using the approaches shown in Figure 2. These assessments are divided into two subgroups: 1) those that involve single-stimulus presentations and 2) those that involve a choice of stimuli that are concurrently available to the child.

### Single Stimulus Presentations

*Evaluation of Stimulus Control and Preference*    Some children respond differently across types of tasks or play materials, presumably because of their idiosyncratic histories of reinforcement. The current result of these idiosyncratic histories is that variable responding occurs within what may at first appear to be the same stimulus situation (e.g., a demanding task). Neef, Shafer, Egel, Cataldo, and Parrish (1983) provided an example of this type of effect by showing that differential responding occurred to "do" and "don't" requests during compliance training.

For some children, engagement in challenging behavior occurs only within specific stimulus conditions. For these children, the results of the functional analysis will be affected by the presence or absence of those specific stimuli during assessment. For example, Taylor, Sisson, McKelvey, and Trefelner (1993) reported that an adolescent girl with multiple disabilities engaged in aggressive behavior toward her classroom teacher only during low social conditions in which the teacher interacted with another adult. The aggressive behavior did not occur during low social conditions in which the teacher interacted with other children. This can be a challenging situation for assessment because, to the caregiver, the same type of request, task, or toy is being presented, and the child's behavior appears to be random. In this case, the child has discriminated the difference among antecedent stimuli, but the caregiver has not made this discrimination. If variable responding is noted within the "same" assessment situation (e.g., variable levels of challenging behavior occur during demands or independent play times), then two approaches to antecedent assessment might be considered.

First, an A-B-C assessment might be conducted to determine whether changes in an antecedent stimulus are correlated with changes in behavior. If so, then these different antecedents might be presented in a counterbalanced order within a multielement design. For example, Tom, a 3-year-old boy whom we evaluated in a preschool setting, was compliant to virtually all requests and tasks and across familiar and unfamiliar caregivers, as long as the requests/tasks were phrased as questions ("Would you pick up _____?"). The same requests, however, often would result in aggression if they were phrased as declaratives ("Pick up _____."). Given these initial findings, a historical interview with the parent revealed that requests at home had always been presented as questions. A subsequent antecedent analysis that was conducted within a multielement design confirmed these findings and suggested that questions functioned as $S^D$s.

A second approach, described by Shore et al. (1994) and Smith, Iwata, Goh, and Shore (1995), is to determine the context in which problematic behavior occurs and then to systematically alter antecedent variables such as setting, task, or person. Differences in responding across changes in the antecedent stimulus demonstrate stimulus control.

The changes in behavior that can occur across different antecedent stimuli can sometimes be quite dramatic. Asmus, Derby, Wacker, Porter, and Ulrich (1993) reported that the function of problematic behavior for Jeff, a 2-year-old boy with multiple disabilities who engaged in self-injury, destruction, and aggression toward adults and children, differed depending on the presence or absence of his sibling. The experimental analysis was conducted by the parent in the home, with coaching from a trained behavior analyst. The results of a functional analysis initially suggested that the function of Jeff's challenging behavior was to escape from social contact with the parent (when directed to complete demands or even to play). No challenging behavior occurred when he was ignored. Jeff's 1-year-old sibling was then introduced into the assessment, and the same conditions were repeated; the opposite effects occurred. When the parent was directed to play with the sibling and to ignore Jeff, Jeff's problematic behaviors increased substantially. Jeff's behavior remained appropriate, however, when his mother interacted with him.

Other antecedent stimuli may not change the results of a functional analysis but may influence the quality of the interactions between the child and the caregivers. In these cases, changes in behavior may be due to the preferences of the child or to idiosyncratic differences in available materials. For example, we evaluated Matt, a 2-year-old child with severe self-injurious (eye poking, ear poking, head banging) and stereotypic behavior that was reported to occur at high frequencies throughout the day. All assessments and interventions were conducted in the child's home. A functional analysis identified that attention (positive reinforcement) maintained challenging behavior.

Intervention consisted of the use of a differential-reinforcement-of-other behavior procedure that also included contingent removal of attention and toys for engagement in self-injury. Over the next 2 months, weekly outreaches to Matt's home were conducted in which his mother implemented the specified intervention procedure, but Matt's self-injury did not decrease. A component analysis of intervention indicated that he responded differently to toys that he played with independently (noninteractive toys, such as a stuffed animal) versus those that he played with cooperatively (interactive toys, such as stacking cups) with his mother. During the component analysis, when Matt played with noninteractive toys, he was more likely to engage in self-injury than when he played with interactive toys. We hypothesized that the noninteractive toys signaled a reduction in parent attention, which was later verified by pairing parent attention with both types of toys.

In this case, the assessment of antecedent variables occurred during intervention rather than prior to intervention, and we evaluated the evoking effects of these variables. We conducted the analysis because variable behavior occurred over the course of intervention, and the assessment proved to be useful for identifying changes in antecedent stimuli that were discriminable to the child but not to the child's caregiver.

A similar approach can be used to show that a child's preference of play activities may influence engagement in challenging behavior. Asmus et al. (1996) provided an example of this situation with Sam, who was 9 years old and was diagnosed as having mild to moderate developmental disabilities. He engaged in high frequencies of stereotypic behavior (face rubbing, lip licking, chewing on clothes) on an apparently random basis throughout the day. A functional analysis suggested that this behavior served an automatic function because it occurred primarily when the child was alone. A preference (concurrent choice) assessment indicated that when he was given preferred toys *plus* attention from his mother, he played appropriately. If he was given either nonpreferred toys or no attention, challenging behavior occurred.

Stimulus control assessments are complex to the extent that it is often unpredictable which stimuli have been paired with reinforcement and have become either S$^D$s or preferred stimuli. If variability in behavior occurs across trials during assessment or intervention, the experimental analysis involves the presentation of distinct antecedent stimuli in either multielement or reversal designs.

***Evaluation of Establishing Operations/Setting Events*** Exposure to alternative sources of a reinforcer may influence the effectiveness of that reinforcer in maintaining behavior during assessment or intervention conditions. In some cases, exposure to a reinforcer prior to an assessment condition may decrease the value of that same reinforcer during assessment, as described by Vollmer and Iwata (1991). Relative to challenging behavior, Berg et al. (1994) demonstrated that the responding of a young boy during low social attention conditions (i.e., when he was ignored) varied according to the presence or absence of positive social attention from an adult in a preceding assessment condition. When high levels of noncontingent attention preceded times when the child was ignored, the child was fine. When the child was left alone without attention in the preceding condition, however, challenging behavior often occurred during a subsequent time period when he was ignored.

It is important to note that an ignore condition provides the S$^D$ for attention (in this case, presence of a caregiver), but behavior is placed on extinction. Thus, an ignore condition is useful for studying the effects of deprivation or satiation of attention (e.g., free play, left alone) without requiring the adult to reinforce (attend to) challenging behavior.

As behavior analysts begin to study variables such as EOs, it will be necessary to begin inspecting dyads of assessment conditions instead of solely studying each discrete condition. In this case, the dyad comparison was free play/ignore versus alone/ignore to study the effects of attention satiation or deprivation on subsequent behavior. As discussed by Smith, Iwata, Goh, and Shore (1995), it is critical that the final condition remain constant, with changes occurring only in the preceding condition.

A similar approach to the assessment of setting or biological events is useful, except that patterns of behavior will be identified over time (in most cases) within reversal designs rather than across conditions via multielement designs. As discussed previously in relation to Carr and Smith (1995), changes in a biological condition (e.g., menses) may result in cyclical changes in behavior. This situation can best be understood by what Michael (1982) referred to as "evoking stimuli." The biological variable (menses) may cause overall distress in the person, which might make routine demands, for example, more aversive than at other times. In operant terms, negative reinforcement (escape/avoidance responding) is active for demands only when the biological variable is in place. Carr and Smith (1995) described this possibility for biological variables, and Kennedy and Itkonen (1993) described it for environmental variables.

One approach to assessment is to again note variability in behavior, especially cyclical changes, and then to generate hypotheses about the active variable. Note if changes in behavior are correlated with changes in the antecedent stimulus, and, if possible, attempt to systematically vary the setting event while continuing all other aspects of a given assessment condition. Wacker et al. (1996) demonstrated this approach with a young girl with severe self-injurious behavior and feeding difficulties. A functional analysis revealed variable challenging behavior across all assessment conditions, including free play. Based on the work of Rast, Johnson, Drum, and Conrin (1981), Wacker et al. hypothesized that food quantity might be related to self-injury. We compared the child's behavior during free-play conditions following small mini-meals with large meals that possibly resulted in gastric distress. Self-injury occurred almost exclusively during play following large meals and almost never during play following the smaller meals. Similar findings occurred after long intervals of time without eating, suggesting that the biological variable of "gastric distress" was evoking self-injury even during play.

## Concurrent Stimulus Presentations

In concurrent stimulus presentations, the individual is given the opportunity to choose among two or more concurrently available alternatives. Assessment procedures that provide choices among stimuli are considered to approximate natural contexts in which individuals have an opportunity to select among concurrently available items or activities (Northup, George, Jones, Broussard, & Vollmer, 1996). The variables that determine relative preference in a given situation, however, can be quite complex. As discussed in the previous sections, an individual's preference for an item may be influenced by a variety of factors. These factors include prior reinforcement history (i.e., stimulus control), differences in relevant reinforcer characteristics (e.g., quantity, quality, delay, effort needed to obtain reinforcer) associated with each choice option, and preceding events that function to influence the reinforcing value of each presented choice option (EOs). Thus, the variables associated with choice are complex and may be influenced by both historic and current schedules of reinforcement.

There are three basic assessment approaches that involve the concurrent presentation of stimuli. The first approach is to evaluate choice (the presence of two or more alternative stimuli) as an active variable by comparing conditions that provide choices with those that do not. The second approach is to use *a priori* preference assessments to provide concurrent stimuli as a method for identifying preferences and to implement this type of preference assessment prior to other assessment or intervention conditions. A third option is to evaluate the effects of various dimensions of reinforcement on response allocation among currently available stimuli.

**Choice as an Active Variable**　The provision of a choice may function similarly to any other type of instruction and may come to signal reinforcement if choices have been paired historically with reinforcement. Thus, like the question versus declarative formats described previously, the offer of a choice may function as an $S^D$ for reinforcement. It makes intuitive sense that, historically, when children are offered choices, there is an increased likelihood that reinforcement also will be provided following those choices. For example, the choices may involve mostly preferred activities or may be offered by adults only when the child's behavior is appropriate and therefore is likely to be reinforced. In either case, the presentation of a choice may come to function as an $S^D$.

A number of researchers have demonstrated relationships between providing opportunities for choice making during concurrent stimulus presentations and positive outcomes (Cooper et al., 1992; Dunlap et al., 1994; Dunlap et al., 1991; Dyer, Dunlap, & Winterling, 1990; Foster-Johnson, Ferro, & Dunlap, 1994; Harding, Wacker, Cooper, Millard, & Jensen-Kovalan, 1994; Kennedy & Haring, 1993). For example, Dyer et al. (1990) compared the effects of teacher-selected versus student-selected tasks and rewards on problem behavior. Conditions in which students were allowed to choose tasks and rewards resulted in lower levels of problem behavior. Cooper et al. (1992) evaluated the effects of choice offers with an elementary school student in a special education classroom for children with disabilities requiring minimal supports and/or with behavior disorders. The results of this study showed that the student's behavior improved in conditions in which he was allowed to select an academic task in comparison to having the teacher assign him a similar task. Thus, for this student, the opportunity to choose between tasks appeared to be more effective in controlling appropriate behavior than conditions in which he was simply assigned a task, even though the assigned task was a relatively preferred activity. Dunlap et al. (1994) also examined the effects of choice making on the responding of elementary school students with emotional and behavioral disabilities. The results showed that choice-making conditions increased task engagement and reduced disruptive behaviors. Harding et al. (1994) conducted an assessment of antecedent intervention components with young children referred to an outpatient clinic for behavior problems. The results of this study showed that giving a preschool-age girl a choice of task materials (e.g., red crayon versus green crayon) resulted in increased compliance to parent requests.

To assess choice as an independent variable, it is critical for preference to remain constant across conditions (Smith, Iwata, & Shore, 1995). In an ideal case, choice versus no-choice conditions would be compared for both high-preference and low-preference activities. This would permit inspection of the relative influences of preferences and choice. Thus, if choice is the active variable, relatively better responding should occur in the choice conditions irrespective of the preference variable. If preference is the active variable, better behavior should occur in the high-preference conditions, regardless of choice. If there is an interaction between preference and choice, then the high preference with choice condition might be followed by low preference with choice, high preference without choice, and low preference without choice conditions. Different hierarchical arrangements of the above conditions might clearly establish for any given child which variable was most important.

**A Priori *Preference Assessments*** The results of an *a priori* preference assessment may generate hypotheses regarding stimuli that currently function as reinforcers within the individual's environment. If preference is considered to be a relative distinction, then a concurrent choice assessment is warranted (Fisher et al., 1992). A number of investigations have used concurrent choice procedures to identify preferred stimuli (Derby et al., 1995; Fisher et al., 1992; Northup et al., 1996; Northup, Jones, Broussard, & George, 1995; Piazza, Fisher, Hagopian, Bowman, & Toole, 1996; Sigafoos & Dempsey, 1992; Wacker, Berg, Wiggins, Muldoon, & Cavanaugh, 1985). For example, Piazza et al. (1996) used a choice assessment to identify the relative preference (high preferred, medium preferred, low preferred) of stimuli presented to four individuals with severe disabilities and behavior disorders. The relative effectiveness of the stimuli as reinforcers then was evaluated by comparing the duration of time each individual spent engaged in concurrently available target responses during each session. The results of this study showed that the preference assessment had utility in predicting the relative reinforcing value of the various stimuli.

The Piazza et al. (1996) study, based on Fisher et al. (1992), showed that preference does not necessarily equal reinforcement. When preference is identified via an arbitrary behavior (e.g., reaching, allocating time in a designated area), it is important to then establish that the same relationship holds for more socially meaningful behavior (e.g., compliance to task demands). By preceding intervention with a preference assessment and incorporating preferred stimuli into intervention, displays of challenging behavior may be reduced or avoided (Steege, Wacker, Berg, Cigrand, & Cooper, 1989).

**Concurrent Stimulus Presentations During Intervention** Concurrent stimulus presentations have been used to evaluate individual responding when differing schedules of reinforcement are arranged simultaneously for two or more responses. Alone, either schedule maintains a particular response, but when operating concurrently, behavior is distributed across the schedules roughly in proportion to the distribution of reinforcers. Applied researchers have demonstrated that allocation of behavior among available alternatives can be influenced by various dimensions of reinforcement including rate (quantity), quality (value), delay, and the response effort required to obtain reinforcement (e.g., Forzano & Logue, 1995; Horner, Day, Sprague, O'Brien, & Heathfield, 1991; Mace, Neef, Shade, & Mauro, 1996; Martens, Lochner, & Kelly, 1992; Neef, Mace, Shea, & Shade, 1992). These dimensions of reinforcement also may interact to affect the probability that an individual will choose to engage in one response alternative over another (Neef, Shade, & Miller, 1994). Analyzing these interactions may make it possible to alter one or more of these dimensions of reinforcement in order to influence responding in a particular direction.

Relative to severe behavior disorders, response alternatives might include engaging in challenging or appropriate behavior, or engaging in a specific topography of challenging or appropriate behavior among the array of options. Changes in the various dimensions of reinforcement, if signaled by the antecedent stimuli associated with the schedules of reinforcement, may increase the probability that an individual will engage in one behavior (desired) over another (challenging) (Mace & Roberts, 1993). Neef et al. (1992) and Mace et al. (1996) provided participants with different colored cards (e.g., green and yellow) as $S^D$s to signal each variable interval (VI) schedule of reinforcement. Martens et al. (1992) facilitated discrimination between VI schedules of reinforcement for students in a classroom by varying the equipment (red versus green clipboard, Batman versus race car stickers) associated with each schedule. Cooper et al. (1995) used different colors of placemats and spoons to signal young children with feeding disorders which option resulted in the highest quantity or quality of reinforcement.

The study by Cooper et al. (1995) showed the value of incorporating $S^D$s into choice procedures. The children all displayed severe food refusal, suggesting that avoidance (negative reinforcement) was the primary maintaining variable. To identify whether positive reinforcers also influenced behavior, two identical target bites of food were offered to the children using different colored materials (placemats, spoons). For example, with one child, each option was paired with different amounts of the same potential reinforcer (one versus two bites of a preferred food). The child's choice responding showed the effects of changes in the positive reinforcers within a reversal design. Thus, if a pink placemat was paired with greater quantity of reinforcement in the first phase, then the second option (green) was paired with the greater quantity of reinforcement during the second phase, followed by a return to pink being paired with the greater quantity of reinforcement. If choice responding varied across the pink and green options according to the amount of positive reinforcement provided, positive reinforcers could be identified. In addition, antecedent stimulus conditions (color of materials) also became $S^D$s, which, over time, may have contributed to the overall reduction in problematic behavior during meals.

The pairing of different types, dimensions, or schedules of reinforcement with distinct antecedent conditions may have heuristic appeal for studying the interaction of variables in establishing interventions for behavior disorders. In a typical home situation, for example, idiosyncratic differences across children and across contexts for the same child may be complex and dynamic. An efficient method for studying these variables within home settings has obvious clinical importance.

Harding et al. (1995) used a choice-making procedure to identify child preferences across a selection of antecedent variables that included item preference, access to parent attention, and task demands. The primary objective of this procedure was to identify variables that increased time allocated to choice options that included compliance to parent requests. Rob, a 4-year-old child who participated in this study, was diagnosed with fragile X syndrome and pervasive developmental disorder. Problem behaviors included noncompliance to parent requests, destruction of property, and self-injury (e.g., finger biting). All assessment procedures were conducted by Rob's mother in his home.

Response allocation was defined as the child's location in one of the two available play areas in his living room. An event recording system was used to measure Rob's completion of parent requests during each session. Prior to conducting the choice-making conditions, Harding et al. (1995) conducted a brief preference assessment of toys based on Piazza et al. (1996). During the subsequent choice-making procedures, Rob was told what was available in each play area. He was allowed to move to either area as often as he desired. The purpose of conducting this assessment was to evaluate the relative influence of parent attention, access to preferred toys, and escape from task demands on his choice responding.

Three choice conditions were then conducted. The first condition involved Rob's choice between 1) directed play (demand) with his mother and high-preference toys or 2) playing alone with low-preference toys. The researchers' question was as follows: Would he tolerate the task demand when he was also provided with parent attention and preferred toys? The answer was yes. The other two conditions were used to further assess the role of preference and increased task demands. Overall, the results of the choice assessment suggested that parent attention was the most salient reinforcer, even when Rob was required to complete more demanding tasks with low-preference items. Given these results, an intervention package was designed in which parent attention and access to preferred activities were used as reinforcers for task completion. Thus, the concurrent choice assessment permitted an evaluation of a complex situation (three distinct independent variables) in a relatively brief period of time and in a natural context without asking the parent to reinforce challenging behavior. This was possible by linking antecedent stimuli to consequences and presenting various combinations of these variables to the child via concurrently available options.

## SUMMARY

This chapter has attempted to provide a conceptual overview of how experimental analyses of antecedents can be based directly on previous research conducted on consequences (functional analyses). We advocate linking the results of assessment to basic processes and schedules of reinforcement. Establishing this link permits inferences to be generated regarding why behavior varies across antecedent conditions in addition to showing improved behavior within designated conditions. The understanding of why behavior changes offers a methodology for more fully predicting when problematic behavior will and will not occur, possibly leading to a preventive model of intervention to augment existing reinforcement-based intervention approaches.

## REFERENCES

Arndorfer, R., & Miltenberger, R. (1993). Functional assessment and treatment of challenging behavior: A review with implications for early childhood. *Topics in Early Childhood Special Education, 13,* 83–105.

Asmus, J., Derby, K.M., Wacker, D.P., Porter, J., & Ulrich, S. (1993, May). The stimulus control effects of siblings during functional analyses conducted in home settings. In C.H. Kennedy (Chair), *Stimulus control of problem behavior.* Symposium presented at the annual conference of the Association for Behavior Analysis, Chicago.

Asmus, J.M., Wacker, D.P., Richman, D., Cooper, L.J., Harding, J., Berg, W., & Andelman, M. (1996, May). The application of concurrent choices to behavior maintained by automatic reinforcement. In T.R. Vollmer (Chair), *Developing treatments based on functional analysis.* Symposium presented at the annual conference of the Association for Behavior Analysis, San Francisco.

Axelrod, S. (1987). Functional and structural analysis of behavior: Approaches leading to reduced use of punishment procedures. *Research in Developmental Disabilities, 8,* 165–178.

Berg, W.K., Peck, S.M., Wacker, D.P., Derby, K.M., Asmus, J., & Richman, D.M. (1994, May). The effects of setting events on responding during assessment and intervention for attention maintained behavior problems. In K.M. Derby (Chair), *Applications of behavioral assessments and treatments with toddlers and preschoolers.* Symposium presented at the annual conference of the Association for Behavior Analysis, Atlanta.

Bijou, S., & Baer, D. (1961). *Child development: A systematic and empirical theory.* Englewood Cliffs, NJ: Prentice Hall.

Bijou, S., Petersen, R., Harris, F., Allen, K., & Johnston, M. (1969). Methodology for experimental studies of young children in natural settings. *Psychological Record, 19,* 177–210.

Carr, E.G. (1977). The motivation of self-injurious behavior: A review of some hypotheses. *Psychological Bulletin, 84,* 800–816.

Carr, E.G., & Durand, V.M. (1985). Reducing behavior problems through functional communication training. *Journal of Applied Behavior Analysis, 18,* 111–126.

Carr, E.G., & Smith, C. (1995). Biological setting events for self-injury. *Mental Retardation and Developmental Disabilities Research Reviews, 1,* 94–98.

Cooper, L.J., McComas, J., Brown, J., Peck, S., Drew, J., & Wacker, D. (1995, May). The application of matching theory to feeding disorders. In L. Kern (Chair), *Novel applications of functional analysis.* Symposium presented at the annual conference of the Association for Behavior Analysis, Washington, DC.

Cooper, L.J., Wacker, D.P., Sasso, G.M., Reimers, T.M., & Donn, L.K. (1990). Using parents as therapists to assess the appropriate behavior of their children: Application to a tertiary diagnostic clinic. *Journal of Applied Behavior Analysis, 23,* 285–296.

Cooper, L.J., Wacker, D.P., Thursby, D., Plagmann, L.A., Harding, J., & Derby, K.M. (1992). Analysis of the role of task preferences, task demands, and adult attention on child behavior in outpatient and classroom settings. *Journal of Applied Behavior Analysis, 25,* 823–840.

Derby, K.M., Wacker, D.P., Andelman, M., Berg, W., Drew, J., Asmus, J., Prouty, A.M., & Laffey, P. (1995). Two measures of preference during forced-choice assessments. *Journal of Applied Behavior Analysis, 28,* 345–346.

Derby, K.M., Wacker, D.P., Sasso, G., Steege, M., Northup, J., Cigrand, K., & Asmus, J. (1992). Brief functional analysis techniques to evaluate challenging behavior in an outpatient setting: A summary of 79 cases. *Journal of Applied Behavior Analysis, 25,* 713–721.

Dunlap, G., dePerczel, M., Clarke, S., Wilson, D., Wright, S., White, R., & Gomez, A. (1994). Choice making to promote adaptive behavior of students with emotional and behavioral challenges. *Journal of Applied Behavior Analysis, 27,* 505–518.

Dunlap, G., Kern-Dunlap, L., Clarke, S., & Robbins, F.R. (1991). Functional assessment, curricular revision, and severe behavior problems. *Journal of Applied Behavior Analysis, 24,* 387–397.

Durand, V.M., & Carr, E.G. (1992). An analysis of maintenance following functional communication training. *Journal of Applied Behavior Analysis, 25,* 777–795.

Dyer, K., Dunlap, G., & Winterling, V. (1990). The effects of choice making on the serious problem behaviors of students with developmental disabilities. *Journal of Applied Behavior Analysis, 23,* 515–524.

Fisher, W.W., Piazza, C.C., Bowman, L.G., Hagopian, L.P., Owens, J.C., & Slevin, I. (1992). A comparison of two approaches for identifying reinforcers for persons with severe and profound disabilities. *Journal of Applied Behavior Analysis, 25,* 491–498.

Forzano, L.B., & Logue, A.W. (1995). Self-control and impulsivity in children and adults: Effects of food preferences. *Journal of the Experimental Analysis of Behavior, 64,* 33–46.

Foster-Johnson, L., Ferro, J., & Dunlap, G. (1994). Preferred curricular activities and reduced problem behaviors in students with intellectual disabilities. *Journal of Applied Behavior Analysis, 27,* 493–504.

Halle, J.W., & Holt, B. (1991). Assessing stimulus control in natural settings: An analysis of stimuli that acquire control during training. *Journal of Applied Behavior Analysis, 24,* 579–589.

Halle, J.W., & Spradlin, J.E. (1993). Identifying stimulus control of challenging behavior. In J. Reichle & D.P. Wacker (Eds.), *Communication and language intervention series: Vol. 3. Communicative alternatives to challenging behavior: Integrating functional assessment and intervention strategies* (pp. 83–109). Baltimore: Paul H. Brookes Publishing Co.

Harding, J., Wacker, D., Berg, W., Derby, K.M., Asmus, J., & Prouty, A.M. (1995, May). An analysis of preference in the assessment of a preschooler's challenging behavior. In K.M. Derby (Chair), *Current applications and extensions of preference assessments.* Symposium presented at the annual convention of the Association for Behavior Analysis, Washington, DC.

Harding, J., Wacker, D.P., Cooper, L.J., Millard, T., & Jensen-Kovalan, P. (1994). Brief hierarchical assessment of potential treatment components with children in an outpatient clinic. *Journal of Applied Behavior Analysis, 27,* 291–300.

Horner, R., Day, H., Sprague, J., O'Brien, M., & Heathfield, L. (1991). Interspersed requests: A nonaversive procedure for reducing aggression and self-injury during instruction. *Journal of Applied Behavior Analysis, 24,* 265–278.

Iwata, B.A. (1994). Functional analysis methodology: Some closing comments. *Journal of Applied Behavior Analysis, 27,* 413–418.

Iwata, B.A., Dorsey, M.F., Slifer, K.J., Bauman, K.E., & Richman, G.S. (1994). Toward a functional analysis of self-injury. *Journal of Applied Behavior Analysis, 27,* 197–209. (Reprinted from *Analysis and Intervention in Developmental Disabilities, 2,* 3–20, 1982.)

Kantor, J. (1980). An analysis of the experimental analysis of behavior. *American Journal of Mental Deficiency, 87,* 458–461.

Kennedy, C.H., & Haring, T.G. (1993). Teaching choice making during social interactions to students with profound multiple disabilities. *Journal of Applied Behavior Analysis, 26,* 63–76.

Kennedy, C.H., & Itkonen, T. (1993). Effects of setting events on the problem behavior of students with severe disabilities. *Journal of Applied Behavior Analysis, 26,* 321–327.

Mace, F.C., & Lalli, J.S. (1991). Linking descriptive and experimental analysis in the treatment of bizarre speech. *Journal of Applied Behavior Analysis, 24,* 553–562.

Mace, F.C., Neef, N.A., Shade, D., & Mauro, B.C. (1996). Effects of problem difficulty and reinforcer quality on time allocated to concurrent arithmetic problems. *Journal of Applied Behavior Analysis, 29,* 11–24.

Mace, F.C., & Roberts, M.L. (1993). Factors affecting selection of behavioral interventions. In J. Reichle & D.P. Wacker (Eds.), *Communication and language intervention series: Vol. 3. Communicative alternatives to challenging behavior: Integrating functional assessment and intervention strategies* (pp. 113–133). Baltimore: Paul H. Brookes Publishing Co.

Martens, B.K., Lochner, D.G., & Kelly, S.Q. (1992). The effects of variable-interval reinforcement on academic engagement: A demonstration of matching theory. *Journal of Applied Behavior Analysis, 25,* 143–151.

Michael, J. (1982). Distinguishing between discriminative and motivational functions of stimuli. *Journal of the Experimental Analysis of Behavior, 37,* 149–155.

Neef, N.A., Mace, F.C., Shea, M.C., & Shade, D. (1992). Effects of reinforcer rate and reinforcer quality on time allocation: Extensions of matching theory to educational settings. *Journal of Applied Behavior Analysis, 25,* 691–699.

Neef, N.A., Shade, D., & Miller, J.S. (1994). Assessing influential dimensions of reinforcers on choice in students with serious emotional disturbance. *Journal of Applied Behavior Analysis, 27,* 575–583.

Neef, N.A., Shafer, M.S., Egel, A.L., Cataldo, M.F., & Parrish, J.S. (1983). The class specific effects of compliance training with "do" and "don't" requests: Analogue analysis and classroom application. *Journal of Applied Behavior Analysis, 16,* 81–89.

Northup, J., George, T., Jones, K., Broussard, C., & Vollmer, T.R. (1996). A comparison of reinforcer assessment methods: The utility of verbal and pictorial choice procedures. *Journal of Applied Behavior Analysis, 29,* 201–212.

Northup, J., Jones, K., Broussard, C., & George, T. (1995). A preliminary comparison of reinforcer assessment methods for children with attention deficit hyperactivity disorder. *Journal of Applied Behavior Analysis, 28,* 99–100.

Peck, S.M., Wacker, D.P., Berg, W.K., Cooper, L.J., Brown, K.A., Richman, D., McComas, J.J., Frischmeyer, P., & Millard, T. (1996). Choice-making treatment of young children's severe behavior problems. *Journal of Applied Behavior Analysis, 29,* 263–290.

Piazza, C.C., Fisher, W.W., Hagopian, L.P., Bowman, L.G., & Toole, L. (1996). Using a choice assessment to predict reinforcer effectiveness. *Journal of Applied Behavior Analysis, 29,* 1–9.

Rast, J., Johnson, J., Drum, C., & Conrin, J. (1981). The relation of food quantity to rumination behavior. *Journal of Applied Behavior Analysis, 14,* 121–130.

Sasso, G.M., Reimers, T.M., Cooper, L.J., Wacker, D., Berg, W., Steege, M., Kelly, L., & Allaire, A. (1992). Use of descriptive and experimental analyses to identify the functional properties of challenging behavior in school settings. *Journal of Applied Behavior Analysis, 25,* 809–821.

Shore, B.A., Iwata, B.A., Lerman, D.C., & Shirley, M.J. (1994). Assessing and programming generalized behavioral reduction across multiple stimulus parameters. *Journal of Applied Behavior Analysis, 27,* 371–384.

Sigafoos, J., & Dempsey, R. (1992). Assessing choice making among children with multiple disabilities. *Journal of Applied Behavior Analysis, 25,* 747–755.

Smith, R.G., Iwata, B.A., Goh, H.-L., & Shore, B.A. (1995). Analysis of establishing operations for self-injury maintained by escape. *Journal of Applied Behavior Analysis, 28,* 433–445.

Smith, R.G., Iwata, B.A., & Shore, B.A. (1995). Effects of subject- versus experimenter-selected reinforcers on the behavior of individuals with profound developmental disabilities. *Journal of Applied Behavior Analysis, 28,* 61–71.

Steege, M.W., Wacker, D.P., Berg, W.K., Cigrand, K.K., & Cooper, L.J. (1989). The use of behavioral assessment to prescribe and evaluate treatments for severely handicapped children. *Journal of Applied Behavior Analysis, 22,* 23–33.

Taylor, J.C., Sisson, L.A., McKelvey, J.L., & Trefelner, J.G. (1993). Situation specificity in attention-seeking problem behavior. *Behavior Modification, 17,* 474–497.

Vollmer, T.R., & Iwata, B.A. (1991). Establishing operations and reinforcement effects. *Journal of Applied Behavior Analysis, 24,* 279–291.

Wacker, D.P. (1996). Behavior analysis research in *JABA*: A need for studies that bridge basic and applied research. *Experimental Analysis of Human Behavior Bulletin, 14*(1), 11–14.

Wacker, D.P., Berg, W.K., Wiggins, B., Muldoon, M., & Cavanaugh, J. (1985). Evaluation of reinforcer preferences for profoundly handicapped students. *Journal of Applied Behavior Analysis, 18,* 173–178.

Wacker, D.P., Harding, J., Cooper, L.J., Derby, K.M., Peck, S., Asmus, J., Berg, W.K., & Brown, K.A. (1996). The effects of meal schedule and quantity on problematic behavior. *Journal of Applied Behavior Analysis, 29,* 79–87.

Wahler, R., & Fox, J. (1981). Setting events in social networks: Ally or enemy in child behavior therapy? *Behavior Therapy, 14,* 19–36.

# ~ *5* ~

# *Experimental Designs to Evaluate Antecedent Control*

## Timothy R. Vollmer and Carole M. Van Camp

Many of the other chapters in this book provide detailed definitions and descriptions of antecedent variables that can influence human behavior. General classes of antecedent variables include physiological factors (see Chapter 6), pharmacological factors (see Chapter 7), establishing operations (EOs; see Chapter 15), and stimulus control (see Chapter 16), among others. This chapter, however, is not intended to define or describe specific antecedent–behavior relationships; rather, the general purpose of the chapter is to outline the experimental logic and experimental designs used to evaluate the influence of antecedent variables.

The scientific and experimental orientation of this chapter is derived from the discipline of behavior analysis. A behavioral analysis is usually accomplished through single-subject experimentation, in which repeated measures of individuals' behaviors are collected during test-and-control or baseline conditions. Independent variables (i.e., environmental events) are manipulated to test the effects on dependent variables (i.e., some measurable dimension of behavior). A *functional relationship* is said to exist when behavior changes as a result of systematically manipulated environmental events. This chapter outlines methods—that is, experimental designs—used to identify functional relationships between antecedent events and behavior. As such, antecedent events are the independent variables of interest, and behavior is the dependent variable of interest.

There are at least four general reasons to conduct experimental analyses related to antecedent control in applied settings: 1) to identify antecedent events that exert control over challenging behavior, 2) to identify situations that do not exert control over desired behavior, 3) to isolate the effects of antecedent manipulations on undesired behavior, and 4) to isolate the effects of antecedent manipulations on desired behavior. The first and second items represent assessment issues because they are related to why the behavior is or is not occurring. The third and fourth items are issues related to interventions or intervention development, specifically how this manipulation changes current levels of behavior. Historically, demonstrating functional relationships between antecedent events and behavior (whether in assessment or intervention) has presented unique challenges to behavior analysts. Behavior analysts have a rich tradition of evaluating the influence of reinforcement contingencies (i.e., consequent events), but to experimentally analyze the role of antecedent events requires that consequent events are held constant during some part of or throughout the experiment.

The following sections discuss principles of experimental logic as they relate to antecedent analyses, principles of experimental design as they relate to antecedent analyses, and examples of designs that could be used to evaluate antecedent control.

## TERMINOLOGY AND EXPERIMENTAL LOGIC

In the most general sense, an *experimental analysis* involves testing the effects of an independent variable on a dependent variable. As implied previously, the independent variables of interest in this discussion include the general class of events called *antecedents*, defined here as those environmental events that precede behavior. The dependent variable of interest is *behavior*, defined here as anything the person does (Catania, 1992).

The term *environment*, as it is used here, includes both ambient and internal (i.e., physiological) events. It is important to note that environmental events may include internal stimulation (e.g., some physiological or pharmacological states) in addition to ambient stimulation; the environment is not restricted to events that occur outside the skin (Skinner, 1974). Environmental events sometimes do and sometimes do not influence behavior. A properly designed experiment should yield information about which events do and which events do not exert control over behavior.

Because the dependency of a variable cannot be judged without measurement, a basic tenet of a behavioral analysis is that behavior can be measured. In fact, behavior has several measurable dimensions that are amenable to experimental analysis, including frequency (how many times the behavior occurs), duration (how long the behavior occurs), and latency (the time period between the presentation of some stimulus and a response), among others (Johnston & Pennypacker, 1980).

Single-subject analyses usually involve repeated measurements of behavior. That is, measures or samples of behavior are taken during some observational interval (the interval could be a week, a day, an hour, several minutes, etc.), and those measurements are repeated over time. For example, the number of aggressive acts per day may be counted for several consecutive days, or the number of self-injurious responses per minute could be counted for several 15-minute observational sessions. When several observational units (repeated measures) have been completed in the same general context, the analyst is able to predict the level of behavior in a given "condition." A *condition* refers to the circumstances making up an experimental phase or series of sessions within an experiment. The upper panel of Figure 1 shows a hypothetical series of repeated measures. (Please note that the figures for this chapter are located in the chapter's appendix.) In this example, the rate of aggression is recorded and plotted for 10 consecutive days. The stability of the baseline allows the analyst to predict the approximate rate of behavior if more measures were taken.

To evaluate the effects of antecedent variables, an experiment must be designed in which behavior can be evaluated with and without the independent variable in place. For example, if the effect of verbal instruction is being tested, the analyst would need to compare the level of behavior during one condition in which instructions were not presented with another condition in which instructions were presented. The condition in which the independent variable is not presented is often called a "baseline" or a "control" condition. The condition in which the independent variable is presented is often called a "test" condition (because the effects of the variable are being tested). The center panel of Figure 1 shows a data path that begins with the same repeated measures series as the upper panel. Suppose the series constitutes a baseline condition in which no verbal instructions were presented. In the next condition, verbal instructions were introduced and behavior changed in a direction not predicted by the baseline measures. Thus, the independent variable may have exerted some influence over behavior.

Another tenet of behavior analysis is that experimental effects should be replicated (Sidman, 1960). Replication involves repeating a previously observed relation or repeating an experiment (Cooper, Heron, & Heward, 1987). In a single-subject design, replication is usually accomplished both within and across participants. For example, the well-known reversal (or ABAB) design involves baseline (A) and test (B) conditions. If the test condition yields differential effects, the test condition is then withdrawn in a return-to-baseline condition. If baseline levels of behavior are reestablished, the test condition then may be implemented again to ensure that behavior change occurs as it did in the initial test. If behavior change correlated with the test condition is replicated, the experimenter has an increased confidence that effects were a function of the independent variable being tested. If the effects are replicated with more individual participants, confidence levels are higher still. The lower panel of Figure 1 shows an example of a typical reversal design testing the effects of independent variables. In the example, decreased aggression rates can be attributed to the introduction of instructions with a degree of confidence because behavior change occurred as the antecedent changed; furthermore, the effects were replicated.

When comparing a test condition to baseline (or to another test condition) in the analysis of antecedent variables, it is essential to hold other variables (e.g., consequences) constant across conditions. For example, Smith, Iwata, Goh, and Shore (1995) tested the effects of instruction rate in the evaluation of self-injurious behavior (SIB) maintained by escape. In one condition, instructions were presented at a low rate (10 trials per session); and in another condition, instructions were presented at a high rate (30 trials per session). Importantly, escape was presented contingent on SIB in *both* conditions. Otherwise, differential effects could not have been attributed to the antecedent variable (instruction rate). The upper panel of Figure 2 depicts a hypothetical experiment designed to test the effects of low-rate versus high-rate instructions. During baseline and test conditions, escape is presented contingent on SIB. During the test conditions, however, instruction rate is manipulated. The effects of the independent variables can be evaluated in comparison to baseline or in comparison to the other test condition. The clear separation in data paths representing high-rate and low-rate instruction provides a demonstration of experimental control. The center and lower panels of Figure 2 are discussed later in the chapter.

## EXPERIMENTAL DESIGN

To arrange a test of an independent variable is to design an experiment. Thus, the method used to systematically evaluate functional relations constitutes an *experimental design*. Three of the most common single-subject designs are the reversal, multi-element, and multiple-baseline designs. A single-subject analysis is rarely constructed to fit a formula or prescribed structure that cannot be influenced by unexpected changes or serendipitous findings (e.g., Johnston & Pennypacker, 1980). As such, the designs described in the following sections should be viewed as general formats to establish experimental control, with the expectation that design changes or modifications may need to be implemented based on visual inspection of the data as those data are collected and plotted graphically. Furthermore, this chapter does not intend to provide an exhaustive review of designs used to test antecedent control; rather, the following sections present some basic designs in order to outline how experimental logic is incorporated into a design. Ultimately, the manner in which an independent variable is introduced, withdrawn, or varied depends on the idiosyncrasies of the experimental question and how that question changes or expands in light of ongoing data analysis.

## Reversal Designs

Recall that a reversal design is depicted in the lower panel of Figure 1. In the traditional use of reversal designs, independent variables of interest have been related to consequent events (i.e., reinforcement, punishment); but the same analytic logic holds for the analysis of antecedent variables. The primary benefit of the reversal design is that the effects of an independent variable can be demonstrated convincingly by essentially "turning on" and "turning off" a behavior (Baer, Wolf, & Risley, 1968). The convincing demonstration of effects results from the within-subject replication that defines a reversal design.

Two concerns are often raised about the use of reversal designs: 1) risks associated with exposing the participant to conditions that had maintained dangerous or otherwise undesired behavior, and 2) irreversibility. From an ethical standpoint, reversals to baseline should be avoided if a participant is placed in a situation of undue risk (e.g., serious injury to self or others). It is also important, however, to recognize that a *failure* to revert to baseline also must be justified ethically. For example, if a medication appears to exert control over behavior, a failure to reverse to baseline (no medication or placebo) leaves some question about the effects of unknown extraneous variables (e.g., a coincidental environmental change that took place at the same time that medication was introduced). If no reversal is attempted, the participant may receive an unneeded medication for an indefinite amount of time. In addition, reversals are ethically justified from a scientific standpoint because the scientific community will need assurance that the observed effects are a result of introducing the independent variable; otherwise individuals around the world may begin receiving erroneously identified interventions.

*Irreversibility,* the second potential concern about reversal designs, may occur if the target behavior contacts new reinforcement contingencies once it is acquired. For example, if a researcher is testing the effects of an instructional videotape on bicycle riding and the viewers (participants) learn to ride a bicycle after viewing the tape, it is unlikely that the viewers could "unlearn" to ride a bike. Similarly, if an educational package is used to teach reading, it is unlikely that students will unlearn their reading skills, presumably because reading can be maintained for numerous reasons independent of contrived antecedent or consequent events (e.g., provides information). Alternative designs may be required when irreversibility is predicted or obtained.

## Multi-element Designs

In a *multi-element design,* two or more conditions are presented in a rapidly alternating fashion (Sidman, 1960). The design is sometimes called *alternating treatments* but the term *multi-element* will be used here. When the term *alternating treatment* is used though, *treatment* is used to connote *condition* rather than an intervention, per se (Barlow & Hayes, 1979). That is, the effects of specific variables can be tested using a multi-element design for the purposes of assessment as easily as for the purposes of intervention. In fact, Iwata, Dorsey, Slifer, Bauman, and Richman (1982/1994) used a multi-element design in their seminal functional analysis study designed to test the effects of various sources of reinforcement on SIB (see Chapter 4 for a detailed discussion of functional analysis methods). The upper panel of Figure 2, involving the hypothetical experiment on instruction rate, depicts a multi-element design because the high-rate instruction condition is alternated with the low-rate instruction condition on a session-by-session basis (the order of the conditions could be alternated, randomized, or counterbalanced). Experimental control is established when a separation is obtained in the data path representing one experimental condition versus the data path representing the other experimental condition(s). The primary benefit of the multi-element design is that experimental control often can be established more rapidly than with a reversal design. For example, if the hypothetical study depicted in the upper panel of Figure 2 were designed using a reversal format, a long series of conditions would be necessary (possibly including reversals to baseline after each test condition). Whereas the reversal design might involve ABACACAB (in which A is baseline, B is high-rate instruction, and C is low-rate instruction), the multi-element design can establish the same sort of experimental control in far fewer sessions.

The center and lower panels of Figure 2 depict variations of multi-element designs. In the center panel, baseline conditions are alternated with tests conditions to serve as a "control," to which independent variable effects can be compared. In the lower panel, the logic of the reversal design and multi-element design is combined to test the effects of the two independent variables.

O'Reilly (1995) applied the Iwata et al. (1982/1994) functional analysis methodology to explicitly test the effects of sleep deprivation as an EO for escape behavior (aggression) using a multi-element design. Some instructional demand sessions were conducted when the participant had less than 5 hours of sleep, and some sessions were conducted when the participant had more than 5 hours of sleep. The high-sleep/low-sleep sessions were alternated among other standard functional analysis test conditions (e.g., attention, alone, escape). Results showed that behavior rates were elevated during escape conditions only and were especially elevated during low-sleep conditions. Using the logic of a multi-element design, O'Reilly was able to draw two conclusions from the results: 1) Aggression was maintained by escape, and 2) escape-maintained aggression was more likely to occur when the participant had less than 5 hours of sleep.

Despite the strengths of the multi-element design, problems may arise when the effects of one condition carry over to another condition (i.e., interaction effects; Higgins Hains & Baer, 1989). For example, Vollmer, Iwata, Duncan, and Lerman (1993) found that response rates were high in some functional analysis sessions only because the effects of previous conditions influenced subsequent conditions. Two strategies are suggested to identify and control for interaction effects when using multi-element designs: 1) Evaluate within-session response patterns (Vollmer, Iwata, Zarcone, Smith, & Mazaleski, 1993), and/or 2) extend the design to a reversal format when necessary to minimize interaction effects (Vollmer, Marcus, Ringdahl, & Roane, 1995).

The upper panel of Figure 3 depicts a hypothetical undifferentiated assessment testing the effects of three antecedent variables (Antecedent A, Antecedent B, and Antecedent C). The following question arises: Are the results undifferentiated because the variables do not exert differential control, or are the results undifferentiated because of interaction effects (i.e., the effects of one condition carry over to another condition)? The center panel of Figure 3 shows a within-session analysis of the hypothetical response patterns from the upper panel assessment. Suppose the sessions were each 10 minutes in duration. The data points in the center panel reflect the frequency of the target behavior during each minute of the first 15 sessions. All sessions that follow the "Antecedent A" test condition begin with a burst of behavior that subsides by the end of the session. The overall session rates are roughly equal across conditions (as seen in the upper panel), but the within-session patterns show that the "Antecedent A" test condition is influencing subsequent sessions (Vollmer, Iwata, Zarcone, et al., 1993). The lower panel of Figure 3 shows an extension of the upper panel assessment using a reversal design. Although early sessions in Antecedents B and C may be influenced by Antecedent A, the effects are eventually diminished as more sessions are conducted within the condition.

Another issue that can arise with multi-element designs used to assess antecedent control is that the design may not correctly treat the antecedent as the independent variable of interest. The upper panel of Figure 4 shows a hypothetical analog functional analysis of aggression with no peer present (left side) and with a peer present (right side). The presence of the peer seems to exert some control over attention-maintained aggression (i.e., perhaps peer presence establishes adult attention as positive reinforcement). Furthermore, there seems to be appropriate experimental control because a multi-element design is used. In this case, however, the independent variable of interest is the absence/presence of peers; thus, no experimental control has been demonstrated, because the sequence of conditions with respect to the independent variable is A-B (no peers–peers). The center panel of Figure 4 offers a more controlled analysis because 1) the effects of attention as reinforcement are demonstrated, and 2) the effects of peers as a controlling antecedent are demonstrated and replicated. The lower panel of Figure 4 offers a more efficient analysis because sessions with peers present are alternated among the other test conditions. The design in the lower panel is analogous to the design used by O'Reilly (1995) to test the effects of sleep deprivation on escape-maintained aggression.

## Multiple-Baseline Designs

When reversals are undesired (due to safety concerns) or unexpected (due to predicted irreversibility), a multiple-baseline arrangement is frequently selected as a design format (Baer et al., 1968). A multiple-baseline design involves the sequential implementation of the test variable across two or more baselines. Commonly, the multiple baselines are taken across settings, participants, or behaviors. Dunlap, Kern-Dunlap, Clarke, and Robbins (1991) reported a good example of a multiple-baseline design to test antecedent control. In that study, a multiple-baseline design was used to test sequentially the effects of a revised curriculum (antecedent intervention) first at night and then during the day. Figure 5 depicts a hypothetical analysis using a standard multiple-baseline design across settings.

Using a multiple-baseline design, a degree of experimental control is established insofar as the effects of the intervention are correlated with the onset of intervention across each of the target settings. In Figure 5, the hypothetical settings are home, school, and child care. Although a degree of experimental control is established, the multiple-baseline design is not as strong (i.e., not as convincing) as the reversal or multi-element format because there is no reversal or within-subject replication of effects in any given setting. The design would be strengthened if a brief reversal to baseline were conducted in one of the settings.

In some cases, when using a multiple baseline, it is difficult to distinguish between generalization effects and a lack of experimental control. Establishing experimental control requires that behavior change is correlated with the onset of intervention across all settings (or participants or behaviors), but generalization effects may account for behavior change in untreated contexts once intervention has been established in one context. Figure 6 depicts a multiple-baseline dilemma: Intervention was implemented in one context (home), but effects were seen in the other test contexts (school and child care) prior to intervention implementation. Are these generalization effects, or is this a failed experiment in which behavior change was brought about by some uncontrolled variable that just happened to coincide with the first implementation of the test variable? Of course, this question cannot be answered given the hypothetical nature of the example, but the question arises whenever such effects are obtained with a multiple baseline. From a clinical standpoint, generalization across settings is obviously desired; from an experimental standpoint, possible generalization effects can spoil a design.

## Combined Designs

The multiple-baseline dilemma presents a good forum for discussing the utility of combining design logic based on the obtained data. The possibility of generalization effects in Figure 6 is itself potentially interesting from a clinical and an experimental standpoint. No intervention was implemented in two of the settings, yet behavior change was observed. The analyst can turn an apparent lack of experimental control into an interesting, if serendipitous, extension of the original research question. If the original question was "Does intervention X influence behavior?" then the results of the study suggest the following extension: Does intervention X (implemented in Setting A) influence behavior in Settings B and C (where it has not been implemented)? Figure 7 depicts a potential solution to the multiple-baseline dilemma. By implementing a reversal, the analyst is able to establish experimental control and is able to establish that intervention in one setting is influencing behavior in another setting (generalization). Had behavior not returned to baseline levels during the reversal to baseline conditions, the analyst could have begun to explore extraneous influences on behavior.

A similar dilemma may arise when a behavior does not return to baseline levels in a reversal design. Just as with the multiple-baseline dilemma, a failure to reverse may be clinically desirable because behavior change has been maintained even when programmed interventions are no longer in effect. But also like the multiple-baseline dilemma, a demonstration of experimental control is sacrificed with a failure to reverse. The upper panel of Figure 8 shows a failure to reverse. Is the intervention so potent that its effects persist when the condition is no longer in effect (e.g., once strengthened, behavior has come in contact with reinforcement extraneous to the contrived intervention), *or* was the initial behavior change caused by some extraneous variable? By beginning simultaneous multiple baselines, the design can be altered to see if behavior change is consistently correlated with the onset of intervention (see Figure 8, center and lower panel). If a failure to reverse is a consistent finding, the analyst may then want to further investigate untested features of the environment that could maintain behavior in the absence of a programmed intervention.

## ADDITIONAL CONCEPTUAL ISSUES

This section discusses some additional conceptual issues about experimental designs as they relate to antecedent control. The principal objective of the section is to evaluate concerns related to design and to suggest potential avenues for future research.

### Antecedent Control

The assumption of this chapter, and of this entire book, is that antecedent events control behavior. If the definition of *control* in this context refers to events that exert influence over behavior, then antecedents do control behavior. When the telephone rings, we pick it up. When the traffic light turns green, we press the car's accelerator. It is important to recognize, however, that antecedent events influence operant behavior in conjunction with consequent events (Skinner, 1953). If we press the accelerator when a traffic light turns green, that behavior produces forward movement (i.e., positive or negative reinforcement depending on what we are moving toward or away from). But if the automobile does not move forward, we would not forever persist in stepping on the accelerator pedal (i.e., the behavior would extinguish). Similarly, antecedent events such as instructions, prompts, food deprivation, and so forth exert control over behavior only if that behavior continues to produce a particular outcome.

From an experimental standpoint, it is important to develop a design that can help to evaluate the independent role of antecedent events. We suggest there are two very general methods, but with numerous variations: 1) Continue to reinforce a behavior in conditions with and without the antecedent variable of interest, and 2) place a behavior on extinction in conditions with and without the antecedent variable of interest.

Figure 9 depicts the hypothetical effects of reinforcement with and without the presentation of a particular antecedent event. In the upper panel, the antecedent stimulus appears to exert control over behavior because, initially, there is a consistently higher rate of responding in that condition. The antecedent in this case is said to exert control because the reinforcement contingency is held constant, and the only factor that can account for differential response rates is the presence of the antecedent stimulus. In the second panel, the antecedent event does not exert differential control over behavior because there is no discernible difference in response rates when the two conditions are compared.

The third and fourth panels of Figure 9 depict the hypothetical effects of extinction with and without the presentation of a particular antecedent event. In the third panel, the antecedent stimulus appears to exert control over behavior initially because there is a consistently higher rate of responding in that condition. As with the prior example, the differential response rates indicate that the antecedent stimulus exerts control over responding (i.e., the stimulus previously correlated with reinforcement makes behavior more resistant to extinction). In the fourth panel, the antecedent event does not exert differential control over behavior because there is no discernible difference in response rates when the two conditions are compared.

Analogous methods may be used to identify differential responding when two antecedent events are compared (while holding the consequence constant). For example, a mother and a father may exert differential control over a child's behavior. As mentioned previously, however, the differential effect of the mother versus the father is only an antecedent effect insofar as the consequence is held constant. Thus, in the clinical context when a parental complaint is "he or she does this (aberrant behavior) more around me than he or she does it around my spouse," one should not presume an antecedent effect; rather, differential reinforcement or differential punishment probably accounts for the stimulus control.

## Parametric Analyses

A *parametric analysis* is an evaluation of the effects of different values of an independent variable on a dependent variable. Parametric analyses may be especially critical in the evaluation of antecedent control because many events that occur prior to behavior influence responding only if they occur at a sufficient magnitude. For example, suppose a particular child's parents present food contingent on SIB because it "calms down" the child (i.e., temporarily stops SIB). A common explanation from the parents may be that the child engages in SIB when he is hungry (i.e., SIB is maintained by access to food, and food deprivation is an EO). One question that may arise from an assessment perspective of antecedent control is this: How much food deprivation is required to establish food as a reinforcer for SIB? The upper panel of Figure 10 depicts how a parametric analysis might be used to evaluate the role of EOs in maintaining the child's SIB.

In the hypothetical parametric analysis, contingent access to food occurs in all conditions (again, holding the consequence constant is essential to an analysis of antecedent variables). Observations are conducted immediately after meals, 1 hour after meals, 2 hours after meals, 3 hours after meals, and 4 hours after meals. Using a reversal-design format, the parametric analysis shows that the 4-hour deprivation condition yielded high rates of SIB. Analogous designs could be used evaluate the magnitude of stimulation needed to establish stimulus control, instructional control, or a variety of other antecedent variables.

## Component Analyses

A component analysis usually involves conducting an experiment to evaluate which aspects (components) of an environmental variable are responsible for behavior change. Component analyses could be especially relevant for antecedent analyses for two general reasons: 1) The separate and combined effects of antecedent and consequent events could be evaluated, and 2) the separate and combined effects of antecedent packages could be evaluated. The center panel of Figure 10 depicts a hypothetical component analysis evaluating the separate and combined effects of antecedent and consequent events. In this example, the effects of antecedent and consequent variables are additive; the antecedent condition increased mand rates compared with baseline, but the addition of a consequence maximized intervention effects (i.e., both are necessary, but neither is sufficient). The lower panel of Figure 10 depicts a hypothetical component analysis of an antecedent-based instructional package for spelling (verbal model + visual model + practice). In this example, the visual model is the necessary and sufficient component of the intervention package.

## Influence at a Temporal Distance

A final point should be made regarding the influence of temporal distance on experimental design. It should not be surprising that behavior is sometimes influenced by temporally remote events. Physical events that occur at Time 1 can exert influence over events that occur at Time 2. Heat emitted by the sun influences the temperature on the earth much later. A breeze on the ocean exerts an effect on waves for an indefinite period of time. Writing a note on Monday may influence some behavior on Friday. Similarly, instructions, illness, sleep deprivation, diet, medication, and so forth can exert influence over behavior long after those events have taken place. Little behavioral research, however, has been conducted to evaluate the influence of such temporally remote events.

One reason that the effects of temporally remote events have not been well studied in behavior analysis could be that the evaluation of such effects requires special considerations in experimental design. Although many of the experimental designs discussed previously in this chapter are appropriate for analyzing remote antecedent events, the isolation of specific independent variables is especially difficult when time passes. For example, suppose the effects of an illness (e.g., flu) on SIB are being evaluated. It is entirely possible that illness is not the only variable to consider; for instance, changes in diet and sleep patterns may co-occur with the flu for a given individual. Also, people may be more disposed to provide contingent attention or contingent escape during an illness (e.g., "I do not make him do that if he is sick"). If differential SIB rates are reliably correlated with illness, do we attribute the differential responding to the illness, per se, or to other factors? There is no simple answer; but to adequately test the effects of remote antecedents, all extraneous factors must be taken into account and, in the best case, held constant. Without such experimental control, antecedent analyses of temporally remote events are correlational at best, and no functional relationships can be assumed.

## CONCLUSIONS

This chapter has described the logic of experimentation as it relates to antecedent control. Furthermore, it has outlined general experimental design strategies and hypothetical examples to suggest methods for evaluating the effects of antecedent variables. In summary, it appears that the critical features of an experimental design involve the isolation of variables (e.g., holding consequent events constant while manipulating antecedent variables) and replication of effects within and across participants. Beyond that, the experimental analysis of antecedent variables can be a creative enterprise charged by the data.

## REFERENCES

Baer, D.M., Wolf, M.M., & Risley, T. (1968). Current dimensions of applied behavior analysis. *Journal of Applied Behavior Analysis, 1,* 91–97.

Barlow, D.H., & Hayes, S.C. (1979). Alternating treatments design: One strategy for comparing the effects of two treatments in a single subject. *Journal of Applied Behavior Analysis, 12,* 199–210.

Catania, A.C. (1992). *Learning* (3rd ed.). Englewood Cliffs, NJ: Prentice Hall.

Cooper, J.O., Heron, T.E., & Heward, W.L. (1987). *Applied behavior analysis.* Columbus, OH: Charles E. Merrill.

Dunlap, G., Kern-Dunlap, L., Clarke, S., & Robbins, F.R. (1991). Functional assessment, curricular revision, and severe behavior problems. *Journal of Applied Behavior Analysis, 24,* 387–397.

Higgins Hains, A., & Baer, D.M. (1989). Interaction effects in multielement designs: Inevitable, desirable, and ignorable. *Journal of Applied Behavior Analysis, 22,* 57–69.

Iwata, B.A., Dorsey, M.F., Slifer, K.J., Bauman, K.E., & Richman, G.S. (1994). Toward a functional analysis of self-injury. *Journal of Applied Behavior Analysis, 27,* 197–209. (Reprinted from *Analysis and Intervention in Developmental Disabilities, 2,* 3–20, 1982.)

Johnston, J.M., & Pennypacker, H.S. (1980). *Strategies and tactics for human behavioral research.* Hillsdale, NJ: Lawrence Erlbaum Associates.

O'Reilly, M.F. (1995). Functional analysis and treatment of escape-maintained aggression correlated with sleep deprivation. *Journal of Applied Behavior Analysis, 28,* 225–226.

Sidman, M. (1960). *Tactics of scientific research.* New York: Basic Books.

Skinner, B.F. (1953). *Science and behavior.* New York: Macmillan.

Skinner, B.F. (1974). *About behaviorism.* New York: Alfred A. Knopf.

Smith, R.G., Iwata, B.A., Goh, H., & Shore, B. (1995). Analysis of establishing operations for self injury maintained by escape. *Journal of Applied Behavior Analysis, 28,* 515–535.

Vollmer, T.R., Iwata, B.A., Duncan, B.A., & Lerman, D.C. (1993). Extensions of multielement functional analysis using reversal-type designs. *Journal of Developmental and Physical Disabilities, 5,* 311–325.

Vollmer, T.R., Iwata, B.A., Zarcone, J.R., Smith, R.G., & Mazaleski, J.L. (1993). Within-session patterns of self-injury as indicators of behavioral function. *Research in Developmental Disabilities, 14,* 479–492.

Vollmer, T.R., Marcus, B.A., Ringdahl, J.E., & Roane, H.S. (1995). Progressing from brief assessments to extended experimental analyses in the evaluation of aberrant behavior. *Journal of Applied Behavior Analysis, 28,* 561–576.

~ *Appendix* ~

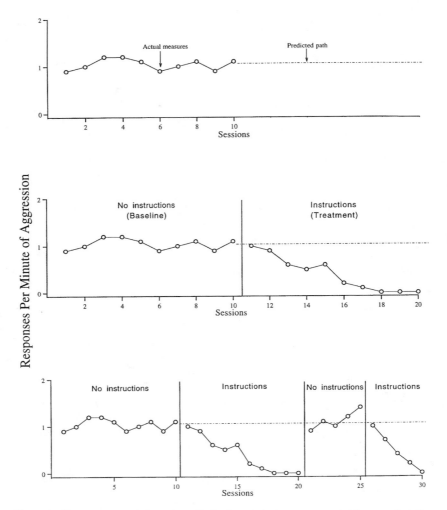

Figure 1. The upper panel shows hypothetical repeated measurements of aggression. The repeated measurements allow the analyst to predict the data path if more observations were conducted. The center panel shows a data path that changes in a direction not predicted by the baseline. The lower panel shows a standard reversal (ABAB) design, in which the effects of implementing an independent variable are replicated.

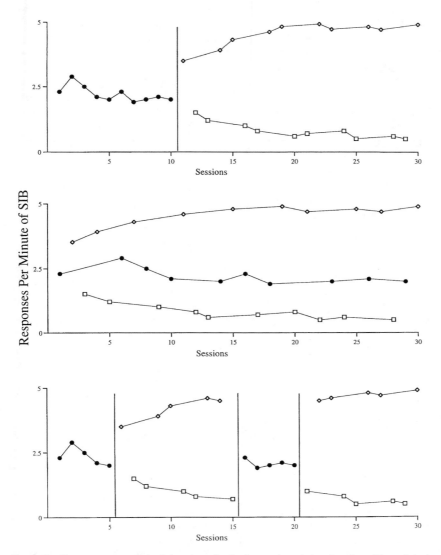

Figure 2. The upper panel depicts a hypothetical experiment showing the differential effects of one antecedent condition versus another in a multi-element experimental design. The center panel shows a variation of the multi-element design, in which baseline conditions are alternated with the test conditions. The lower panel depicts a combined multi-element and reversal design. (Key: ●, Baseline [Moderate rate], ◇, High rate, □, Low rate.)

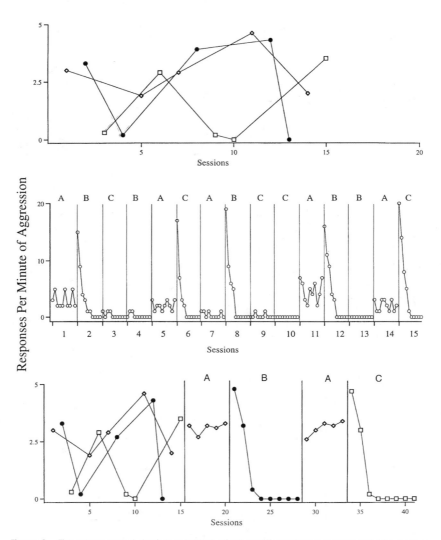

Figure 3. The upper panel depicts a hypothetical undifferentiated assessment. The center panel shows that a within-session (minute-by-minute) data display may reveal interaction effects that produced the undifferentiated results in the upper panel. The lower panel depicts a reversal design, in which the interaction effects are minimized because of repeated exposure to various test conditions. (Key: ◇, Antecedent A; ●, Antecedent B; □, Antecedent C.)

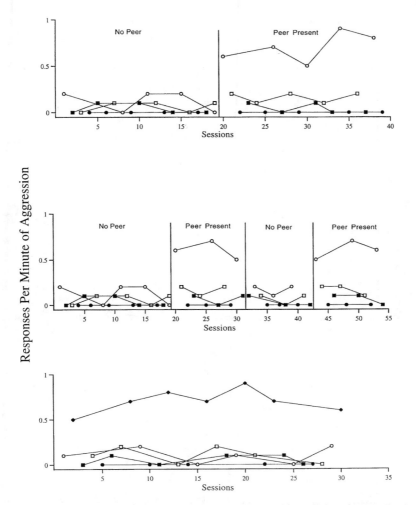

Figure 4. The upper panel depicts a hypothetical analysis of the effects of peers. The hypothetical experiment does not adequately demonstrate control because the design is A-B with respect to peers as independent variable. The center and lower panels depict appropriate experimental designs to test interactions between two independent variables (in this case, attention and peers present/absent). (Key: ○, Attention without peer; ♦, Attention with peer; ■, Escape; □, Materials; ●, Control.)

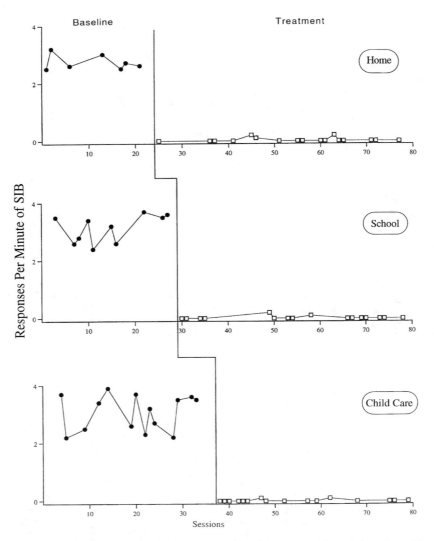

Figure 5. This figure depicts a standard multiple-baseline across settings design. Control is demonstrated if behavior change is correlated with the implementation of the independent variable.

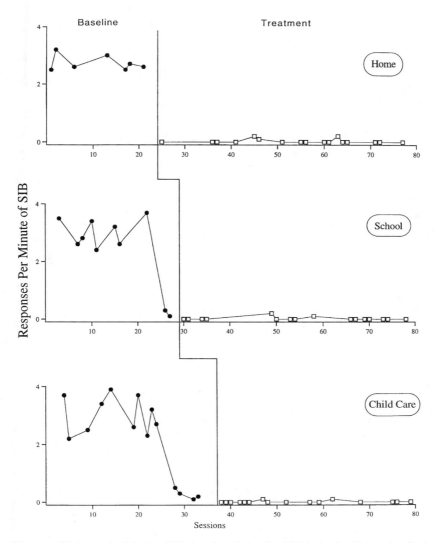

Figure 6. This figure depicts a multiple-baseline design in which behavior change in all settings is correlated with the implementation of the independent variable in one setting only.

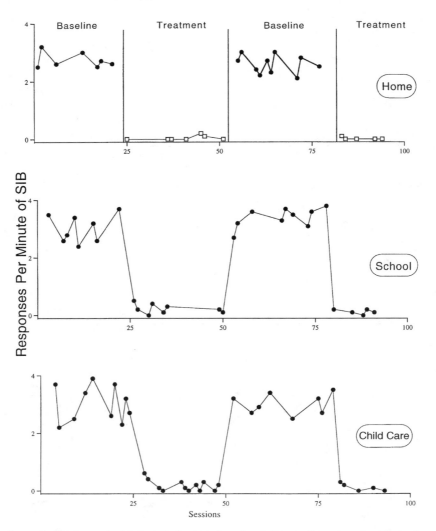

Figure 7.   This figure depicts how the multiple-baseline ''dilemma'' can be solved by implementing a reversal design. The independent variable influences behavior in settings that are
not explicitly tested.

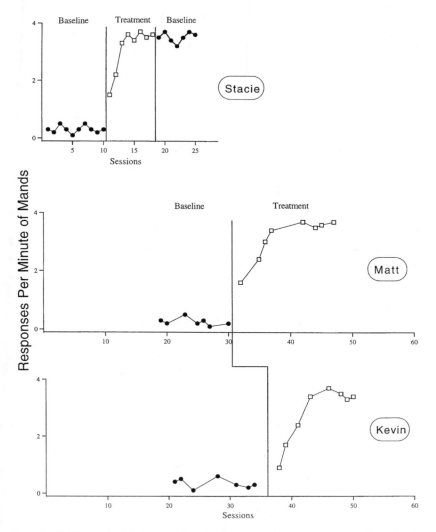

Figure 8.   This figure depicts how a failure to reverse can be accommodated by using the logic of a multiple-baseline design. Behavior change is correlated with the onset of intervention across all three participants.

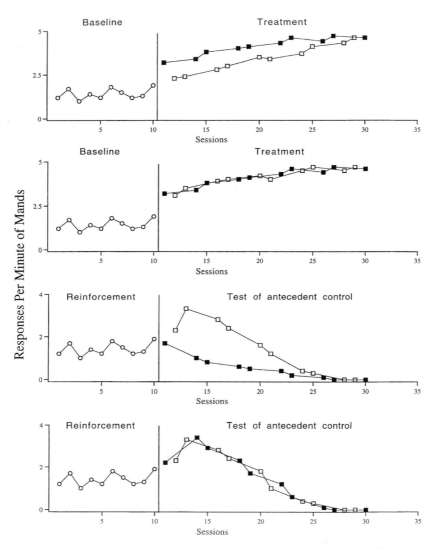

Figure 9. The upper and second panels depict hypothetical experiments showing the differential effects (and noneffects) of an antecedent variable. In the hypothetical experiment, consequent variables (reinforcement) are held constant. The third and lower panels depict hypothetical experiments showing the differential effects (and noneffects) of an antecedent variable. In the lower two panels, extinction is held constant so that any differential effects must be attributed to antecedent factors. (Key: ○, Baseline; ■, With antecedent; □, Without antecedent.)

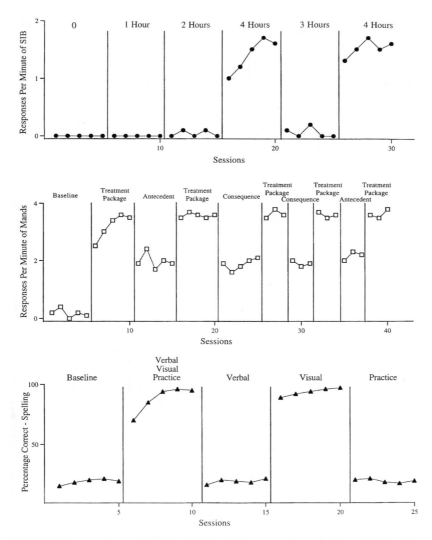

Figure 10. The upper panel depicts a hypothetical parametric analysis in which food deprivation levels are tested at varying durations. Four hours serves as an establishing operation. The center panel depicts a hypothetical component analysis in which the effects of antecedent and consequent factors are additive. The lower panel depicts a hypothetical component analysis in which one component of an intervention package is sufficient to obtain intervention effects.

# ~ *III* ~

## *Issues of Intervention*

### Physical and Medical Influences

# ~ *6* ~

## *Physiological State as Antecedent*
### Utilization in Functional Analysis

## Raymond G. Romanczyk and Amy L. Matthews

Analyzing antecedents of behavior in conceptualizing and formulating clinical interventions is an important endeavor and, historically, has not received sufficient attention. Whereas there were some early research efforts (e.g., Gaylord-Ross, Weeks, & Lipner, 1980; Goren, Romanczyk, & Harris, 1977), significant interest has emerged primarily in the 1990s. Perhaps one reason for this relative inattention to the analysis of relevant antecedent events is the powerful nature of consequence manipulation. Another reason is that, assuming a nonstatic model, the process of analyzing relevant antecedent events is made difficult because of the number of possible antecedents and the resulting possible permutations. Furthermore, analysis of physiological state has received very little systematic attention, no doubt due to the conceptual and technical problems associated with such an analysis.

The history of the analysis of antecedents of behavior is varied and complex and is beyond the scope of this chapter. The analysis, however, has proceeded along some systematic routes. For example, in our own research and clinical work, certain systematic themes have arisen. One theme has been manipulation of the "teaching" environment, in which there has been a strong emphasis in the literature on task difficulty and task demand with respect to problematic behavior (e.g., Weeks & Gaylord-Ross, 1981). Some of our work in the 1980s

---

We thank Wayne Kashinsky for his invaluable assistance in the design and construction of the hardware and software used in our clinical and research efforts. We also want to thank the staff and students of the Institute for Child Development for their continuing cooperation and support and, in particular, Meredith Cochran, who assisted in several of the case studies presented in this chapter.

used computer-assisted instruction to focus directly on this issue. By utilizing computer-assisted instruction, we were able to unconfound the social interaction aspects of a human teacher with the task difficulty and demand characteristics of the teaching lesson itself. These results were quite striking. It became clear that, with respect to challenging behavior among children with developmental disabilities, the presence of the human instructor was a significant variable. Human instructor presence was found to be significant even for such behaviors as self-stimulation (for which physiological state is often invoked as an explanatory mechanism), which up to that point had almost universally been seen as nonreactive to social variables. We found, however, that the relationship between level of interaction and challenging behavior was not simple and, in fact, varied not only with task difficulty but also with the teaching method and presence of instructor (i.e., human versus computer) (Plienis & Romanczyk, 1985).

Further clinical application and research in our laboratory consistently indicated the power of the functional analysis approach, especially with respect to understanding important controlling variables. Furthermore, the approach provided a mechanism for comprehending the complexity of the interactions that may take place among controlling variables with respect to changing proportional contributions (e.g., Romanczyk, Colletti, & Plotkin, 1980; Taylor, Ekdahl, Romanczyk, & Miller, 1994; Taylor & Romanczyk, 1994). Perhaps of most importance in our series of studies is work done in the 1990s, which indicated that the "standard" functions of task avoidance, social avoidance, and attention seeking are quite inadequate as comprehensive categories. Similar to the work of quantum physicists who seem to be on a never-ending path of discovering smaller and smaller components of the atom, we also are finding more and more combinations of functional behavior relationships that tend to be quite idiosyncratic for given individuals. Thus, although the importance of antecedent events is underscored, we believe that the complexity of the analysis process and the diversity of the patterns has been understated in the literature.

Parallel with this research, for many years we have also pursued the use of psychophysiological monitoring (e.g., Romanczyk, Gordon, Crimmins, Wenzel, & Kistner, 1980) as an additional variable to be used in our antecedent analyses. Early on we were struck by the degree of individual variability and the degree to which there is disagreement in the field as to appropriate measures of psychophysiological monitoring. This is due to the complex issues surrounding use of a construct such as anxiety. Even when using a more descriptive term, such as *arousal*, problems in measurement and interpretation abound.

Even given these difficulties, however, previous research studies in our laboratory indicated that the use of psychophysiological measures were not only intriguing but also provided assistance in a conceptual analysis of challenging behavior. This, then, is the focus of our chapter. The chapter first presents an overview of some of the important methodological and conceptual issues, then reviews specific research, presents several clinical examples, and offers suggestions for clinical utilization. Many of the examples refer to individuals with autism, but the conceptual and methodological issues raised have generic implications applicable to other clinical populations.

## PSYCHOPHYSIOLOGY

Psychophysiological measurements focus on the detection of physiological events as they relate to behavior (Surwillo, 1990). The occurrence of physiological events may be considered antecedents, determinants, concomitants, or the result of behavior. Physiological phenomena and psychological events often occur together but are not necessarily correlated. In some cases, however, physiological responses may reliably precede certain behaviors. If behavior could be predicted from physiological states, then challenging behaviors could potentially be preempted through physiological monitoring in a feedback process. Psychophysiological assessment provides unique information that allows analysts to learn about that which cannot be observed directly but which can be useful in understanding and, possibly, predicting behavior.

The process of assessment of physiological states is specific to the research or clinical question of interest. Issues such as diagnosis, construct description, and the behavior–physiology relationship should be considered in utilizing an assessment of physiological state. Ultimately, the important question to ask is, "What is the explanatory value of physiological data, and what new information can the data provide?" Physiological variables may play an important role in challenging behaviors maintained by sensory or multiple functions, and physiological assessment as part of the functional assessment process may serve to influence the creation of effective intervention programs that include components that may not otherwise be addressed (Freeman & Horner, 1996).

Physiological data have been explored primarily by conducting global evaluations of groups of individuals to learn which characteristics a given population may share. For example, some studies have examined the physiological states of children with autism to determine whether consistent patterns are evident that could provide diagnostic or intervention information. Unfortunately, results of numerous studies have provided little consistency regarding physiological patterns of individuals with autism as a whole. Furthermore, little research has been conducted examining the clinical utility of physiological assessment on an individual basis for individuals with autism.

Psychophysiological measurement and interpretation is a highly complex topic area, particularly with people with developmental disabilities. Nevertheless, an overly cautious atmosphere with respect to research and clinical utilization of physiological measurement seems to have resulted (Romanczyk, Lockshin, & O'Connor, 1990).

## PHYSIOLOGICAL MEASUREMENT

The use of physiological measures can seem cumbersome and confusing when one considers the many decisions required and the information needed to conduct a psychophysiological assessment. A brief comparison of three commonly used techniques, however, may provide perspective. Because of space limitations, only heart rate, skin temperature, and electrodermal activity (EDA) are reviewed here (see Andreassi, 1989, for a review of other physiological measures).

### Heart Rate

Heart rate is simply a measure of frequency of contractions of the heart initiated by spontaneous depolarization in the sinoatrial node per unit time. Cardiac activity often has been thought to parallel level of arousal; however, there is not a simple linear relationship between heart rate and arousal. Heart rate can be influenced by many factors such as stress, emotion, and movement (Wolf, 1979). There is also a high degree of individual variability and differential responses to type of stimuli presented.

Heart rate is affected by the balance between the sympathetic and parasympathetic branches of the autonomic nervous system (ANS) (Fowles, 1993). Increases in heart rate are related to activation of the sympathetic division of the ANS. Decreases in heart rate are related to activation of the parasympathetic division, specifically from the vagus nerve. Heart rate measurement typically uses electrodes, which are placed in an "adhesive" connection to the individual. A photoplethysmograph transducer is much easier to use because it is in simple "mechanical" contact with the skin, typically the finger or ear lobe; but it is easily disturbed, which can cause error. Many potential artifact problems exist for heart rate measurement (Romanczyk et al., 1990), and therefore heart rate as a psychophysiological assessment tool is not suitable for many clinical situations because it can be difficult to unconfound artifact from a "pure" response to a given stimuli. Cardiac activity, however, has frequently been used successfully in biofeedback to measure fear and anxiety.

## Skin Temperature

The measurement of skin temperature most frequently has been used to provide biofeedback along with electromyogram readings (i.e., measurement of muscle tension). New technology has made measurement quick and simple through the use of temperature sensitive liquid crystals (TSLCs). Few studies, however, have been conducted to examine the utility of these new devices, which are commercially available and are typically used in the context of stress reduction and personal biofeedback.

As part of a study conducted in our laboratory, skin temperature was used as an adjunct with galvanic skin conductance (GSC). The study involved five undergraduate students participating in a range of activities while GSC and skin temperature were measured via TSLCs to determine differential response across activities and measurement sites (right versus left hand). The activities included moving the right and left hand differentially, resting, blowing up a balloon, popping a balloon, relaxing, and using emotional imagery. Wide individual variations were found for GSC across participants and activities. However, there was virtually no variation of skin temperature across activities using the TSLCs, indicating differential sensitivity compared with GSC. Due to the limited research in this area and our results, if one is attempting to measure behavior-specific variation, the measurement of skin temperature using the TSLC method should be considered with caution.

## Electrodermal Activity

One of the most popular physiological measures of arousal, EDA, seems to be integrally linked with registration of stimulus input (Venables & Christie, 1973). It is also inconsistently measured and presented in the literature (Fowles et al., 1981). EDA is an indirect measure of arousal (arousal is related to sweat gland activity, and GSC is directly related to sweat gland activity). The eccrine sweat glands are of most interest. The secretory portion of the eccrine sweat gland has a profuse nerve supply via cholinergic fibers of the sympathetic nervous system (SNS) (Andreassi, 1989). EDA strongly reflects SNS activity, and behavioral researchers often interpret EDA as indicative of arousal level or emotional reactivity of an organism. EDA measures are viewed as reflecting the activity of sweat glands, which are solely innervated by the sympathetic branch of the ANS (Fowles, 1993). Thus sweating in response to psychological stimuli has sometimes been termed *arousal* sweating and has adaptive value (Andreassi, 1989). Changes in EDA will occur with a wide variety of sensory and psychological stimuli. The momentary fluctuations of EDA that occur with stimulation are termed *phasic responses*, whereas the relatively stable EDA is referred to as the *tonic level* (Venables & Christie, 1973; Venables & Martin, 1967).

Sweat gland secretions contain large amounts of salt, which makes skin electrically conductive. The more sweat on the skin, the more conductive skin is to electricity. The greatest density of sweat glands is on soles of feet and palms of hands (Fowles, 1986). It is recommended that skin conductance be recorded from palmar sites with silver-silver chloride electrode paste consisting of a sodium chloride electrolyte in a neutral ointment cream medium. The area of contact with the skin should be controlled, and time should be allowed for stabilization of the skin-electrode interface. Of most importance is the need to standardize placement and size of electrodes to maximize comparability of measurement across sessions (Lykken & Venables, 1971). Palm placement of electrodes can be difficult due to skin flexing, so finger placement is commonly used. There is less total surface area on fingers, however, so electrode preparation, size, and placement become more critical.

EDA is measured by passing an external electrical current through the skin to obtain skin conductance or skin resistance readings (exosomatic) (Venables & Christie, 1980). These readings indicate the amount of electrical current that the skin will allow to pass. Skin conductance and skin potential are similar processes and are used interchangeably in research. Skin conductance is usually favored because equipment and technique are easier. Units of conductance are preferred by many investigators instead of resistance values. One reason for this is that conductance values are more suitable for averaging and other statistical manipulations. In addition, conductance increases with higher levels of arousal or activity of the organism and decreases at low levels—a relationship that is more logical for most people than resistance measurement, which is inversely related to arousal.

There are three analyses often used in skin conductance interpretation. First, the average level of conductance during a given period of time is termed "skin conductance level" (SCL); it is also referred to as "tonic level." Second, the number of conductance changes that have a waveform characterized by specific onset and decay time and amplitude above a specified threshold during a given time period is termed "skin conductance response" (SCR), also referred to as a "phasic response." Third is magnitude of the SCR, defined as positive increase as indexed to the tonic level immediately preceding the SCR (Andreassi, 1989). Therefore, EDA is composed of slow tonic changes in baseline level and fast changes reflected in phasic response. Both are mediated by the SNS.

Because EDA is reactive to a variety of factors such as room temperature, humidity, and movement, comparison across sessions can be difficult. In addition, skin factors such as dry skin, calluses, and washing can also affect EDA. Problems can also arise with the use of psychophysiological measurement as the individual becomes bored, curious, or displeased with wearing the monitoring device and could, themselves, precipitate a change in EDA. Equipment and transducer constraints can be prohibitive with respect to use by some individuals, especially those who are uncooperative or display high-frequency and/or high-intensity disruptive behavior. Devices for EDA measurement are continually being refined, however, and are becoming minimally intrusive. Greater mobility and less intrusiveness will reduce the reactivity to the measurement, which can often serve as a problematic confounding variable. Although there are always potential problems with the use of EDA (or any other measurement), standardization for each individual is the key to interpretation and generalizability of data across sessions. That is, clinical utilization is concerned less with "absolute" measurement in order to compare someone with other individuals; rather, emphasis is placed on within-subject changes and reproducible measurement procedures and pattern of responses.

It is important to emphasize that EDA should be regarded not as a unitary variable but as one reflecting different aspects of arousal, which can be most useful as part of a comprehensive evaluation (Stevens & Gruzelier, 1984).

## AROUSAL

Arousal is the result of activation of the sympathetic branch of the ANS. Arousal activation is reflected by an increase in sweat gland activity, increased heart rate, increased blood pressure, dilation of the pupils, and other glandular responses that prepare an individual for a quick response to a stressful event (Andreassi, 1989). On the one hand, a variety of behavior responses are related to varying levels of arousal, and a moderate amount of physiological arousal is required for optimal learning to occur. On the other hand, high arousal can lead to an extreme anxiety response, resulting in anxiety disorders such as panic attacks. Therefore, understanding how physiological arousal is linked to different behaviors could prove to have clinical utility.

Arousal theories have been postulated to explain a number of aspects of autism such as self-injury, social avoidance, and escape behavior. Research into autism has embraced three possible arousal dysfunctions: underarousal (Rimland, 1964), overarousal (Hutt, Hutt, Lee,

& Ousted, 1964), and poor modulation of arousal (Ornitz & Ritvo, 1968). There have been little data on the physiological functioning of children with autism to support any of these theories. Research has indicated that physiological responsivity was diminished and correlated with behavioral unresponsiveness (Bernal & Miller, 1971). Opposing findings, however, have also been reported with some studies showing elevated SCLs. For example, Palkowitz and Wisenfeld (1980) found that a group of 10 individuals with autism displayed significantly higher resting SCLs and more spontaneous SCRs than a group of 10 typically developing individuals of the same chronological age. Elevated heart rate was sometimes found in both children with autism and in children without autism but who had other disorders (Cohen & Johnson, 1977; James & Barry, 1984). Other studies have detected normal heart rate (Palkowitz & Wisenfeld, 1980) and SCL (van Engeland, Roelofs, Verbaten, & Slangen, 1991). Interpretation of results is difficult, as children with autism may be reacting to the stress of being tested. Heterogeneity in age and functioning level of children with autism may also play a role in the differences among studies (James & Barry, 1980).

## Application of Arousal to a Model

Increased levels of arousal may serve to motivate escape and avoidance behavior. Escape or avoidance behaviors that serve to alleviate aversive arousal may include gaze avoidance, aggression, and self-injury. If physiological measurement could be utilized to detect variations in arousal level, then escape and avoidance behavior may be analyzed more precisely; then more appropriate behaviors could be taught to take their place, given knowledge of the behavior's function. The complex behavioral, or operant/respondent, model (Romanczyk, 1986, 1992; Romanczyk, Kistner, & Plienis, 1982) incorporates escape and avoidance mechanisms in the context of arousal. A specific example with respect to self-injurious behavior (SIB) is presented here as an illustration of the hypothesized mechanisms.

*Operant/Respondent Model* The operant/respondent model emphasizes respondent aspects of SIB and, in particular, emphasizes the role of arousal as an important maintaining factor. Previous research has described the possible relationship between arousal and SIB (Davenport & Menzel, 1963; Frankel & Simmons, 1976; Gluck & Sackett, 1974; Levinson, 1970; Newsom, Carr, & Lovaas, 1977; Romanczyk & Goren, 1975; Tinklepaugh, 1928), but difficulty in conducting specific research investigations with humans has limited the impact of this hypothesis. By emphasizing the contribution of both operant and respondent components, the conceptualization is that SIB may be initially elicited by arousal, which in turn is elicited by stressors in the environment. As SIB is emitted, environmental events shape and maintain the behavior through operant conditioning. Physiological variables serve to mediate arousal.

This is perhaps best illustrated in the case of individuals who have undergone a period of severe restraint as a protective mechanism for their SIB. Such individuals are often seen to behave in a frenzied fashion when restraints are removed. Their SIB appears quite uncontrollable, and the individuals display severe distress and what may be termed panic. Given the operant/respondent model, the hypothesis is that experience with restraint has led to a conditioning history wherein restraint is associated with the removal of demands and aversive environmental events as well as the cessation of SIB. Because SIB produces pain, which in turn produces arousal, it is therefore the case, in a respondent fashion, that restraint is associated with the reduction of arousal and thus becomes a powerful positive conditioned stimulus. In Figure 1, the process is illustrated wherein SIB, quite paradoxically, can be seen as its own eliciting event and serves to illustrate the frenzied SIB characteristic of some individuals when removed from restraint.

As indicated in Figure 1, SIB produces an unconditioned stimulus, pain. This is immediately followed by the unconditioned response of arousal, which in turn serves to motivate escape behavior. Escape behavior is selected from a hierarchy of behavior that has been effective in the past in producing escape from the aversive state or stimuli. For an individual with a history of restraint, seeking restraint is an effective method of arousal reduction. Once achieved, the negative reinforcement value of arousal reduction serves to increase the probability that this form of escape behavior will be utilized in the future. Of course, because the behavior that results in restraint is SIB, this completes the vicious circle. Over time, the degree to which overt arousal can be observed may be significantly reduced.

This form of learning via the mechanism of escape and/or avoidance is very powerful. As Krasner and Ullmann stated,

> A person may avoid situations without experiencing any physiological arousal; or, to put it differently, he may avoid situations in order not to be aroused. In college certain professors or courses are reputed to be tough and are accordingly avoided. A student may go to great lengths to avoid these ogres without ever having had any experience with the professors or the subject matter they teach. (1973, p. 98)

Thus, this model attributes both respondent and operant properties to SIB. Initial occurrences of SIB are respondents and may be elicited thereafter. Environmental events, however, also act to shape and main-

## Operant/Respondent Components

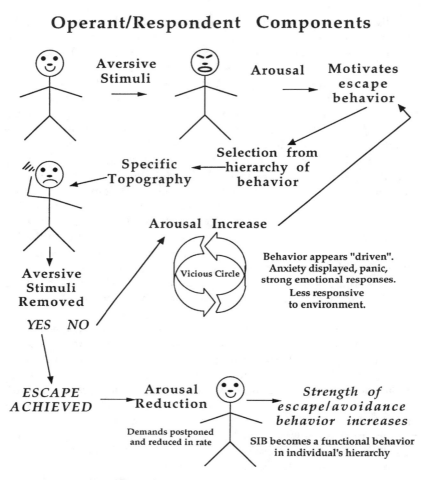

Figure 1. Schematic of the operant/respondent model as applied to self-injurious behavior.

tain responding through operant conditioning. Development of this model of SIB is further complicated by the possibility of predisposing physiological variables (e.g., dysfunction of sensory stimulation modulation, neurological and biochemical influences) that may increase the probability of SIB. Early experience with painful stimuli, such as otitis media or simple accidents, may also play an important role.

The end result, therefore, is that SIB becomes an ever increasingly functional behavior in the individual's behavioral hierarchy. With respect to higher-order conditioning, it is a relatively simple process by which arousal of any type will elicit SIB such that one may not see a simple relationship to restraint removal, but rather restraint removal becomes one of many circumstances that elicit intense SIB. It is also critical to emphasize that although the example given here is restraint in a physical/mechanical sense, this is not necessarily its only form. The calming effects often seen with the application of restraint are also seen in the application of effective acutely rapid deceleration procedures such as physical punishment. The same calming effect is often observed, and it may be because in one sense the individual is being restrained from self-injury. Thus, within this model, it would be an error to view restraint as simply response prevention via physically encumbering the limbs.

It is important to emphasize that the operant/respondent model is not an either/or model with respect to its two learning process emphases. The question is not which component is "true" for a given individual, but rather what is the relative contribution of each learning component to the SIB of a given individual. Furthermore, this model is not exclusive of biological influences. Specifically, both the operant and, in particular, the respondent processes can be significantly influenced by the various biological variables. It is important to emphasize the multiprocess etiology for SIB. It is highly doubtful, for even the most "simple" or "clear" cases of SIB, that a single maintaining mechanism is operating or that there is a single etiological factor present. As we have learned from the long history of the "nature-nurture" debate, it is not a question of which is correct but rather the complex interrelationship of learning and biology that should be the focus of our attention.

## Arousal Research

Discrepant findings in arousal research, which may arise from a number of factors that have been inadequately reported in the literature, were reported in a review by James and Barry (1980). There has been inconsistency in diagnostic terminology and classification without enough reporting of individual characteristics to assist in interpretation of data. In addition, obtaining reliable physiological data from young children with severe disabilities can be complicated and time consuming. Within each study, experimenters utilize different ways to reduce participant movement, fear responses, and escape responses. Various acclimatization procedures are likely used but are infrequently reported. James and Barry (1980) also pointed out that differences in results may be related to medication effects.

There are significant individual differences in psychophysiological response patterning in typical individuals, thus making differences among individuals with developmental disabilities even more difficult to interpret. Multidisciplinary studies are needed to evaluate possible associations among behavioral, clinical, and psychophysiological data and to determine how they relate to sensory, perceptual, and cognitive processes (James & Barry, 1980).

Overall, a review of the literature indicates that no characteristic of CNS functioning can be definitively linked to autism (James & Barry, 1980). The one pattern that has emerged from the research is that children with autism display responses that are different from children without autism. The precise nature of the differences, however, has yet to be discerned. Turpin (1989) suggested that researchers are moving away from general arousal theories to examination of stimulus–response relationships to provide more specific explanations of behavior. It may be more useful, therefore, to utilize physiological assessment on an individual basis to determine relationships among behavioral, environmental, and physiological events.

Population differences, although elusive, do merit continued research. As an example, Belser and Sudhalter (1995) investigated the issue of arousal modulation in males with fragile X syndrome. They noted that their search of the literature since the mid-1980s "failed to identify a single publication with both the words 'arousal' and 'fragile x syndrome' in its abstract" (p. 271). This is in contrast to speculation about the role of arousal (Braden, 1992; Romanczyk, 1992; Scharfenaker, Braden, & Hickman, 1991), which again underscores the interest in conceptualizations using arousal/anxiety and also emphasizes the great difficulty associated with doing well-controlled research in this area.

Belser and Sudhalter (1995) assessed arousal using observation and rating scale procedures in 10 males with Down syndrome and in 10 males with fragile X syndrome of similar chronological age and with similar scores on the Vineland Adaptive Behavior Scales (VABS) (Sparrow, Balla, & Cicchetti, 1984). Individuals participated in a social situation, and results indicated that "males with fra(x) exhibit significantly more anxious behavior during conversations than do males with DS [Down syndrome] who had been matched as closely as possible for age and VABS" (Belser & Sudhalter, 1995, p. 276). In Part 2 of their study, four individuals participated—two with fragile X syndrome and two without. GSC was used to assess arousal during conversations wherein eye contact was or was not maintained by the experimenter. Results indicated that the two participants with fragile X syndrome displayed greater arousal as measured by GSC during eye contact versus non–eye contact conditions. This pattern was not seen for the control participants. These data provide support for the importance of population-specific investigations and also underscore the specificity of assessment conditions. Furthermore, the difficulty in conducting such research serves to produce small sample sizes, such as in this case in which 20 individuals participated when arousal assessment was performed via observation, whereas only 4 individuals participated when direct physiological measurement was used.

**Relaxation Techniques** The importance of investigating arousal is also inferred from the successful use of relaxation for challenging behaviors (e.g., Cautela & Baron, 1973; Cautela & Groden, 1978; Groden & Baron, 1991; Steen & Zuriff, 1977). Within individuals with developmental disabilities, these studies indicate, although indirectly, that anxiety and arousal as possible antecedent factors need to be considered within the development of interventions. Physiological measurement may be able to indicate the critical times when relaxation techniques should be used. Relaxation as an intervention or intervention component for SIB has been used for quite some time, but without the explicit conceptual underpinning. Thus, relaxation or counterconditioning procedures would appear to be a very reasonable intervention approach. Although a number of studies have used relaxation as a component for intervention, few published studies have assessed arousal directly with psychophysiological measurement in conjunction with their intervention programs (Romanczyk et al., 1990). This is likely due to the continued complexity of using physiological equipment and methods in a clinical setting.

## CASE EXAMPLES

Kohlenberg, Levin, and Belcher (1973) studied the relationship between SIB and GSC for a 7-year-old girl who had mental retardation requiring extensive supports, was nonverbal, and had been in restraint for several years because of the severity of her SIB. This was an experimental investigation as opposed to a clinical intervention. Consistent with the model presented earlier concerning arousal, they found consistent increases in GSC level when restraints were removed. They stated that based on their data,

> The lack of relationship, however, between rates of self-destructive behavior or amount of increase in skin conductance level to the initial arousal levels measured immediately before removal of restraints, does not support the arousal hypothesis. That is, if an optimal arousal level is responsible for self-destructive behavior, then higher initial values of arousal should result in lower rates of self-destruction. The data do not support such a contention. (Kohlenberg et al., 1973, p. 13)

Freeman and Horner (1996) conducted a study examining the utility of heart rate as a predictor of challenging behavior in two adult men with mental retardation and severe challenging behaviors. They utilized a consumer-grade, "over-the-counter" heart rate measurement device commonly used by athletes. Results indicated that for these participants, heart rate was an indicator of negative emotional arousal and was highly associated with perceived distress (note that this would not necessarily be the case for a given individual in a given situation; that is, increased heart rate can occur to affectively positive events, such as anticipation of a desired item or arrival of a preferred individual). In addition, behaviors maintained by similar functions had different heart rate patterns. This underscores that physiological measures are more useful for individual assessment than for group consistency. These researchers concur with our previous recommendations of using psychophysiological measures as part of a functional analysis to assist in designing clinical interventions.

We have attempted to use physiological measures within our clinical work and research to determine if this type of assessment is useful in contributing to our understanding of behavior. We have found that children vary widely in their physiological responses, and, therefore, the measures have always been used only on an individual basis to examine the relationship between a particular child's physiological response and behavior. We use a setup that permits us to achieve elements of in vivo observation, biofeedback, and archival recording to permit later more detailed analysis than is possible during assessment sessions (see Figure 2).

For two children with severe behavior problems but non–life-threatening SIB—a 3-year-old girl with autism and a 10-year-old girl with a dual diagnosis of mental retardation and schizophrenia—we employed GSC as the measure of choice because heart rate was too difficult to obtain. GSC, however, proved to be relatively easy to obtain, although as mentioned previously, significant problems with respect to obtaining valid physiological measurement exist with individuals who display severe behavior problems. In the first encounter with the 3-year-old girl, her SIB was quite intense (e.g., finger biting, self-slapping, occasional head banging). SIB was episodic and occurred more in social/teaching contexts than in solitary activities. Initially, psychophysiological monitoring was attempted in the context of having her teacher engage in habilitative activities. Some overall patterns emerged such that high arousal levels tended to precede bouts of SIB. The pattern, however, was more of interest rather than clinically significant. Subjectively, there still appeared to be some variation and cyclicity to her behavior, although the pattern was not stable. Given the occasional relationship between ear infections and SIB and given the child's sporadic history of ear infections, consultation

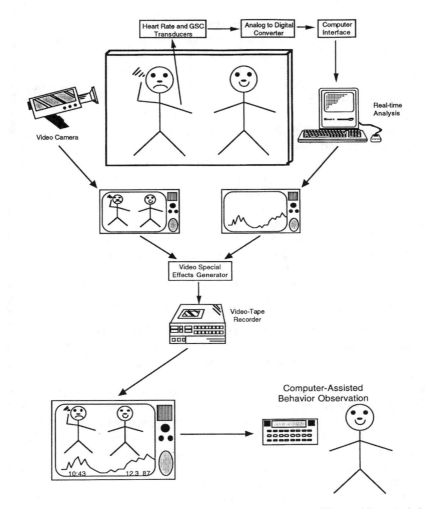

Figure 2. A "typical" psychophysiological assessment set up, permitting real-time analysis and feedback as well as archival recording on videotape.

was obtained with the child's physician to ensure that ear infection was not a current problem; assessment was negative. Given that the child was reasonably compliant with the assessment procedures, however, a tympanogram, which can be used to detect ear infection by recording middle-ear pressure on the eardrum, was then obtained on a daily basis (although typically a tympanogram is used for routine screening and not on a daily basis). Wide variations in the tympanogram were found, and it appeared that the child was experiencing strong inner-ear pressure in the absence of easily diagnosed external signs of ear infection. Consultation with the physician resulted in a more aggressive medication regimen and, subsequently, levels of intensity of SIB began to attenuate. This type of assessment indicates the complexity of variables associated with challenging behaviors. The assessment did not result in the elimination of SIB, but it allowed for reduction.

For the second child, SIB was very intense and resulted in bleeding wounds and disfigurement. Intense head banging was further cause for concern. She would often avoid interaction but would approach and engage in intense aggressive behavior. Staff described her as "unpredictable." She had participated in an extreme range of polypharmacy for both self-injurious and aggressive behaviors with no result.

GSC was utilized and assessment took place in a structured teaching situation. Arousal levels rose in response to physical contact and close physical proximity. Rises in arousal could also be seen after periods of noninteraction. Thus she appeared to be both attention seeking as well as socially avoidant, and difficulty in arousal modulation was hypothesized.

The initial intervention procedure established a very low demand situation with only child and therapist, in which aggressive and self-injurious behavioral episodes did not terminate interaction. A reduction in such outbursts was seen, and given this reduction, it was possible to observe behavior patterns. In vivo systematic desensitization enabled closer and closer physical proximity, task demand, social interaction, and general commotion (e.g., movement of people in room, noise from conversations and activities, common environmental sounds) to occur. Then a clearly delineated physical space was made available as a "retreat," and she was taught to modulate her arousal by changing the physical distance among her and other children and staff. Eventually self-control was encouraged through a symbolic system in which she could earn time to be by herself for increasing tolerance of social interaction and physical contact. During this phase, a telemetric device was utilized to transmit GSC measurement to a computer in the classroom that monitored arousal level on-line and continuously displayed GSC for staff to use to assist in choreographing the physical and social environment. This was done not to minimize arousal but rather to ensure that it was kept at a moderate level for which she could exert control successfully. Results were excellent, and outbursts attained near-zero rates with concomitant substantial increases in social interaction and participation in school and recreational activities.

## Psychophysiological Measurement

We conducted an assessment with two young children with autism who were exhibiting erratic serious challenging behaviors with no clear environmental antecedent based on our "typical" functional analysis. Because of the puzzling nature of the behavior and the difficulty determining the function and cause, it was decided that GSC measures would be taken in a variety of situations in an attempt to identify whether arousal was associated differentially with specific activities and/or settings.

Each of the two children participated in a total of 24 sessions over the course of 3 weeks. In the first part of the assessment, an easy task and a difficult task were alternated every 5 minutes for 20 minutes within a classroom setting. In the second part of the assessment, the tasks continued to be alternated; but half of the sessions were presented in the classroom, and the other half were presented in a novel environment. For the final part of the assessment, the difficult task and unstructured play were alternated.

During all conditions, the child wore silver-silver chloride electrodes on two fingers that connected to a custom micro-miniature computer (size: $2\frac{1}{2}'' \times 4\frac{1}{2}'' \times \frac{3}{4}''$; weight: 5 ounces). Once GSC data were collected, the data were downloaded to an Apple Macintosh computer for data analysis. Data were analyzed by a specially designed computer program that summarized and plotted data for each minute (see Figure 3). The program summarized and graphed the number of SCRs (see Figure 3) and SCLs for a session. It also created a summary table that included descriptive statistics and an overall visual display of the GSC data.

An important aspect of clinical use is that the data analysis produces information in a highly usable and compact form. That is, clinical analysis is quite different from a group study in which results are based on aggregation of many individuals over many sessions. Thus our data analysis process was designed to produce a session document that was easily shared among interested parties of widely diverse backgrounds and levels of sophistication with respect to psychophysiological assessment. Therefore, it incorporates both simple visual display as well as error detecting and statistical tables. Most important, however, is that definition of phasic versus tonic and signal error detection are quantified and performed by the computer so as to eliminate the ever-present possibility of observer bias that is associated with hand scoring.

Unfortunately, in this case, the results were disappointing but were informative with respect to physiological measurement. Signifi-

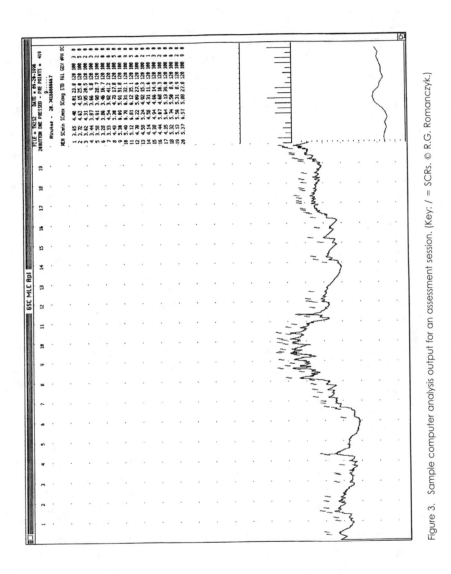

Figure 3. Sample computer analysis output for an assessment session. (Key: / = SCRs. © R.G. Romanczyk.)

cant time was spent preparing for the case studies, collecting data, and analyzing data. Although approximately half of the total time spent was "recyclable" in the sense that it could be applied to other individuals and thus was a "one time" expense, the per-session, per-child time (24 sessions multiplied by 2 children) was still substantial. Thus the results were disappointing both because of the staff time costs associated with assessment as well as the fact that it was difficult to discern any clear or predictable pattern within the data that could assist us in clinical decision making. Table 1 presents these costs.

In addition, many problems occurred within the data collection, which prevented us from obtaining reliable GSC data from each session. The two children in this study were identified as having significant behavior problems that were interfering with their participation in social and learning settings. We discovered that similar behavior made it quite difficult to collect GSC data because the children would interfere with data collection by refusing to wear the electrodes, playing with them, damaging equipment, and so forth. Therefore, the very behaviors we were attempting to study were also the behaviors that were preventing us from obtaining accurate data. In addition, the exciting new technology that allowed us to be portable in our data collection also created some problems because the device was somewhat fragile and did not respond well when it was the focus of the children's disruptive behavior.

Table 1. Time summary for psychophysiological assessment of two children

| Procedure | Staff hours | Recyclable |
| --- | --- | --- |
| **General preparation** | | |
| Hardware | 30.00 | Yes |
| Software—data collection | 12.00 | Yes |
| Software—data analysis | 60.00 | Yes |
| Staff training | 8.00 | Yes |
| Sum | **110.00** | |
| **Child general preparation** | | |
| Acclimation—physiological transducers | 1.50 | No |
| Acclimation—assessment procedures | 2.00 | No |
| Sum | **3.50** | |
| **Per session** | | |
| Prepare equipment | 0.25 | No |
| Prepare child | 0.25 | No |
| Postsession—equipment | 0.25 | No |
| Postsession—child | 0.25 | No |
| Data analysis | 0.10 | No |
| Sum | **1.10** | |

Although these results seem discouraging, we viewed them as evidence that physiological measurement and clinical usage are in their infancy. Although patterns of responding within sessions were apparent, interpretation was difficult with the combination of technological difficulties and child behaviors. Technology has advanced a great deal to allow us to measure physiological responses using portable and sensitive equipment. The electrodes used were disposable to reduce preparation time and make consistency easier to achieve in comparison with standard reusable electrodes, and we used a soft protective covering for the electrodes and computer to minimize child interference with the equipment. Even further advances, however, may be necessary before physiological measures can be easily used within a clinical setting in which the focus is on severe challenging behavior. The time required for preparation of individuals and equipment would be overwhelming within the average educational/clinical setting. For example, most children require a period of acclimatization before they will willingly wear the electrodes. Some children become accustomed to the electrodes after a brief period of exposure, although others require days of repetition before becoming used to the electrodes. The pragmatic limitations of physiological measurement for clinical purposes remain substantial.

## CLINICAL UTILIZATION

There is a critical need to consider conceptual validity (i.e., psychological understanding) as well as clinical utility (i.e., prediction and development of an intervention program) to determine the contribution of psychophysiological data to behavior assessment. There is some evidence of conceptual validity but little at this time for clinical utility (Turpin & Clements, 1993). More theoretical models are needed to drive psychophysiological research, and methods of assessment need continued advancement. Generalizability must be considered because most physiological studies take place within a carefully controlled research environment, unlike the case study presented here.

Psychophysiological assessment can provide objective information about arousal or emotional states. There is not always a good relationship, however, between psychophysiological measures and behavior measures. It must be part of a multimodal assessment. It has been evident across research studies that there is a wide range of variability to physiological measures across individuals. Within a study of 14 children with autism conducted in our laboratory, each child had a different response to assessment conditions within and across days. Some children never showed a reactive physiological response regardless of situation ($n=3$), other children were highly reactive with no apparent consistency across time and day ($n=7$), whereas still other children had more consistent reactivity across time and/or day ($n=4$). Comparisons among children, therefore, even within a given population such as autism, do not seem to be useful, and physiological measurement in normative environments appears to serve best as a tool for individual assessment.

Choosing a physiological measure may seem a difficult task. Selection involves considering the rationale behind the decision to use a physiological measure and the definition of the arousal construct. Theories of arousal are few and limited, with little research to assist the clinician in choosing a psychophysiological assessment measure. A reasonable choice should result from observations of behavior and the specific activity or task required (e.g., heart rate and high rates and/or range of movement cannot be separated). It is important to consider the context of the assessment and also the practical considerations such as instrumentation, cost-benefit analysis, time-course, and scale.

Researchers also should consider issues of individual differences in activation and reactivity. Comparisons should be made within individuals involving the examination of patterns of responses rather than absolute values. At this time, psychophysiological assessment is not sensitive enough to be related to more universal psychological characteristics, and comparisons across individuals can be difficult because there appears to be a high degree of individual variability. Psychophysiological assessment may find its best clinical use in the assessment of the individual to determine patterns of responses and their relationship to environmental events, especially when the individual may have poor communication skills or display what appears to be highly erratic behavior.

## CONCLUSIONS

In our clinical and research activities we have obtained about a 50/50 ratio of success to failure in using psychophysiological analysis, which is a satisfactory level. Success in this context means that the information was useful in our decision making and conceptualizations. At times this means ruling out physiological state as an important variable. It is usually technical and procedural problems that account for the 50% "failure."

As technology advances and physiological studies continue to be conducted, assessments may more routinely include the use of measures such as GSC to validate the conceptual underpinnings of various interventions. In addition, psychophysiological assessment may prove useful to help predict and prevent challenging behaviors before they occur, as we have illustrated. We look forward to continued research in this area and to the expanded possibilities of its use on a more routine and cost effective basis.

## REFERENCES

Andreassi, J.L. (1989). *Psychophysiology: Human behavior and physiological response.* Hillsdale, NJ: Lawrence Erlbaum Associates.

Belser, R., & Sudhalter, V. (1995). Arousal difficulties in males with fragile X syndrome: A preliminary report. *Developmental Brain Dysfunction, 8,* 270–279.

Bernal, M.E., & Miller, W.H. (1971). Electrodermal and cardiac responses of schizophrenic children to sensory stimuli. *Psychophysiology, 7,* 155–168.

Braden, M.L. (1992). Behavioral assessments. In R.J. Hagermann & P. McKenzie (Eds.), *1992 International Fragile X conference proceedings.* Dillon, UT: Spectra.

Cautela, J.P., & Baron, M.G. (1973). Multifaceted behavior therapy of self-injurious behavior. *Journal of Behavior Therapy and Experimental Psychiatry, 4,* 125–131.

Cautela, J.P., & Groden J. (1978). *Relaxation: A comprehensive manual for adults, children, and children with special needs.* Champaign, IL: Research Press.

Cohen, D.J., & Johnson, W.T. (1977). Cardiovascular correlates of attention in normal and psychiatrically disturbed children. *Archives of General Psychiatry, 34,* 56–57.

Davenport, R.K., & Menzel, E.W. (1963). Stereotyped behavior in the infant chimpanzee. *Archives of General Psychiatry, 8,* 99–104.

Fowles, D.C. (1986). The eccrine system and electrodermal activity. In M.G.H. Coles, E. Donchin, & S.W. de Porges (Eds.), *Psychophysiology systems, processes, and applications* (pp. 51–96). New York: Guilford Press.

Fowles, D.C. (1993). Electrodermal activity and antisocial behavior: Empirical findings and theoretical issues. In J.C. Roy, W. Boucsein, D.C. Fowles, & J.H. Gruzelier (Eds.), *Progress in electrodermal research* (pp. 223–237). New York: Plenum.

Fowles, D.C., Christie, M.J., Edelberg, R., Grings, W.W., Lykken, D.T., & Venables, P.H. (1981). Publication recommendations for electrodermal measurements. *Psychophysiology, 18,* 232–239.

Frankel, F., & Simmons, J.Q. (1976). Self-injurious behavior in schizophrenic and retarded children. *American Journal of Mental Deficiency, 80,* 512–522.

Freeman, R., & Horner, R.H. (1996, May). *The relationship between physiological arousal and problem behavior.* Paper presented at the 22nd annual meeting of the Association for Behavior Analysis, San Francisco.

Gaylord-Ross, R., Weeks, M., & Lipner, C. (1980). An analysis of antecedent, response, and consequence events in the treatment of self-injurious behavior. *Education and Training of the Mentally Retarded, 5,* 35–42.

Gluck, J.P., & Sackett, G.P. (1974). Frustration and self-aggression in social isolate rhesus monkeys. *Journal of Abnormal Psychology, 83,* 331–334.

Goren, E.R., Romanczyk, R.G., & Harris, S.L. (1977). A functional analysis of echolalic speech: The effects of antecedent and consequent events. *Behavior Modification, 1,* 481–498.

Groden, G., & Baron, M.G. (Eds.). (1991). *Autism: Strategies for change—a comprehensive approach to the education and treatment of children with autism and related disorders.* New York: Gardner Press.

Hutt, C., Hutt, S.J., Lee, D., & Ousted, C. (1964). Arousal and childhood autism. *Nature, 204,* 908–909.

James, A.L., & Barry, R.J. (1980). A review of psychophysiology in early onset psychosis. *Schizophrenia Bulletin, 6,* 506–525.

James, A.L., & Barry, R.J. (1984). Cardiovascular and electrodermal responses to simple stimuli in autistic, retarded, and normal children. *International Journal of Psychophysiology, 1,* 179–193.

Kohlenberg, R.J., Levin, M., & Belcher, S. (1973). Skin conductance changes and the punishment of self-destructive behavior: A case study. *Mental Retardation, 11,* 11–13.

Krasner, L., & Ullmann, L. (1973). *Behavior influence and personality: The social matrix of human action.* New York: Holt, Rinehart & Winston.

Levinson, C.A. (1970). The development of headbanging in a young rhesus monkey. *American Journal of Mental Deficiency, 75,* 323–328.

Lykken, D.T., & Venables, P.H. (1971). Direct measurement of skin conductance: A proposal for standardization. *Psychophysiology, 8,* 656–672.

Newsom, C.D., Carr, E.G., & Lovaas, O.I. (1977). The experimental analysis and modification of autistic behavior. In R.S. Davidson (Ed.), *Modification of pathological behavior* (pp. 109–187). New York: Gardner Press.

Ornitz, E.M., & Ritvo, E.R. (1968). Perceptual inconstancy in early infantile autism. *Archives of General Psychiatry, 2,* 389–399.

Palkowitz, R.J., & Wisenfeld, A.R. (1980). Differential autonomic responses of autistic and normal children. *Journal of Autism and Developmental Disorders, 10,* 347–360.

Plienis, A., & Romanczyk, R.G. (1985). Analysis of performance, behavior, and predictors for severely disturbed children: A comparison of adult vs. computer instruction. *Analysis and Intervention in Developmental Disabilities, 5,* 345–356.

Rimland, B. (1964). *Infantile autism.* New York: Appelton-Century-Crofts.

Romanczyk, R.G. (1986). Self-injurious behavior: Conceptualization, assessment and treatment. In K.D. Gadow (Ed.), *Advances in learning and behavioral disabilities* (Vol. 5., pp. 29–56). Greenwich, CT: JAI Press.

Romanczyk, R.G. (1992, June). *The role of arousal and anxiety in self-injurious behavior: Implications for treatment.* Paper presented at the Third International Fragile X Conference, Snowmass, CO.

Romanczyk, R.G., Colletti, G., & Plotkin, R. (1980). Punishment of self-injurious behavior: Issue of behavior analysis, generalization, and the right to treatment. *Child Behavior Therapy, 2,* 37–54.

Romanczyk, R.G., Gordon, W.C., Crimmins, D.B., Wenzel, Z.M., & Kistner, J.A. (1980). Childhood psychosis and 24-hour rhythms: A behavioral and psychophysiological analysis. *Chronobiologica, 7,* 1–14.

Romanczyk, R.G., & Goren, E.R. (1975). Severe self-injurious behavior: The problem of clinical control. *Journal of Consulting and Clinical Psychology, 43,* 730–739.

Romanczyk, R.G., Kistner, J.A., & Plienis, A. (1982). Self-stimulatory and self-injurious behavior: Etiology and treatment. In J. Steffen & P. Karoly (Eds.), *Advances in child behavioral analysis and therapy* (Vol. 2, pp. 189–256). Lexington, MA: D.C. Heath.

Romanczyk, R.G., Lockshin, S., & O'Connor, J. (1990). Psychophysiology and issues of anxiety and arousal. In J.K. Luiselli, J.L. Matson, & N.M. Singh (Eds.), *Assessment, analysis, and treatment of self-injury* (pp. 93–121). New York: Springer-Verlag.

Scharfenaker, S., Braden, M., & Hickman, L. (1991). An integrated approach to intervention. In R.J. Hagerman & A.C. Cronister-Silverman (Eds.), *Fragile X syndrome: Diagnosis, treatment, and research* (pp. 327–372). Baltimore: The Johns Hopkins University Press.

Sparrow, S., Balla, D., & Cicchetti, D. (1984). *Vineland Adaptive Behavior Scales (VABS)*. Circle Pines, MN: American Guidance Service.

Steen, P.L., & Zuriff, G.E. (1977). The use of relaxation in the treatment of self-injurious behavior. *Journal of Behavior Therapy and Experimental Psychiatry, 8,* 447–448.

Stevens, S., & Gruzelier, J. (1984). Electrodermal activity to auditory stimuli in autistic, retarded, and normal children. *Journal of Autism and Developmental Disabilities, 14,* 245–260.

Surwillo, W.W. (1990). *Psychophysiology for clinical psychologists.* Norwood, NJ: Ablex.

Taylor, J., Ekdahl, M., Romanczyk, R.G., & Miller, M. (1994). Escape behavior in task situations: Task versus social antecedents. *Journal of Autism and Developmental Disorders, 24,* 331–344.

Taylor, J., & Romanczyk, R.G. (1994). Generating hypotheses about the function of student problem behavior by observing teacher behavior. *Journal of Applied Behavior Analysis, 27,* 251–265.

Tinklepaugh, O.L. (1928). The self-mutilation of a male macaques monkey. *Journal of Mammalogy, 9,* 293–300.

Turpin, G. (Ed.). (1989). *Handbook of clinical psychophysiology.* New York: John Wiley & Sons.

Turpin, G., & Clements, K. (1993). Electrodermal activity and psychopathology: The development of the palmar sweat index (PSI) as an applied measure for use in clinical settings. In J. Roy, W. Boucsein, D.C. Fowles, & J.H. Gruzelier (Eds.), *Progress in electrodermal research* (pp. 49–59). New York: Plenum.

van Engeland, H., Roelofs, J.W., Verbaten, M.N., & Slangen, J.L. (1991). Abnormal electrodermal reactivity to novel visual stimuli in autistic children. *Psychiatry Research, 38,* 27–38.

Venables, P.H., & Christie, M.J. (1973). Mechanisms, instrumentation, recording techniques and quantification of responses. In W.F. Prokasy & D.C. Raskin (Eds.), *Electrodermal activity in psychological research* (pp. 1–124). New York: Academic Press.

Venables, P.H., & Christie, M.J. (1980). Electrodermal activity. In I. Martin & P.H. Venables (Eds.), *Techniques in psychophysiology* (pp. 3–67). New York: John Wiley & Sons.

Venables, P.H., & Martin, I. (1967). The relation of palmar sweat gland activity to level of skin potential and conductance. *Psychophysiology, 3,* 302–311.

Weeks, M., & Gaylord-Ross, R. (1981). Task difficulty and aberrant behavior in severely handicapped students. *Journal of Applied Behavior Analysis, 14,* 449–463.

Wolf, S. (1979). Anatomical and physiological basis for biofeedback. In J.V. Basmajian (Ed.), *Biofeedback principles and practice for clinicians* (pp. 5–30). Baltimore: Williams & Wilkins.

# ~ 7 ~

# Psychopharmacology and Steady-State Behavior

Nirbhay N. Singh, Cynthia R. Ellis, and Philip K. Axtell

Many individuals with developmental disabilities who are referred to nonmedical clinicians for therapeutic, educational, and related services are on psychotropic medication for their behavior problems or psychiatric disorders. Given that the prevalence of psychiatric disorders in individuals with developmental disabilities is at least three or four times as high as their peers without disabilities, it is to be expected that proportionately greater numbers of them will be on psychotropic medication. Furthermore, some individuals with developmental disabilities have intractable behavior problems that require pharmacological management for short periods until alternative treatment modalities can be implemented. This situation arises particularly with those individuals who have self-injurious, aggressive, and violent explosive behaviors. The motivations for their challenging behaviors are often not readily apparent through a functional analysis and, therefore, are unable to be controlled through systematic behavior management procedures. Regardless of the treatment modality used, the aim is always to provide integrated, person-centered services in the most facilitative environment so that individuals with developmental disabilities can enjoy an enhanced quality of life in the community.

This chapter begins with an introduction to setting events because setting events provide the conceptual basis for understanding behavior–drug–environment interactions that underlie psychopharmacological treatment. This discussion is followed by brief sections on psychopharmacology and developmental disabilities, some general principles of psychopharmacology, and selected factors that affect the outcome of psychopharmacological treatment. Each section briefly discusses the clinical implications of various setting events and their impact on psychopharmacological treatment of individuals with developmental disabilities. This is a complex and rapidly developing area of investigation, and interested readers may find our earlier papers to be useful background to this field (e.g., Singh & Aman, 1990; Singh & Ellis, 1995; Singh & Repp, 1988). We use the term *psychotropic drug* in this chapter to refer to any pharmacological agent that is prescribed for the explicit purpose of bringing about behavioral, cognitive, or emotional changes in the individual. The term *psychoactive drug* is used in a more general sense to refer to any pharmacological agent that may bring these effects regardless of the physician's intent when prescribing this type of medication. We use the term *individual* in a lifespan context.

## SETTING EVENTS AS THE CONTEXT OF PSYCHOPHARMACOLOGY

Behavior is contextual, and—to understand the motivation for a behavior—we must investigate it in the context of its occurrence. Similarly, treatment is contextual, and—to understand steady-state behavior that follows treatment—we must investigate it within the context in which treatment is provided. In behavioral treatment, we need to understand the behavior–environment–treatment interactions and interrelationships; and, in psychopharmacological treatment, we need to understand the behavior–environment–drug interactions and interrelationships.

Ecobehavior analysis provides an elegant methodology for understanding the interactions and interrelationships among behavior, environment, and psychopharmacological treatment(s). Although its history is very short in terms of psychopharmacology, ecobehavior analysis has been an accepted part of the research methodology in a number of fields, including psychology (Barker, 1968; Willems, 1974), education (Brophy, 1979), and behavior analysis (Martens & Witt, 1988; Rogers-Warren & Warren, 1977; Wahler & Graves, 1983). This approach emphasizes the study of people within their biological, physical, social, and cultural contexts and provides a methodology for describing the interactions and interrelationships that occur among individuals and their behaviors, cultural and social settings, and internal states.

In ecobehavior analysis, the concept of setting events has been used to investigate and understand environment–behavior interactions (see Schroeder, 1990). The early work of Bijou and Baer (1961) and Kantor (1959) led to the seminal work by Wahler and Fox (1981) on setting events, which provided the impetus for the study of environment–behavior interactions of individuals. Bijou and Baer defined a setting event as "a stimulus-response interaction which, simply because it has occurred, will affect other stimulus–response relationships which follow" (1961, p. 21). In broadening the concept of setting events, Wahler and Fox advanced the notion that setting events include "complex antecedent conditions, events, and stimulus–response interactions which may overlap with or entirely precede subsequent behaviors that they affect" (1981, p. 331). Singh and Repp (1988) took it a step further by suggesting that setting events can be of at least four different types, all lying along and often overlapping on a continuum of time relative to the behaviors that they subsequently or concurrently affect. They suggested that the following could be setting events: 1) events or stimulus–response interactions totally removed in time (e.g., by weeks, months, or even years), 2) events or stimulus–response interactions close in time (e.g., events that occur up to a few days before or just prior to subsequent behavior), 3) concurrent stimulus events (e.g., when the stimulus condition, setting, or activity is present concurrently with the behavior it affects), and 4) concurrent stimulus–response interactions (e.g., when stimulus–response interactions set the occasion for the target behavior to occur).

The concept of setting events provides a useful way of understanding some of the environment–behavior interactions and interrelationships that occur prior to, during, and subsequent to psychopharmacological treatment of individuals with developmental disabilities. For example, in addition to the physical, social, and cultural contexts of the target individual, the individual him- or herself, his or her disease state(s), and concurrent therapies provide the setting event for the assessment and prescription of psychopharmacological treatment, along with adjunctive psychosocial and educational interventions. The concept of steady-state behavior in terms of psychopharmacological treatment takes on added significance because of the multitude of variables, both biological and nonbiological, that have the potential to alter steady-state plasma concentration levels and subsequent behavior. Given space limitations, this chapter considers only selected variables and their clinical implications.

## PSYCHOPHARMACOLOGY AND DEVELOPMENTAL DISABILITIES

Psychopharmacology is slowly achieving the status of a valid, adjunctive treatment modality in developmental disabilities. With its origins as a magic bullet for serious behavior problems, psychopharmacology had established itself at least until the 1980s as the treatment of choice for individuals with developmental disabilities who were incarcerated in large, understaffed residential facilities. The use of psychotropic medication reached such extensive proportions that several U.S. courts provided guidelines for its use in state residential facilities (Singh, Guernsey, & Ellis, 1992). For example, in the 1972 landmark ruling in the case of *Wyatt v. Stickney*, a federal court in Alabama ruled that "medication shall not be used as punishment, for the convenience of staff, as a substitute for a habilitation program, or in quantities that interfere with the resident's habilitation program." The *Wyatt* standards continue to be used in the 1990s, often with major extensions and clarifications, by many federal district courts as the basis for their rulings regarding the use of psychotropic drugs in state facilities.

The extensive use of psychotropic medications in residential facilities was not based on data attesting to their efficacy. In the absence of alternative treatments, psychopharmacological treatments appeared to be effective in residential and community settings for controlling severe behavior problems, such as self-injury and aggression, but their efficacy proved questionable when compared with placebo in well-controlled studies. Indeed, there are limited data to suggest that the antipsychotics, the most-used class of drugs in this population, provide long-term benefit for the majority of individuals with mental retardation who have severe behavior problems (Schatzberg & Cole, 1986; Schroeder, 1988).

In the late 1990s, our understanding is that sometimes psychopharmacological treatment is necessary but not sufficient to improve the quality of life of individuals with developmental disabilities who exhibit behavior problems or psychiatric disorders. Data from the 1990s suggest that the numbers of individuals with developmental disabilities on psychotropic medication has been declining since the late 1970s and early 1980s. Following the seminal work of Lipman (1970) on the use of psychotropic drugs in residential facilities, a large number of prevalence studies have reported the use of psychoactive medication in residential and community facilities for individuals with developmental disabilities. Overall, institutional surveys show that psychotropic drug usage ranges from a low of 19% to a high of 86%, with the majority of studies reporting prevalence rates between 30% and 50%. The use of seizure medication in institutions ranges from a low of 24% to a high of 56%, although typically it is between 25% and 45%. Together, psychotropic and antiepileptic medication usage in institutions ranges from 50% to 70%, with some individuals being prescribed both types of drugs concurrently (Singh & Winton, 1989).

Overall, fewer community surveys have been conducted than institutional studies, and these show that psychotropic drug usage with children ranges from 2% to 7%, and for adults it ranges from 14% to 36%. The use of seizure medication in community settings ranges from 12% to 31% for children and from 18% to 24% for adults. The combined prevalence of psychotropic and antiepileptic medications ranges from 19% to 33% for children and from 36% to 48% for adults (Aman & Singh, 1991).

Singh, Ellis, and Wechsler (1998) noted that various factors influence psychotropic medication prescription in individuals with developmental disabilities. For example, increasing dosages have been found to correlate highly with increasing age and decreasing intellectual impairment. There is a strong relationship between the type of residential facility and the use of medication to control behavior problems, with more medication being used in larger facilities and in facilities with very restrictive environments. Furthermore, there is a strong positive correlation between the number and severity of an individual's behavior and psychiatric problems and the use of medication (Aman & Singh, 1988). For example, those who exhibit aggression, hyperactivity, self-injury, screaming, or anxiety are more likely to receive drug treatment than those who exhibit milder and less disruptive problems, such as noncompliance.

Given that psychopharmacology remains a standard treatment for many individuals with developmental disabilities, it is important for clinicians and direct services staff working with this population to remain current with the research literature in this field. Although we do not think that it is critical for nonmedical clinicians to be experts in the psychopharmacology of developmental disabilities, it may be helpful for them to have a working knowledge of basic concepts in the field so that their collaboration with physicians can be more meaningful. For example, it may help them to better understand the theoretical bases of the choices made by a psychiatrist in the selection of specific agents for treating single or multiple behavior problems or psychiatric disorders. Furthermore, it may be helpful if they understand that many factors, such as medication compliance and smoking, influence drug effects once steady-state dosing has been reached. If clinicians and direct care staff are knowledgeable about the factors that modulate the effects of psychotropic medication in individuals with developmental disabilities, they can be relied on not only to assist the prescribing physician but also to make environmental and programmatic changes that will enhance the therapeutic effects of medication. After all, like any other treatment modality, psychopharmacological treatment is used to improve the individual's general functioning and quality of life rather than strictly to reduce an undesirable behavior (Singh, 1995).

Often, we assume that psychiatric treatment and the prescription of psychotropic medication is solely in the domain of psychiatrists and that their services will form a part of an integrated service plan for individuals with developmental disabilities. The fact is, however, that the majority of prescriptions for psychotropic medication written for psychiatric disorders are by family practice and primary care physicians who have limited training in mental health (Beardsley, Gardocki, Larsen, & Hidalgo, 1988). Psychologists and other clinicians assume a major role in the baseline assessment of the individual with developmental disabilities and contribute to the case formulation. In addition, they are often responsible for monitoring the individual's response to medication (Ellis, Singh, & Singh, 1997). Because they are the primary therapists for individuals' psychosocial treatments, psychologists are in an ideal position to monitor symptomatic improvement, observe the emergence of side effects, and assess medication compliance. Having a good knowledge of psychopharmacology enables psychologists and other clinicians to play an active collaborative role in recommending medication and dosage changes to the individual's physician.

Although there is still a paucity of well-controlled studies on the use of psychotropic drugs in the treatment of behavior problems and psychiatric disorders of children and adults with developmental disabilities, psychopharmacology is considered an integral part of a person-centered service plan (Singh, 1997). Given our understanding that medication alone is rarely sufficient in the treatment of behavior problems in this population, in the late 1990s, pharmacotherapy is considered an important, and often necessary, part of a multimodal treatment plan (Ellis et al., 1997). Clinicians who espouse the biopsychosocial model of psychopathology understand that psychopharmacology, like any other single-modality treatment, is limited in scope because it focuses on only one aspect of the individual. Given that children and adults with developmental disabilities live in an interactional biological, social, and cultural matrix, effective interventions must be multimodal, multifocused, and multidisciplinary in nature (Singh, Parmelee, Sood, & Katz, 1993).

## GENERAL PRINCIPLES OF PSYCHOPHARMACOLOGY

When psychotropic drugs are prescribed primarily for psychiatric disorders, they are intended to affect the mental processes of the individual (i.e., to sedate, stimulate, or otherwise change mood, thinking, or behavior). *Psychopharmacology* is a subspecialty of pharmacology that deals with the chemistry, disposition, actions, and clinical pharmacology of psychotropic drugs. The two most important branches of psychopharmacology include pharmacokinetics and pharmacodynamics. Pharmacogenetics, which can be considered a component of pharmacodynamics, is increasingly viewed as being very important in our understanding of the effects of psychoactive drugs (Singh & Ellis, in press).

## Pharmacokinetics

*Pharmacokinetics* describes the time course of drug concentrations and the effects of drugs and their metabolites on the body. Thus, it describes what the body does to a drug.

**Pharmacokinetic Factors** The most important pharmacokinetic factors that affect the time course and the effects of drugs on individuals include the following: 1) *absorption,* which is the process that determines how a drug travels from the site of administration to the site of measurement (e.g., plasma, whole blood); 2) *first-pass effect,* which is the hepatic extraction of orally administered drugs before they reach the systemic circulation; 3) *distribution,* which indicates how much of a drug is distributed to the various organs or sites of action throughout the body; 4) *steady-state concentration,* which indicates the concentration of the drug when the amount administered is equal to the amount eliminated per unit time; 5) *half-life,* which is the time required for the concentration of the drug in plasma or whole blood to fall by one half; 6) *elimination rate constant,* which is the proportion of the drug in the body that is eliminated per unit time; 7) *clearance,* which provides a measure of elimination of the drug from the body and is calculated by multiplying the amount of drug in the body by the elimination rate constant; 8) *first-order kinetics,* which occurs when the amount of the drug eliminated per unit time is directly proportional to its plasma concentration; and 9) *zero-order kinetics,* which occurs only when a fixed amount of the drug is eliminated per unit time regardless of plasma concentration. Data on these factors can be used to draw a unique kinetic profile of a given drug.

**Steady-State Condition** As the name implies, an individual taking prescribed medication on a regular dosage schedule will reach a steady-state condition. In principle, 50% of the eventual steady-state plasma drug concentration is reached in one half-life of the drug, 87.5% in three half-lives, and more than 97% in five half-lives. As an example, if a drug has a half-life of 24 hours, its steady state level in an individual can be estimated on days 5 or 6. When steady-state is reached, the individual's mean plasma drug concentration will remain constant as long as his or her dosing schedule and drug clearance do not change. Physicians often use the mean steady-state drug concentration to predict the likelihood of therapeutic efficacy or adverse effects, such as toxicity (Friedman & Greenblatt, 1986).

Several factors may alter an individual's steady-state condition. For example, unless the prescribed drug is given by continuous intravenous infusion, it is likely that the individual will experience interdose fluctuation in his or her mean plasma drug concentration because he or she will be on discrete multiple doses. Under these conditions, his or her plasma drug concentration will rise above and fall below the mean steady-state value during each dosage interval. Just how much fluctuation occurs depends on many factors, including the half-life value and absorption profile of the drug. For example, greater interdose fluctuations occur with drugs that have short half-life values (e.g., stimulants) than those with long half-life values (e.g., antipsychotics). Clinically, this means that the daily dosage of drugs with short half-life values may need to be given more frequently in subdivided doses. An alternative is to use sustained release formulations of the same drugs because their slow absorption profile will reduce the interdose fluctuation in plasma drug concentration.

Many psychotropic drugs have pharmacologically active metabolites, which reduce interdose fluctuation at steady-state because the active metabolites usually fluctuate less than their parent drug (Caccia & Garattini, 1990). One of the practical implications of such drugs is that the relationship between plasma drug concentration and clinical outcome becomes more complicated because the levels of both the parent drug and those of its active metabolites must be considered simultaneously. Given that some active metabolites may have a longer half-life than the parent drug, drug effects may persist well beyond the clearance of the parent drug at discontinuation because of the sustained levels of the long half-life metabolites. For example, pharmacokinetic studies show that the effects of norfluoxetine persist when fluoxetine, the parent drug, has cleared from the body (Plato, Murphy, & deVane, 1991).

Clinicians must also be aware of time-dependent kinetics, which refers to changes in the rates of pharmacokinetic processes over time, because these may alter steady-state drug concentrations. For example, there is some enthusiasm for using carbamazepine for its psychotropic effects in treating serious behavior problems of individuals with developmental disabilities (see Ellis et al., 1997). Research on plasma kinetics of carbamazepine shows that the drug may induce its own metabolism. That is, the half-life of carbamazepine is longer in individuals just starting therapy than in those who have used it chronically, suggesting that steady-state drug concentrations decrease over time (Eichelbaum, Ekbom, Bertilsson, Ringberger, & Rane, 1975). This finding has important implications in terms of dosing and clinical outcome across individuals.

Other concurrent events that may alter steady-state drug concentrations include disease states, such as cardiac, renal, and liver disorders, which can markedly alter the kinetics of psychotropic drugs through changes in the metabolism, excretion, distribution, and protein binding of the drugs. Clinically, this means that dose adjustments may be necessary when these disease states occur (Bennett, 1988; Williams & Benet, 1980). For example, clinicians often use creatinine clearance as a measure of renal function to estimate a dose adjustment for many drugs in renal failure (Bennett, 1988).

## Pharmacodynamics

*Pharmacodynamics* deals with the relationship between drug dosage or concentration in the body and its drug effects, both desirable and undesirable. Thus, it deals with the mechanism(s) of drug action and generally describes what a drug does to the body.

**Pharmacodynamic Factors**  The most important pharmacodynamic considerations include the following: 1) *receptor mechanism,* which describes how the drug binds at the cellular level and initiates its pharmacodynamic effects; 2) *dose-response curve,* which provides a plot of the drug concentration against the effects of the drug, and it allows the comparison of the efficacy and potency of drugs; 3) *therapeutic index,* which provides a relative measure of the toxicity and safety of a drug and is calculated by dividing the median toxic dose by the median effective dose; 4) *lag time,* which is the time taken for the full therapeutic effects of a given drug to appear, and the reasons for a delay in effects may be pharmacokinetic, pharmacodynamic, or both; and 5) *tolerance,* which refers to the responsiveness of an individual to a particular drug as it is administered over time.

**Pharmacogenetics**  *Pharmacogenetics* deals with idiosyncratic or unusual drug responses that have a hereditary basis (Kalow, 1990). Responses to psychotropic and other drugs are modulated by their genetic predisposition. This is because "genes encoding enzymes or proteins that play a role in the drug response differ in some respect from one individual to the next" (Nebert & Weber, 1990, p. 469). When all other variables are held constant, an individual's pharmacogenetic response reflects a genetic difference in the metabolic rate when compared with that of a control participant. For example, Zhou, Koshakji, Silberstein, Wilkinson, and Wood (1989) compared the physiologic effects and the pharmacological disposition of the drug propranolol in a group of Caucasian Americans and a group of Chinese Asians. They reported that the Chinese participants were more responsive to the drug, displaying a larger reduction in the heart rate and blood pressure because they metabolized the drug more efficiently than the participants in the Caucasian group.

According to Nebert and Weber (1990), idiosyncratic drug responses that may be due to genetic variation in any of the subcellular steps involved in pharmacokinetics include the following mechanisms: 1) transport (absorption, plasma protein binding); 2) transducer mechanism (receptors, enzyme induction, or inhibition); 3) biotransformation; and 4) excretory mechanisms (renal and biliary transport). Typically, clinical observations, family or twin studies, protein polymorphisms, animal modeling, and deoxyribonucleic acid (DNA) polymorphism characterizations are methods used to discover new atypical drug responses that may have a pharmacogenetic basis.

The clinical importance of pharmacogenetics is that clinicians should be aware of the possibility of differences in drug response and in dose requirements among individuals with developmental disabilities from various ethnic and racial groups.

## OTHER FACTORS AFFECTING THE OUTCOME OF PHARMACOTHERAPY

The effects of psychotropic drugs are seldom determined solely by their pharmacological properties, such as those discussed in previous sections. Indeed, psychotropic medication is prescribed and used within a transactional system among the child with developmental disabilities, his or her family, physician, and other clinicians, as well as others (e.g., teachers, peers) who are significant in the life of the individual (Moerman, 1979; Singh & Aman, 1990). Of course, we must remember that individuals with developmental disabilities often do not request assistance from physicians directly; their parents and other caregivers do. The individual's views of the treatment process, his or her therapeutic alliance with the physician, and his or her attributions of the effects of medication are also important and may be responsible for at least some of the effects of pharmacotherapy (Towbin, 1995). Furthermore, other factors, such as compliance, placebo effects, and sociocultural factors are important in treatment outcome. Almost all studies on the psychopharmacology of developmental disabilities, however, have focused on biological, behavioral, and learning variables to the exclusion of virtually all others.

Singh and Aman (1990) noted that our knowledge of the intended effects of psychotropic medication in children often is based on an assessment of the changes in the target behavior, symptoms, and syndrome as a result of a controlled trial of a given drug. They criticized this approach on the grounds that it does not include the study of interactions and interrelationships among environment, behavior, and drugs. The majority of psychopharmacological research being done in the late 1990s, in general, focuses on the consequences of specific drugs or drug combinations on the target behavior or diagnosis, without regard to the setting events or contextual variables that may influence the effects of the medication. A transactional analysis would require that the effects of pharmacotherapy be explained in terms of setting events; that is, the relevant contextual variables that transact to determine treatment outcome.

There are a large number of contextual variables that may contribute to the outcome of psychopharmacological treatment in developmental disabilities. Although all variables cannot be covered here, we present diverse examples to show that assessment of treatment outcome is much more complex than has hitherto been noted in psychopharmacological research in this population.

## Behavioral Teratogenesis

Young women of child-bearing age are always cautioned about the potential interaction among pregnancy and nursing, the course of a psychiatric disorder, and psychotropic treatment (Coyle, Wayner, & Singer, 1976; Schou, 1990). With some drugs (e.g., lithium, valproic acid), there is a real possibility of a drug–pregnancy interaction, which increases the risk of malformations in the unborn child and the potential for later developmental anomalies. For example, lithium may increase the risk of fetal macrosomia, premature delivery, and perinatal mortality (Schou, 1990); the teratogenic effects of valproic acid on exposed fetuses include a 1%–2% incidence of spina bifida (Centers for Disease Control, 1983).

There has always been concern about women with developmental disabilities having children (Dowdney & Skuse, 1992). With the *Zeitgeist* for community placement and the prohibition of involuntary sterilization of women with developmental disabilities, the population of women of child-bearing age who have developmental disabilities and live in the community has increased substantially during the 1990s (Tymchuk & Feldman, 1991). Given estimates of behavior problems and psychiatric disorders among individuals with mental retardation, we can expect a number of these women to be on psychotropic medication for their mental health needs. Behavioral teratogenesis is a major risk for the children of women on psychotropic medication during pregnancy, especially when their mental health treatment needs are coupled with their limited knowledge about conception and fetal development. Thus, clinicians must consider the pregnancy status of women with developmental disabilities before prescribing psychotropic medications and monitor this throughout the course of psychotropic drug treatment.

This risk of teratogenesis from in utero psychotropic drug exposure may have a direct effect on the treatment outcome of a woman of child-bearing potential because many clinicians will consider the benefit of a specific medication against the risk it may cause should the woman become pregnant. Should the woman get pregnant, clinicians will limit their use of known teratogenic medications or use them only after alternative medications have been unsuccessful. Thus, medications that might otherwise be efficacious may not be considered or used as frequently in these women because of the possible teratogenic effects on the child. Furthermore, expectant mothers may also introduce other factors that may alter the outcome of psychotropic drug treatment. For example, if a woman knows that the medication prescribed for her has the possibility of causing harm to her child, she may well be noncompliant to medication.

In terms of contextual analysis, the mother's disease state or psychiatric disorder is the setting event for her treatment with psychotropic drugs. The interactions among the mother's disease state, psychotropic drug treatment, and conception provide the distal setting event for any teratogenic effects on the child. This is a case of the setting events occurring months prior to the effects being evident in the child.

## Behavioral Toxicity

The term *behavioral toxicity* refers to the undesirable effects of essentially therapeutic levels of medication clinically indicated for a given disorder (DiMascio, Soltys, & Shader, 1970). These undesirable effects may include anticholinergic effects, alpha-adrenergic blockade, and dopaminergic effects, among others. In behavioral terms, behavioral toxicity can be classified as a concurrent stimulus event that affects the ongoing learning and interactions of the individual. For example, take the case of a child with developmental disabilities who is on medication for a seizure disorder. The drowsiness produced by his anticonvulsant medication (e.g., Phenobarbital) may cause him to function more poorly than he might in its absence. Thus, in this case, behavioral toxicity may operate concurrently with classroom instruction or activities at home.

Given that learning is a major problem for individuals with developmental disabilities, clinicians must pay particular attention to therapeutic regimens that may diminish their learning capacity even further. For example, in clinically effective doses, initial and repeated administrations of benzodiazepines induce not only central nervous system depression but also a wide variety of cognitive impairments (Taylor & Tinklenberg, 1987). These impairments include, but are not limited to, 1) the reduced ability to learn new information, 2) the difficulty in acquiring verbal as well as visual information, 3) the reduced speed (but not accuracy) of retrieving verbal information from short-term memory, 4) vigilance ability, and 5) divided attention. Benzodiazepines also generally impair driving performance. Many individuals with mild mental retardation need to drive to work, and all perform tasks that require the use of their cognitive abilities. Some of these individuals may be at risk for behavioral toxicity if they are on therapeutic doses of benzodiazepines.

In assessing the effects of psychopharmacotherapy, clinicians should include measures indicative of possible behavioral toxicity because it will assist the individual's treatment planning team to arrive at risk-to-benefit treatment decisions on the basis of data. For example, the treatment team will be faced with such issues as balancing lithium's blunting of life against the control of suicidal thoughts or other forms of self-destructive behavior during an individual's manic episodes. Although most often the side effects of therapeutic levels of psychotropic medication are within typical variations in life, in some cases they are behaviorally toxic. In these cases, the individual and his or her person-centered treatment planning team must assess the risk-to-benefit ratio and determine whether that particular psychopharmacological treatment regimen is in the best interests of the individual.

## Compliance

*Compliance* is the degree to which an individual adheres to the recommended treatment plan of the treating physician. Compliance with medication in individuals with developmental disabilities is typically partial because they tend to take medication irregularly or less often than is prescribed. This is a problem that is not unique to individuals with developmental disabilities; for example, about 40% of individuals without disabilities receiving psychotropic medications are noncompliant with the prescribed medication regimen (Preskorn, Burke, & Fast, 1993). The reasons for medication noncompliance can be categorized as "rational, capricious, absolute refusal, confusion or iatrogenic" (Janicak, Davis, Preskorn, & Ayd, 1993, p. 49). Often, noncompliance occurs because of unpleasant side effects of the medication and the perceived stigma associated with taking medication in school. Some individuals believe that taking medication somehow lessens their control over their own lives or that the medication determines what they do. In behavioral terms, compliance (or noncompliance) is a reciprocal concurrent setting event. That is, the individual's disorder is the setting event for the psychopharmacological treatment, and the individual–drug–psychosocial environment interaction provides the reciprocal concurrent setting event for compliance or noncompliance. These reciprocal concurrent setting events are typically psychosocial in nature and affect the outcome of psychopharmacological treatment.

Medication compliance in individuals with developmental disabilities can be increased by 1) having the individual actively participate in treatment planning, 2) explaining the expected side effects of the medication to the individual before treatment begins, 3) emphasizing the positive aspects of taking the medication as prescribed, and 4) having the simplest drug regimen (e.g., prescribing long-acting drugs to facilitate once-a-day dosing).

For individuals with developmental disabilities living with their families, medication compliance can be increased by involving the family in the treatment process. Although the research literature on psychosocial management of medication noncompliance in individuals with developmental disabilities is almost nonexistent, we can extrapolate from the wealth of research findings with other populations. The best data comes from individuals with schizophrenia or psychotic disorders (McEvoy et al., 1996), which strongly suggests that a family-based psychoeducational program regarding the individual's disorder and its treatment is an essential requirement. Furthermore, this psychoeducation needs to be provided periodically throughout the individual's course of illness. As in the general population, individuals with developmental disabilities come from diverse backgrounds, and clinicians must ensure that the psychoeducation program takes into account the cultural, educational, vocational, and clinical issues that are important to the individual and his or her family (Anderson, Reiss, & Hogarty, 1986; Xiang, Ran, & Li, 1994). It is critical that what is taught is not in conflict with the family's cultural beliefs about the cause of the illness and its appropriate treatment (Singh, 1998). In addition to family involvement, clinicians must be aware that nothing works quite as well as a good therapeutic alliance between the individual and his or her physician to increase and maintain medication compliance (Frank & Gunderson, 1990). The human side of the physician–individual relationship appears to be the key ingredient, suggesting that some of the best interventions are still as much an art as a science.

## Comorbidity

*Comorbidity*, which is the presence of disorders other than the one targeted for treatment, affects treatment outcome because the additional disorders change the simple disorder–drug–environment inter-action to a more complex $disorder_1$–drug–environment–$disorder_2$ in-teraction, if there is just one comorbid disorder. This interaction may mean that a second treatment, which could be pharmacotherapy or an alternative, is necessary to control a comorbid disorder, resulting in $disorder_1$–$drug_1$–environment–$disorder_2$–$drug_2$ interaction. Of course, other interactions may also occur, including changes in the physiologically determined susceptibilities of the drugs to interact with the environment to produce certain unintended, positive or ad-verse effects (i.e., side effects). This suggests that the individual must be adequately assessed not only for the target symptoms, syndrome, or disorder but also for comorbid disorders.

It is evident that physicians are increasingly using multiple psy-chotropic agents, particularly in individuals with comorbid psychiat-ric disorders and treatment-resistant behavior problems. This practice is known as polypharmacy and has generally not been looked upon very favorably in clinical practice. For example, Werry suggested that "polypharmacy should raise doubts in the minds of parents about the prescribing physician's competence" (1993, p. 18). Combined targeted drug therapy, however, is gaining momentum because of our in-creased understanding of the mechanism of action of different drugs and the synergistic effects of multiple agents. Under some conditions, the use of multiple psychotropic agents may well have beneficial ef-fects. For example, when an individual with depressive symptoms is responding well to fluoxetine but is still having problems with insom-nia, the use of low-dose trazadone may be useful. In some cases, an individual's diagnosis may indicate the need for combined targeted drug therapy. For example, an individual who is depressed and has psychotic symptoms may need a combination of cyclic antidepressant and an antipsychotic agent.

In behavioral terms, comorbid disorders are concurrent setting events that occasion complex multiple interactions among the dis-orders, treatments, and the environment. As an example of the com-plex multiple interactions predicted by a setting events analysis, drug–drug interactions occur when the pharmacological action of $drug_1$ is altered by the concurrent administration of $drug_2$. This may result in one of several possibilities, including the known effects of either or both drugs increasing or decreasing or the emergence of a new effect that is not predicted on the basis of either drug alone. These drug–drug interactions are usually classified in terms of their primary mechanism of action. Both pharmacokinetic and pharmacodynamic interactions may occur with concurrently administered medications. As would be expected, on the one hand, the pharmacokinetic interactions occur as the drug is transported to and from its site of action, resulting in a change in the plasma level or tissue distribution of the drug. On the other hand, the pharmacodynamic interactions occur at the receptor sites, resulting in a change in the pharmacological effect of a given plasma level of the drug. In addition, there are idiosyncratic interactions in a small percentage of individuals that cannot be predicted from the known pharmacological actions of the individual drugs. Although the mechanisms of the drug–drug interactions in such cases remain to be determined, we suspect that pharmacogenetics may be involved.

What we have discussed is the $drug_1$–$drug_2$ interactions of the $disorder_1$–$drug_1$–environment–$disorder_2$–$drug_2$ interaction. The picture becomes very complex when we factor in the environmental transactions, the individual's genetic predispositions, the disorders and their interactions across time, and the interactions that the components have with each other over time. Although we have separated the different interactions for the sake of clarity of presentation, we emphasize that these interactions are continuous, dynamic, and inseparable, and that a setting events analysis provides us only with a crude methodology for understanding these interactions. In any case, clinicians using multiple psychotropic drugs to treat comorbid psychiatric disorders or treatment-resistant behavior problems must remember that they are setting up multiple concurrent interactions, most of which we do not understand. There are a few guidelines, however, that they can follow to make good clinical decisions. For example, a number of factors have been gleaned from clinical experience that suggest an increased likelihood of significant drug–drug interactions, including drugs that 1) induce or inhibit hepatic microsomal enzymes, 2) have a low therapeutic index, and 3) have a multiplicity of pharmacological action (Callahan, Fava, & Rosenbaum, 1993). Clinicians can anticipate adverse interactions when using multiple agents if they have some understanding of the setting events that may precipitate these effects.

## Placebo Effects

The *placebo effect* in pharmacology is the phenomenon that is observed when an individual exhibits a clinically significant response to a pharmacologically inert substance when used as a nonspecific treatment control (White, Tursky, & Schwartz, 1995). In psychopharmacology studies, a placebo response can be defined as a reduction in psychiatric symptoms from baseline in the placebo-treated group of participants (Brown, 1994). Although it is a well-recognized phenomenon in medicine, there is little consensus on its conceptualization. What we do know is that the placebo response is not due to the psycho-pharmacological properties of the drug; that is, the outcome is not due to the effects of the prescribed intervention. Indeed, it has been suggested that the curative elements associated with the placebo response arise from a "healing ritual" that promotes positive expectations (Frank & Frank, 1991). It results from purely psychological effects as a consequence of expectancy of an outcome from the treatment. Although a majority of the placebo effects are established simply by asking the individual if he or she is feeling better or by having him or her complete a rating scale that provides a measure of his or her subjective well-being, often placebo effects can also be measured objectively. That is, placebos produce a change not only in the mind but also in the body. For example, individuals given placebo treatment for anxiety disorder often show less autonomic nervous system arousal (e.g., decrease in heart rate, lower blood pressure).

The placebo response is not a rare phenomenon as it may account for 20%–70% (mean of 30%–40%) of the therapeutic responses observed in psychopharmacological treatment (Laporte & Figueras, 1994). In addition, the placebo response varies across different psychiatric disorders. Controlled studies show low placebo response rates for schizophrenia, Alzheimer's disease, dementia, and obsessive-compulsive disorder (Mavissakalian, Jones, & Olson, 1990) and higher rates for mild depression, generalized anxiety disorder, and panic disorder (Loebel, Hyde, & Dunner, 1986). Unfortunately, there have been no well-controlled studies designed to investigate placebo response rates in the pharmacological treatment of behavior problems in individuals with mental retardation.

There have been a number of attempts to identify predictors of placebo response. As would be expected from a setting events analysis, no consistent differences have been reported among placebo responders and nonresponders because of the number of complex, dynamic interactions that occur across multiple variables. Careful analyses of the research literature, however, have revealed that there may be a number of variables associated with each psychiatric disorder that may *reduce* placebo response. For example, the following variables may reduce the placebo response in individuals with depression: 1) duration of current depressive episode, with longer duration of episode being predictive of lower placebo response (Khan & Brown, 1991); 2) severity of the presenting episode, with greater severity being predictive of lower placebo response; 3) chronicity of depression, with recurring major depression being predictive of lower placebo response (Bialik, Ravindran, & Lapierre, 1995); and 4) psychomotor retardation, with its presence being indicative of poor placebo response (Bialik et al., 1995; Joyce & Paykel, 1989).

Clearly, the placebo effect has important clinical implications. Not only does it provide the setting event for clinically significant improvements of uncertain duration in some individuals, it appears to be a major mediator of treatment response of which clinicians must be aware when initiating, modifying, and evaluating the effects of psychopharmacological treatment. Although we can say that being able to differentiate a *true* drug response from a placebo response would enable the physician to better develop a treatment regimen that has long-term efficacy, this can be a particularly difficult task with individuals with increasing levels of developmental disabilities.

## Reciprocal Interactions

In behavioral terms, *reciprocal interactions* are concurrent stimulus–response contexts that set the occasion for further interactions. This is an important variable that affects the course of psychopharmaco-therapy because the initial effects of drugs on an individual may also have an effect on the *reactions* of others who interact with him or her. This phenomenon was clearly illustrated in the stimulant treatment of children with attention-deficit/hyperactivity disorder in which 1) the drug increased a child's compliance with parent demands; and 2) the parents, in turn, reduced their commands and disciplinary behaviors, while increasing their positive interactions with the child (Barkley & Cunningham, 1979; Cunningham & Barkley, 1978). This phenomenon highlights the importance of assessing drug effects on reciprocal interactions of the child with significant others in the individual's environment (e.g., parents, siblings, peers, teachers).

The effects of reciprocal interactions can be a potent treatment variable in the care of individuals with developmental disabilities, especially in cases in which parents or direct care staff perceive the individual as difficult to manage. For example, individuals labeled as being difficult are often treated as being difficult even though their actual behavior may be normative among their peers (e.g., all individuals in a vocational workshop). To take advantage of reciprocal interactions, clinicians should stress the expected changes due to psychopharmacological treatment as a setting event for changes in the behavior of the caregivers toward the individual, which, in turn, may lead to changes in the individual's interaction with the staff, and so forth. Thus, positive reciprocal interactions can be used as a modulator of drug response in individuals with mental retardation.

## Social Vices

Like people in the general population, individuals with developmental disabilities engage in behaviors that could be considered social vices, including smoking, drinking alcohol, or using recreational drugs. These social vices may interfere with the individual's psychopharmacological treatment. Using smoking as an example, we know that a number of individuals with developmental disabilities smoke cigarettes. Indeed, in many residential facilities for individuals with mental retardation, cigarettes often are used as reinforcers for good behavior. Although the prevalence of smoking in the United States as a whole is about 26% (Morbidity and Mortality Weekly Report, 1994), a 1997 study showed that 30% of individuals with mild mental retardation and 37% of those with borderline mental retardation in a sample of individuals with mental retardation and mental illness were regular smokers (Hymowitz, Jaffe, Gupta, & Feuerman, 1997).

When compared with the nonsmokers in this study, the smokers were significantly more likely to drink alcohol, use other drugs, and be sexually active (Hymowitz et al., 1997). Multiple regression analyses showed that level of mental retardation and a diagnosis of schizophrenia were significant predictors of smoking in the study sample. These findings are to be expected given that smokers as a group have been found to be somewhat different from nonsmokers in the general population. For example, when compared with nonsmokers, smokers have been found to drink more coffee and alcohol; eat more meat; eat less fruit, vegetables, and dietary fiber; exercise less; sleep less; and have significant sociodemographic differences (e.g., socioeconomic status, level of education, occupation) (Fisher & Gordon, 1985; Kato, Tominaga, & Suzuki, 1989; Subar, Harlan, & Mattson, 1990). Indeed, many studies have revealed extraordinarily high rates of smoking in people diagnosed with schizophrenia (Goff, Henderson, & Amico, 1992). Although still speculative, it has been suggested that people with schizophrenia smoke more because the dopamine augmenting effect of nicotine may counterbalance a relative dopamine deficiency that is usually found in this population (Glassman, 1993).

Of more importance is the fact that smoking provides the setting event for the effects of some psychotropic medications used in the treatment of psychiatric disorders; that is, response to psychotropic medication differs in smokers when compared with nonsmokers. For example, the new antipsychotic, clozapine, is increasingly used for treating mania and psychotic disorder. Nicotine from cigarette smoking induces the isozyme P4501A2, the same enzyme that is primarily responsible for metabolizing clozapine. When a cigarette smoker is administered clozapine, the plasma concentration of the drug is typically lower than in a nonsmoking control participant because of the enzyme-induction effect of the nicotine. That is, the nicotine provides the interactive setting event for the plasma concentration of the drug. In addition, it has been found that smokers need higher doses of neuroleptic medications than nonsmokers to reach the same levels of treatment efficacy (Vinarova, Vinar, & Kalvach, 1984). The mechanism responsible for this interaction is unknown, as the neuroleptics are not metabolized primarily by the isozyme P4501A2.

Knowing the interactive effects of nicotine from cigarette smoking will assist physicians in developing an effective psychopharmacological treatment regimen for individuals with developmental disabilities who may need antipsychotic and other medications. Furthermore, human services staff need to be made aware of the effects that nicotine has on the health and well-being of smokers so that they can take active steps to curb its use, especially as a reinforcer for good behavior, in individuals with developmental disabilities.

## Sociodemographic Variables

There are a number of sociodemographic variables that affect the outcome of psychopharmacological treatment, including age, disease state, gender, and ethnicity. Some of these variables increase the effects of psychotropic medication by altering the pharmacokinetics of the prescribed drug. Age is an excellent example of such a variable. Changes in older adults, such as a decrease in intracellular water, protein binding, and tissue mass, along with an increase in total body fat, act synergistically to increase the effects of most psychotropic drugs in this population. Furthermore, in older adults, there is a substantial lengthening of the half-life of drugs that undergo extensive biotransformation prior to elimination. This means that elimination of such drugs in older adults takes longer, making them more susceptible to toxicity on the same drug and dose (Janicak et al., 1993). This also occurs with disease states that alter the physiological mechanisms that subserve the various pharmacokinetic phases.

There is emerging evidence that there are gender differences in psychotropic drug metabolism, suggesting possible gender differences in drug response (Pollock, 1997). For example, there are gender differences in a drug's volume of distribution. Women have enhanced metabolic clearance because of their increased volume of distribution (Greenblatt, Sellers, & Shader, 1982). Furthermore, there is an age-by-gender interaction in a drug's volume of distribution, thus increasing the half-life of lipid soluble drugs such as diazepam. For example,

Sweet, Pollock, Wright, Kirshner, and deVane (1995) found that the volume of distribution of bupropion in older women was twice that reported in young males. Furthermore, when compared with the young males, the plasma half-life of bupropion in the women increased with age much more than the decrease in the clearance of the drug. In general, nonmetabolic factors that may interact with gender and affect drug disposition include gastrointestinal transit (Hutson, Roehrkasse, & Wald, 1989) and protein binding (Kristensen, 1983; Wilson, 1984). In addition, metabolic differences that are gender related include exogenous estrogen (Abernethy, Greenblatt, & Shader, 1984), menstrual cycle (Kimmel, Gonsalves, Youngs, & Gidwani, 1992; Wilson, Oram, Horth, & Burnett, 1982), and pregnancy (Wisner, Perel, & Wheeler, 1993).

There is a dearth of data on the interactive effects of psychotropic drugs and gender-related variables, such as pregnancy, menstrual cycle, and hormonal therapy, in women in the general population. Furthermore, there is a major gap in our knowledge of the effects of psychotropic drugs in postmenopausal women. Needless to say, our knowledge of any of these effects in women with developmental disabilities who are on psychotropic medication is almost nonexistent.

Given the racial and ethnic diversity of our world, it is important that clinicians also appreciate the importance of pharmacogenetic effects, particularly in individuals such as those with mental retardation requiring extensive supports who cannot inform us of the effects that psychotropic drugs may have on their internal states. There is remarkable inter-individual and inter-ethnic variability in the therapeutic and adverse effect profiles of most psychotropic drugs that are commonly used for treating psychiatric disorders (Greenblatt, 1993; Kalow, 1992; Lin & Poland, 1995; Rudorfer, 1993)—drugs that are also used to treat individuals with developmental disabilities. We do not understand very well the mechanisms that underlie these differences, and we do not have practical methods to predict clinical response in individuals of different racial and ethnic backgrounds. The pace of research in pharmacogenetics, however, is accelerating, and we appear to be on the verge of major breakthroughs in this field (Lin, Poland, Wan, Smith, & Lesser, 1996). This not only will help us in understanding the basic mechanisms of action but also, at a more practical level, will guide our dosing practices of psychotropic medications.

## SUMMARY

The concept of setting events provides a useful framework for discussing the various factors that alter drug response in individuals with developmental disabilities. Singh and Aman (1990) ushered in the era of ecobehavior analysis of pharmacotherapy, which is based on the concept of setting events. They noted that past research in psychopharmacology and developmental disabilities focused on the consequences of drugs on the behavior of individuals by controlling contextual conditions and holding them as constant as possible. Thus, ecological or contextual variables were treated as confounding variables, or noise—essentially, as having a nuisance value. There is considerable worth, however, in placing a much greater emphasis on these contextual variables in an attempt to gain a more comprehensive understanding of relevant drug effects. In this chapter, we have discussed a number of antecedent and concurrent setting events that directly or indirectly affect the outcome of pharmacotherapy. Our aim has been to show that many of these antecedent or concurrent conditions occur at the physiological level and that by having a knowledge of the mechanism of action of these variables, we are in a much better position to make appropriate and informed clinical judgments that will produce the best quality-of-life outcomes for individuals with developmental disabilities.

## REFERENCES

Abernethy, D.R., Greenblatt, D.J., & Shader, R.I. (1984). Imipramine disposition in users of oral contraceptive steroids. *Clinical Pharmacology and Therapeutics, 35*, 792–797.

Aman, M.G., & Singh, N.N. (1988). *Psychopharmacology of the developmental disabilities.* New York: Springer-Verlag.

Aman, M.G., & Singh, N.N. (1991). Pharmacological intervention: An update. In J.L. Matson & J.A. Mulick (Eds.), *Handbook of mental retardation* (2nd ed., pp. 347–372). New York: Pergamon.

Anderson, C., Reiss, D., & Hogarty, G. (1986). *Schizophrenia in the family: A practitioner's guide to psychoeducation and management.* New York: Guilford Press.

Barker, R.G. (1968). *Ecological psychology.* Stanford, CA: Stanford University Press.

Barkley, R.A., & Cunningham, C. (1979). The effects of Ritalin on the mother–child interactions of hyperactive children. *Archives of General Psychiatry, 36*, 201–208.

Beardsley, R.S., Gardocki, G.J., Larsen, D.B., & Hidalgo, J. (1988). Prescribing of psychotropic medication by primary care physicians and psychiatrists. *Archives of General Psychiatry, 45*, 1117–1119.

Bennett, W.M. (1988). Guide to drug dosage in renal failure. *Clinical Pharmacokinetics, 15*, 326–354.

Bialik, R.J., Ravindran, A.V., & Lapierre, Y.D. (1995). A comparison of placebo responders and nonresponders in subgroups of depressive disorder. *Journal of Psychiatry and Neuroscience, 20*, 265–270.

Bijou, S.W., & Baer, D.M. (1961). *Child development: Vol. 1. A systematic and empirical theory.* Englewood Cliffs, NJ: Prentice Hall.

Brophy, J.E. (1979). Teacher behavior and its effects. *Journal of Educational Psychology, 71,* 733–750.

Brown, W.A. (1994). Placebo as a treatment for depression. *Neuropsychopharmacology, 10,* 265–269.

Caccia, S., & Garattini, S. (1990). Formation of active metabolites of psychotropic drugs: An updated review of their significance. *Clinical Pharmacokinetics, 18,* 434–459.

Callahan, A.M., Fava, M., & Rosenbaum, J.F. (1993). Drug interactions in psychopharmacology. *Psychiatric Clinics of North America, 16,* 647–671.

Centers for Disease Control. (1983). Valproate: A new cause of birth defects—Report from Italy and followup from France. *Morbidity and Mortality Weekly Report, 32,* 438–439.

Coyle, I., Wayner, M.J., & Singer, G. (1976). Behavioral teratogenesis: A critical evaluation. *Pharmacology, Biochemistry and Behavior, 4,* 191–200.

Cunningham, C., & Barkley, R. (1978). The effects of methylphenidate on the mother–child interactions of hyperactive identical twins. *Developmental Medicine and Child Neurology, 20,* 634–642.

DiMascio, A., Soltys, J.J., & Shader, R.I. (1970). Psychotropic drug side effect in children. In R.I. Shader & A. DiMascio (Eds.), *Psychotropic drug side effects* (pp. 235–269). Baltimore: Williams & Wilkins.

Dowdney, L., & Skuse, D. (1992). Parenting provided by adults with mental retardation. *Journal of Child Psychology and Psychiatry, 34,* 25–47.

Eichelbaum, M., Ekbom, K., Bertilsson, L., Ringberger, V.A., & Rane, A. (1975). Plasma kinetics of carbamazepine and its epoxide metabolite in man after single and multiple doses. *European Journal of Clinical Pharmacology, 8,* 337–341.

Ellis, C.R., Singh, Y.N., & Singh, N.N. (1997). Use of behavior-modifying drugs. In N.N. Singh (Ed.), *Prevention and treatment of severe behavior problems: Models and methods in developmental disabilities* (pp. 149–176). Pacific Grove, CA: Brooks/Cole.

Fisher, M., & Gordon, T. (1985). The relation of drinking and smoking habits to diet: The lipid research clinics prevalence study. *American Journal of Clinical Nutrition, 41,* 623–630.

Frank, A.F., & Gunderson, J.G. (1990). The role of the therapeutic alliance in the treatment of schizophrenia. *Archives of General Psychiatry, 47,* 228–235.

Frank, J.D., & Frank, J.B. (1991). *Persuasion and healing: A comparative study of psychotherapy.* Baltimore: The Johns Hopkins University Press.

Friedman, H., & Greenblatt, D.J. (1986). Rational therapeutic drug monitoring. *Journal of the American Medical Association, 256,* 2227–2233.

Glassman, A.H. (1993). Cigarette smoking: Implications for psychiatric illness. *American Journal of Psychiatry, 150,* 546–553.

Goff, D.C., Henderson, D.C., & Amico, E. (1992). Cigarette smoking in schizophrenia: Relationship to psychopathology and medication side effects. *American Journal of Psychiatry, 149,* 1189–1194.

Greenblatt, D.J. (1993). Basic pharmacokinetic principles and their application to psychotropic drugs. *Journal of Clinical Psychiatry, 54*(Suppl.), 8–13.

Greenblatt, D.J., Sellers, E.M., & Shader, R.I. (1982). Drug disposition in old age. *New England Journal of Medicine, 306,* 1081–1088.

Hutson, W.R., Roehrkasse, R.L., & Wald, A. (1989). Influence of gender and menopause on gastric emptying and motility. *Gastroenterology, 96,* 11–17.

Hymowitz, N., Jaffe, F.E., Gupta, A., & Feuerman, M. (1997). Cigarette smoking among patients with mental retardation and mental illness. *Psychiatric Services, 48,* 100–102.

Janicak, P.G., Davis, J.M., Preskorn, S.H., & Ayd, F.J. (1993). *Principles and practice of psychopharmacology.* Baltimore: Williams & Wilkins.

Joyce, P.R., & Paykel, E.S. (1989). Predictors of drug response in depression. *Archives of General Psychiatry, 46,* 89–99.

Kalow, W. (1990). Pharmacogenetics: Past and future. *Life Sciences, 47,* 1385–1397.

Kalow, W. (1992). *Pharmacogenetics of drug metabolism.* New York: Pergamon.

Kantor, J.R. (1959). *Interbehavioral psychology.* Bloomington, IN: Principia.

Kato, I., Tominaga, S., & Suzuki, T. (1989). Characteristics of past smokers. *International Journal of Epidemiology, 18,* 345–354.

Khan, A., & Brown, W.A. (1991). Who should receive antidepressants: Suggestions from placebo treatment. *Psychopharmacology Bulletin, 27,* 271–274.

Kimmel, S., Gonsalves, L., Youngs, D., & Gidwani, G. (1992). Fluctuating levels of antidepressants premenstrually. *Journal of Psychosomatic Obstetrics and Gynecology, 13,* 277–280.

Kristensen, C.B. (1983). Imipramine serum protein binding in healthy subjects. *Clinical Pharmacology and Therapeutics, 34,* 689–694.

Laporte, J.R., & Figueras, A. (1994). Placebo effects in psychiatry. *Lancet, 344,* 1206–1208.

Lin, K.M., & Poland, R.E. (1995). Ethnicity, culture, and psychopharmacology. In F.E. Bloom & D.I. Kupfer (Eds.), *Psychopharmacology: The fourth generation of progress* (pp. 1907–1919). New York: Raven Press.

Lin, K.M., Poland, R.E., Wan, Y.J.Y., Smith, M.W., & Lesser, I.M. (1996). The evolving science of pharmacogenetics: Clinical and ethnic perspectives. *Psychopharmacology Bulletin, 32,* 205–217.

Lipman, R.S. (1970). The use of psychopharmacological agents in residential facilities for the retarded. In F.J. Menolascino (Ed.), *Psychiatric approaches to mental retardation* (pp. 387–398). New York: Basic Books.

Loebel, A.D., Hyde, T.S., & Dunner, D.L. (1986). Early placebo response in anxious and depressed patients. *Journal of Clinical Psychiatry, 47,* 230–233.

Martens, B.K., & Witt, J.C. (1988). Ecological behavior analysis. In M. Hersen, R.M. Eisler, & P.M. Miller (Eds.), *Progress in behavior modification* (Vol. 22, pp. 115–140). Newbury Park, CA: Sage Publications.

Mavissakalian, M.R., Jones, B., & Olson, S. (1990). Absence of placebo response in obsessive-compulsive disorder. *Journal of Nervous and Mental Disorders, 178,* 268–270.

McEvoy, J., Weiden, P., Smith, T., Carpenter, D., Kahn, D., & Frances, A. (1996). The expert consensus guidelines series: Treatment of schizophrenia. *Journal of Clinical Psychiatry, 57*(Suppl. 12B).

Moerman, D.E. (1979). Anthropology of symbolic healing. *Currents in Anthropology, 20,* 59–80.

Morbidity and Mortality Weekly Report. (1994). Cigarette smoking among adults: United States, 1992, and changes in definition of smoking. *Journal of the American Medical Association, 272,* 14.

Nebert, D.W., & Weber, W.W. (1990). Pharmacogenetics. In W.B. Pratt & P. Taylor (Eds.), *Principles of drug action* (pp. 469–531). New York: Churchill Livingstone.

Plato, M.T., Murphy, D.L., & deVane, C.L. (1991). Sustained plasma concentrations of fluoxetine and/or norfluoxetine four and eight weeks after fluoxetine discontinuation. *Journal of Clinical Psychopharmacology, 11,* 224–225.

Pollock, B.G. (1997). Gender differences in psychotropic drug metabolism. *Psychopharmacology Bulletin, 33,* 235–241.

Preskorn, S.H., Burke, M.J., & Fast, G.A. (1993). Therapeutic drug monitoring: Principles and practice. *Psychiatric Clinics of North America, 16,* 611–645.

Rogers-Warren, A., & Warren, S.F. (1977). *Ecological perspectives in behavior analysis.* Baltimore: University Park Press.

Rudorfer, M.V. (1993). Pharmacokinetics of psychotropic drugs in special populations. *Journal of Clinical Psychiatry, 54*(Suppl.), 50–54.

Schatzberg, A.F., & Cole, J.O. (1986). *Manual of clinical psychopharmacology.* Washington, DC: American Psychiatric Press.

Schou, M. (1990). Lithium treatment during pregnancy, delivery, and lactation: An update. *Journal of Clinical Psychiatry, 51,* 410–412.

Schroeder, S.R. (1988). Neuroleptic medications for persons with developmental disabilities. In M.G. Aman & N.N. Singh (Eds.), *Psychopharmacology of the developmental disabilities* (pp. 82–100). New York: Springer-Verlag.

Schroeder, S.R. (1990). *Ecobehavioral analysis and developmental disabilities: The twenty-first century.* New York: Springer-Verlag

Singh, N.N. (1995). Moving beyond institutional care for individuals with developmental disabilities. *Journal of Child and Family Studies, 4,* 129–145.

Singh, N.N. (1997, November). *Person-centered planning in mental health: A holistic approach to service delivery.* Invited address presented at the 7th Annual Virginia Beach Conference on Children and Adolescents with Emotional and Behavioral Disorders, Virginia Beach, Virginia.

Singh, N.N. (1998). Cultural diversity: A challenge for evaluating systems of care. In M.H. Epstein, K. Kutash, & A. Duchnowski (Eds.), *Community based programming for children with serious emotional disturbance and their families: Research and evaluations.* Austin, TX: PRO-ED.

Singh, N.N., & Aman, M.G. (1990). Ecobehavioral assessment of pharmacotherapy. In S.R. Schroeder (Ed.), *Ecobehavioral analysis in developmental disabilities* (pp. 182–200). New York: Springer-Verlag.

Singh, N.N., & Ellis, C.R. (1995). Ecobehavioral analysis of pharmacotherapy: A research methodology. *Society of Teachers of Family Medicine Research News, 9,* 10–22.

Singh, N.N., & Ellis, C.R. (in press). Pharmacological therapies. In T.H. Ollendick (Ed.), *Comprehensive clinical psychology: Vol. 4. Children and adolescents: Clinical formulation and treatment.* New York: Elsevier.

Singh, N.N., Ellis, C.R., & Wechsler, H.A. (1998). Psychopharmacoepidemiology in mental retardation. *Journal of Child and Adolescent Psychopharmacology, 7,* 255–266.

Singh, N.N., Guernsey, T.F., & Ellis, C.R. (1992). Drug therapy for persons with developmental disabilities: Legislation and litigation. *Clinical Psychology Review, 12,* 665–679.

Singh, N.N., Parmelee, D.X., Sood, A., & Katz, R.C. (1993). Collaboration of disciplines. In J.L. Matson (Ed.), *Handbook of hyperactivity in children* (pp. 305–322). Needham Heights, MA: Allyn & Bacon.

Singh, N.N., & Repp, A.C. (1988). The behavioral and psychopharmacological management of problem behaviors in people with mental retardation. *Irish Journal of Psychology, 9,* 264–285.

164 ~ Singh, Ellis, and Axtell

Singh, N.N., & Winton, A.S.W. (1989). Behavioral pharmacology. In J.K. Luiselli (Ed.), *Behavioral medicine and developmental disabilities* (pp. 152–179).
New York: Springer-Verlag.

Subar, A.F., Harlan, L.C., & Mattson, M.E. (1990). Food and nutrient intake
differences between smokers and nonsmokers in the U.S. *American Journal
of Public Health, 80,* 1323–1329.

Sweet, R.A., Pollock, B.G., Wright, B., Kirshner, M., & deVane, C. (1995). Single
and multiple dose bupropion pharmacokinetics in elderly patients with depression. *Journal of Clinical Pharmacology, 35,* 876–884.

Taylor, J.L., & Tinklenberg, J.R. (1987). Cognitive impairment and benzodiazepines. In H.Y. Meltzer (Ed.), *Psychopharmacology: The third general of progress*
(pp. 1449–1454). New York: Raven Press.

Towbin, K.E. (1995). Evaluation, establishing the treatment alliance, and informed consent. *Child and Adolescent Psychiatric Clinics of North America, 4,*
1–14.

Tymchuk, A.J., & Feldman, M.A. (1991). Parents with mental retardation and
their children: A review of research relevant to professional practice. *Ca-
nadian Psychology/Psychologie Canadienne, 32,* 486–496.

Vinarova, E., Vinar, O., & Kalvach, Z. (1984). Smokers need higher doses of
neuroleptic drugs. *Biological Psychiatry, 19,* 1265–1268.

Wahler, R.G., & Fox, J.J. (1981). Setting events in applied behavior analysis:
Toward a conceptual and methodological expansion. *Journal of Applied Behavior Analysis, 14,* 327–338.

Wahler, R.G., & Graves, M.G. (1983). Setting events in social networks: Ally
or enemy in child behavior therapy? *Behavior Therapy, 14,* 19–36.

Werry, J.S. (1993). Introduction: A guide for practitioners, professionals, and
public. In J.S. Werry & M.G. Aman (Eds.), *Practitioner's guide to psychoactive
drugs for children and adolescents* (pp. 3–21). New York: Plenum.

White, L., Tursky, B., & Schwartz, G.E. (1995). *Placebo: Theory, research and
mechanisms.* New York: Guilford Press.

Willems, E.P. (1974). Behavioral technology and behavioral ecology. *Journal of
Applied Behavior Analysis, 7,* 151–165.

Williams, R.L., & Benet, L.Z. (1980). Drug pharmacokinetics in cardiac and
hepatic disease. *Annual Review of Pharmacology and Toxicology, 20,* 389–413.

Wilson, K. (1984). Sex-related differences in drug disposition in man. *Clinical
Pharmacokinetics, 9,* 189–202.

Wilson, K., Oram, M., Horth, C.E., & Burnett, D. (1982). The influence of the
menstrual cycle on the metabolism and clearance of methaqualone. *British
Journal of Clinical Pharmacology, 14,* 333–339.

Wisner, K.L., Perel, J.M., & Wheeler, S.B. (1993). Tricyclic dose requirements
across pregnancy. *American Journal of Psychiatry, 150,* 1541–1542.

*Wyatt v. Stickney,* 344 F. Supp. 387, 400 § 22d (M.D. Ala., 1972).

Xiang, M., Ran, M., & Li, S. (1994). A controlled evaluation of psychoeducational family intervention in a rural Chinese community. *British Journal of
Psychiatry, 165,* 544–548.

Zhou, H.H., Koshakji, R.P., Silberstein, D.J., Wilkinson, G.P., & Wood, A.J.
(1989). Racial differences in drug response: Altered sensitivity to and clearance of propranolol in men of Chinese descent as compared with American
whites. *New England Journal of Medicine, 320,* 565–570.

# ~ *IV* ~

## *Issues of Intervention*

### Language-Based Approaches

# ~ *8* ~

# Setting Events to Improve Parent–Teacher Coordination and Motivation for Children with Autism

Robert L. Koegel,
Cynthia M. Carter, and Lynn Kern Koegel

Behavioral antecedents are recognized as vital components in research and intervention programs. These behavioral antecedents include context variables and setting events that may temporarily alter the value of a reinforcer (see Carr, Reeve, & Magito-McLaughlin, 1996; Horner, Vaughn, Day, & Ard, 1996). Clearly, contextual variables are numerous, of different types, and not always obvious or easy to amend. By manipulating certain known behavioral antecedents, however, positive setting events can be constructed to set a context that is likely to result in an increased number and value of reinforcers. This chapter focuses on antecedent manipulations that improve learning and reduce disruptive behavior for children with autism through a combination of antecedent procedures that appear to increase the children's motivation to interact socially, communicatively, and academically.

It is well documented that children with autism fail to respond to and avoid many types of language and academic interactions (Koegel, Koegel, Frea, & Smith, 1995). Because this avoidance behavior frequently occurs at the start of an interaction, it is possible to hypothesize that negative antecedents have been previously established. These negative antecedents and resulting failure to respond to everyday environmental stimuli, which appear as a widespread motiva-

Portions of the research described in this chapter were funded by PHS Research Grant No. MH 28210 from the National Institute of Mental Health and by the U.S. Department of Education Grant No. G0087C0234.

tional problem, may not only have an impact on a child's communicative and scholastic activities but also can be profoundly detrimental to a child's social development. Children with autism who are lacking in social skills may be excluded from everyday social interactions and are, in turn, unlikely to learn conversational competence and to develop age-appropriate language (Koegel, 1995). Thus, antecedent variables that improve motivation may be critical in working with children with autism who, because of uncontrolled variation in these setting events, may be contradictorily described as appearing uncommonly intelligent in certain circumstances and appearing as having severe mental retardation in others (Koegel & Mentis, 1985). Hence, such children may be placed in educationally inappropriate settings with inappropriate educational goals (Koegel, Koegel, & Smith, 1997) and may be viewed by others as lacking competence in social situations. In actuality, they may be lacking in motivation to respond under specific antecedent conditions (Koegel et al., 1995).

By altering variables that influence a child's motivation to interact in stimulus situations (e.g., social, language, or difficult academic interactions), however, positive antecedent conditions can be created that decrease or eliminate disruptive attempts to avoid interactions (Koegel & Johnson, 1989; Koegel & Mentis, 1985; Koegel et al., 1989; Schreibman, 1988). This approach also lends itself to the provision of positive behavioral support, rather than needing to rely on aversive consequences as a response to the children's disruptive behavior.

## MOTIVATION AS A PIVOTAL RESPONSE

Motivation has often been described as a pivotal behavior in the literature (see Koegel et al., 1995; Koegel, Koegel, & Schreibman, 1991; Koegel et al., 1989; Schreibman, Stahmer, & Pierce, 1996). *Pivotal behaviors* are those that are central to wide areas of functioning, such that a change in the pivotal behavior will result in widespread and positive effects across many other behaviors. Pivotal behaviors may be described, in essence, as tapping into the crux of the child's problem by developing antecedent procedures that change the context by providing positive setting events. These setting events create an environment that increases the likelihood of an appropriate response rather than disruptive avoidance responding. Thus, setting events have been manipulated to positively affect disruptive behavior. Clearly, then, the identification and assessment of pivotal behaviors is vital for children with autism and other related severe disabilities. Because these children have large numbers of target behaviors that require remediation, to conduct individual interventions for one behavior at a time is not only lengthy and impractical but may indeed be unrealistic if the intervention is to result in socially significant gains (Koegel et al., 1991). Thus, addressing pivotal behaviors to gain antecedent control is critical so that children can make widespread gains in a practical fashion. The following sections describe approaches that deal with antecedent control over variables that affect motivation as a pivotal behavior, which have been shown to result in dramatically greater learning and decreased disruptive behavior in children with autism.

## CREATING POSITIVE BEHAVIORAL ANTECEDENTS IN LANGUAGE INTERVENTION

Language interventions historically have relied on artificial approaches to produce desired verbal responses (e.g., drill procedures using picture cards). These methods were unpleasant for the children involved and often produced speech that sounded unnatural and that was not of a conversational nature. By altering known behavioral antecedents in language intervention approaches to produce positive learning environments for the child, however, dramatic gains can be achieved in all facets of language production.

### Motivation

Antecedent variables known to influence *motivation*, broadly defined as an increase in initiations and responsiveness to social and environmental stimuli, have been shown to enhance the outcomes of language interventions. An initial step in the language-learning process may involve creating antecedent setting events such that the child learns to use communication to obtain wanted items and to fulfill basic needs (Howlin, 1989; Koegel, 1995). The learning environment, however, can be expanded gradually so that children become motivated to use language to fulfill social needs and to obtain linguistic and academic knowledge from others (Koegel, Camarata, Valdez-Menchaca, & Koegel, in press; Sigman & Kasari, 1995).

### Motivational Variables

As mentioned in the opening paragraphs, certain antecedent variables—child choice, reinforcing attempts, shared control and turn-taking, interspersing maintenance tasks, and the use of natural and direct reinforcers—have been identified, which, when modified from traditional language training procedures, have been shown to increase a child's responsivity to environmental stimuli and, thus, appear to increase the child's motivation during language interactions. Moreover, research has demonstrated that techniques that use these antecedent variables decrease disruptive behavior during language intervention (Koegel, Koegel, & Surratt, 1992). This finding is of considerable value because children with autism often exhibit disruptive behavior to escape new or difficult language tasks. Indeed, noncompliance is one of the most commonly reported behavior challenges in children with autism and related severe developmental disabilities (Mace et al., 1988). The following sections discuss specific antecedent variables in detail.

**Child Choice**    The term *child choice* refers to the use of child-preferred materials, topics, and toys and to following the child's lead (i.e., attention, interest). The manipulation of this variable—in contrast to traditional analog language training procedures, wherein the child is directed to attend to a stimulus that is chosen by the clinician—to instead using stimuli that are selected by the child has been reported to increase responsiveness in language interactions and to decrease avoidance behavior by providing an antecedent signal for increased reinforcement (Koegel & Koegel, 1995; Koegel, Dyer, & Bell, 1987; Koegel & Mentis, 1985). For example, a traditional language training procedure to increase vocabulary would typically involve a drill practice, wherein a clinician directs a child to name items shown in a series of picture cards chosen by the clinician. This repetitive, arbitrary format may come to serve as a negative setting event for the child, as the task demands contain few reinforcers inherent in the interactions, per se. In contrast, child choice during language interventions shifts behavioral antecedents to a positive context by allowing the child to choose stimulus items from a pool of previously determined desired items (e.g., toys, books, playdough, blocks) that are likely to possess reinforcing properties, thereby increasing the likelihood of reinforcement during the teaching interactions. Thus, language learning occurs in a naturally reinforcing conversational context, and the child is provided with contingent opportunities to play with the items that were previously selected. It is important to note that although the child has choice throughout this type of interaction, the language task itself is carefully constructed by the clinician so that the desired target behaviors are incorporated while using the positive antecedent stimuli selected by the child. Thus, systematic teaching still occurs, but the child is less likely to avoid the interaction. As such, child choice is an important behavioral antecedent because in allowing the child to select the teaching stimuli for the relevant target behavior, setting events become positive for the child, and responsivity to language interactions increases.

**Reinforcing Attempts**    Reinforcing communicative attempts also has been shown to be an important antecedent variable (Koegel & Johnson, 1989; Koegel & Mentis, 1985; Koegel, O'Dell, & Dunlap,

1988). By reinforcing communicative attempts, as opposed to reinforcing correct responses only, children with autism show an increased responsiveness to language intervention as the teaching progresses. It is possible that reinforcing communicative attempts serves as an antecedent to signify that a response in the child's repertoire will efficiently produce a reinforcer. Reinforcing attempts as a behavioral antecedent, then, may be especially important for children with autism, whose lack of motivation may stem from previous repeated failure at tasks (Clark & Rutter, 1979). Koegel and Koegel (1995) also called to attention an interactive effect combining child choice and reinforcing attempts: Permitting a child to choose desired stimuli will undoubtedly increase the probability of verbal response attempts because there is increased interest in the antecedent stimulus. This, followed by immediate reinforcement for any attempt to communicate—no matter how distant it is from the exact response—would result in an expanded number of responses and attempts at the communicative goal (Koegel & Koegel, 1995). Thus, by combining these antecedent variables, responsivity and subsequent reinforcement for language communication is increased significantly.

**Shared Control and Turn Taking**   Changing the behavioral antecedents so that the child has some control over conversational interactions in the language intervention has been shown to improve social responsivity (Koegel & Johnson, 1989; Koegel & Mentis, 1985). This can be accomplished by teaching the children to initiate social interactions (e.g., by asking questions) or by initiating appropriate child-preferred topic shifts during conversation (Koegel, 1995; Koegel, Dyer, & Bell, 1987). Shared control during language interaction appears to be a necessary part of natural conversation, and preliminary research suggests that children who do not engage in reciprocal shared control are not viewed by others as functioning appropriately (Shoshan, Koegel, & Koegel, 1996). Therefore, whereas analog language procedures have traditionally focused on clinician control of the environment, consideration of both the clinician and child in intervention practices expands child responsivity in natural language interactions by allowing for greater and natural reinforcements for participation in conversational interactions. In using natural conversational exchanges (e.g., turn taking), as opposed to employing analog language intervention in which language is directed at the child in a conversationally artificial climate, the child is granted increased opportunity to direct language interactions. Thus, behavioral antecedents are changed to signify a greater likelihood of reinforcement in the conversational interaction. In turn, a greater responsivity during the social exchanges elicits a more natural conversational interaction and extended responsiveness to environmental stimuli.

***Interspersing Maintenance Tasks*** Variation of task sequencing to include maintenance tasks (i.e., previously learned tasks) has been shown to be an important antecedent variable influencing responding in children with autism (Carr, Newsom, & Binkoff, 1980; Dunlap & Koegel, 1980; Koegel & Koegel, 1986; Koegel & Johnson, 1989). Initial research demonstrated that children with autism responded more favorably (i.e., with increased enthusiasm and interest) when previously mastered tasks were interspersed with acquisition trials on new targeted tasks, rather than when the children were presented with the same new target task in a massed series of trials (Dunlap, 1984; Dunlap & Koegel, 1980). By interspersing maintenance tasks, the setting event is changed from one in which new and unlearned tasks are exclusively presented, to one in which the child encounters previously learned tasks randomly and frequently interspersed among new tasks. This shift appears to result in the child's experiencing a high degree of success for initial responding, and this success sets the context for a further increased likelihood of obtaining reinforcement, ultimately leading to increased responsiveness.

Repeated success of an antecedent variable also may relate to theories of behavioral momentum in children with severe developmental disabilities (see Kennedy, Itkonen, & Lindquist, 1995; Mace et al., 1988; Nevin, 1996; Singer, Singer, & Horner, 1987). Behavioral momentum refers to the tendency for behavior to persist following a change in setting events. For example, altering behavioral antecedents by preceding a difficult task with a series of short and easy tasks that have a high probability of being followed (Singer et al., 1987) results in the child's achieving repeated success and building momentum for improving responding through obtaining repeated reinforcements. This antecedent variable then ultimately leads to decreased escape behavior and increased positive responsiveness to difficult tasks.

***Natural and Direct Reinforcers*** Most children whose language develops typically receive a number of social reinforcers from language interactions. Children with autism, who encounter difficulties learning language, however, may not experience the minimum degree of social reinforcement necessary to serve as a positive antecedent to increase the likelihood of future interactions. In an attempt to rectify this problem, early behavioral approaches for teaching language to children with autism focused on response consequences relying heavily on arbitrary extrinsic reinforcers (e.g., food). It is now documented that in rearranging antecedents by using a stimulus that naturally provides a task-appropriate consequence, children show more rapid acquisition of target behaviors. That is, learning is enhanced when the target behavior is a direct and natural part of the chain leading to the reinforcer (Koegel & Williams, 1980). As a result, a child may learn the necessary association between responding and reinforcement. That is, children may discriminate that there is a consequence to their behaviors such that they may associate positive outcomes with their own direct responding (Koegel & Koegel, 1995). This change in antecedent stimuli ultimately increases reinforcement for the child in the natural environment. It also has been suggested that using a reinforcer that is inherently related to the response may shorten the delay between the response and the reinforcer, making the antecedent stimuli and the reinforcer more salient (Kazdin, 1977; Koegel & Koegel, 1995). By drawing the child's attention to the relevant cues, the probability of subsequent responding is thereby raised under relevant stimulus conditions.

## NATURAL LANGUAGE PARADIGM

The Natural Language Paradigm (NLP) is a behavioral intervention approach that alters traditional analog language teaching by incorporating a combination of the antecedent variables discussed in the previous sections (Koegel, O'Dell, & Koegel, 1987). Although its basic premise is to arrange the environment to increase children's opportunities to use language under natural conditions (e.g., school, home), the overriding importance of NLP is its manipulation of a number of antecedent variables in an overall language package to increase responsivity during language interactions. Procedures similar to the NLP, which manipulate antecedents to cause positive behavior change, have been proven to be effective in language interventions with diversified populations of children with disabilities, ranging from mild to severe (see Camarata, 1993, 1996; Camarata, Nelson, & Camarata, 1994; Kaiser & Hester, 1994; Valdez-Menchaca & Whitehurst, 1988; Yoder et al., 1995). Furthermore, naturalistic language models incorporating motivational techniques to increase responsivity have been extended to classroom applications (see Yoder et al., 1995), and preliminary research suggests that these variables also may be important components in developing an active and maintained use of augmentative communication systems (Stiebel, 1997). Natural language teaching has also been found to be preferable to analog conditions in generalization and retention of language learning in adults with autism (Elliott, Hall, & Soper, 1991).

Because the NLP intervention is specifically meant for use in natural environments, it is ideally suited for use in the child's home, and it can be easily implemented by parents (Laski, Charlop, & Schreibman, 1988). It also is noteworthy that research in the area of parent education suggests that parental stress is reduced when parents be-come proficient at implementing the NLP procedures (Koegel, Bim-bela, & Schreibman, 1996). Although one tends to think of intervention only in terms of the child directly, it may also be necessary to view behavioral antecedents in the broader context of the child's commu-nity and family. Because these children need ongoing therapeutic in-teractions during much of their waking hours, it may be necessary for parents to take an active role in the habilitative process so that be-havioral antecedents are arranged to promote learning opportunities in home routines (Koegel, Koegel, Kellegrew, & Mullen, 1996). High parental stress, which results in a negative antecedent condition, how-ever, impair the parents' ability to be effective in the habilitation pro-cess (Robbins, Dunlap, & Plienis, 1991). Thus, the importance of de-veloping procedures that arrange stimulus conditions to promote therapeutic interactions and simultaneously decrease parental stress is of considerable importance (Koegel, Bimbela, & Schreibman, 1996). Previous interventions often neglect family stress issues, thereby de-creasing many possible opportunities for antecedent control of lan-guage use within the home setting. As mentioned, the techniques in-corporated into the NLP build on arranging the environment to increase children's opportunities and natural reinforcement for using language (Koegel, 1995; Koegel, Bimbela, & Schreibman, 1996). Thus, the setting events are constructed in such a way as to maximize the child's desire, need, and opportunity for language use. This type of intervention also has resulted in the widespread generalization of in-tervention gains and decreases in disruptive behavior (Koegel et al., 1992).

It is interesting to note that similar manipulations of antecedent variables to increase responsivity have been investigated across a va-riety of language behaviors, including the intelligible use of speech sounds during conversation. For instance, a study to be published in 1998 compared the use of a naturalistic language teaching approach (incorporating the previously mentioned types of changes in antece-dent variables to increase motivation) versus an analog (traditional, structured motor drills) language teaching approach for increasing speech intelligibility in children with autism (Koegel, Camarata, Koe-gel, Ben-Tall, & Smith, in press). It is also interesting to note that al-though both procedures resulted in some increases in the targeted speech sounds in the clinic setting, only the naturalistic approach pro-duced gains in intelligible speech sounds during natural conversation. That is, manipulating antecedent variables within the context of speech sound intervention also appears to produce the desired effect of increased opportunities for reinforcement in natural language interactions and increased speech sound gains when compared with an analog motor drill teaching approach. The resulting improvement in speech intelligibility appears to "unlock a bottleneck" and to promote further interactions with the child by peers without disabilities, teachers, and family members.

## Antecedent Question Asking

Another area of language that has been repeatedly discussed as problematic is self-initiation of language use. Children with autism typically exhibit a severe lack of initiations, including the failure to use questions to seek information as well as the failure to initiate and maintain conversation (Sigman, 1996; Tager-Flusberg, 1994, 1996). As mentioned previously, a lack of motivation to initiate is severely detrimental to a child's social and language development, such that a lack in initiation skills will preclude a child from naturally obtaining social and language proficiencies that would usually be learned in everyday conversational interactions with peers and others. For example, typical children begin to request names of items from caregivers during their second year of life by asking "What's that?" (usually expressed as "dat?" while pointing at an object) (Koegel, 1995). Thus, a characteristic "vocabulary spurt" is seen in typical children at this time of development. Later, "where" and "whose" develop, further expanding social and language skills and, hence, a child's communicative competence (Koegel, 1995). Unfortunately, such questions are used infrequently, if at all, by children with autism. As such, a focus of researchers has become to teach question-asking (i.e., self-initiated queries) to children with autism (see Carter, Koegel, & Koegel, 1996; Koegel, 1993).

Koegel (1993, 1995) discussed procedures—which increased motivation by incorporating ideas from the NLP—to teach self-initiated queries to children with autism who have language delays. For example, to teach "What's that?" to increase expressive vocabulary labels, highly desired items (e.g., toys, candies) were placed in an opaque bag, and a child was prompted to ask, "What's that?" After the child asked the question, a desired item was removed from the bag, shown to the child, and labeled. The child then was allowed to take the item if he or she desired. Progressively, this prompt was faded when the child was using the query at a high frequency. Next, the child was prompted to repeat the name of the highly desired item before it was removed and shown. This prompt was also faded gradually. At that point, the child was asking the question "What's that?" then labeling the item at a high rate. Then, new items that the child did not label correctly were gradually interspersed with the familiar desired items beginning with every fourth item, then third, and so on until all of the items represented new items with targeted vocabulary labels. Finally, the bag was faded so that the items were simply placed on the table. Following this intervention, children with autism showed dramatic increases in vocabulary; but perhaps more important, they begin to use the query spontaneously in their natural environments. Similar procedures have been developed to other questions, such as "Where is it?" to learn prepositions, "Whose is it?" to learn possessives and pronouns, and "What's happening?" and "What happened?" to learn verb conjugations, and to expand verb diversity. Thus, by utilizing the antecedent procedures of teaching the children to use questions, subsequent learning opportunities are substantially increased as children learn a tool for gaining access to linguistic and social competencies through ongoing reinforcing reciprocal interactions (for further discussion, see Koegel, 1995).

## Antecedent Stimulus Variables During Testing

It is widely known among learning theorists that children who are unmotivated will perform poorly. Children with autism, who often exhibit a generalized lack of appropriate responses under antecedent conditions associated with standardized testing, may perform in a way that severely underestimates their abilities. It is possible, however, to manipulate antecedent variables that influence motivation and attention to relevant test cues in order to produce a more accurate assessment of children's abilities on standardized tests. Specifically, Koegel, Koegel, and Smith (1997) functionally assessed antecedent variables causing disruptive behavior during standardized testing. Based on the results of the functional assessment, individual antecedent conditions were arranged for each child, such as having the child repeat the test question before responding or changing the location of the testing. Substantial increases in the children's test scores occurred following these antecedent manipulations.

Although the use of standardized tests has often been criticized in the literature (Berliner, 1988; California Association of School Psychologists, 1987; Lambert, 1981; Rothman & Cohen, 1988; Turnbull, 1993; Williams, 1983; Zigler, Abelson, Trickett, & Seitz, 1982), in reality, standardized tests are used often in practice. Unfortunately, inaccurate or misleading results obtained from these measures can lead to inappropriate educational goals and placements. Thus, if standardized testing is implemented, the use of antecedent manipulations to promote meaningful test results is critical.

## CREATING POSITIVE BEHAVIORAL ANTECEDENTS TO INCREASE ACADEMIC RESPONDING AND DECREASE INAPPROPRIATE BEHAVIORS

Interventions that use positive behavioral antecedents are shown to be effective in increasing academic responding and in decreasing inappropriate behaviors. Positive methods include priming, both to increase academic success and to increase social initiations, and using antecedent physical exercise to decrease self-stimulatory and stereotypic behaviors.

### Priming

Priming is a method of intervention that previews information or activities with which a child is likely to have difficulties (Wilde, Koegel, & Koegel, 1992). That is, priming focuses on antecedent events that are likely to stimulate a child's interest in an activity, increase competence in a given area, and deter any escape or avoidance behaviors a child may demonstrate when presented with new material. There are three variables that often lead to successful priming: 1) The priming session is conducted prior to the activity, 2) the priming session is low demand, and 3) the priming session is rich in potential sources of reinforcement (Zanolli, Daggett, & Adams, 1996). Priming can be used as a method of altering the antecedents for a variety of different behaviors.

***Priming to Increase Academic Success***    In applications used in the 1990s, priming is used most often in academic settings for children with disabilities who are fully included in general preschool and grade-school classrooms, but priming can be used with any child experiencing difficulty in classroom activities (Koegel, Koegel, et al., 1996). For example, consider a preschool student who is displaying disruptive behavior (e.g., not attending to teaching tasks, aggressing toward peers, turning his back to the teacher) during storybook time in class (Wilde et al., 1992). To incorporate priming techniques, the child's parents and teacher change the antecedent events by coordinating materials so that the child has access to course materials before the next day's class. In a relaxed, nondemanding manner, the parent reads the book that is to be read the next day in class. This can be incorporated into an evening family routine, perhaps as a bedtime story.

Preliminary research suggests that when such priming sessions are implemented, disruptive behavior is reduced or eliminated when the story is read the next day in class. In control sessions in which a parent read a story that was different from the one read by the teacher the next day in class, disruptive behavior remained at the previous high levels. Furthermore, primed sessions always resulted in higher listening comprehension. Thus, this antecedent manipulation shows the common inverse relationship between improved learning and reduced disruptive behavior. It is also important to note that if a parent is not able or willing to participate in this type of home–school coordination, equally effective outcomes have resulted when special education personnel (e.g., resource specialist, school psychologist, speech-language pathologist) implemented the priming sessions after school hours.

Priming also has proved to be effective with a variety of academic tasks (e.g., writing, appropriate free play, math) with children of a variety of ages (preschool through high school) and with a variety of severity of disabilities. Furthermore, anecdotal reports of success suggest that this procedure also may be very effective for children without disabilities who are experiencing temporary difficulties. This success suggests important new ways of thinking about homework as an antecedent manipulation rather than as a consequence-oriented follow-up to class assignments.

**Priming to Increase Social Initiations**   In addition, research has shown that priming can be an effective intervention for increasing social initiations to peers for children with autism (Zanolli et al., 1996). As noted previously, social initiations (e.g., question asking, initiating conversation with peers) are critical in developing language because through initiations, children increase their opportunities for learning new vocabulary, obtaining communicative competence, and learning age-appropriate rules of language. Unfortunately, studies of initiations in autism have consistently reported children with autism to be lacking in frequency of social initiations (Hauck, Fein, Waterhouse, & Feinstein, 1995; Koegel, 1995; Sigman, 1996; Tager-Flusberg, 1996). Priming social skills as an antecedent to increase initiations, therefore, appears to show considerable promise.

In a study investigating spontaneous initiations in children with autism (Zanolli et al., 1996), priming sessions with children with autism and peers who were typically developing were conducted immediately prior to general preschool activities. Specifically, peers were first taught to respond socially to initiations from children with autism (e.g., "Hi [child with autism's name]"; "Way to go"; "High five") and to give brief access to a preferred item previously identified for the children with autism. Then, priming sessions were conducted in which the children with autism were prompted by a teacher to look at a peer's face, smile at the peer, say the peer's name, and engage in appropriate play after the teacher modeled these behaviors. Subsequently, activity sessions were conducted in which a child with autism and a peer were brought to an area of the classroom in which they played with one of the child-preferred items. Here, the teacher asked the child with autism and peer to greet each other and play in the area for 5 minutes. Each time the child with autism spontaneously directed an initiation to the peer, the peer delivered the prescribed consequences. If the peer did not deliver consequences contingently (i.e., within 1 second), the teacher prompted the peer to respond by saying something such as "John [child with autism] talked to you, what do you do?" and waited 1 second. If the peer still did not respond, the teacher said, "Say something, and give him a treat." Behaviors then were assessed during regular free-play time, when all of the children enrolled in the classroom were present. Results indicated spontaneous initiations by children with autism to typically developing peers increased to above the average rate of initiations among typical peers in the same activities and showed considerable variety. That is, priming had an effect on the variety of spontaneous initiation topographies, including previously prompted behaviors (e.g., looking at the peer's face, smiling at the peer, saying "Give me that," touching the peer, saying the peer's name), as well as several behaviors that had not been prompted (e.g., "I want that," "I want crayon," "Hi") (Zanolli et al., 1996). Thus, by priming to change behavioral antecedents to include reinforcing conversational interactions, subsequent social initiations by children with autism may be increased.

**Other Priming Methods**  There have been other methods of priming for social skills reported in the literature. For example, Kamps, Leonard, Vernon, Dugan, and Delquadri (1992) investigated the use of a social skills group to train high-functioning students with autism to facilitate peer interaction in an inclusive classroom. A number of appropriate social skills were selected for instruction including initiating, responding, keeping an interaction going, greeting others, giving and accepting compliments, taking turns, asking for help and helping others, and including others in activities. The intervention providers included the first author in the study, the classroom teacher, and a special education teacher. Training occurred in the first 10 minutes of 20-minute play groups incorporated into the daily routine of a general first-grade classroom, four times per week. Intervention involved teaching the social skills mentioned by modeling to three boys with autism and their peers without disabilities. Results of the study indicated that in changing behavioral antecedents by employing priming for social skills, social performance was much improved in both frequency and duration of social interactions. There was also an increase in responsivity of children with autism to their typical peers, and vice versa.

In summary, developing home–school coordination to prime various functions as an antecedent manipulation to prevent challenging behaviors may be an effective and desirable alternative to using home time for remediating academics that the child has missed due to disruptive in-school conduct (Koegel, Koegel, et al., 1996).

## Using Antecedent Physical Exercise

Another application of antecedent conditions producing positive behavior changes has been discussed in the literature regarding the effects of physical exercise on the behavior of children with autism (Kern, Koegel, & Dunlap, 1984; Kern, Koegel, Dyer, Blew, & Fenton, 1982). Many children with autism display inappropriate behaviors, such as hand flapping and body rocking. These behaviors, often termed *stereotypic* or *self-stimulatory* behaviors, appear to interfere with these children's development. Although the predominance of effective early intervention methods for these behaviors had initially focused on manipulation of response consequences (e.g., Foxx & Azrin, 1972; Luiselli & Krause, 1981; Mulhern & Baumeister, 1969), later investigations began to examine manipulation of antecedent events. For example, Kern and colleagues (1982) investigated the use of antecedent physical exercise (jogging) as a possible method of decreasing subsequent self-stimulatory behavior in children with autism. They found that not only did self-stimulatory behavior decrease markedly but resulting decreases in stereotypic behavior also covaried with increases in appropriate behaviors. That is, while antecedent jogging decreased subsequent self-stimulatory behaviors, it also increased subsequent appropriate play and academic responding. Therefore, it is unlikely that the decrease in stereotypic behavior occurred as a result of fatigue, because play and academic responding increased.

In light of this research showing the benefits of physical exercise on stereotypic behavior, an ensuing study (Kern et al., 1984) examined the type of antecedent exercise required to obtain these beneficial effects in children with autism. In comparing 15-minute intervals of mild exercise (ball playing) with the same interval of continuous and vigorous exercise (jogging), results indicated that the specific type of physical activity did have a differential effect on the subsequent behavior of the children in the study. Specifically, mild exercise had little or no influence on the children's subsequent stereotypic responding, whereas vigorous exercise was always followed by reductions in stereotypic behaviors.

Thus, another viable method of changing behavioral antecedents may be to incorporate vigorous exercise into the routine of children who display stereotypic behaviors. These decreases in stereotypic responding, which also covary with appropriate play and academic responding, may be a positive alternative to the use of aversive response consequences (see also Koegel & Covert, 1972; Koegel, Firestone, Kramme, & Dunlap, 1974; Koegel & Koegel, 1989; Watters & Watters, 1980).

## Functional Analysis of Antecedent Stimulus Conditions Related to Sibling Aggression

Other changes in antecedent stimuli to increase appropriate behavior have also been explored in the literature. For example, Koegel, Stiebel, and Koegel (in press) examined a multicomponent antecedent manipulation including environmental changes and functional communication training to reduce aggression in children with autism toward their infant and toddler siblings. After a functional assessment of antecedent stimuli leading to aggression was conducted for each of the participants in the study in their own homes during problematic times, individual intervention plans were determined. For each child, intervention plans were then implemented by the parent, using a parent–professional consultation model, for the setting events that consistently resulted in aggression (three or four setting events for each child). For example, one child whose aggression occurred at mealtime required a combination of appropriate setting event changes (e.g., replacing the metal plate with a plastic one on the sibling's high chair to reduce noise) and functional communication instruction to teach the aggressive child appropriate verbal behavior in place of aggression (e.g., saying, "baby needs help" to a parent when the infant was crying). Appropriate nonverbal responses also were taught, such as teaching the child with autism to hand the infant sibling a pacifier or bottle, so that the child with autism could attend to the infant's needs him- or herself. Results of the study indicated that the antecedent intervention brought about significant reductions or eliminated the children's aggression toward their infant or toddler siblings and brought about increases in parent and child happiness levels (Koegel, Stiebel, & Koegel, in press). This study and others show that functional assessment of antecedent variables can facilitate the design of effective intervention programs. As mentioned previously, involving families as active participants may be a necessary and vital component to speed up the process of analyzing antecedent setting events. Furthermore, the family involvement appears to be a critical component in implementing programs that will result in widespread lifestyle changes in antecedent context variables so that challenging behaviors can be prevented, reduced, and eliminated.

## SUMMARY

Children with autism present many challenges during interventions focusing on language, academic, and social areas. These challenges are often the result of the children's generalized avoidance of seemingly difficult aspects of these types of interactions. In the past, the children's disruptive avoidance behaviors often resulted in frequent, intensive, and painful response consequences in an attempt to eliminate the avoidance responding so that teaching could occur. In contrast, expanding interventions to include analyses of antecedent stimuli that may precipitate the occurrence of avoidance responding results in positive behavioral support procedures that maintain the dignity of individuals while increasing their motivation to engage in even difficult language, academic, and social tasks. The types of procedures described in this chapter, including variables related to motivation and child initiations, not only reduce challenging behaviors but inherently increase the children's active involvement in the habilitation process.

## REFERENCES

Berliner, D.C. (1988). Meta-comments: A discussion of critiques of L.M. Dunn's monograph Bilingual Hispanic children on the U.S. mainland. [Special issue: Achievement testing: Science versus ideology.] *Hispanic Journal of Behavioral Sciences, 10,* 273–299.

California Association of School Psychologists. (1987). *Documentation and recommendations.* Millbrae: Author.

Camarata, S. (1993). The application of naturalistic conversation training to speech production in children with speech disabilities. *Journal of Applied Behavior Analysis, 26,* 173–182.

Camarata, S.M. (1996). On the importance of integrating naturalistic language, social intervention, and speech intelligibility training. In L.K. Koegel, R.L. Koegel, & G. Dunlap (Eds.), *Positive behavioral support: Including people with difficult behavior in the community* (pp. 333–351). Baltimore: Paul H. Brookes Publishing Co.

Camarata, S.M., Nelson, K.E., & Camarata, M.N. (1994). Comparison of conversational recasting and imitative procedures for training grammatical structures in children with specific language impairment. *Journal of Speech and Hearing Research, 37,* 1414–1423.

Carr, E.G., Newsom, C.D., & Binkoff, J.A. (1980). Escape as a factor in the aggressive behavior of two retarded children. *Journal of Applied Behavior Analysis, 18,* 111–126.

Carr, E.G., Reeve, C.E., & Magito-McLaughlin, D. (1996). Contextual influences on problem behavior in people with developmental disabilities. In L.K. Koegel, R.L. Koegel, & G. Dunlap (Eds.), *Positive behavioral support: Including people with difficult behavior in the community* (pp. 403–423). Baltimore: Paul H. Brookes Publishing Co.

Carter, C.M., Koegel, L.K., & Koegel, R.L. (1996, May). *Generalized effects of question asking on acquisition of language structures.* Poster session presented at the annual meeting of the Association for Behavior Analysis, San Francisco.

Clark, P., & Rutter, M. (1979). Task difficulty and task performance in autistic children. *Journal of Child Psychology and Psychiatry and Allied Disciplines, 20,* 271–285.

Dunlap, G. (1984). The influence of task variation and maintenance tasks on the learning and affect of autistic children. *Journal of Experimental Child Psychology, 37,* 41–64.

Dunlap, G., & Koegel, R.L. (1980). Motivating autistic children through stimulus variation. *Journal of Applied Behavior Analysis, 13,* 619–627.

Elliott, R.O., Jr., Hall, K., & Soper, H.V. (1991). Analog language teaching versus natural language teaching: Generalization and retention of language learning for adults with autism and mental retardation. *Journal of Autism and Developmental Disorders, 21,* 433–447.

Foxx, R.M., & Azrin, H.H. (1972). Restitution: A method of eliminating aggressive-disruptive behavior of retarded and brain damaged patients. *Behaviour Research and Therapy, 10,* 15–27.

Hauck, M., Fein, D., Waterhouse, L., & Feinstein, C. (1995). Social initiations by autistic children to adults and other children. *Journal of Autism and Developmental Disorders, 25,* 579–595.

Horner, R.H., Vaughn, B.J., Day, H.M., & Ard, W.R., Jr. (1996). The relationship between setting events and problem behavior: Expanding our understanding of behavioral support. In L.K. Koegel, R.L. Koegel, & G. Dunlap (Eds.), *Positive behavioral support: Including people with difficult behavior in the community* (pp. 381–402). Baltimore: Paul H. Brookes Publishing Co.

Howlin, P. (1989). Changing approaches to communication training with autistic children. *British Journal of Disorders of Communication, 24,* 151–168.

Kaiser, A.P., & Hester, P.P. (1994). Generalized effects of enhanced milieu teaching. *Journal of Speech and Hearing Research, 37,* 1320–1340.

Kamps, D.M., Leonard, B.R., Vernon, S., Dugan, E.P., & Delquadri, J.C. (1992). Teaching social skills to students with autism to increase peer interactions in an integrated first grade classroom. *Journal of Applied Behavior Analysis, 25,* 281–288.

Kazdin, A.E. (1977). The influence of behavior preceding a reinforced response on behavior change in the classroom. *Journal of Applied Behavior Analysis, 10,* 299–310.

Kennedy, C.H., Itkonen, T., & Lindquist, K. (1995). Comparing interspersed requests and social comments as antecedents for increasing student compliance. *Journal of Applied Behavior Analysis, 28,* 97–98.

Kern, L., Koegel, R.L., & Dunlap, G. (1984). The influence of vigorous versus mild exercise on autistic stereotyped behaviors. *Journal of Autism and Developmental Disorders, 14,* 57–67.

Kern, L., Koegel, R.L., Dyer, K., Blew, P.A., & Fenton, L.R. (1982). The effects of physical exercise on self-stimulation and appropriate responding in autistic children. *Journal of Autism and Developmental Disorders, 12,* 399–419.

Koegel, L.K. (1993). *Teaching children with autism to use a self-initiated strategy to learn expressive vocabulary.* Unpublished doctoral dissertation, University of California at Santa Barbara.

Koegel, L.K. (1995). Communication and language intervention. In R.L. Koegel & L.K. Koegel (Eds.), *Teaching children with autism: Strategies for initiating positive interactions and improving learning opportunities* (pp. 17–32). Baltimore: Paul H. Brookes Publishing Co.

Koegel, L.K., & Koegel, R.L. (1986). The effects of interspersed maintenance tasks on academic performance in a severe childhood stroke victim. *Journal of Applied Behavior Analysis, 19,* 425–430.

Koegel, L.K., & Koegel, R.L. (1995). Motivating communication in children with autism. In E. Schopler & G.B. Mesibov (Eds.), *Learning and cognition in autism* (pp. 73–87). New York: Plenum.

Koegel, L.K., Koegel, R.L., Kellegrew, D., & Mullen, K. (1996). Parent education for prevention and reduction of severe problem behaviors. In L.K. Koegel, R.L. Koegel, & G. Dunlap (Eds.), *Positive behavioral support: Including people with difficult behavior in the community* (pp. 3–30). Baltimore: Paul H. Brookes Publishing Co.

Koegel, L.K., Koegel, R.L., & Smith, A. (1997). Variables related to differences in standardized test outcomes for children with autism. *Journal of Autism and Developmental Disorders, 27,* 233–244.

Koegel, L.K., Stiebel, D., & Koegel, R.L. (in press). Using functional assessment and parent-implemented intervention plans to reduce aggression in children with autism toward infant or toddler siblings. *Journal of The Association for Persons with Severe Handicaps.*

Koegel, R.L., Bimbela, A., & Schreibman, L. (1996). Collateral effects of parent training on family interactions. *Journal of Autism and Developmental Disorders, 26,* 347–359.

Koegel, R.L., Camarata, S., Koegel, L.K., Ben-Tall, A., & Smith, A.E. (in press). Increasing speech intelligibility in children with autism. *Journal of Autism and Developmental Disorders.*

Koegel, R.L., Camarata, S.M., Valdez-Menchaca, M.C., & Koegel, L.K. (in press). Setting generalization of question-asking by children with autism. *American Journal on Mental Retardation.*

Koegel, R.L., & Covert, A. (1972). The relationship of self-stimulation to learning in autistic children. *Journal of Applied Behavior Analysis, 5,* 381–387.

Koegel, R.L., Dyer, K., & Bell, L. (1987). The influence of child-preferred activities on autistic children's social behavior. *Journal of Applied Behavior Analysis, 20,* 243–252.

Koegel, R.L., Firestone, P.B., Kramme, K.W., & Dunlap, G. (1974). Increasing spontaneous play by suppressing self-stimulation in autistic children. *Journal of Applied Behavior Analysis, 7,* 521–528.

Koegel, R.L., & Johnson, J. (1989). Motivating language use in autistic children. In G. Dawson (Ed.), *Autism: Nature, diagnosis, and treatment* (pp. 310–325). New York: Guilford Press.

Koegel, R.L., & Koegel, L.K. (1989). Community referenced research on self-stimulation. In E. Cipani (Ed.), *The treatment of severe behavior disorders: Be-*

*havior analysis approaches* (pp. 129–150). Washington, DC: American Association on Mental Retardation.

Koegel, R.L., Koegel, L.K., Frea, W.D., & Smith, A.E. (1995). Emerging interventions for children with autism: Longitudinal and lifestyle implications. In R.L. Koegel & L.K. Koegel (Eds.), *Teaching children with autism: Strategies for initiating positive interactions and improving learning opportunities* (pp. 1–15). Baltimore: Paul H. Brookes Publishing Co.

Koegel, R.L., Koegel, L.K., & Schreibman, L. (1991). Assessing and training parents in teaching pivotal behaviors. *Advances in Behavioral Assessment of Children and Families, 5,* 65–82.

Koegel, R.L., Koegel, L.K., & Surratt, A. (1992). Language intervention and disruptive behavior in children with autism. *Journal of Autism and Developmental Disorders, 22,* 141–152.

Koegel, R.L., & Mentis, M. (1985). Motivation in childhood autism: Can they or won't they? *Journal of Child Psychology and Psychiatry, 26,* 185–191.

Koegel, R.L., O'Dell, M.C., & Dunlap, G. (1988). Producing speech use in nonverbal autistic children by reinforcing attempts. *Journal of Autism and Developmental Disorders, 18,* 525–538.

Koegel, R.L., O'Dell, M.C., & Koegel, L.K. (1987). A natural language teaching paradigm for nonverbal autistic children. *Journal of Autism and Developmental Disorders, 17,* 187–200.

Koegel, R.L., Schreibman, L., Good, A., Cerniglia, L., Murphy, C., & Koegel, L.K. (1989). *How to teach pivotal behaviors to children with autism: A training manual.* Santa Barbara: University of California.

Koegel, R.L., & Williams, J. (1980). Direct vs. indirect response–reinforcer relationships in teaching autistic children. *Journal of Abnormal Child Psychology, 4,* 537–547.

Lambert, N.M. (1981). The clinical validity of the process for assessment of effective student functioning. *Journal of School Psychology, 19,* 323–334.

Laski, K.E., Charlop, M.H., & Schreibman, L. (1988). Training parents to use the natural language paradigm to increase their autistic children's speech. *Journal of Applied Behavior Analysis, 21,* 391–400.

Luiselli, J.K., & Krause, S. (1981). Reduction in stereotypic behavior through a combination of DRO, cueing, and reinforced isolation procedures. *Behavior Therapist, 4,* 2–3.

Mace, F.C., Hock, M., Lalli, J.S., West, B.J., Belfiore, P., Pinter, E., & Brown, D.K. (1988). Behavioral momentum in the treatment of noncompliance. *Journal of Applied Behavior Analysis, 21,* 123–141.

Mulhern, T., & Baumeister, A.A. (1969). An experimental attempt to reduce stereotypy by reinforcement procedures. *American Journal of Mental Deficiency, 74,* 69–74.

Nevin, J.A. (1996). The momentum of compliance. *Journal of Applied Behavior Analysis, 29,* 535–547.

Robbins, F.R., Dunlap, G., & Plienis, A.J. (1991). Family characteristics, family training, and the progress of young children with autism. *Journal of Early Intervention, 15,* 173–184.

Rothman, R.W., & Cohen, J. (1988). Teaching test taking skills. *Academic Therapy, 23,* 341–348.

Schreibman, L. (1988). *Autism.* Newbury Park, CA: Sage Publications.

Schreibman, L., Stahmer, A.C., & Pierce, K.L. (1996). Alternative applications of pivotal response training: Teaching symbolic play and social interaction skills. In L.K. Koegel, R.L. Koegel, & G. Dunlap (Eds.), *Positive behavioral support: Including people with difficult behavior in the community* (pp. 353–371). Baltimore: Paul H. Brookes Publishing Co.

Shoshan, Y., Koegel, L.K., & Koegel, R.L. (1996, May). *Prognostic factors for children with autism.* Poster session presented at the annual meeting of the Association for Behavior Analysis, San Francisco.

Sigman, M. (1996). Communication/social/emotional development. *Journal of Autism and Developmental Disorders, 26,* 140–144.

Sigman, M., & Kasari, C. (1995). Joint attention across contexts in normal and autistic children. In C. Moore & P.J. Dunham (Eds.), *Joint attention: Its origins and role in development* (pp. 189–203). Hillsdale, NJ: Lawrence Erlbaum Associates.

Singer, G.H.S., Singer, J., & Horner, R.H. (1987). Using pretask requests to increase the probability of compliance for students with severe disabilities. *Journal of The Association for Persons with Severe Handicaps, 12,* 287–291.

Stiebel, D. (1997). *Augmentative communication teaching procedures for children with autism.* Manuscript in preparation, University of California at Santa Barbara.

Tager-Flusberg, H. (1994). Dissociations in form and function in the acquisition of language by autistic children. In H. Tager-Flusberg (Ed.), *Constraints on language acquisition: Studies of atypical children* (pp. 175–194). Hillsdale, NJ: Lawrence Erlbaum Associates.

Tager-Flusberg, H. (1996). Brief report: Current theory and research on language and communication in autism. *Journal of Autism and Developmental Disorders, 26,* 169–172.

Turnbull, H.R., III. (1993). *Free appropriate public education: The law and children with disabilities.* Denver, CO: Love.

Valdez-Menchaca, M.C., & Whitehurst, G.J. (1988). The effects of incidental teaching on vocabulary acquisition by young children. *Child Development, 59,* 1451–1459.

Watters, R.G., & Watters, W.E. (1980). Decreasing self-stimulatory behavior with physical exercise in a group of autistic boys. *Journal of Autism and Developmental Disorders, 10,* 379–387.

Wilde, L.D., Koegel, L.K., & Koegel, R.L. (1992). *Increasing success in school through priming: A training manual.* Santa Barbara: University of California.

Williams, T.S. (1983). Some issues in the standardized testing of minority students. *Journal of Education, 165,* 192–208.

Yoder, P.J., Kaiser, A.P., Goldstein, H., Alpert, C., Mousetis, L., Kaczmarek, L., & Fischer, R. (1995). An exploratory comparison of milieu teaching and responsive interaction in classroom applications. *Journal of Early Intervention, 19,* 218–242.

Zanolli, K., Daggett, J., & Adams, T. (1996). Teaching preschool age autistic children to make spontaneous initiations to peers using priming. *Journal of Autism and Developmental Disorders, 26,* 407–422.

Zigler, E., Abelson, W.D., Trickett, P.K., & Seitz, V. (1982). Is an intervention program necessary in order to improve economically disadvantaged children's IQ scores? *Child Development, 53,* 340–348.

# ~ *9* ~

## *Choice Making and Personal Selection Strategies*

### Jeff Sigafoos

Choice making is an integral and important part of daily life (Brown, Belz, Corsi, & Wenig, 1993; Shevin & Klein, 1984; Wilson, 1992). Indeed, the nature and extent of choice-making skills and opportunities are often seen to reflect the quality of one's lifestyle (Brown, Bayer, & Brown, 1992; Cummins, 1991; Parmenter, 1994; Raphael, Brown, Renwick, & Rootman, 1996; Schalock, 1993; Whitaker, 1989). In addition, meaningful participation in most aspects of daily living involves some degree of choice making (Jenkinson & Nelms, 1994; Kishi, Teelucksingh, Zollers, Park-Lee, & Meyer, 1988). Furthermore, choice making often requires the mediation of others; for example, others may provide the opportunity for choice making or deliver a chosen item. In such circumstances, choice making involves a social–communicative interaction, and participation in these opportunities requires effective skills in communicating one's choices. It therefore stands to reason that restricted choice-making opportunities and skills could negatively influence quality of life, limit participation in daily life, and reduce social–communicative interactions with others.

Other negative by-products may arise from restricted choice-making skills and opportunities. For example, it has been suggested that limited opportunities to make choices, and hence, limited opportunities to exert some degree of control over the environment, could lead to a phenomenon known as learned helplessness (Guess, Benson, & Siegel-Causey, 1985; Wilson, 1992). Among people with develop-

Preparation of this chapter was supported by a grant from the Australian Commonwealth, Department of Human Services and Health.

mental disabilities, learned helplessness may present as extreme lethargy or passivity. Restricted choice making also may contribute to the development and strengthening of challenging behaviors, such as aggression, self-injury, property destruction, and severe tantrums. Such behaviors may be provoked by interactions with others that focus on directing and controlling, rather than on autonomy and choice making (Carr et al., 1994). If restricted skills and opportunities for choice making can lead to challenging behavior, then enhancement of such skills and opportunities may lead to amelioration and prevention of some problematic behavior. It therefore stands to reason that antecedent control procedures focused on increasing choice-making skills and opportunities would represent logical components in the behavioral support of individuals with challenging behavior (Horner et al., 1990).

## CHOICE-MAKING OPPORTUNITIES FOR PEOPLE WITH DEVELOPMENTAL DISABILITIES

Kishi et al. (1988) and Parmenter, Briggs, and Sullivan (1991) documented limited choice-making opportunities for people with developmental disabilities. These two studies assessed the extent to which people with mental retardation living in community-based group homes made various types of choices (e.g., what to eat, what to wear, how to spend leisure time). To assess choice making, a self-report questionnaire was administered. In cases in which the individual had limited communication skills, support staff answered the questionnaire on his or her behalf. In both studies, people with mental retardation had significantly less opportunity for choice making when compared with people without mental retardation. Kishi et al. (1988) also found that staff reported the fewest opportunities for choice making among people with disabilities requiring more extensive supports.

The results of these studies should be interpreted with caution, however, because Stancliffe (1995) demonstrated that self-reports and staff reports may not be equivalent. He also found more opportunities for choice making among his sample of 47 people with mental retardation in comparison with those reported by Kishi et al. (1988) and Parmenter et al. (1991). Stancliffe's sample, however, included people in semi-independent living situations, in which more opportunities for choice making might be expected. All of these studies are further limited because they involved indirect assessment of choice-making opportunities.

Houghton, Bronicki, and Guess (1987) assessed opportunities more directly. They made observations in 12 classrooms for children with disabilities requiring extensive supports. A total of 37 students and 48 school personnel were involved. Observers recorded the occurrence of choice making and expression of preferences among the students in relation to staff responses. Results showed that staff rarely responded to student-initiated expressions of choice and preference. The low rates of staff responsivity may have stemmed from the fact that many of the behaviors said to indicate choice and preference were relatively unconventional (e.g., head, arm, and leg movements; facial grimaces). It is possible that the school personnel involved in this study were not aware or did not consider that these bodily movements and facial expressions functioned as indications of choice and preference. Indeed, it remained unclear whether these responses did in fact function as valid indications of choice and preferences among the students observed.

In a related study focused on choice-making opportunities, Shaddock et al. (1993) observed people with mental retardation requiring extensive supports in vocational and community access programs. Each of 38 individuals was observed during four 12-minute sessions to estimate the nature and extent of their choice-making skills and opportunities. Shaddock et al. observed what they considered to be relatively little choice making (i.e., 140 choices across the 152 sessions). Most of these 140 choices involved fairly simple expressions of preferences or indications of need (e.g., eat, drink, toilet). The opportunities provided by staff varied across individuals and appeared to be determined by several factors, including the expectations of the staff person as to whether or not the person could make choices. In addition, people who engaged in disruptive behavior tended to receive fewer choice-making opportunities.

Overall, the results from these studies suggest that in some cases, people with developmental disabilities have limited opportunities for choice making. In addition, when initiations of choice and preference consist of idiosyncratic and unconventional response forms, others may fail to recognize the functional nature of these responses. If these types of personal selection responses are emitted but not reinforced, then choice making and expressions of preference may eventually cease due to the prevailing extinction schedule. When opportunities and reinforcement are limited, so too may be the acquisition of more conventional choice-making skills (Dunst, Cushing, & Vance, 1985). Maintenance of existing strategies for indicating choice and preference also would be compromised. These factors may contribute to increased challenging behavior among some individuals with developmental disabilities (Stokes, Osnes, & DaVerne, 1993).

## Factors Related to Limited Choice Making

There may be several reasons for restricted choice making among people with developmental disabilities. Part of the problem no doubt stems from limited skills and opportunities. Given that many choice-making opportunities require the mediation of another person, the amount of choice afforded an individual will depend to some extent on the number and types of opportunities provided by others. In some cases, these others (e.g., parents, teachers, support staff, peers) may lack the knowledge and skills that would enable them to provide meaningful choice-making opportunities (Parsons, McCarn, & Reid, 1993; Reid & Parsons, 1991). In other cases, there is anecdotal evidence from Kishi et al. (1988) and Shaddock et al. (1993) to suggest that opportunities are limited because others do not expect the individual to make a choice or are sure that the person would make a "bad" choice (Brown, 1991b). Such expectations could arise if previous attempts to occasion choice making have been unsuccessful, either because the person to whom the opportunity was directed did not respond in a recognizable manner or made a choice that others did not find acceptable.

### Addressing Limited Choice Making

Limited provision of choice-making opportunities may be addressed through teaching appropriate choice-making skills. In addition, parents, teachers, peers, and support staff may need to learn how to provide meaningful and effective opportunities for choice making to people with developmental disabilities. It also may be necessary to ensure that those providing opportunities learn to recognize and respond appropriately to the personal selection and choice-making strategies that may already be part of an individual's repertoire. In short, support for individuals with developmental disabilities in the area of choice making will require a comprehensive curriculum that focuses on the reciprocal and social interactive nature of choice making. The remainder of this chapter delineates theoretical and conceptual issues underlying considerations of choice making and personal selection strategies in interventions for challenging behavior. The chapter also focuses on the implementation of various relevant components of a comprehensive choice-making curriculum for people with developmental disabilities and challenging behaviors.

## OVERVIEW OF CHAPTER

Only since the 1980s has the importance of choice making been emphasized in relation to the education of people with developmental disabilities (Bannerman, Sheldon, Sherman, & Harchik, 1990; Guess et al., 1985; Harchik, Sherman, Sheldon, & Bannerman, 1993; Shevin & Klein, 1984). And only in the 1990s has there been an emergence of objective data on the effects of choice-making opportunities on the behavior and achievement of people with developmental disabilities, including the influence of choice making on challenging behavior. Studies are beginning to document effective strategies for incorporating choice-making interventions into comprehensive behavioral support plans for individuals with developmental disabilities and challenging behaviors. This chapter focuses on the literature that explores incorporation of effective choice-making opportunities into support plans and examines the theoretical, conceptual, and applied issues relevant to the application of choice making as an antecedent control procedure in the prevention of and intervention for challenging behavior.

## THEORETICAL AND CONCEPTUAL ISSUES

Several theoretical and conceptual issues arise when considering the application of choice making in behavioral support. There is, of course, the obvious need to define choice making. Other important issues include the operant and continuous nature of choice-making behaviors. After considering these issues, the chapter next describes the range of behaviors that might be used to indicate choice and preference among people with developmental disabilities. For some individuals, challenging behaviors could be viewed as operant behaviors that function to indicate choice and preference. This latter part of the chapter also reviews the effects of opportunity for choice making on problematic and more appropriate alternative behaviors among people with developmental disabilities.

### Definition of Choice Making

Choice making seems to be one of those concepts that is familiar and easy to recognize. Certain specific acts, such as ordering a meal from a menu or selecting clothes from a wardrobe, are such obvious examples of the concept that it would appear that little more is required by way of definition. Indeed, Shevin and Klein (1984) noted that studies focused on choice making among people with developmental disabilities have not always included an explicit definition of the concept. The lack of a common definition, however, can be problematic. For example, analysis of the effects of choice making and the development of effective interventions to enhance choice making would seem to require an operational definition of the concept.

**Direct Choice Making** Shevin and Klein defined *choice making* in operational terms as *"the act of an individual's selection of a preferred alternative from among several familiar options"* (1984, p. 160, italics in original). This definition is consistent with the typical choice paradigm used to assess preferences among people with developmental disabilities. Parsons and Reid (1990), for example, described what could be considered a prototypic choice paradigm. Their study focused on assessing preferences for foods and beverages among adolescents and adults with mental retardation requiring pervasive supports. The procedure involved presenting various pairs of objects (e.g., applesauce and pudding, banana and corn chips) and allowing the individual to select one of the two items. Within relatively few such pairings, (e.g., 20–30 trials), preferences for one of the items in each pair tended to emerge. Similar arrangements have been used to assess choice making and identify preferences among children with disabilities requiring extensive or pervasive supports (Sigafoos, Laurie, & Pennell, 1995; Windsor, Piche, & Locke, 1994). In studies of this type, it is assumed that items selected more frequently are preferred over items selected less frequently. Indeed, further evidence suggests this is often the case. That is, items selected more frequently from pairs tend to be more effective types of reinforcement for that individual (Paclawskyj & Vollmer, 1995; Piazza, Fisher, Hagopian, Bowman, & Toole, 1996). The definition of choice making offered by Shevin and Klein (1984), therefore, appears consistent with the way in which choice making has been operationalized in several relevant studies involving people with developmental disabilities.

**Indirect Choice Making** Of course, there will be many situations when the alternatives are not presented directly to the individual. For example, choices often need to be made when the individual is asked whether he or she wants water or lemonade, wants to vacuum or dust, or wants to stay home or go shopping. Making a choice under these conditions no doubt requires different types of skills in comparison with selecting directly one of two or more offered items. When attempting to develop choice-making skills in people with developmental disabilities, one should not assume that these two situations are equivalent. Along these lines, Vaughn and Horner (1995) showed that choice making increased and problem behavior decreased when a young man with autism was presented with concrete representations of the available choices (i.e., pictures of several food items from which to choose) as compared with when these same choices were presented verbally by staff (e.g., "Do you want ham or turkey or tuna?").

## Choice Making as Operant Behavior

Consistent with the operational definition provided in the previous section, the act of making a choice could be conceptualized as an operant response maintained by access to preferred items or events. The opportunity to exert some degree of control over the environment via choice making could also be the functional reinforcer in some cases. This conceptualization has several important implications for the provision of services to people with developmental disabilities.

First, choices may reveal one's personal preferences. These preferred items may, in turn, represent effective types of reinforcement. Knowledge of preferences should therefore enable others to enrich that person's environment and improve his or her quality of life by ensuring the availability of preferred items, be they objects, activities, or companions. Identification of more effective types of reinforcement also may improve the effectiveness of skill training and other habilitative programs (Green et al., 1988; Pace, Ivancic, Edwards, Iwata, & Page, 1985). Seen in this light, the development and implementation of individualized habilitation plans, including behavioral support plans, need not be incompatible with the enhancement of personal liberties. Both may occur when choice-making skills and opportunities are extended (see Bannerman et al., 1990).

Second, conceptualization as operant behavior implies that choice making will change in response to various contingencies of reinforcement. This allows for the possibility of increasing choice making by arranging the proper contingencies. This latter point is consistent with a definition of *choice* as the probability of making one response rather than another when presented with two mutually exclusive courses of action (Pierce & Epling, 1995). Experimental studies have shown that the probability of choosing one response over another in a two-choice situation is determined by, among other variables, preference for the consequence associated with each response and by the amount, delay, and rate of reinforcement associated with each alternative (Forzano & Logue, 1995; Herrnstein, 1961; Mace, 1994).

## Choice Making Is Continuous

Choice can be viewed as a discrete selection response to a specific choice-making situation, but others have correctly pointed out that choice also can be viewed as a more continuous aspect of behavior (Belfiore, Browder, & Mace, 1994). Individuals initiate and terminate various actions, and such changes may indicate that a choice has been made. In addition, there may be times when an individual chooses not to choose, so to speak.

Although choice making also may involve decisions concerning when to initiate and terminate behavior and whether to act in the first place, one should not assume that all behavior is necessarily the result of a deliberate choice-making process. When a person engages in aggression or self-injury, for example, it is perhaps tempting to assume that the person has chosen to engage in such behavior. This implies, first, that the individual's behavioral repertoire includes challenging behavior as well as functionally equivalent courses of action but that, for some reason, the person has chosen to engage in challenging behavior rather than in some alternative. Evidence reviewed in other chapters of this book suggests, however, that challenging behavior is often functionally related to impairments in alternative skills. Even if the person's behavioral repertoire contained alternatives, an instance of challenging behavior may not necessarily indicate that the person has, therefore, chosen to engage in challenging behavior rather than in some more appropriate alternative. Instead, an occurrence of challenging behavior could suggest that the environment contains stimuli that have in the past set the occasion for challenging behavior and that these same stimuli have not yet come to occasion more appropriate alternative responses.

Second, instead of challenging behavior reflecting the outcome of a deliberate choice, it may be that for some individuals, challenging behavior is the means by which the person has learned to indicate choice and preference. That is, challenging behavior may be acquired as a personal or idiosyncratic selection strategy. The next section reviews the various means by which people with developmental disabilities may indicate choice and preference.

### Personal Selection Strategies

In the context of this chapter, *personal selection strategies* refer to the means by which an individual makes choices and indicates his or her preferences. This definition allows for a range of behaviors that could be described as personal selection strategies. For example, one might make a choice or indicate a preference by asking for or requesting one item over another, by not accepting or more actively rejecting an offered item, or by expressing interest in a particular object or event (e.g., "Oh, I like that jacket"). As these examples illustrate, choices often are made in the context of a social–communicative interaction with the choice-making response consisting of conventional verbal behavior.

There are other times, of course, when choices are made and preferences are indicated more directly. For example, the person may simply reach out and take one of several items, may approach or avoid certain objects or events, or may choose to engage in, or disengage from, a particular activity. These latter examples do not necessarily involve social–communicative interaction but rather require adaptive skills of another sort.

People with developmental disabilities experience impairments in many adaptive skill areas, including expressive and receptive language. As a result, such individuals will no doubt have difficulty making choices and indicating preferences in conventional ways. Children with disabilities who require pervasive supports, however, may be capable of making certain unconventional or idiosyncratic responses that could be developed as personal selection strategies for choice making. Table 1 lists responses that have been observed in the repertoires of people with developmental disabilities. In some cases it appears that these actions represent personal selection strategies for indicating choice and preference (Houghton et al., 1987; Pace et al., 1985; Sigafoos, Roberts, Couzens, & Kerr, 1993).

Although some people with developmental disabilities may engage in idiosyncratic gestures of the types listed in Table 1, an important empirical question is whether such acts constitute valid means of making choices and indicating preferences. Along these lines, Sigafoos and Dempsey (1992) described an assessment procedure to determine whether various idiosyncratic gestures functioned as valid choice-making responses among three children with disabilities and pervasive support needs. Opportunities were provided for the children to choose between pairs of preferred foods (e.g., cake versus cookie) and beverages (e.g., milk versus juice) during their regular morning snack time. Choice making was recorded if the child reached for, moved toward, or looked at one of the two offered items. If any one or more of these gestures occurred in response to the choice-making opportunity, the child was given one of the items and observed to determine whether that item was then accepted or refused.

In the Sigafoos and Dempsey (1992) study, choice making was observed under two conditions. In the first (matched) condition, the child was given the item that he or she had previously reached for,

Table 1.  Examples of personal selection strategies

| Type | Examples |
|---|---|
| Vocalization | Laugh, cry, groan, hum, sigh |
| Head nod | Left/right, up/down, roll |
| Facial expressions | Smile, frown, purse lips, grimace |
| Body movement | Move toward, move away, wiggle |
| Contact | Touch or drop object, tighten grip |
| Eye gaze | Look at, look away, open/close |
| Challenging behavior | Aggression, tantrum, self-injury |

moved toward, or looked at. During the second (mismatched) condition, however, the child was given the wrong item. That is, if the child reached for the juice, he or she was given the milk. The rationale for this procedure was relatively straightforward: If reaching for, moving toward, and looking at one of two offered items did in fact constitute valid choice-making responses, then the children should be more likely to accept the item under the first condition and more likely to refuse the wrong item during the second condition. The results provided some support for this hypothesis. In general, the children were more likely to accept the item that they had previously reached for, moved toward, or looked at (matched condition), and they were more likely to refuse the wrong item in the mismatched condition. Based on these results, it would appear that these idiosyncratic gestures did in fact represent valid, albeit somewhat unconventional, choice-making responses.

Although the Sigafoos and Dempsey (1992) study suggested that some people with developmental disabilities may acquire idiosyncratic gestures that function as valid choice-making responses, others may lack any such skills. Even if idiosyncratic gestures of the type listed in Table 1 occur frequently, these may not necessarily represent deliberate or valid indicators of choice or preference. It is possible that some such gestures represent motor movements unrelated to the occurrence of choice making or other communicative opportunities (Fraser, Hensinger, & Phelps, 1990).

## Responses to Personal Selection Strategies

Nonetheless, given a conceptualization of choice making as operant behavior, it is also possible that if others react consistently to such gestures as if they were in fact valid indicators of choice and preference, then over time these gestures could become conditioned as effective personal selection strategies. For example, others may give a person items that he or she has looked at or moved toward in the belief that the person wanted or needed the items. Assuming that receipt of certain items represents an effective type of positive reinforcement, then the individual may become more likely to look at and move toward these items in the future. At other times, activities may cease or items may be removed if the person is observed to engage in gestures that others interpret as acts of refusal. For example, a young boy may turn away as he is offered a cup of soup, leading his mother to withdraw the offer. If the removal of soup represented an effective type of negative reinforcement, then turning away from nonpreferred objects will be more likely to occur on future such occasions. With repeated exposure to these types of positive and negative reinforcement contingencies, it should not be long before the idiosyncratic gestures come to represent effective personal selection strategies for indicating choice and preference. A related issue is whether problematic topographies also might be acquired inadvertently as effective indicators of choice and preference via similar processes.

## Challenging Behavior as Personal Selection Strategies

There is growing evidence to suggest that parents, teachers, and staff are affected by and react to aggression, self-injury, tantrums, and other challenging behaviors in ways that may inadvertently strengthen these problematic topographies (Carr & Taylor, 1991; Taylor & Carr, 1992a, 1992b). Consider a child with developmental disabilities prone to self-injurious head banging. During an instructional lesson, the child may start head banging, which perhaps leads the adult to abandon the session. If withdrawal of the task demands represented negative reinforcement, perhaps because the task itself was not highly preferred, then the child may be more likely to head bang when confronted with nonpreferred objects or activities in the future. The child's head banging, over time, could come to represent an idiosyncratic way of indicating rejection or refusal of nonpreferred objects or activities (Carr & Newsom, 1985; Carr, Newsom, & Binkoff, 1980; Doss & Reichle, 1989). Adults also may be less inclined to involve the child in such tasks in the future because they, too, may have been reinforced for removing the task by the cessation of self-injury.

Further evidence from Hastings and his colleagues (Hastings & Remington, 1994a, 1994b; Hastings, Remington, & Hall, 1995) indicates that staff involved in the habilitation of people with developmental disabilities and challenging behaviors often interpret problematic actions as if these were the individuals' ways of indicating needs. Staff also may reason that these needs should be met so as to stop the behavior (Hastings et al., 1995). For example, a person who "uses" challenging behavior to indicate a preference for one item over another would, according to this logic, be given the preferred item, thereby satisfying the need and also eliminating the reason for the challenging behavior. Although this seemingly logical approach may in fact lead to momentary cessation of challenging behavior, one would also expect an increased future probability of the behavior owing to the reinforcing effects of receiving the preferred item. Under this scenario, challenging behavior could be shaped and maintained as a personal selection strategy for indicating choice and preference.

Although the scenario in the previous paragraph is speculative, it is consistent with a functional taxonomy of challenging behavior that has emerged since the 1970s (Carr, 1977; Iwata, Dorsey, Slifer,

Bauman, & Richman, 1982; Wieseler, Hanson, Chamberlain, & Thompson, 1985). There is substantial evidence to support the conclusion that much of the challenging behavior observed among people with developmental disabilities represents learned behavior maintained by positive, negative, and/or automatic reinforcement (Iwata et al., 1994). In particular, many of the positive and negative reinforcers that come to maintain challenging behavior—reinforcers such as attention, access to preferred objects, and removal of nonpreferred activities— require the mediation of others, and, thus, these problematic responses could be interpreted as rather unconventional forms of communication (Carr et al., 1994; Durand, 1993; Sigafoos, Reichle, & Light-Shriner, 1994). As indicated previously, effective choice making often requires a socially mediated context. It is possible, therefore, that some of the personal selection strategies for making choices and indicating preferences that may be developed in people with developmental disabilities might include unconventional forms of communication, such as aggression, self-injury, or extreme tantrums.

In addition to the possibility that challenging behaviors may be shaped and maintained as personal selection strategies for indicating choice and preference, the extent of choice-making opportunities and skills also might represent independent variables that influence the probability of challenging behavior. For example, challenging behavior may represent a form of countercontrol in response to interactions that contain little opportunity for choice (Halle, 1995). In addition, the lack of opportunities for choice may represent a setting event that influences the probability of challenging behavior. As reviewed next, there is evidence that the opportunity to make choices and indicate preferences can affect a range of responses, including challenging behavior.

## Effects of Choice Making on Behavior

The effects of choice making on the behavior of people with developmental disabilities have been studied by observing the frequency of a certain behavior and whether opportunities for choice exist. Within this general paradigm, investigators have examined the effects of the provision of choice-making opportunities on participation in functional activities and the frequency of challenging behavior. After a brief review of some key studies in this area, this section considers the possible mechanisms underlying these observed effects. Analysis of the possible mechanisms underlying the observed effects has implications for the behavioral support of individuals with developmental disabilities and challenging behaviors.

Increased participation in functional activities is an important aim in the education and habilitation of people with developmental disabilities (Cipani & Spooner, 1994; Orelove & Sobsey, 1991). For individuals with existing and appropriate personal selection strategies, the provision of choice-making opportunities in the context of functional activities can represent an effective antecedent control procedure to achieve this aim. For example, Mithaug and colleagues (Mithaug & Hanawalt, 1978; Mithaug & Mar, 1980) demonstrated that adults with mental retardation requiring extensive supports showed individual preferences for certain vocational tasks over others. When given a choice, these adults were more likely to select and work on preferred tasks. Working on vocational tasks also can be increased by providing opportunities for choice (Bambara, Ager, & Koger, 1994; Parsons, Reid, Reynolds, & Bumgarner, 1990). In the leisure domain, Realon, Favell, and Lowerre (1990) found that the opportunity to choose materials (e.g., toys versus videocassettes) leads to increased responding during a structured leisure activity among three adults with multiple disabilities requiring pervasive supports. Other researchers also found that the opportunity for choice can increase engagement with leisure materials (Dattilo & Rusch, 1985). As a final example, Dunlap et al. (1994) examined the effects of choosing versus not choosing academic assignments on task engagement in two 11-year-old boys who attended a self-contained classroom for students with emotional disabilities. Both boys also engaged in disruptive behaviors (e.g., leaving their seats, talking out, noncompliance). Task engagement increased for both boys during sessions when they could choose the assignment. In addition, as task engagement increased, disruption showed collateral decreases during the choice condition.

Although engagement in functional activities is important in its own right, the study by Dunlap et al. (1994) is particularly relevant because it also demonstrated collateral reductions in challenging behavior. This finding extends the results of an important study that showed that serious problem behaviors (e.g., aggression, self-injury, extreme tantrums) in three children with autism and mental retardation requiring extensive supports was reduced when these children chose the instructional tasks and reinforcers (Dyer, Dunlap, & Winterling, 1990). Mason, McGee, Farmer-Dougan, and Risley (1989) had previously shown that challenging behavior in young children with autism was effectively reduced by allowing the children to choose their own reinforcers. More generally, additional types of evidence (e.g., correlational and quasi-experimental data) have suggested a relationship between increased opportunities for choice making and reduced challenging behavior in people with developmental disabilities (Ip, Szymanski, Johnston-Rodriguez, & Karls, 1994; Kearney, Durand, & Mindell, 1995).

Reductions in challenging behavior, however, may not always occur merely as a function of providing or increasing opportunities for choice making. As noted by Harchik et al. (1993), the reasons for such negative effects remain unclear. As of 1998, there appears to have been no investigation into learner characteristics or environmental variables that may predict the effectiveness of choice making as an intervention for challenging behavior. Even when positive results are obtained, as in the studies by Dunlap et al. (1994) and Dyer et al. (1990), there are several plausible explanations that could account for the observed effects.

## Explaining the Effects of Choice Making on Challenging Behavior

To further the application of choice making in behavioral support, it is important to understand the mechanisms underlying the effects of choice making on challenging behavior. The next four sections consider possible explanations for why the provision of choice-making opportunities may lead to reductions in challenging behavior. In considering these explanations, it is important to bear in mind that they are neither exhaustive nor mutually exclusive. In addition, although these explanations are consistent with the available data, alternative and perhaps more satisfactory accounts may emerge from future studies.

**Preference**   One possible explanation for why the provision of choice-making opportunities may lead to reductions in challenging behavior is related to preference. Depending on the alternatives available, choice may enable the individual to gain access to preferred objects or activities, which, in turn, may lead to increased participation and collateral reductions in challenging behavior. Evidence by Koegel, Dyer, and Bell (1987) supports this interpretation. They examined the influence of preferred versus arbitrarily selected activities on the rate of problematic social avoidance in children with developmental disabilities. Avoidance included attempts by the child to escape from social interactions with an adult by looking or moving away or pushing the adult, for example. Adults interacted with the child in the context of arbitrary (e.g., playing with a toy airplane, talking about sports) or child-preferred activities (e.g., playing with a toy telephone, talking about television shows). The amount of social avoidance was negatively correlated with the amount of time the child spent in preferred activities (Study 1). When arbitrary and child-preferred activities were alternated in an ABAB reversal design, social avoidance was considerably lower during sessions when child-preferred activities were incorporated into the social interaction (Study 2). Prompting the child to engage in child-preferred activities was also effective in reducing social avoidance in community settings (Study 3). These results suggest that the provision of preferred activities rather than choice, per se, may be sufficient to reduce challenging behavior in some instances.

Although choice is clearly related to preference, a second study by Dunlap et al. (1994) showed that choice making has effects on challenging behavior over and above the influence of preference. Specifically, they found increased engagement and reduced disruption when choice was given, even though the child in this study was given access to preferred items during the no-choice condition as well. Nonetheless, the resulting access to preferred objects and activities is no doubt an important component in maintaining choice making. In addition, providing access to preferred objects and activities may be one way to enrich the environment. And enriched environments may help to induce appropriate responses and reduce challenging behavior (Horner, 1980).

**Choice Sets the Occasion for Alternative or Incompatible Responses**  A second possibility is that the environmental effects of making a choice set the occasion for alternative or incompatible behavior (Meyer, Evans, Wuerch, & Brennan, 1985). After choosing a particular leisure item, for example, a child should be more likely to play with that item (Realon et al., 1990). Provided the child has acquired play skills appropriate to that item and assuming that playing with the item is automatically reinforcing (Vollmer, 1994), then access to the toy should set the occasion for appropriate play. In some instances, appropriate play includes topographies that are incompatible with challenging behavior. For example, using both hands to push a toy truck or play a xylophone is incompatible with self-injurious face slapping. Under this hypothesis, challenging behavior is displaced by access to a chosen item, which sets the occasion for the automatic reinforcement of alternative or incompatible responses.

**Choice Making as Functional Communication**  A third possibility is that choice making represents a form of communication that is functionally equivalent to the learner's challenging behavior. By strengthening choice making, challenging behavior is therefore replaced. There is evidence to support the classification of some challenging behavior as unconventional communication (Carr et al., 1994; Durand, 1993). For example, some learners may engage in self-injury or aggression because, in the past, these behaviors have been reinforced by attention, access to preferred objects, or escape from non-preferred activities. When access to these reinforcers requires the mediation of others (i.e., someone must give attention, deliver the preferred object, or remove the nonpreferred activity), then the challenging behavior could be viewed as a form of communication. More specifically, these examples would constitute unconventional mands or requests (Skinner, 1957). As indicated previously, when choice making requires the mediation of others, it also represents a mand or request. Thus, choice making may lead to reductions in challenging behavior because it represents an alternative form of manding that may be more efficient or effective for the individual (Horner & Day, 1991).

**Choice Making Promotes Control and Autonomy** A final possibility for why the provision of choice-making opportunities may lead to increased participation and decreased challenging behavior is related to control and autonomy (Bannerman et al., 1990). Choice making gives the individual a means by which to exert some degree of control over the environment, including influence over others with whom he or she interacts. Choice making also may allow the individual opportunities to express preferences, which could be viewed as fundamental to the concept of personal autonomy. Some writers have speculated that the lack of control and autonomy may contribute to increased levels of challenging behavior among some people with developmental disabilities (Gunnar-Vongnechten, 1978; Harchik et al., 1993). If so, increasing control and autonomy through the provision of choice would function to decrease challenging behavior.

It remains to be determined if attention to each of the aforementioned factors does in fact increase the effectiveness of choice making as an intervention for challenging behavior. It is clear, however, that choice making can have beneficial effects. This alone would seem to warrant the inclusion of choice making in the behavioral support of individuals with developmental disabilities who exhibit challenging behaviors (Dunlap et al., 1994). Of course, the provision of choice-making opportunities may not be all that is required for effective intervention for challenging behavior. Additional research will be needed before the general utility of choice making as an intervention for challenging behavior is known.

Nonetheless, there is sufficient empirical validation of the effects of choice making on challenging behavior to recommend its general use as an antecedent control procedure for the behavioral support of people with developmental disabilities. The next section outlines a model for implementing choice making for behavioral support and reviews studies that illustrate the application of choice making in interventions for challenging behavior among people with developmental disabilities.

## INTERVENTION APPLICATION

There is growing consensus that choice making represents a useful addition to behavioral support plans (Carr et al., 1994; Dunlap et al., 1994). In addition, studies on interventions for challenging behavior are beginning to incorporate opportunities for choice making as part of the intervention plan (e.g., Bambara, Koger, Katzer, & Davenport, 1995; Brown, 1991a; Carr & Carlson, 1993; Taylor, O'Reilly, & Lancioni, 1996). As indicated in this final part of the chapter, these intervention applications offer useful guidelines for incorporating choice making into behavioral support plans.

### A Model for Implementing
### Choice Making for Behavioral Support

Comprehensive curricula focused on enhancing choice making among learners with developmental disabilities have yet to be fully developed (see Gothelf, Crimmins, Mercer, & Finocchiaro, 1994). More specifically, there are few guidelines for implementing choice making as an antecedent control procedure for the prevention of and intervention for challenging behavior. Figure 1 is an initial attempt to delineate a model for implementation that may be useful for this latter purpose. The steps outlined in Figure 1 may assist practitioners in the initial application of choice making in interventions for challenging behavior among people with developmental disabilities. Although some aspects of the recommendations included in this model are based on empirical evidence, it is important to note that the model as a whole has not yet been put to any empirical test. In addition, the four steps are not entirely distinct nor are they meant to be implemented sequentially. It is no doubt highly desirable to implement some steps concurrently with others. In addition, implementing the model outlined in Figure 1 involves a number of issues that need to be considered in greater detail.

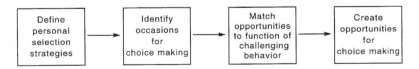

Figure 1.  Proposed steps of a model for the application of choice-making in interventions for challenging behavior.

***Define Personal Selection Strategies*** To enhance choice making, it is important to first define the target of intervention. One goal of the intervention model outlined in Figure 1 is to increase appropriate forms of choice making. To this end, assessments of the type conducted by Sigafoos and Dempsey (1992) could be used to determine if any existing responses within the learner's behavioral repertoire function as valid personal selection strategies for indicating choice and preference. If so, and if these existing strategies are socially acceptable, then they should be strengthened and maintained. Of course, on the one hand, the target behaviors would have to be defined in objective, measurable terms so that others would be able to create opportunities for choice making and identify and respond appropriately to the learners' indications of choice and preference. On the other hand, if the person did not appear to have any existing or appropriate personal selection strategies, then additional interventions would be needed to teach effective choice-making skills.

Procedures for teaching choice-making skills have been described in the literature. For example, Gothelf et al. (1994) outlined 10 steps for teaching choice-making skills to students who are deaf and blind. Each of the 10 steps is based on an associated principle. The principle associated with Step 1, for example, is that choice making should occur in natural environments. Therefore, when teaching children to choose what to eat, instruction would occur in the same locations in which the student would typically eat (e.g., kitchen table, school cafeteria, restaurant). In many respects, the model outlined by Gothelf et al. is similar to procedures (as described in previous sections) that have been used to assess preferences among people with developmental disabilities (e.g., Parsons & Reid, 1990; Sigafoos et al., 1995; Windsor et al., 1994). Gothelf et al., however, also described prompting, shaping, and fading procedures to extend choice making beyond merely selecting one of two offered items. That is, a child might be presented with two foods, one to the left and one to the right. After sampling both items by touching, smelling, and tasting, the child is verbally prompted to "Pick the one you want for lunch." Sampling is repeated if the child attempts to select both items or does not choose. In due course, the child is also prompted to indicate choices in a more sophisticated manner. For example, instead of just reaching for an item, the child might be prompted to make the sign for the chosen item. Over successive opportunities the length of the communicative response may be increased and the amount of prompting systematically decreased, thereby extending the child's choice-making skills. Although field tests indicated that the procedures "worked" (Gothelf et al., 1994, p. 14), more objective data on the effectiveness of these procedures were not presented.

In another study, Kennedy and Haring (1993) presented data on the effectiveness of response prompting and stimulus change for teaching four children with multiple disabilities to use microswitches to make choices. During one phase of the study, the children were given a preferred leisure item (e.g., music, computer game, magazine) and a microswitch. Pressing the microswitch operated a taped message (e.g., "Let's try something new") and resulted in the removal of one item and presentation of a different leisure item. To teach the response, the child was physically prompted to press the microswitch when he or she had stopped playing with the item for 5 seconds. The 5-second pause could be viewed as an indication that the child was finished with the item. Three of the four children showed rapid acquisition of the response, indicating the reinforcing effects of controlling the presentation and withdrawal of leisure items. In addition, the added degree of control was associated with increased engagement in the leisure activity. Thus, when acceptable and valid personal selection strategies are not already part of the individual's repertoire, systematic instructional procedures can be applied to teach effective choice-making skills.

In some cases, challenging behavior may reflect a means of indicating choice and preference. As with other unconventional and idiosyncratic responses, it is imperative to verify the function of challenging behavior before designing an intervention. If the results of such assessments reveal that an individual's challenging behavior functions as a means of indicating choice and preference, then a logical intervention goal would be to replace the challenging behavior by teaching alternative personal selection strategies. For example, if challenging behavior were used to indicate preference for one task over another, then intervention could focus on teaching the individual to select which of several tasks he or she wanted to complete.

Alternative forms of choice making might include vocal, gesture, or graphic mode communication systems. In the past, the form of the communicative response was considered relatively unimportant. What mattered more was the function. Although this is true to some extent, when attempting to replace challenging behavior with functionally equivalent alternative behaviors, the form of the alternative behavior may have an impact on the effectiveness of the intervention. That is, interventions may have greater effect when the alternative response is more efficient than the challenging behavior. Thus, in addition to being readily interpreted and socially acceptable (Butterfield, Arthur,

& Sigafoos, 1995), the alternative response should be easier to perform, and it should produce more consistent reinforcement than the challenging behavior (Horner & Day, 1991).

In other cases, challenging behavior will be maintained by positive, negative, or automatic reinforcement in the form of attention and tangibles, escape and avoidance, and perceptual and sensory consequences, respectively. Intervention for these types of challenging behaviors also might focus on teaching functionally equivalent alternative responses. Again, systematic instructional procedures have been applied to teach such alternative, replacement skills (e.g., Bird, Dores, Moniz, & Robinson, 1989; Carr & Durand, 1985; Durand & Carr, 1991; Horner & Budd, 1985; Sigafoos & Meikle, 1996). Even when challenging behavior does not appear to function as a direct means of indicating choice and preferences, however, the provision of choice-making opportunities, matched to the function of the challenging behavior, may still be a useful addition to comprehensive behavioral support plans. This latter point is expanded in describing the third step of Figure 1.

**Identify Occasions for Choice Making** An important step in developing appropriate personal selection strategies is to identify occasions for choice making. To increase the functional benefits of increased control and autonomy, choice making would ideally come to be controlled by a range of naturally arising discriminative stimuli. Consistent with the procedures outlined by Gothelf et al. (1994), this might be accomplished by making use of the occasions that arise naturally within the individual's daily routine. For example, mealtime sets the occasion for choosing what to eat; the stimuli associated with having just showered set the occasion for choosing what to wear; arriving at work is a discriminative stimulus for selecting a vocational task; and settling into the couch at home may set the occasion for choosing to watch television, to read a book, or to listen to music. When existing personal selection strategies are limited or socially unacceptable, systematic instructional procedures would be implemented in the presence of these naturally arising discriminative stimuli so that the individual learns to make choices and to indicate preferences through more appropriate means.

Effective implementation of choice making as an antecedent control procedure for behavioral support requires identification of the conditions that set the occasion for challenging behavior. The conditions that evoke challenging behavior may provide additional occasions for promoting appropriate choice making skills. Bringing appropriate personal selection strategies for indicating choice and preference under the control of the same stimuli or setting events that currently evoke challenging behavior also may represent an effective antecedent control procedure for reducing challenging behaviors.

Some individuals are more likely to engage in challenging behavior under conditions of low attention (Taylor & Carr, 1992a). This may indicate that occasional reinforcement in the form of attention is responsible for maintaining the problem behaviors. If so, challenging behavior might be replaced by strengthening more appropriate forms of attention seeking. Procedures could be implemented to bring more appropriate forms of attention seeking under the control of discriminative stimuli associated with conditions of low attention. When the person has acquired an appropriate means of recruiting attention, he or she also should have some choice and control over the initiation of social interactions. This added choice and control over social interactions may help to maintain low rates of challenging behavior.

Different strategies would be needed to address challenging behavior related to other conditions. For example, some learners engage in challenging behavior when presented with task demands. For these situations, an opportunity to choose the task, materials, or reinforcers may represent effective antecedent control procedures for reducing challenging behavior. Of course, it is important to provide the opportunity for choice at the right time. This means identifying the specific conditions that control the challenging behavior. Consider the individual who will work at a task for a few minutes and then engage in challenging behavior. Although this behavior is also related to task demands, it is not the presentation of demands that sets the occasion for challenging behavior but rather the length of time worked. In situations such as this, the individual might be given the choice of whether to stop or continue the task. If the opportunity to make this choice is provided just before the time when challenging behavior is likely to occur, the resulting control over the duration of the task would perhaps eliminate the conditions that previously evoked challenging behavior (DePaepe, Reichle, & O'Neill, 1993; Doss & Reichle, 1989).

### Match Opportunities to the Function of Challenging Behavior

Choice making can and should be integrated with the results of a prior functional assessment. The results of functional analyses and assessment procedures often enable the operant function of an individual's challenging behavior to be determined. It is important to conduct such analyses because intervention efficacy is enhanced when interventions are matched to the function of the challenging behavior (Iwata et al., 1994). Figure 2 provides a few examples of how opportunities for choice making might be matched to various functional categories.

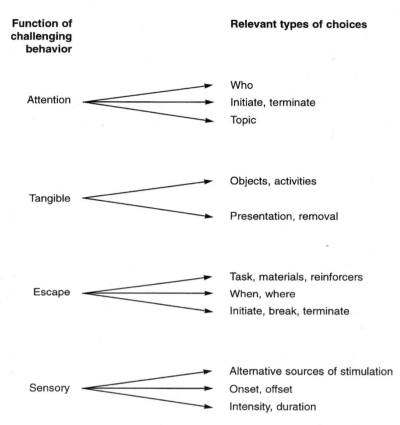

**Function of
challenging
behavior**

**Relevant types of choices**

Attention

Who
Initiate, terminate
Topic

Tangible

Objects, activities

Presentation, removal

Escape

Task, materials, reinforcers
When, where
Initiate, break, terminate

Sensory

Alternative sources of stimulation
Onset, offset
Intensity, duration

Figure 2.   Examples of matches between the type of choice-making opportunity and the function of challenging behavior.

Whether the types of choices illustrated in Figure 2 actually function to reduce challenging behavior is an empirical question that would need to be determined at the individual level. The potential for increasing the effectiveness of interventions based on choice making—by matching the type of choice to the function of the challenging behavior—however, would appear sufficient to warrant additional research.

**Create Opportunities for Choice Making**   As noted in the chapter's opening paragraphs, opportunities for choice making often are limited for people with developmental disabilities. This could be due to several factors, including the lack of effective choice-making skills in the learner's repertoire or the possibility that parents, teachers, staff, and peers do not know how to create effective opportunities for choice making. For learners who lack skills in this area, opportunities will need to be created and structured to promote the acquisition of appropriate personal selection strategies. In addition, increasing the number of opportunities for choice making and incorporating these opportunities into the natural routine will be necessary to ensure functional use, long-term maintenance, and appropriate generalization of existing or newly acquired personal selection strategies. Thus, choice-making interventions will no doubt often need to include a component that focuses on assisting others with the difficult task of creating effective opportunities for choice making.

Learners with disabilities requiring extensive supports or those with limited or negative past experiences in choice making may initially require fairly structured opportunities to benefit from choice-making interventions. Structured opportunities involve systematic presentation of discriminative stimuli, response prompts, and reinforcing consequences. First, discriminative stimuli should be presented that make it clear that a choice response is expected. Sigafoos et al. (1995) suggested that one reason why some individuals with disabilities requiring extensive supports may fail to indicate a choice during a structured opportunity is because the stimuli associated with the task are insufficient to occasion a selection response. Second, procedures to prompt an appropriate choice-making response often will be necessary. Prompting will most likely be required during the early, acquisition stage of intervention when the individual is perhaps unlikely to make a choice independently. Application of verbal or gesture prompts, modeling, and physical assistance will ensure that these individuals experience the consequences of making choices. If prompting is required initially, then systematic fading procedures may be needed to eliminate response prompts and to develop more independent choice making. Third, choice making should be reinforced. That is, for example, the consequences associated with choice making should function to increase the person's degree of control and autonomy in obtaining a selected item or activity. The added control and resulting access to preferred objects and activities are likely to be effective types of reinforcement (Bambara et al., 1995; Dunlap et al., 1994; Koegel et al., 1987)—which lead to acquisition and maintenance of independent choice making.

Procedures encompassing these three components have been developed for creating structured choice-making opportunities. The steps listed in Table 2 represent an attempt to synthesize procedures common to a number of studies that have focused on the provision of structured choice-making opportunities to people with developmental disabilities (e.g., Dattilo, 1986; Dattilo & Mirenda, 1987; Mithaug & Hanawalt, 1978; Parsons & Reid, 1990; Sigafoos et al., 1995). This general approach to the provision of structured choice-making

Table 2. Structured choice-making protocol

1. **Offer**—Offer the person two items spaced some distance apart. A small sample of each item might also be provided initially.
2. **Ask**—While making an offer, ask the person which option he or she would prefer.
3. **Wait**—Wait a reasonable amount of time (e.g., 5, 10, 30 seconds) for the person to make a choice.
4. **Response**—A choice occurs when the person makes any voluntary motion toward one of the items (e.g., points, reaches), maintains physical contact, or looks at one item for at least 3 seconds.
5. **Reinforce**—When a choice occurs, give the person the selected item.
6. **Prompt**—If the person does not make a choice within the allocated time interval, assist him or her to sample each item and then make a second offer. As an alternative, present one item at a time and provide verbal, gesture, model, or physical assistance to prompt selection of the item.

From Sigafoos, J., Roberts, D., Couzens, D., & Kerr M. (1993). Providing opportunities for choice-making and turn-taking to adults with multiple disabilities. *Journal of Developmental and Physical Disabilities, 5*, 300; adapted by permission.

opportunities has proven to be an effective way of assessing preferences and increasing choice making among learners with developmental disabilities.

After demonstrating that even learners with disabilities requiring extensive or pervasive supports were able to participate in and benefit from structured choice-making opportunities (Parsons & Reid, 1990; Sigafoos et al., 1995), efforts have turned to assisting others to create effective opportunities for choice making and to incorporate these into the learner's natural routine. Reid and Parsons (1991), for example, demonstrated that structured choice-making opportunities could be incorporated without undue difficulty into the natural mealtime routines of three adult women with mental retardation requiring pervasive supports. Staff at the residential facility in which these three women lived altered the mealtime routine to include opportunities for the women to make choices (e.g., french fries with or without ketchup). The number of choices provided by staff and the number of choices made by the women increased as a result of incorporating structured choice-making opportunities at mealtimes.

Procedures for teaching staff how to create choice-making opportunities have been developed in conjunction with efforts to incorporate opportunities into natural routines. Table 3 summarizes procedures that have been used for this purpose. For example, Parsons et al. (1993) used in-service training, in vivo classroom training, monitoring, and feedback to teach staff how to incorporate opportunities for choice making at breaktime in four classrooms for adults with disabilities requiring extensive supports. Sigafoos et al. (1993) also used in-service training consisting of verbal and written explanation,

Table 3. Procedures for teaching staff how to provide structured choice-making opportunities

**In-service training**
- Use verbal explanations of the importance of choice making and rationale for increasing choice making.
- Make written and verbal descriptions of generic steps involved in providing opportunities for structured choice making (see Table 2).
- Identify routines into which opportunities for choice making could be incorporated.
- Specify how generic steps would be applied in identified routines.

**In vivo training**
- Demonstrate procedures for providing structured choice-making opportunities (e.g., demonstrate steps outlined in Table 2).
- Have staff practice procedures that were demonstrated, and provide feedback.
- Continue practice until procedures are implemented correctly.

**Feedback**
- Implementation of procedures is monitored on a regular basis.
- Feedback is provided to staff during monitoring session.
- Procedures are modified and extended in response to learner's changing needs.
- Reinforcement is provided to maintain implementation.

modeling, and feedback to teach staff how to provide opportunities for choice making to five young adults with multiple disabilities during a snack routine. In both studies, the training procedures were effective in increasing the number of opportunities provided by staff. In addition, the number of choices made by the participants also increased as they received more opportunities.

In working to teach family members, staff, or peers how to create opportunities for choice making, it is important to consider ecological factors and personal values that may influence the types of choices that could be increased. In some families, for example, it may be too disruptive to allow choices as to when or what to eat because the parents operate with set mealtimes and menus. Thus even if challenging behaviors appeared to be related to lack of choice over when and where to eat, it may not be acceptable to the family to incorporate such choices into their existing routine. For these reasons, procedures of the type outlined in Table 3 need to allow for input from parents, staff, and peers as to the types of choices that could be accommodated.

Although the exact nature and types of choices may be constrained by certain ecological considerations, systematic implementation of the curriculum model outlined here may represent a starting point for increasing choice making among people with developmental disabilities. By carefully defining appropriate personal selection strategies, identifying occasions for choice making, matching opportunities to the function of the challenging behavior, and creating opportunities for choice making, more effective behavioral support plans may result.

## Examples of Incorporating Choice Making into Behavioral Support Plans

Components of the choice-making curriculum outlined in the previous section have been incorporated into studies focused on the intervention for challenging behavior in people with developmental disabilities. Carr and Carlson (1993) included choice making as part of multicomponent interventions for three young men with autism who had histories of challenging behavior (e.g., aggression, screaming, tantrums, self-injury) when shopping for groceries in supermarkets. In relation to the shopping task analysis, staff identified antecedents that appeared to evoke challenging behavior. Hypotheses as to the possible functions of the challenging behaviors were generated, and intervention strategies based on these hypotheses were developed for those antecedent conditions that consistently evoked challenging behavior.

Some of these intervention strategies focused on creating opportunities for choice. For example, one participant would enter the store but then attempt to exit. If prevented from leaving the store, he would engage in challenging behavior. It was hypothesized that challenging behavior in this situation represented an attempt to escape from the task. The intervention strategy for this particular antecedent condition involved giving the learner choice over the initial activity. Before entering the store, he was asked what he would like to do first. The options included looking at magazines or browsing the shelves containing pens and pencils—two activities he seemed to enjoy. For some of the other conditions that set the occasion for challenging behavior (e.g., learner attempted to obtain prohibited item, learner asked to move on to another step of the task), different choice options were created and matched to the hypothesized function of the challenging behavior (e.g., learner could choose from among some alternative items, learner could choose the next step). After identifying conditions that set the occasion for problem behavior, opportunities for choice making were created and incorporated into the grocery shopping task analysis. In addition, choice opportunities were matched to the hypothesized function of the challenging behavior. The intervention led to increased participation and reduced challenging behavior. By the end of the study, each participant completed lengthy shopping excursions on a regular basis with only rare instances of challenging behavior.

Of course, because choice making was only one of the five strategies included in the multicomponent intervention, it is difficult to ascertain the precise contribution that the provision of choice made to the overall effectiveness of the intervention package. Nonetheless, because the specific situations in which choice making were used no longer evoked challenging behavior on a consistent basis, incorporating choice into these conditions was likely a functional component of the intervention package.

Taylor et al. (1996) also included choice opportunities within a multicomponent intervention for a 5-year-old boy with autism who engaged in aggression, screaming, and self-injury. Functional assessments indicated that these challenging behaviors were most likely to occur when instructional demands were made, which suggested an escape function. Following a baseline phase, the teacher was taught to present the task demands after a sequence of less-aversive requests (e.g., "Get the ball. Let's go for a walk") that the child was likely to follow. During the target task, the boy was informed of the required behavior and the reinforcers that would follow. He also received specific verbal praise ("Good boy. You are sitting and playing with the blocks"). The final intervention component involved two types of choice opportunities. First, he was allowed to choose the target activity (e.g., puzzle versus blocks). Second, if he showed inappropriate behavior (e.g., standing on the table), he was prompted to choose an alternative behavior (e.g., "You can't stand on the table, but you can play with the puzzle or blocks"). As the teacher increased her use of these strategies, correct responding to the task demands increased from zero to the 70%–80% level, whereas challenging behavior decreased to near-zero levels. Again, given the multifaceted nature of the intervention, it is difficult to isolate the effects of including choice opportunities. The opportunity to select the task, however, was consistent with the hypothesized function (i.e., escape from task demands) of the child's challenging behavior (see Figure 2). An intriguing and innovative element of this study was the provision of opportunities to choose alternative responses to inappropriate behaviors. Because two types of choices were implemented concurrently, however, the effects of this latter type of choice opportunity on challenging behavior cannot be determined without further research.

Bambara et al. (1995) incorporated opportunities for choice into various household chores after a functional analysis suggested that the lack of choice and control was contributing to reduced participation and increased yelling, profanity, and aggression in a 50-year-old man with intellectual disability requiring extensive supports. Functional analyses across a variety of household tasks (e.g., making juice, setting the table, taking out the trash) showed that *direct* (e.g., "Al, you need to make the juice now") and *indirect* (e.g., "Al, would you make the juice now?") instructions were associated with little or no task initiations and high rates of challenging behavior. In contrast, *choice* (e.g., "Would you like to make juice or set the table?") and *conditional choice* (e.g., "Al, if you feel like it, make the juice please") produced high rates of task initiations and no instances of challenging behavior. Bambara et al. (1995) hypothesized that it was the lack of choice and control that evoked challenging behavior, not the tasks, per se. This hypothesis was supported by the results of a subsequent intervention in the context of vacuuming, dusting, and preparing snacks. Various types of choices (e.g., choosing which room to vacuum, selecting which outlet to plug the vacuum cleaner into, deciding which area to start vacuuming) were incorporated into the tasks. When these types of choices were allowed, participation increased and challenging behavior decreased.

The use of numerous and various choice points within natural routines is also supported by case descriptions supplied by Brown (1991a). Although some individuals may prefer a structured daily schedule, others may react with challenging behavior. Brown (1991a), therefore, recommended creating opportunities for choice and control with respect to the time, content, and sequence of activities within the daily schedule. These manipulations were proposed as one way of preventing challenging behavior. For example, one case involved Bob, a young adult male with autism who engaged in self-injurious head banging. Self-injury was observed when he was prompted to initiate activities (e.g., brush teeth, shower, clean room), especially if the task demand interrupted his ritualistic arrangement of objects in the environment. Similar to Al in the Bambara et al. (1995) study, it appeared that Bob did not like being told what to do. Bob's intervention allowed him to choose what activities to perform and when. That is, choice was provided in the time and content dimensions of his daily schedule. Brown (1991a) reported that these types of antecedent control procedures were effective in reducing challenging behavior among several individuals.

As these studies indicate, opportunities for choice have been incorporated into behavioral support plans for individuals with developmental disabilities. Although often only one of several components in a multifaceted intervention package, the provision of choice-making opportunities appeared to be functional and effective. Creating opportunities for choice and incorporating these into situations that evoke challenging behavior would appear to represent an effective antecedent control procedure in interventions for challenging behavior in people with developmental disabilities. The effectiveness of this strategy may depend on matching the type of choice opportunity to the function of the challenging behavior, creating opportunities in those situations that evoke challenging behavior, and ensuring that more appropriate personal selection strategies occur and are reinforced in those situations, so as to preempt and replace challenging behavior.

## CONCLUSIONS

This chapter has focused on issues related to choice making and the strategies that people with developmental disabilities may use to indicate choice and preference. Several conclusions can be made from this review:

- Compared with people without disabilities, people with developmental disabilities often have severely restricted choice-making skills. They may also have limited opportunities to make choices, gain access to preferred objects and activities, and exert control.
- Limited choice reduces a person's overall quality of life by restricting his or her participation in functional activities and social interactions. In addition, limited choice may result in learned helplessness and increased challenging behavior. For some individuals, challenging behavior may represent personal selection strategies for indicating choice and preference.
- The opportunity for choice and control can have powerful and predictable effects on participation and challenging behavior. In general, increased opportunity for choice and control leads to increased participation and decreased challenging behavior.
- People with developmental disabilities can be taught appropriate personal selection strategies for indicating choice and preference.
- The provision of opportunities to make choices, indicate preferences, and exert control can be effective antecedent control procedures in interventions for challenging behavior among people with developmental disabilities.

Enhancing choice is important in its own right. Increasing opportunities for choice and developing appropriate skills in this area may give people with developmental disabilities greater control and autonomy in their lives. Unfortunately, many people with developmental disabilities have restricted opportunities in numerous areas due to serious challenging behavior. For these individuals, it is also important, and indeed critical, to provide effective intervention focused on reducing serious challenging behaviors (Van Houten et al., 1988).

There has been some suggestion that habilitative programs in general, and behavioral approaches to the intervention for challenging behaviors in particular, are incompatible with the enhancement of choice and autonomy (Bannerman et al., 1990; Lovett, 1996). This is not the case. Choice making is operant behavior and can be conceptualized in behavioral terms. The reasons behind the often limited choice in the lives of people with developmental disabilities may be largely explained in terms of behavior deficits: People with developmental disabilities often lack appropriate choice-making skills, and others with whom they interact may lack the skills needed to create effective opportunities for choice making. These impairments can be overcome by systematic application of behavioral procedures. The strategies for enhancing choice outlined in this chapter show that behavioral interventions and personal control and autonomy are compatible. These and the other types of lifestyle enhancing strategies described in this book will no doubt become increasingly important in the behavioral support of people with developmental disabilities.

## REFERENCES

Bambara, L.M., Ager, C., & Koger, F. (1994). The effects of choice and preference on the work performance of adults with severe disabilities. *Journal of Applied Behavior Analysis, 27,* 555–556.

Bambara, L.M., Koger, F., Katzer, T., & Davenport, T.A. (1995). Embedding choice in the context of daily routines: An experimental case study. *Journal of The Association for Persons with Severe Handicaps, 20,* 185–195.

Bannerman, D.J., Sheldon, J.B., Sherman, J.A., & Harchik, A.E. (1990). Balancing the right to habilitation with the right to personal liberties. *Journal of Applied Behavior Analysis, 23,* 79–89.

Belfiore, P.J., Browder, D.M., & Mace, C. (1994). Assessing choice-making and preference in adults with profound mental retardation across community and center-based settings. *Journal of Behavioral Education, 4,* 217–225.

Bird, F., Dores, P.A., Moniz, D., & Robinson, J. (1989). Reducing severe aggression and self-injurious behaviors with functional communication training. *American Journal on Mental Retardation, 94,* 37–48.

Brown, F. (1991a). Creative daily scheduling: A nonintrusive approach to challenging behaviors in community residents. *Journal of The Association for Persons with Severe Handicaps, 16,* 75–84.

Brown, F. (1991b, November). *Teaching service providers to increase choice opportunities within the daily routine.* Paper presented at the annual meeting of The Association for Persons with Severe Handicaps, Washington, DC.

Brown, F., Belz, P., Corsi, L., & Wenig, B. (1993). Choice diversity for people with severe disabilities. *Education and Training in Mental Retardation, 28,* 318–326.

Brown, R.I., Bayer, M.B., & Brown, P.M. (1992). *Empowerment and developmental handicaps: Choices and quality of life.* Toronto: Captus Press.

Butterfield, N., Arthur, M., & Sigafoos, J. (1995). *Partners in everyday communicative exchanges.* Sydney: MacLennan and Petty.

Carr, E.G. (1977). The motivation of self-injurious behavior: A review of some hypotheses. *Psychological Bulletin, 84,* 800–816.

Carr, E.G., & Carlson, J.I. (1993). Reduction of severe behavior problems in the community using a multicomponent treatment approach. *Journal of Applied Behavior Analysis, 26,* 157–172.

Carr, E.G., & Durand, V.M. (1985). Reducing behavior problems through functional communication training. *Journal of Applied Behavior Analysis, 18,* 111–126.

Carr, E.G., Levin, L., McConnachie, G., Carlson, J.I., Kemp, D.C., & Smith, C.E. (1994). *Communication-based intervention for problem behavior: A user's guide for producing positive change.* Baltimore: Paul H. Brookes Publishing Co.

Carr, E.G., & Newsom, C.D. (1985). Demand-related tantrums: Conceptualization and treatment. *Behavior Modification, 9,* 403–426.

Carr, E.G., Newsom, C.D., & Binkoff, J.A. (1980). Escape as a factor in the aggressive behavior of two retarded children. *Journal of Applied Behavior Analysis, 13,* 101–117.

Carr, E.G., & Taylor, J.C. (1991). The effects of severe behavior problems in children on the teaching behavior of adults. *Journal of Applied Behavior Analysis, 24,* 523–535.

Cipani, E.C., & Spooner, F. (Eds.). (1994). *Curricular and instructional approaches for persons with severe disabilities.* Needham Heights, MA: Allyn & Bacon.

Cummins, R.A. (1991). The Comprehensive Quality of Life Scale—Intellectual Disability: An instrument under development. *Australia and New Zealand Journal of Developmental Disabilities, 17,* 259–264.

Dattilo, J. (1986). Computerized assessment of preferences for severely handicapped individuals. *Journal of Applied Behavior Analysis, 19,* 445–448.

Dattilo, J., & Mirenda, P. (1987). An application of a leisure preference assessment protocol for persons with severe handicaps. *Journal of The Association for Persons with Severe Handicaps, 12,* 306–311.

Dattilo, J., & Rusch, F.R. (1985). Effects of choice on leisure participation for persons with severe handicaps. *Journal of The Association for Persons with Severe Handicaps, 10,* 194–199.

DePaepe, P., Reichle, J., & O'Neill, R. (1993). Applying general-case instructional strategies when teaching communicative alternatives to challenging behavior. In J. Reichle & D.P. Wacker (Eds.), *Communication and language intervention series: Vol. 3. Communicative alternatives to challenging behavior: Integrating functional assessment and intervention strategies* (pp. 237–262). Baltimore: Paul H. Brookes Publishing Co.

Doss, S., & Reichle, J. (1989). Establishing communicative alternatives to the emission of socially motivated excess behavior: A review. *Journal of The Association for Persons with Severe Handicaps, 14,* 101–112.

Dunlap, G., DePerczel, M., Clarke, S., Wilson, D., Wright, S., White, R., & Gomez, A. (1994). Choice making to promote adaptive behavior for students with emotional and behavioral challenges. *Journal of Applied Behavior Analysis, 27,* 505–518.

Dunst, C.J., Cushing, P.J., & Vance, S.D. (1985). Response-contingent learning in profoundly handicapped infants: A social systems perspective. *Analysis and Intervention in Developmental Disabilities, 5,* 33–47.

Durand, V.M. (1993). Problem behavior as communication. *Behaviour Change, 10,* 197–126.

Durand, V.M., & Carr, E.G. (1991). Functional communication training to reduce challenging behavior: Maintenance and application in new settings. *Journal of Applied Behavior Analysis, 24,* 251–264.

Dyer, K., Dunlap, G., & Winterling, V. (1990). Effects of choice making on the serious problem behaviors of students with severe handicaps. *Journal of Applied Behavior Analysis, 23*, 515–524.

Forzano, L.B., & Logue, A.W. (1995). Self-control and impulsiveness in children and adults: Effects of food preferences. *Journal of the Experimental Analysis of Behavior, 64*, 33–46.

Fraser, B.A., Hensinger, R.N., & Phelps, J.A. (1990). *Physical management of multiple handicaps: A professional's guide* (2nd ed.). Baltimore: Paul H. Brookes Publishing Co.

Gothelf, C.R., Crimmins, D.B., Mercer, C.A., & Finocchiaro, P.A. (1994). Teaching choice-making skills to students who are deaf-blind. *Teaching Exceptional Children, 26*(4), 13–15.

Green, C.W., Reid, D.H., White, L.K., Halford, R.C., Brittain, D.P., & Gardner, S.M. (1988). Identifying reinforcers for persons with profound handicaps: Staff opinion versus systematic assessment of preferences. *Journal of Applied Behavior Analysis, 21*, 31–43.

Guess, D., Benson, H.A., & Siegel-Causey, E. (1985). Concepts and issues related to choice-making and autonomy among persons with severe disabilities. *Journal of The Association for Persons with Severe Handicaps, 10*, 79–86.

Gunnar-Vongnechten, M.R. (1978). Changing a frightening toy into a pleasant toy by allowing the infant to control its actions. *Developmental Psychology, 14*, 157–162.

Halle, J.W. (1995). Innovations in choice-making research: An editorial introduction. *Journal of The Association for Persons with Severe Handicaps, 20*, 173–174.

Harchik, A.E., Sherman, J.A., Sheldon, J.B., & Bannerman, D.J. (1993). Choice and control: New opportunities for people with developmental disabilities. *Annals of Clinical Psychiatry, 5*, 151–162.

Hastings, R.P., & Remington, B. (1994a). Rules of engagement: Towards an analysis of staff responses to challenging behavior. *Research in Developmental Disabilities, 15*, 279–298.

Hastings, R.P., & Remington, B. (1994b). Staff behaviour and its implications for people with learning disabilities and challenging behaviours. *British Journal of Clinical Psychology, 33*, 423–438.

Hastings, R.P., Remington, B., & Hall, M. (1995). Adults' responses to self-injurious behavior: An experimental analysis using a computer-simulation paradigm. *Behavior Modification, 19*, 425–450.

Herrnstein, R.J. (1961). Relative and absolute strength of response as a function of frequency of reinforcement. *Journal of the Experimental Analysis of Behavior, 4*, 267–272.

Horner, R.D. (1980). The effects of an environmental "enrichment" program on the behavior of institutionalized profoundly retarded children. *Journal of Applied Behavior Analysis, 13*, 473–491.

Horner, R.H., & Budd, C.M. (1985). Acquisition of manual sign use: Collateral reduction of maladaptive behavior, and factors limiting generalization. *Education and Training of the Mentally Retarded, 20*, 39–47.

Horner, R.H., & Day, H.M. (1991). The effects of response efficiency on functionally equivalent competing behaviors. *Journal of Applied Behavior Analysis, 24*, 719–732.

Horner, R.H., Dunlap, G., Koegel, R.L., Carr, E.G., Sailor, W., Anderson, J., Albin, R.W., & O'Neill, R.E. (1990). Toward a technology of "nonaversive" behavioral support. *Journal of The Association for Persons with Severe Handicaps, 15,* 125–132.

Houghton, J., Bronicki, G.J., & Guess, D. (1987). Opportunities to express preferences and make choices among students with severe disabilities in classroom settings. *Journal of The Association for Persons with Severe Handicaps, 12,* 18–27.

Ip, S.M.V., Szymanski, E.M., Johnston-Rodriguez, S., & Karls, S.F. (1994). Effects of staff implementation of a choice program on challenging behaviors in persons with developmental disabilities. *Rehabilitation Counseling Bulletin, 37,* 347–357.

Iwata, B.A., Dorsey, M.F., Slifer, K.J., Bauman, K.E., & Richman, G.S. (1982). Toward a functional analysis of self-injury. *Analysis and Intervention in Developmental Disability, 2,* 3–20.

Iwata, B.A., Pace, G.M., Dorsey, M.F., Zarcone, J.R., Vollmer, T.R., Smith, R.G., Rodgers, T.A., Lerman, D.C., Shore, B.A., Mazaleski, J.L., Goh, H.L., Cowdery, G.E., Kalsher, M.J., McCosh, K.C., & Willis, K.D. (1994). The functions of self-injurious behavior: An experimental-epidemiological analysis. *Journal of Applied Behavior Analysis, 27,* 215–240.

Jenkinson, J., & Nelms, R. (1994). Patterns of decision-making behaviour by people with intellectual disability: An exploratory study. *Australia and New Zealand Journal of Developmental Disabilities, 19,* 99–109.

Kearney, C.A., Durand, V.M., & Mindell, J.A. (1995). It's not where but how you live: Choice and adaptive/maladaptive behavior in persons with severe handicaps. *Journal of Developmental and Physical Disabilities, 7,* 11–24.

Kennedy, G.H., & Haring, T.G. (1993). Teaching choice making during social interactions to students with profound multiple disabilities. *Journal of Applied Behavior Analysis, 26,* 63–76.

Kishi, G., Teelucksingh, B., Zollers, N., Park-Lee, S., & Meyer, L. (1988). Daily decision making in community residences: A social comparison of adults with and without mental retardation. *American Journal on Mental Retardation, 92,* 430–435.

Koegel, R.L., Dyer, K., & Bell, L.K. (1987). The influence of child-preferred activities on autistic children's social behavior. *Journal of Applied Behavior Analysis, 20,* 243–252.

Lovett, H. (1996). *Learning to listen: Positive approaches and people with difficult behavior.* Baltimore: Paul H. Brookes Publishing Co.

Mace, F.C. (1994). Basic research needed for stimulating the development of behavioral technologies. *Journal of the Experimental Analysis of Behavior, 61,* 529–550.

Mason, S.A., McGee, G.G., Farmer-Dougan, V., & Risley, T.R. (1989). A practical strategy for ongoing reinforcer assessment. *Journal of Applied Behavior Analysis, 22,* 171–179.

Meyer, L.H., Evans, I.M., Wuerch, B.B., & Brennan, J.M. (1985). Monitoring the collateral effects of leisure skill instruction: A case study in multiple-baseline methodology. *Behavior Research and Therapy, 23,* 127–138.

Mithaug, D.E., & Hanawalt, D.A. (1978). The validation of procedures to assess prevocational task preferences in retarded adults. *Journal of Applied Behavior Analysis, 11,* 153–162.

Mithaug, D.E., & Mar, D.K. (1980). The relation between choosing and working prevocational tasks in two severely retarded young adults. *Journal of Applied Behavior Analysis, 13,* 177–182.

Orelove, F.P., & Sobsey, D. (Eds.). (1991). *Educating children with multiple disabilities: A transdisciplinary approach* (2nd ed.). Baltimore: Paul H. Brookes Publishing Co.

Pace, G.M., Ivancic, M.T., Edwards, G.L., Iwata, B.A., & Page, T.J. (1985). Assessment of stimulus preference and reinforcer value with profoundly retarded individuals. *Journal of Applied Behavior Analysis, 18,* 249–255.

Paclawskyj, T.R., & Vollmer, T.R. (1995). Reinforcer assessment for children with developmental disabilities and visual impairment. *Journal of Applied Behavior Analysis, 28,* 219–224.

Parmenter, T.R. (1994). Quality of life as a concept and measurable entity. *Social Indicators Research, 33,* 9–46.

Parmenter, T.R., Briggs, L., & Sullivan, R. (1991). Quality of life: Intellectual disabilities and community living. *Evaluation Journal of Australia, 3,* 12–25.

Parsons, M.B., McCarn, J.E., & Reid, D.H. (1993). Evaluating and increasing meal-related choices throughout a service setting for people with severe disabilities. *Journal of The Association for Persons with Severe Handicaps, 18,* 253–260.

Parsons, M.B., & Reid, D.H. (1990). Assessing food preferences among persons with profound mental retardation: Providing opportunities to make choices. *Journal of Applied Behavior Analysis, 23,* 183–195.

Parsons, M.B., Reid, D.H., Reynolds, J., & Bumgarner, M. (1990). Effects of chosen versus assigned jobs on the work performance of persons with severe handicaps. *Journal of Applied Behavior Analysis, 23,* 253–258.

Piazza, C.C., Fisher, W.W., Hagopian, L.P., Bowman, L.G., & Toole, L. (1996). Using a choice assessment to predict reinforcer effectiveness. *Journal of Applied Behavior Analysis, 29,* 1–9.

Pierce, W.D., & Epling, W.F. (1995). The applied importance of research on the matching law. *Journal of Applied Behavior Analysis, 28,* 237–241.

Raphael, D., Brown, I., Renwick, R., & Rootman, I. (1996). Assessing quality of life of persons with developmental disabilities: Description of a new model, measuring instruments, and initial findings. *International Journal of Disability, Development and Education, 43,* 25–42.

Realon, R.E., Favell, J.E., & Lowerre, A. (1990). The effects of making choices on engagement levels with persons who are profoundly multiply handicapped. *Education and Training in Mental Retardation, 25,* 299–305.

Reid, D.H., & Parsons, M.B. (1991). Making choice a routine part of mealtimes for persons with profound mental retardation. *Behavioral Residential Treatment, 6,* 249–261.

Schalock, R.L. (1993). Viewing quality of life in the larger context. *Australia and New Zealand Journal of Developmental Disabilities, 18,* 201–208.

Shaddock, A.J., Zilber, D., Guggenheimer, S., Dowse, L., Bennett, M., & Browne, F. (1993). Opportunities for choice in day programs for adults with severe intellectual disabilities. *Australasian Journal of Special Education, 17,* 48–56.

Shevin, M., & Klein, N.K. (1984). The importance of choice-making skills for students with severe disabilities. *Journal of The Association for Persons with Severe Handicaps, 9,* 159–166.

Sigafoos, J., & Dempsey, R. (1992). Assessing choice making among children with multiple disabilities. *Journal of Applied Behavior Analysis, 25,* 747–755.

Sigafoos, J., Laurie, S., & Pennell, D. (1995). Preliminary assessment of choice making among children with Rett syndrome. *Journal of The Association for Persons with Severe Handicaps, 20,* 175–184.

Sigafoos, J., & Meikle, B. (1996). Functional communication training for the treatment of multiply determined challenging behavior in two boys with autism. *Behavior Modification, 20,* 60–84.

Sigafoos, J., Reichle, J., & Light-Shriner, C. (1994). Distinguishing between socially and nonsocially motivated challenging behavior: Implications for the selection of intervention strategies. In M.F. Hayden & B.H. Abery (Eds.), *Challenges for a service system in transition: Ensuring quality community experiences for persons with developmental disabilities* (pp. 147–169). Baltimore: Paul H. Brookes Publishing Co.

Sigafoos, J., Roberts, D., Couzens, D., & Kerr, M. (1993). Providing opportunities for choice-making and turn-taking to adults with multiple disabilities. *Journal of Developmental and Physical Disabilities, 5,* 297–310.

Skinner, B.F. (1957). *Verbal behavior.* New York: Appleton-Century-Crofts.

Stancliffe, R.J. (1995). Assessing opportunities for choice-making: A comparison of self- and staff reports. *American Journal on Mental Retardation, 99,* 418–429.

Stokes, T., Osnes, P.G., & DaVerne, K.C. (1993). Communicative correspondence and mediated generalization. In J. Reichle & D.P. Wacker (Eds.), *Communication and language intervention series: Vol. 3. Communicative alternatives to challenging behavior: Integrating functional assessment and intervention strategies* (pp. 299–315). Baltimore: Paul H. Brookes Publishing Co.

Taylor, I., O'Reilly, M., & Lancioni, G. (1996). An evaluation of an ongoing consultation model to train teachers to treat challenging behaviour. *International Journal of Disability, Development and Education, 43,* 203–218.

Taylor, J.C., & Carr, E.G. (1992a). Severe problem behaviors related to social interaction I: Attention seeking and social avoidance. *Behavior Modification, 16,* 305–335.

Taylor, J.C., & Carr, E.G. (1992b). Severe problem behaviors related to social interaction II: A systems analysis. *Behavior Modification, 16,* 336–371.

Van Houten, R., Axelrod, S., Bailey, J.S., Favell, J.E., Foxx, R.M., Iwata, B.A., & Lovaas, O.I. (1988). The right to effective behavioral treatment. *The Behavior Analyst, 11,* 111–114.

Vaughn, B., & Horner, R.H. (1995). Effects of concrete versus verbal choice systems on problem behavior. *Augmentative and Alternative Communication, 11,* 89–92.

Vollmer, T.R. (1994). The concept of automatic reinforcement: Implications for behavioral research in developmental disabilities. *Research in Developmental Disabilities, 15,* 187–207.

Whitaker, S. (1989). Quality of life and people with a very profound handicap. *British Journal of Mental Subnormality, 35,* 3–7.

Wieseler, N.A., Hanson, R.H., Chamberlain, T.P., & Thompson, T. (1985). Functional taxonomy of stereotypic and self-injurious behavior. *Mental Retardation, 23,* 230–234.

Wilson, E. (1992). Contemporary issues in choice making for people with a learning disability. *Mental Handicap, 20,* 31–33.

Windsor, J., Piche, L.M., & Locke, P.A. (1994). Preference testing: A comparison of two presentation methods. *Research in Developmental Disabilities, 15,* 439–455.

# ~ *10* ~

## *Correspondence Training and Verbal Mediation*

### Freddy A. Paniagua

The relationship between what an individual says that he or she will do and what he or she actually does or between what he or she does and later says that he or she has done is termed *correspondence between verbal and nonverbal behavior* (Israel, 1978; Paniagua, 1990a). Basic research in this area suggests that correspondence training procedures can produce rapid changes in nonverbal (target) behavior by strengthening the expected verbal–nonverbal relationship (Baer, Williams, Osnes, & Stokes, 1984; Israel, 1973; Israel & O'Leary, 1973; Paniagua & Baer, 1982; Paniagua, Stella, Holt, Baer, & Etzel, 1982; Ribeiro, 1989; Risley & Hart, 1968; Williams & Stokes, 1982). The clinical utility of verbal–nonverbal correspondence training also has been documented (Baer, Osnes, & Stokes, 1983; Finney, Russo, & Cataldo, 1982; Jewett & Clark, 1979; Keogh, Burgio, Whitman, & Johnson, 1983; Paniagua, 1985, 1987; Paniagua, Pumariega, & Black, 1988; Whitman, Scibak, Butler, Richter, & Johnson, 1982).

The general goals of correspondence training procedures are to develop nonverbal behaviors, to increase current nonverbal behaviors, or to decrease problematic nonverbal behaviors through direct reinforcement of verbal–nonverbal correspondences. These goals often are achieved under controlled conditions, in which the reinforcer is programmed on one or more behaviors in the verbal–nonverbal chain (Paniagua & Baer, 1982). The most important goal of correspondence training procedures, however, is to establish verbal behavior as an antecedent event for the occurrence of nonverbal behavior (Paniagua, 1997; Ward & Stare, 1990). The fulfillment of this goal not only indicates that language is a mediator of corresponding nonverbal behavior (Stokes & Baer, 1977) but also provides convincing evidence regarding the social validity or external validity of intervention effects previously established under controlled conditions (Mook, 1992; Wolf, 1978). To put it simply, verbal–nonverbal correspondence training helps to determine whether behavior changes found under a controlled condition also can be replicated in the "real world."

The literature identifies five techniques used to establish the function of verbal behavior as behavioral antecedents in the development of prosocial behaviors and in the reduction of problematic behaviors: 1) Reinforcement of Do-Report Correspondence, 2) Reinforcement of Report-Do Correspondence, 3) Reinforcement Set-up on Reports, 4) Immediate Reinforcement of Intermediate Behaviors (IBs), and 5) Reinforcement Set-up on IBs (Paniagua, 1990a). During the introduction of verbal–nonverbal correspondence training techniques, participants earn reinforcers if they behave (i.e., the "do" in the Do-Report or Report-Do Correspondence) consistently with their reports (i.e., the "report" in the Do-Report or Report-Do Correspondence) about past or future behaviors. Verbal–nonverbal relationships demonstrated during this intervention phase are called *contingency-governed behaviors* (Barkley, 1987; Paniagua, 1987; Skinner, 1969). In this phase of the intervention plan, individuals learn that some rules or instructions given by the clinician serve as *antecedent events* for expected verbal–nonverbal relationships rather than rules that were already formulated by the individual.

For example, a rule selected by the clinician would be, "You can say and do what you elect to say and do, but if you want the reinforcer, you have to say and do what I expect" (e.g., Paniagua, 1987; Risley & Hart, 1968). A rule in which the verbal–nonverbal relationship is selected by the participant would be, "If I say that I want to do X (or not to do X), then I would have to do it (or not do it) if I want the reinforcer" (e.g., Paniagua & Baer, 1982). During the contingency-governed behavior phase (verbal–nonverbal relationships leading to reinforcement), these rules are affected by the same contingency of reinforcement that controls the verbal–nonverbal correspondence relationships. Eventually, these rules take the form of verbalizations mediating nonverbal behaviors (Stokes & Baer, 1977). When rules take this form, usually during the generalization and maintenance phases, the resulting process is termed *rule-governed behavior*, in which rules involving discriminated verbal–nonverbal correspondences are transformed into generalized and maintained correspondence rules (e.g., Deacon & Konarski, 1987; Guevremont, Osnes, & Stokes, 1986a, 1986b; Paniagua & Black, 1990; Ward & Stare,

1990). This chapter describes the contingency- and rule-governed behavioral functions of verbal–nonverbal correspondence as methods of antecedent control over challenging behaviors and illustrates the clinical aspects of the techniques with emphasis on the reduction of problematic behaviors and the development of prosocial behaviors.

## SELECTION OF BEHAVIORS

Before correspondence training techniques are introduced, it is crucial to determine what exactly individuals receiving this training are expected to achieve during the contingency-governed behavior phase of the intervention plan and whether what is learned during this phase could be generalized and/or maintained during the rule-governed phase of the intervention. Prior to commencing intervention, clinicians and target participants should reach agreement with regard to the expected behavior chain necessary to demonstrate a match between verbal behavior and its corresponding nonverbal behavior.

In verbal–nonverbal correspondence training, the behavior chain includes four classes of behaviors (Paniagua & Baer, 1982). The first class emphasizes behaviors that *precede* both the verbal and the nonverbal behavior in a Preceding-Do-Report sequence. For example, preceding behaviors necessary to assist a child with completing a set of math problems would be to train the child to ask for books and pencils, which are necessary to achieve this task; to bring these materials to his or her table; and to sit down to work on this particular task.

The second class involves the *target verbal behavior,* which is a report about the performance of either future or past nonverbal behaviors. In the previous example, the child would display the preceding behaviors and, after the completion of the task, would make a report about past behavior (e.g., "I completed 10 math problems in 15 minutes") in a Preceding-Do-Report sequence. In the same example, preceding behaviors would be followed by a report about future behaviors (e.g., "I'll complete. . .") in a Preceding-Report-Do sequence.

The third class of behaviors in verbal–nonverbal correspondence training is termed *intermediate behaviors.* These are behaviors that occur between a report about future behaviors and corresponding nonverbal behaviors in a Report-IB-Do sequence. When a behavior is to be managed by contingencies operating only on subsequent reports about that behavior, the essential prior activities are called *preceding behaviors.* These behaviors would function as examples of IBs when a behavior is to be managed relative to a report about future behavior in a Report-Do sequence. Therefore, labeling a behavior as preceding versus intermediate depends on the position of this particular behavior in the verbal–nonverbal chain. For example, in the previous example of the child who asks for materials (e.g., books) and brings materials to the table, the display of in-seat behaviors would be termed *IBs* if they are scheduled immediately after the report to perform the task. In this specific case, the child would make a report (e.g., "I'll complete. . .") and then display the necessary IBs (e.g., collecting materials) leading to the reported behavior (i.e., completion of math problems).

The fourth, and most important, class of behavior includes behaviors that are expected to match the corresponding verbal behavior in a given verbal–nonverbal behavior chain. In the previous example, the expected target *nonverbal behavior* is the completion of 10 math problems in 15 minutes.

In the field of verbal–nonverbal correspondence training, the selection of behaviors is a matter of determining which behaviors in the verbal–nonverbal chain are essential antecedent events in controlling verbal–nonverbal relationships (Paniagua, 1997). Initially, only two behaviors in that chain appear crucial: the verbal behavior and its corresponding nonverbal behavior. If after several verbal–nonverbal correspondence training sessions an individual is not able to perform the reported behavior, preceding or IBs would be added to the procedures. The following discussion illustrates specific verbal–nonverbal training procedures, with an emphasis on process of selecting preceding and IBs.

## DESCRIPTION AND CLINICAL APPLICATIONS OF CORRESPONDENCE TRAINING PROCEDURES

The following sections discuss different types of correspondence training procedures including Reinforcement of Do-Report Correspondence, Report-Do Correspondence, Reinforcement Set-up on Reports, Immediate Reinforcement of IBs, and Reinforcement Set-up on IBs. Each of these procedures is discussed in detail, and examples of each are provided in the sections that follow.

### Reinforcement of Do-Report Correspondence

Using the Do-Report Correspondence technique, the reinforcer is delivered when an individual's *doing* corresponds with his or her *reporting about doing* in a Do-Report sequence (Risley & Hart, 1968). For example, Paniagua (1985) used this technique to develop self-care skills and helping behaviors among six juvenile delinquents living in a group home. Self-care skills were divided into two classes, namely Self-Care Skills I and Self-Care Skills II. Self-Care Skills I included going to bed and getting up on time, placing personal items (e.g., shoes, towels) in designated areas (e.g., closets, racks), and cleaning one's bedroom (e.g., removing dust from all flat surfaces). In the case of Self-Care Skills II, the individual had to write six entries on a personal datasheet (e.g., the amount of time requested for visiting friends outside the home, the date of that visit, time the individual returned from that visit). Helping behaviors included cleaning the bathroom (e.g., washing the toilet bowl daily), cleaning the dining room (e.g., cleaning dust from the floor, vacuuming or sweeping the floor daily), cleaning the kitchen (e.g., cleaning and scouring the sinks after each meal), and removing trash (e.g., placing the day's trash in the garage).

During baseline observations, self-care skills and helping behaviors were noted on a datasheet, and at the end of each observation the participants were questioned (one at a time) about Self-Care Skills I (e.g., "Did you make your bed today?"), about Self-Care Skills II (e.g., "Did you sign out/in and return on time each time you went out?"), and about helping behaviors (e.g., "Did you do your chore today?"). During this baseline phase, praise and tokens were given noncontingently after the individuals' verbalizations about past nonverbal (expected) behaviors (e.g., instances of self-care skills). Points allowed participants to gain access to a series of privileges such as watching television, using the stereo, and receiving an allowance of $7.00 per week. During the Do-Report Correspondence phase, points were given contingently on *true reports* about past behaviors in a Do-Report sequence. Individuals who reported about a specific nonverbal behavior (e.g., "I cleaned my room today") but had not actually fulfilled the expected behavior were told, "You didn't really do that, did you?" By contrast, those individuals who reported the expected nonverbal behavior and had actually fulfilled it were told, "You really did that, didn't you!" (Paniagua & Baer, 1982; Risley & Hart, 1968). During the Reinforcement of Do-Report Correspondence phase (i.e., the contingency-governed condition), nonverbal behaviors increased substantially relative to baseline observations. In this phase, the display of expected nonverbal behavior (doing) served as an antecedent event for the emission of subsequent verbalizations about this behavior.

In the same study, a follow-up phase was programmed during which the maintenance of expected nonverbal behaviors (e.g., instances of self-care skills) continued across 6 consecutive days in the absence of direct reinforcement for verbal–nonverbal matching. During this phase, individuals continued reporting about the expected nonverbal behaviors and maintained the expected verbal–nonverbal correspondence. In this phase, verbalizations functioned not only as antecedent events for the emission of subsequent instances of self-care skills and helping behaviors in subsequent days but also as mediators of expected nonverbal behaviors.

Another application of this procedure is the management of disruptive behaviors among children diagnosed as having attention-deficit/hyperactivity disorder (ADHD). Two important clinical issues should be considered prior to the programming of these procedures in interventions for children with ADHD (Paniagua, 1992). First, it is important to ensure that the child can understand exactly what he or she has to do to receive the reinforcer contingently on expected verbal–nonverbal correspondences. For example, an intervention plan designed to reduce "hyperactivity" using correspondence training procedures may not work simply because the child would have difficulty understanding this term when asked "Did you show hyperactivity in the classroom this morning?" In this example, a better approach would be to select nonverbal behaviors that the child could *tact* (for a more thorough discussion, see Paniagua, 1990b; Skinner, 1957) during the verbalization period. One example of a nonverbal behavior that the child could con*tact* during the verbalization period would be an emphasis on "grid changes" (i.e., assessing whether the child crossed a gridline placed on the floor) as an index for the absence versus presence of "hyperactivity" (Paniagua et al., 1988; Zentall, 1985). In this example, a child would be considered "hyperactive" in terms of the percentage of intervals during which he or she "crosses a gridline under [his or her] own power; both feet must be completely in a new quadrant" (Paniagua, 1987, p. 5). During the verbalization period, the question would be "Did you cross *this* line this morning?"

The second point to consider in using correspondence training procedures in interventions for children with ADHD is to establish a criterion for the delivery of the reinforcer (Whitman et al., 1982) and to increase the length of this criterion gradually across days or sessions until verbal–nonverbal correspondences are displayed at the expected levels. The main reason for this recommendation is that children with ADHD "have a strong inclination to seek immediate, direct gratification" (Douglas, 1985, p. 50). That is, with these children, immediate reinforcement seems more effective than delayed reinforcement. Therefore, it is assumed that the effectiveness of correspondence training procedures would be enhanced in those instances when children with ADHD are exposed to the reinforcer as soon as possible. For example, instead of requiring that a child with ADHD display on-task behavior (the expected nonverbal behavior) across an entire 10-minute observational period (i.e., 100% on-task) for the delivery of the reinforcer contingent on verbal–nonverbal correspondences, a better alternative would be to require the child to meet a minimal criterion (e.g., 30% on-task). The child would receive the reinforcer during earlier intervention sessions at the minimal criterion and then gradually increase this criterion in subsequent sessions until the maximum criterion level is reached (e.g., 30%, 60%, 85%, 100%).

Paniagua (1987) used the Reinforcement of Do-Report Correspondence technique to manage inattention (e.g., off-task behavior, activity changes) and overactivity (e.g., grid changes, out-of-seat behavior) in two children with clinical diagnoses of ADHD (American Psychiatric Association, 1980). In a multiple-baseline design across participants, baseline sessions were conducted in an intervention room and in a classroom (to assess the generalization of intervention effects). During these sessions, instances of inattention and overactivity were recorded across 10 consecutive minutes divided into twenty 30-second intervals. At the end of this observational period, participants were questioned about their prior nonverbal behavior (inattention and overactivity) in such settings (e.g., "Did you change activities without permission from your teacher?" "Did you sit still in your chair?" "Did you cross this line?"), but consequences for verbal–nonverbal correspondences were not programmed. The correspondence training technique was programmed only in the intervention room, and an assessment of the generalization of intervention effects was conducted in the classroom. During the introduction of the technique in the intervention room, a tangible reinforcer (e.g., a toy car) was delivered contingent on participants' reports about prior nonverbal behaviors, but only if the following two points were noted: 1) The child's report corresponded with the actual absence of inattention and overactivity in the past (Risley & Hart, 1968), and 2) the child did not show instances of inattention and overactivity across a preestablished criterion level.

In this particular example, each criterion level was established in terms of a percentage of intervals for the nonoccurrence of inattention and overactivity, relative to the total number of intervals for recording (i.e., twenty 30-second intervals). Once the child fulfilled a given criterion level across a given number of sessions (e.g., Criterion 1 = 30%), subsequent criterion levels were introduced gradually (e.g., Criterion 2 = 60%, Criterion 3 = 85%, Criterion 4 = 100%). Exposing the child to these criteria gradually over time facilitated the immediate delivery of the reinforcer during the final sessions of verbal–nonverbal correspondence training. In general, substantial decreases in instances of inattention and overactivity were noted in the intervention room during the introduction of the technique, relative to baseline observations. These decreases in target behaviors were generalized to the classroom, suggesting that children's reports play the role of mediators of nonverbal (expected) behaviors in the classroom. The maintenance of non-verbal changes was assessed during a follow-up phase programmed in both settings. During this phase, children's behavior continued to match their reports, again suggesting that verbal behavior serves as a mediator to the corresponding nonverbal behavior.

## Reinforcement of Report-Do Correspondence

In a Reinforcement of Report-Do Correspondence technique, participants make a report about future behavior, examiners make an assessment of the corresponding nonverbal behavior, and the reinforcer is delivered contingent on the Report-Do Correspondence (Deacon & Konarski, 1986; Osnes, Guevremont, & Stokes, 1987; Paniagua et al., 1988; Whitman et al., 1982; Williams & Stokes, 1982). For example, Osnes et al. (1987) used this technique with a 4-year-old girl with developmental disabilities. An assessment of expected nonverbal behaviors revealed that this child had impairments in three areas: 1) She had infrequent verbal communication with other children, 2) she stayed away from other children, and 3) she rarely participated in group activities (e.g., science activities, songs, fingerplays). The goal of the technique was to increase her frequency of talking to peers, her proximity to peers, and her participation in large-group activities (e.g., encourage hand raising), using an ABACA (follow-up) design (A = baseline, B = correspondence training with positive consequence, C = correspondence training with positive and negative consequences). In baseline observations, impairments in the child's behaviors were noted in the absence of a verbalization period in which there was a discussion about expected behaviors and consequences.

During the B phase, the child was prompted to say, "I'm going to talk to the other kids a lot." These prompts were used only during the first 2 days of baseline. To assess the generalized effects of the technique, the child was not asked questions about proximity to peers or about hand raising in large-group activities. The child's report was followed by the instruction, "Okay, you can go play," and an observational period of 15 minutes was scheduled during which talking to peers, proximity to peers, and hand raising were recorded. At the end of this observational period, the child was praised and instructed to pick up a reinforcer (e.g., a piggy-back ride) from a "Happy Sack" only if she demonstrated the verbal–nonverbal correspondence required for the delivery of the reinforcer (i.e., a verbal promise to talk to other peers and the actual display of this behavior). The correspondence between report about proximity to other peers or hand raising during large-group activities and actual (nonverbal) proximity/hand raising was not required for the delivery of the reinforcer. If the child failed to show the required verbal–nonverbal correspondence, she was told "You said you were going to talk a lot today in play, but you didn't. So, you can't pick from the Happy Sack. Go back to play."

During the C phase, a negative consequence was added contingent on the child's failure to show the required verbal–nonverbal correspondence. If the child did not talk to peers, she was told, "You said you were going to talk a lot today, but you didn't. You have to sit out of play now." The child was escorted to a chair located near the play area and instructed to sit for 3 consecutive minutes. In general, dramatic increases in peer-directed talk were noted only during the programming of verbal–nonverbal correspondence training in combination with the 3 minutes of time-out from positive reinforcement. This combination of techniques also substantially increased the child's proximity to peers and hand raising, suggesting the generalized effects of the verbal–nonverbal correspondence training technique in controlling behaviors that were not directly managed with verbal–nonverbal training. During a 30-day follow-up phase, the child continued to report about her intention to talk to peers and displayed the intended behavior, which provided support for the role of verbal behavior as a mediator of behavior changes in the absence of reinforced verbal–nonverbal relationships.

Additional examples of the clinical utility of this procedure include the management of inattention, overactivity, aggression, noise, and destruction of property in children with diagnoses of ADHD and conduct disorder (e.g., Paniagua, Morrison, & Black, 1990); the development of on-task behavior among individuals with mental retardation (e.g., Whitman et al., 1982); and the management of poor nutritional habits among preschool children (Friedman, Greene, & Stokes, 1990).

## Reinforcement Set-up on Reports

In the correspondence training techniques discussed in the previous sections, the reinforcer is presented and delivered after the completion of the verbal–nonverbal chain, in a Do-Report or Report-Do sequence. In the Reinforcement Set-up on Reports technique, the reinforcer is presented or shown to the participant immediately after the report (the set-up condition) and later delivered contingent on a Report-Do Correspondence training sequence (Israel & O'Leary, 1973; Karoly & Dirks, 1977; Paniagua, 1987; Paniagua & Baer, 1982; Paniagua et al., 1988). For example, Paniagua et al. (1988) used this technique to reduce the frequency of overactivity, inattention, and noise displayed by a 6-year-old boy diagnosed as having ADHD (American Psychiatric Association, 1980). In a multiple-baseline design across two settings (an intervention room and a general classroom), baseline observations were collected during a period of verbalizations about the inhibition of target (nonverbal) behaviors followed by a recording period of 10 minutes during which the occurrence versus nonoccurrence of these behaviors was noted in the absence of consequences. During the Reinforcement Set-up on Report phase, a tangible reinforcer was shown to the child contingent on a report about the inhibition of his maladaptive behaviors in target settings. During this condition, the child made the required report about future behavior (e.g., "I'll sit still in my chair") and was told, "You promised that you're going to sit still in your chair. I will put this toy in your bedroom. You may take this toy later only if you keep your promise." At the end of 10 minutes of observation, the therapist presented the datasheet simultaneously with the comments, "This page shows that you sat still in this room. You can take the toy I put in your bedroom earlier." If the child failed to reach the preestablished criterion level for the expected nonverbal behavior (e.g., Criterion 1 = 30% of total intervals displaying in-seat behavior), the therapist said, "This page shows that you sat still in your chair. But you cannot take the toy, because you did not sit still in your chair for a long period of time." This procedure was compared with the Reinforcement of Do-Report technique, and the results indicated greater behavior changes across all dependent measures during the set-up condition relative to baseline observations. Both procedures, however, led to continued maintenance of behavior changes during a follow-up phase in which the child continued reporting about future (expected) nonverbal behaviors and behaving according to these verbalizations.

In a nonclinical study reported by Paniagua and Baer (1982), setting up the reinforcer on a report about future behavior (and the delivery of the reinforcer contingent on verbal–nonverbal correspondence) was also more effective in controlling the nonverbal behavior than the Reinforcement of Do-Report Correspondence training technique. Paniagua and Baer suggested that when the reinforcer is set up (i.e., shown or presented) on a report about future behavior, then the reinforcer is actually programmed on two points in the verbal–nonverbal chain: once for the report and again for fulfillment of the promised (nonverbal) behavior (e.g., absence of instances of inattention and overactivity in the near future). By contrast, when the reinforcer is delivered contingent on true reports about past (nonverbal) behaviors (e.g., true reports about the absence of overactivity in the past), the reinforcer is programmed at only one point in the chain: immediately after reports about the nonverbal behavior. Therefore, one would expect greater behavior (nonverbal) changes during the set-up condition because a more powerful contingency is programmed during the introduction of the reinforcer at two levels in the verbal–nonverbal chain. In addition, the placement of the reinforcer immediately after the report and the instruction "You may take this toy later only if you keep your promise" may function as powerful antecedent events for subsequent (expected or promised) behaviors in the future. Therefore, the present (set-up) technique would be strongly recommended for children with ADHD who do not respond to reinforcement contingencies operating at only one point in that chain (e.g., the Reinforcement of Do-Report technique).

**Research Directions** A promising area of research is the programming of reinforcement contingencies on IBs and an assessment of the effects of this experimental manipulation on language as mediator of behavior (Paniagua, 1990a). Two correspondence training techniques that emphasize these behaviors are immediate reinforcement of IBs and Reinforcement Set-up on IBs. Clinical applications of these techniques are not available in the literature. Procedures reported with nonclinical studies, however, could be easily transferred to clinical applications in interventions for individuals with developmental disabilities. This point is illustrated by the following examples.

## Immediate Reinforcement of Intermediate Behaviors

In the Immediate Reinforcement of IBs technique, expected behavior changes may be achieved by placing the reinforcer on IBs leading to the target nonverbal behavior in a Report-IBs-Do sequence. For example, in the study by Paniagua et al. (1982), children's reports about their intention to engage in a series of activities (e.g., "I'll paint") were immediately followed by a set of IBs necessary for the fulfillment of the nonverbal behavior (e.g., bringing paint pots, picking up brushes, collecting papers, arranging easels). Each IB was immediately reinforced, and at the end of the last IB, children were observed for a brief period to record their actual performance on the promised (nonverbal) behavior. This procedure resulted in substantial increases of correspondences between reporting about painting and its corresponding nonverbal behavior (actually painting) across sessions, relative to baseline observations.

Because verbal–nonverbal relationships are not directly reinforced in the Immediate Reinforcement of IBs technique, it is assumed that the control of nonverbal behaviors (e.g., painting) is a matter of establishing IBs as *necessary* evocative events (i.e., a case of establishing operations) in the verbal–nonverbal chain. Therefore, the *selection* of this procedure to manage a given clinical case would be recommended in those cases in which substantial changes that are expected in nonverbal behaviors may occur only when IBs are programmed in the verbal–nonverbal chain. For example, if after several sessions of the Reinforcement of Report-Do Correspondence procedure (in which IBs are not selected or emphasized) a child diagnosed as having oppositional defiant disorder (American Psychiatric Association, 1994) continues to have difficulties with the completion of a given task (e.g., completion of math problems), the following IBs would be established to facilitate the completion of the task: 1) asking for task materials, 2) walking to a desk, and 3) placing materials on the desk. In this example, the teacher would ask, "Are you going to complete these 10 math problems during this class period?"; and the child's report (e.g., "Yes, I'll complete these problems") may be followed by the instruction, "Okay, you need to ask for your workbook, pencils, and paper. Walk toward your desk, and place the book, pencils, and paper on it. Then start working on your math problems." The child is allowed to display each IB, which would be followed by praise (e.g., "Good, you're asking for your materials to work on your math problems") and a token. At the end of the last IB, the child is told, "You said that you will complete these problems, and you have already done lots of things to complete these problems, such as asking for the materials you need to start working on these problems. I will give you this toy car for these three tokens you have earned. Go ahead and start working." At the end of the preselected observational period (e.g., 15 minutes allowed for the child to complete the math problems), no additional consequences are programmed.

It should be noted that in the technique discussed in the previous paragraph, the reinforcer is contingent on the report about a future behavior (e.g., "I'll complete. . .") *and* IBs leading to the individual's performance of the expected nonverbal behavior. Therefore, in using the Immediate Reinforcement of IBs procedure, the reinforcer is delivered regardless of the occurrence of nonverbal behavior in the verbal–nonverbal chain. The main assumption, however, is that nonverbal behavior could be placed under the control of verbal behavior by establishing IBs as powerful antecedent events in the verbal–nonverbal chain. In clinical applications of this procedure, however, it is reasonable to expect that an individual would not respond to the technique (i.e., expected behavior changes are not achieved) because of the absence of consequences for failure to display the expected nonverbal behavior. Under such a condition, the antecedent control of IBs would be "weak." One alternative to strengthen the controlling function of IBs is to use a procedure in which the reinforcer is not delivered unless the individual displays three behaviors in the chain: The individual 1) reports about future behavior, 2) displays IBs leading to the re-

ported behavior, and 3) performs the actual nonverbal (expected) behavior. An example of this procedure is described in the following
section.

## Reinforcement Set-up on Intermediate Behaviors

In the Reinforcement Set-up on IBs technique, two correspondences
are required for the actual delivery of the reinforcer: 1) the correspondence between a report of future behavior and its corresponding IBs,
and 2) the correspondence between the report and the occurrence of
the target nonverbal behavior (i.e., "do" in the chain) in the report-
IBs-do chain (Paniagua, 1990a). For example, in a study by Paniagua
and Baer (1982), children reported about playing with a number of
items (e.g., blocks) and were instructed to display a number of IBs
leading to actual play (e.g., walking to the target setting, picking up
the blocks, placing blocks on the floor). Each IB was followed by a
token plus a statement by the experimenter describing the participant's behavior (e.g., "You're picking up your blocks"). Tokens were
given only for the behaviors that successfully led to the final IB (which
was always placing the blocks on the floor). When the final IB occurred, the experimenter said, "I'll change these tokens for this toy,
which I will put outside the door. You may take the toy later." Participants who had made a report about their intention to participate in
the activity displayed the expected IBs, and children who behaved
according to their prior report were allowed to take the toy at the end
of the training session. These procedures emphasize the contingency-
governed behavior phase of the study. A test of verbal behavior as a
mediator of corresponding nonverbal behavior would imply that there
is a condition in which verbalizations alone lead to both the emission
of IBs and the actual nonverbal (related) behavior in the verbal–IB–
nonverbal chain (Paniagua, 1990a).

In the case of the clinical vignette about the child who refuses to
complete a set of math problems in the classroom, the child would be
instructed to make a report about his or her intention to fulfill this
task (e.g., "I'll complete 10 math problems within 15 minutes"), which
would be followed by the child's display of a series of IBs (e.g., asking
for materials). Each IB may be followed by one token, praise, and a
verbal description of specific IBs (e.g., "Good, you're asking for your
materials. Here is one token"). At the end of the last IB, the child
would be told, "You said [repeat what the child said]. Here is your
toy. But you may take this toy only after you have completed these
math problems." This is the "set-up" condition. If the expected nonverbal behavior is not displayed (e.g., a failure to complete the set of
specified math problems), the child would be told, "You said [repeat

what the child said], and you made lots of effort to complete this task; for example, you asked for your materials. But you cannot keep this toy because you did not complete this task today."

The Reinforcement Set-up on IBs procedure is very similar to the Reinforcement Set-up on Report technique, with one critical exception: The reinforcer is programmed at three points in the verbal–nonverbal chain (i.e., on a report about future behaviors, on IBs, and again for fulfillment of the reported behaviors). Therefore, in the clinical management of challenging behaviors among individuals with developmental disabilities, the selection of the Set-up of Reinforcement on IBs condition should be the first choice of intervention—simply because a greater control of behavior would be expected in those conditions when the reinforcer is programmed at three points in the verbal–nonverbal chain.

As noted previously, when behaviors are required prior to an individual's performance of the expected nonverbal behavior in a Do-Report sequence, these behaviors may be termed "preceding" behaviors. For example, in the management of on-task behavior among children with behavior difficulties (e.g., children with ADHD), a child would be required to ask for materials necessary to fulfill the expected task, which may be followed by an observational period of 10 minutes during which the expected nonverbal behavior is recorded. This observation then is followed by a verbalization period during which the child is asked about past (expected) nonverbal behavior. In this condition, "collecting" materials prior to actual performance on expected behavior constitutes the preceding condition. The performance of the task during that observation is the "do" element in the chain, and the child's report about past performance is the "verbal" component in a Preceding-Do-Report sequence. This example illustrates the Reinforcement of Do-Report Correspondence procedure in which preceding behaviors may function as antecedent events for the occurrence of the expected nonverbal behavior (e.g., on-task).

Preceding behaviors also may be programmed during the introduction of the Reinforcement of Report-Do Correspondence training. For example, an individual would display behaviors (e.g., asking for materials to engage in a given task, walking toward a desk, placing materials on the desk, sitting down), and the last preceding behavior would be followed by the question, "Are you going to complete. . .?" The report about the completion of the task is recorded (e.g., "I'll complete. . ."), and the occurrence of the reported behavior is noted during a given observational period. At the end of this observation period, the reinforcer would be delivered on the expected verbal–nonverbal correspondences in a Preceding-Report-Do sequence.

## STRENGTHS AND LIMITATIONS OF
## CORRESPONDENCE TRAINING PROCEDURES

A critical advantage of verbal–nonverbal training procedures is that they can be programmed to decrease problem behaviors *and* to increase prosocial behaviors within the same experimental condition (Paniagua, 1987; Whitman et al., 1982). For example, when these procedures are used to decrease inattention and overactivity among children with ADHD, controlling verbal–nonverbal relationships during the rule-governed behavior phase across sessions or days also may lead to increases in on-task behavior. In this respect, these procedures may have advantages over other behavioral interventions such as time-out from positive reinforcement, response cost, and extinction, which are limited to decreasing behavior (Sulzer-Azaroff & Meyer, 1977).

Another important advantage of verbal–nonverbal training techniques is that verbal behavior may be established as a critical antecedent event for the development of self-control of nonverbal behavior. The term *self-control* often is inferred from either the generalization phase or the maintenance phase (follow-up). That is, when verbal–nonverbal training is programmed during the rule-governed behavior phase of the intervention plan, individuals' verbalizations do not mediate their corresponding nonverbal behavior. During this phase, individuals simply behave consistently with their verbalizations in order to earn reinforcers. If individuals receiving this training behave consistently with their reports about past or future behaviors during the generalization or maintenance conditions, one would assume that their verbalizations are mediators of their nonverbal behavior. A demonstration of verbal behavior as an antecedent mediating event for nonverbal behavior is a case of "self-control," in which expected nonverbal behavior is controlled not by direct reinforcement contingency but by a process of rule-governed behavior (Barkley, 1981; Skinner, 1969). Because individuals learn those rules through direct reinforcement contingent on verbal–nonverbal correspondences, the development of verbal behavior as a mediator of nonverbal behavior is actually programmed during the contingency-governed behavior phase of the intervention plan. For this reason, Stokes and Baer classified verbal–nonverbal correspondence training procedures as an example of generalization techniques (which they termed "mediated generalization" [1977, p. 361]) recommended to plan the generalization and maintenance of intervention effects rather than to hope that behavior changes will continue over time after the removal of the intervention.

Verbal–nonverbal correspondence training may be particularly valuable in those cases in which time constraints or other exigencies prevent clinicians, teachers, or parents from implementing more traditional behavioral interventions. For example, restitution overcorrection (Foxx & Azrin, 1973), which is generally recommended for interventions for challenging behaviors among individuals with mental retardation, usually would take more time to implement than any of the correspondence training techniques reviewed in the previous sections. An example in which a correspondence training technique could be used instead of a restitution overcorrection technique is in the case of throwing food at the dinner table—a maladaptive behavior often displayed by individuals with mental retardation (Matson & Coe, 1991). In this case, the individual would be required to pick up the food from the floor and the table and also to wash the floor and the table each time the maladaptive behavior occurs. If correspondence training is used in this case, the individual would be instructed to make a report about the absence of that behavior (e.g., "I will not throw food on the table"). A brief period of observation would be programmed to record the absence of this (reported) behavior, and at the end of this observation period, the reinforcer would be delivered contingent on expected verbal–nonverbal correspondences. This is the Reinforcement of Report-Do technique. Because "appropriate eating behavior" regularly implies a chain of responses that naturally occur in the environment (e.g., walking toward the dining room, picking up the tray, walking to the table, placing the tray on the table, sitting still) (Stokes & Baer, 1977), an alternative technique would be to take advantage of these naturally occurring behaviors and to use correspondence training techniques that emphasize IBs (e.g., the Reinforcement Set-up on IBs procedure).

Despite the advantages of correspondence training listed in the previous paragraphs, correspondence training procedures are limited in several areas. The first limitation of correspondence training techniques is that these procedures would not be recommended in the management of behaviors that require *immediate* control. These procedures emphasize the shaping of expected verbal–nonverbal relationships over an extended period of time (e.g., from 10 to 16 days in the study by Osnes et al., 1987). Therefore, it may be impractical to recommend these procedures in the management of severe physical aggression, destruction of property, self-injurious behavior, and other behaviors requiring immediate intervention.

A second limitation is that correspondence training often requires the development of expressive and receptive language among target participants. Thus, an individual must be able to understand and produce language prior to the programming of verbal–nonverbal training. An alternative to this limitation was suggested by Whitman et al.

(1982). In this study, four children with mental retardation (IQ scores ranging from 56 to 68) with attentional problems and expressive language impairments served as participants. During correspondence training, rather than instructing the child to report about a future behavior (e.g., sitting still and looking at the task), the child was instructed to *show* (nonverbally) the expected nonverbal behavior in the immediate future. The child was asked, "Do you remember what the teacher said about paying attention?" Affirmative responses (e.g., saying "yes") from the child were followed by the instruction, "Show me how you are going to pay attention to your work." Children who "showed" the expected nonverbal behavior and then behaved according to this demonstration of corresponding nonverbal behavior (e.g., on-task) received praise and nonverbal approval contingent on the showing–nonverbal correspondences. This variant of verbal–nonverbal training led to substantial increases in on-task behavior, relative to baseline observations. In addition, behavior changes were maintained and generalized over time in the absence of direct reinforcement for showing–nonverbal correspondences, suggesting the function of "showing" how to be on-task is a powerful antecedent event for training subsequent behavior.

A third limitation is that correspondence training requires the accurate measurement of target nonverbal behaviors. If clinicians, teachers, and parents cannot directly record the corresponding nonverbal behavior in the verbal–nonverbal chain, it would be difficult to control for the accidental delivery of reinforcers in those instances in which individuals report about past or future behaviors but do not actually behave according to those reports. If the relationship between verbal and nonverbal behavior cannot be recorded *accurately*, a potential negative outcome could be the development of lying among individuals receiving this training (Paniagua, 1990a).

## SUMMARY AND CONCLUSIONS

This chapter discusses five experimental conditions to establish verbal behavior as a mediator of nonverbal behavior. Basic and applied correspondence training research suggests the effectiveness of these techniques in establishing, decreasing, or increasing verbal–nonverbal relationships during the contingency-governed behavior phase of an intervention and the generalization and maintenance of intervention effects during the rule-governed behavior condition.

Correspondence training techniques that emphasize IBs have yielded substantial behavior changes during the contingency-governed behavior phase (e.g., Paniagua & Baer, 1982; Paniagua et al.,

1982). One may argue that the discriminative function of IBs (i.e., an IB is the signal for the emission of the next behavior) could enhance the role of verbal behavior as a mediator of behavior in those cases in which participants are instructed not only to report about what they plan to do (or not to do) but to display specific IBs during the assessment of generalization and maintenance of intervention effects (i.e., the rule-governed behavior phase of the study). Future clinical research is needed to explore the potential impact of IBs in terms of enhancing verbal mediation of related nonverbal behavior.

## REFERENCES

American Psychiatric Association. (1980). *Diagnostic and statistical manual of mental disorders* (3rd ed.). Washington, DC: Author.

American Psychiatric Association. (1994). *Diagnostic and statistical manual of mental disorders* (4th ed.). Washington, DC: Author.

Baer, R.A., Osnes, P.G., & Stokes, T.F. (1983). Training generalized correspondence between verbal behavior at school and nonverbal behavior at home. *Education and Treatment of Children, 6,* 379–388.

Baer, R.A., Williams, J.A., Osnes, P.G., & Stokes, T.F. (1984). Delayed reinforcement as an indiscriminable contingency in verbal/nonverbal correspondence training. *Journal of Applied Behavior Analysis, 17,* 429–440.

Barkley, R.A. (1981). *Attention deficit hyperactivity disorder: A handbook for diagnosis and treatment.* New York: Guilford Press.

Barkley, R.A. (1987). Attention deficit-hyperactivity disorder. In E.J. Mash & R.A. Barkley (Eds.), *Treatment of childhood disorders* (pp. 39–72). New York: Guilford Press.

Deacon, J.R., & Konarski, E.A. (1987). Correspondence training: An example of rule-governed behavior. *Journal of Applied Behavior Analysis, 20,* 391–400.

Douglas, V.I. (1985). The response of ADD children to reinforcement: Theoretical and clinical implications. In L.W. Bloomingdale (Ed.), *Attention deficit disorder: Identification, course, and rationale* (pp. 49–66). New York: Medical & Scientific Books.

Finney, J.W., Russo, D.C., & Cataldo, M.F. (1982). Reduction of pica in young children with lead poisoning. *Journal of Pediatric Psychology, 7,* 197–207.

Foxx, R.M., & Azrin, N. (1973). The elimination of self-stimulatory behavior by overcorrection. *Journal of Applied Behavior Analysis, 6,* 1–14.

Friedman, A.G., Greene, P.G., & Stokes, T.F. (1990). Improving dietary habits of children: Effects of nutrition education and correspondence training. *Journal of Behavior Therapy and Experimental Psychiatry, 21,* 263–268.

Guevremont, D.C., Osnes, P.G., & Stokes, T.F. (1986a). Preparation for effective self-regulation: The development of generalized verbal control. *Journal of Applied Behavior Analysis, 19,* 99–104.

Guevremont, D.C., Osnes, P.G., & Stokes, T.F. (1986b). Programming maintenance after correspondence training interventions with children. *Journal of Applied Behavior Analysis, 19,* 215–219.

Israel, A.C. (1973). Developing correspondence between verbal and nonverbal behavior: Switching sequences. *Psychological Reports, 32,* 1111–1117.

Israel, A.C. (1978). Some thoughts on correspondence between saying and doing. *Journal of Applied Behavior Analysis, 11,* 271–273.

Israel, A.C., & O'Leary, K.D. (1973). Developing correspondence between children's words and deeds. *Child Development, 44,* 575–581.

Jewett, J., & Clark, H.B. (1979). Teaching preschoolers to use appropriate dinnertime conversation: An analysis of generalization from school to home. *Behavior Therapy, 10,* 589–605.

Karoly, P., & Dirks, M.J. (1977). Developing self-control in preschool children through correspondence training. *Behavior Therapy, 8,* 398–405.

Keogh, D., Burgio, L., Whitman, T., & Johnson, M. (1983). Development of listening skills in retarded children: A correspondence training program. *Child & Family Behavior Therapy, 5,* 51–71.

Matson, J.L., & Coe, D.A. (1991). Mentally retarded children. In T.R. Kratochwill & R.J. Morris (Eds.), *The practice of child therapy* (pp. 298–327). New York: Pergamon.

Mook, D.G. (1992). In defense of external validity. In A. Kazdin (Ed.), *Methodological issues and strategies in clinical research* (pp. 119–136). Washington, DC: American Psychological Association.

Osnes, P.G., Guevremont, D.C., & Stokes, T.F. (1987). Increasing a child's prosocial behaviors: Positive and negative consequences in correspondence training. *Journal of Behavior Therapy and Experimental Psychiatry, 18,* 71–76.

Paniagua, F.A. (1985). Development of self-care skills and helping behaviors through correspondence training. *Journal of Behavior Therapy and Experimental Psychiatry, 16,* 237–244.

Paniagua, F.A. (1987). Management of hyperactive children through correspondence training procedures: A preliminary study. *Behavioral Residential Treatment, 2,* 1–23.

Paniagua, F.A. (1990a). A procedural analysis of correspondence training techniques. *Behavior Analyst, 13,* 107–119.

Paniagua, F.A. (1990b). Skinner's senses of "guessing." *New Ideas in Psychology, 8,* 73–79.

Paniagua, F.A. (1992). Verbal–nonverbal correspondence training with ADHD children. *Behavior Modification, 16,* 226–252.

Paniagua, F.A. (1997). Verbal–nonverbal correspondence training as a case of experimental antecedents. In D.M. Baer & E.M. Pinkston (Eds.), *Environment and behavior* (pp. 43–48). Boulder, CO: West Press.

Paniagua, F.A., & Baer, D.M. (1982). The analysis of correspondence training as a chain reinforceable at any point. *Child Development, 53,* 786–798.

Paniagua, F.A., & Black, S.A. (1990). Management and prevention of hyperactivity and conduct disorder in 8–10 year-old boys through correspondence training procedures. *Child and Family Behavior Therapy, 12,* 23–56.

Paniagua, F.A., Morrison, P.B., & Black, S.A. (1990). Management of a hyperactive-conduct disordered child through correspondence training: A preliminary study. *Journal of Behavior Therapy and Experimental Psychiatry, 21,* 63–68.

Paniagua, F.A., Pumariega, J.A., & Black, S.A. (1988). Clinical effects of correspondence training in the management of hyperactive children. *Behavioral Residential Treatment, 3,* 20–40.

Paniagua, F.A., Stella, E.M., Holt, W.J., Baer, D.M., & Etzel, B.C. (1982). Training correspondence by reinforcing intermediate and verbal behavior. *Child and Family Behavior Therapy, 4,* 127–139.

Ribeiro, A. (1989). Correspondence in children's self-report. Tacting and manding aspects. *Journal of the Experimental Analysis of Behavior, 51,* 361–367.

Risley, T.R., & Hart, B. (1968). Developing correspondence between the nonverbal and verbal behavior of preschool children. *Journal of Applied Behavior Analysis, 1,* 267–281.

Skinner, B.F. (1957). *Verbal behavior.* New York: Appleton-Century-Crofts.

Skinner, B.F. (1969). *Contingencies of reinforcement: A theoretical approach.* Upper Saddle River, NJ: Prentice Hall.

Stokes, T.F., & Baer, D.M. (1977). An empirical technology of generalization. *Journal of Applied Behavior Analysis, 10,* 349–367.

Sulzer-Azaroff, B., & Meyer, G.R. (1977). *Applying behavior-analysis procedures with children and youth.* New York: Holt, Rinehart & Winston.

Ward, W.D., & Stare, S.W. (1990). The role of verbalization in generalized correspondence. *Journal of Applied Behavior Analysis, 23,* 129–136

Whitman, T.L., Scibak, J.W., Butler, K.M., Richter, R., & Johnson, M.R. (1982). Improving classroom behavior in mentally retarded children through correspondence training. *Journal of Applied Behavior Analysis, 15,* 545–564.

Williams, J.A., & Stokes, T.F. (1982). Some parameters of correspondence training and generalized verbal control. *Journal of Applied Behavior Analysis, 4,* 11–32.

Wolf, M. (1978). Social validity: The case for subjective measurement or how applied behavior analysis is finding its heart. *Journal of Applied Behavior Analysis, 11,* 203–214.

Zentall, S.S. (1985). A context for hyperactivity. In K.D. Gadows (Ed.), *Advances in learning and behavioral disabilities* (pp. 273–343). Greenwich, CT: JAI Press.

# ~ V ~

## Issues of Intervention

### Additional Strategies

## ~ *11* ~

## *Supported Routines*

### Richard R. Saunders and Muriel D. Saunders

In 1909, the maternal grandmother of the first author of this chapter began a 36-year teaching career with 35 students from seven grades in a one-room school house in rural North Carolina. When asked how she accomplished that feat and, in particular, how she maintained classroom discipline (she was 17 years old when she began teaching), she described a model that today would be labeled "peer tutoring." It was peer tutoring with a special twist, however. She reported,

> During instructional periods in which I taught the students from one grade a new lesson, I assigned other students to help their younger classmates with exercises from lessons I had already taught. During some periods, I assigned third-grade students to assist first-grade students, fourth-grade students to assist second-grade students, and seventh-grade students to assist fifth-grade students, leaving me free to teach the sixth-grade students. I used a schedule of who was to tutor whom that allowed all of the children to receive assistance from more advanced students and also receive daily instruction directly from me on new material. When I had a child who learned more slowly, I was careful about who that student tutored and what instructional material was assigned. This approach ensured that my students who were providing the tutoring were always assisting with lessons they had already mastered. I also chose exercises for the tutored children in which they were nearing proficiency. In this way, I made sure that both the tutor and the tutored students could be successful during tutoring. Successful students are rarely a problem, so if I could arrange to keep them busy being successful for much of the day, I avoided a lot of discipline problems. (C.D. McCollum, personal communication, October 1979)

Preparation of this chapter was supported in part by National Institute of Child Health and Human Development Grants Nos. 5-P30HD02528 and 1-P01HD26927 to the Schiefelbusch Institute for Life Span Studies, University of Kansas.

In summary, all students spent most of the day behaving competently in a socially valued manner, thereby ensuring that they spent most of the day engaging in behavior that she desired to reinforce.

This teacher scheduled her students' day so that most expected performances could be emitted easily, and thus they could perform competently throughout much of the day. Although this schedule of activities may be fairly easy to create with typically developing elementary school students, creating a daily schedule of competently performed routines may be far more difficult for children and adults with developmental disabilities, particularly for extended periods of time. This is especially true for those with the most severe cognitive or physical impairments and for those with poor receptive language. Nevertheless, it is our clinical experience that, to the degree these individuals perform competently, undesirable behavior is reduced proportionately.

Undesirable or challenging behavior is a topic of particular concern among those who educate and support people with developmental disabilities. Changes in the location of support services since the 1960s have not diminished the prevalence of the problem. In fact, as the settings for supportive services have shifted, the need for broadly effective and durable interventions has taken on a greater urgency. Indeed, the impact of challenging behavior on achieving independence, productivity, and social acceptance can increase with greater integration if certain preparations are not made.

This chapter suggests that, among such preparations, the most critical is provision of the opportunity for individuals to develop repertoires of behavior that are socially valuable and that can be performed competently. Since the early 1990s, we have had the opportunity to encourage practitioners to treat challenging behavior by addressing how all of the individual's nonchallenging behavior is supported and to develop intervention plans for the challenging behavior only if it persists following the broader intervention. Specifically, we have assisted practitioners to create and implement comprehensive strategies for increasing competence in individuals with developmental disabilities. Clinically significant reductions and, in many cases, elimination of the challenging behavior have followed from these interventions (e.g., Saunders, Butterfield, Eiler, Lingwood, & Tucker, 1992; Saunders, O'Meara, Fovel, Allen, & Isley, 1994).

Our strategies derive from a general concept called "supported routines" introduced by Saunders and Spradlin (1991). Saunders and Spradlin primarily supported their concept with practical observations and considerations. This chapter attempts to draw together seemingly disparate research literature to provide a more empirically based explanation for the observed success with supported routines. The chapter also describes in detail the specific strategies we refer to collectively as the "supported routines approach" and summarizes research involving supported routines.

## THEORETICAL AND CONCEPTUAL ISSUES

The concept of developing other repertoires to reduce challenging behaviors is not new to intervention methodology. Goldiamond (1974) described a set of intervention procedures, referred to as a "constructional approach," that could be utilized when intervention procedures directed at the target behavior are not particularly successful. Goldiamond listed four components of a constructional approach: 1) selecting new outcomes or targets, 2) identifying current usable repertoires, 3) selecting implementation procedures that are suitable for the new targets, and 4) creating consequences that will maintain the expected behavioral outcomes.

A commonly employed and often effective constructional approach is the differential reinforcement of behavior other than the challenging behavior (DRO). With DRO procedures, the behavior reinforced is whatever behavior is being emitted when the absence of the individual's challenging behavior meets a temporal contingency. That is, when the individual has not engaged in challenging behavior for some prescribed interval or is not engaging in challenging behavior at the end of some interval, a reinforcer is delivered (e.g., Cowdery, Iwata, & Pace, 1990; Foxx, McMorrow, Fenlon, & Bittle, 1986; Mazaleski, Iwata, Vollmer, Zarcone, & Smith, 1993; Vollmer, Iwata, Zarcone, Smith, & Mazaleski, 1993). Thus, in a DRO contingency, whatever the individual is doing at the moment of reinforcer delivery is presumably strengthened. Perhaps an important aspect of the effectiveness of DRO procedures is that reinforcement is delivered for behavior already in the individual's repertoire; the acquisition of a new response is not required. A problem with DRO procedures, however, is that the effects of the contingency are capricious—no particular pattern of behavior or repertoire is strengthened.

In contrast, functional equivalence training could be considered a constructional approach that strengthens a specific behavior or behavior class. *Functional equivalence training* generally establishes a socially relevant response as a to-be-reinforced alternative to some challenging behavior. The most commonly reinforced alternative is a communication response, often because the assessed function (e.g., Iwata, Dorsey, Slifer, Bauman, & Richman, 1994) of the challenging behavior appears communicative (e.g., requesting to escape or avoid task demands). The trained response is referred to as equivalent because it has the same function as the challenging behavior. For example, Carr and Durand (1985) demonstrated the effectiveness of these procedures with aggressive, self-injurious, and disruptive behaviors, and Durand and Carr (1987) extended the demonstration to stereotyped behaviors. Although functional equivalence interventions can be quite effective in reducing the rate of challenging behavior, they also often have the result of ending the individual's participation in a socially relevant task (e.g., household chores, work, bathing).

Most functional equivalence interventions employ a negative reinforcement contingency, and the rates of the challenging and equivalent behavior are measured and reported. It is interesting to note that of the research published in the late 1980s and 1990s in which a *positive reinforcement* contingency was introduced to strengthen alternatives to challenging behavior, the rates of reinforcement and the effects of the contingency on the rates of the alternative behavior were reported infrequently (Saunders, 1998). Without exception, however, these studies described the effects of each intervention on the challenging behavior (Saunders, 1998). Thus, the literature published in the 1990s has provided far more information on the direct effects of contingencies on challenging behavior than on the effects of contingencies on the rest of the individual's behavior. This is somewhat analogous to a football announcer reporting only what happened to the player with the ball and ignoring feints, blocks, and diversions that were highly relevant to what the player with the ball accomplished.

## Comprehensive Enablement

Saunders and Spradlin (1991) suggested a constructional approach that they labeled as supported routines. Saunders and Spradlin suggested that people with developmental disabilities often have ample repertoires of potentially functional behavioral sequences but opportunities and adaptations are rarely made available to create occasions for the behavioral sequences to be required and reinforced. They observed that in typical habilitation and intervention settings, people with developmental disabilities often spend much of their time waiting to participate in *the staff's* routines rather than staff enabling *their* routines. Supported routines was conceptualized as a method of enabling competent performances, which would lead to the establishment of more pervasive opportunities to reinforce socially relevant behavior. Enabling in this context means creating the conditions under which the individual can do something for him- or herself. Saunders and Spradlin viewed these supported routines as vehicles through which an individual is enabled to perform competently throughout increasingly larger segments of the day. It also was conceptualized as having the characteristic of rapidly establishing the individual's providers and supporters as discriminative for reinforcement, a condition critical for successful enablement and generalization of newly acquired skills.

Enablement of competence can be accomplished by teaching specific skills with differential reinforcement or prompt fading procedures. Often, however, enablement is effected more easily by offering the opportunity to perform a sequence that is already in the person's repertoire. Such performances also can be facilitated with the aid of environmental adaptations, nonverbal demonstrations or prompts, or a combination of these and other means, including training. Saunders and Spradlin suggested that comprehensive enabling with opportunities and adaptations could establish a functional repertoire of existing performances within which training of a few new skills could be more successful (e.g., Neef, Iwata, & Page, 1977; see Stoddard, 1982). In other words, comprehensive enabling works in much the same way that a tennis coach works to establish a relatively effective performance at one level before teaching components of a more advanced technique. Thus, a primary requirement for developing an effective supported routine is that most skills necessary to complete the basic routine already must be in the repertoire.

## Delay Reduction

Saunders and Spradlin (1991) also suggested that tasks requiring critical behavioral sequences not currently in the individual's repertoire be bridged. That is, initially the problem sequence would be completed by others so that the individual's performance could produce its intended function without interruption or delay. This may be an essential aspect of this approach for several reasons. First, uninterrupted or fluid behavioral sequences become established behavior chains more rapidly when followed by reinforcement (see Sidman, 1960). Second, elimination of delay may serve as a reinforcer for other behavior, such as requesting (e.g., Charlop, Schreibman, & Thibodeau, 1985; Charlop & Trasowech, 1991; Goetz, Gee, & Sailor, 1985; Halle, Baer, & Spradlin, 1982; Halle, Marshall, & Spradlin, 1979; Schussler & Spradlin, 1991; Sigafoos, Reichle, Doss, Hall, & Pettitt, 1990). Third, studies on the effects of brief time-out from reinforcement have demonstrated that interruptions or delays in moving through reinforced behavioral sequences have aversive properties and may themselves occasion self-injury or aggression (e.g., Barton, Guess, Garcia, & Baer, 1970; Bostow & Bailey, 1969; Foxx & Shapiro, 1978; Wolf, Risley, & Mees, 1964).

Saunders and Spradlin (1991) further suggested that the proportion of sequences to be taught rather than bridged be held to the proportion generally observed among people of comparable age without disability. In addition, those sequences selected for training should have a good prognosis for acquisition, based on the results of current assessments. When this advice is followed, skill training consumes relatively small portions of each day, and the remaining time is allocated to improving the fluency of already acquired skills. Saunders and Spradlin referred to these results of an enabling approach as the production of *competence* to distinguish it from the concept of *independence.* Independence is a concept historically associated with intervention approaches that emphasize skill building or deficit reduction to the general exclusion of enablement (e.g., *active treatment*). Descriptively, competence refers to *functional performances initiated independently and performed fluently, with outside assistance sufficient only to maintain fluency*—outcomes consistent with personal control and environmental mastery. It is obvious, then, that competence increases with reinforced practice.

## Response Fluency and Behavioral Efficiency

Even when powerful reinforcement contingencies can be arranged, they can be effective in altering the rate of a behavior only to the degree that the individual's potential performance is not inhibited by inherent human limitations (e.g., sensorimotor coordination). Weeks and Gaylord-Ross (1981) found that increased task difficulty was associated with higher rates of challenging behavior (see also Carr, Newsom, & Binkoff, 1976; Durand & Carr, 1987; Mace, Browder, & Lin, 1987). Weeks and Gaylord-Ross also found that within-task errors and challenging behaviors could be minimized in visual discrimination tasks with an errorless learning procedure but not in perceptual motor tasks. Research has shown, however, how fluency in motor tasks can be increased with task design remediation and motion-economy–based task analysis (Belfiore, Lim, & Browder, 1994; Belfiore & Toro-Zambrana, 1995). This is an example of using functional assessments that measure the interaction of purposeful behavior and elements of the environment (Halpern & Fuhrer, 1984). Such assessments detect discrepancies between task requirements and the individual's current skills (e.g., Guidubaldi, Perry, & Walker, 1989). Increased fluency means shorter task duration, fewer errors, less wasted motion, and increased productivity.

Dictionary definitions of *fluency* include "flowing smoothly" and "flowing effortlessly" (Soukhanov et al., 1984). The motor performances of humans in typical daily activities have certain observable and measurable characteristics such as length of interresponse time within a behavioral sequence (e.g., shredding five pieces of paper), topography of hand movements (e.g., coordinated two-handed work versus working only with one hand), sequencing errors, error correction responses, and the pattern of latencies of sequence onset. Changes in aspects of some of these characteristics of performance can lead to tighter, smoother, and faster sequences. Thus, temporally shorter but nevertheless effective performances would reflect one aspect of increased fluency.

Another aspect of fluency is reduced physical effort. The symptoms of fatigue often are used to measure changes in effort. In natural environments, exposure to a work task may lead to fatigue and fatigue may be indicated by increases in off-task behavior, including challenging behavior. Prior to increases in challenging behavior, however, we may observe changes in the length of the latency between the end of one behavioral sequence and initiation of the next sequence. Just as increases in these latencies may show increasing fatigue, reductions in these latencies across time should indicate that completing the behavioral sequence requires less effort over time.

A term closely related to fluency is *efficiency*. One dictionary definition of efficiency is "the ratio of the effective or useful output to the total input in a system" (Soukhanov et al., 1984; see also Gilbert, 1996). Thus, *increased efficiency* in the behavioral sense could mean increasing reinforcement while holding effort constant or decreasing effort while maintaining the same frequency of reinforcement. Increases in fluency can affect efficiency in two ways. First, when reinforcers are acquired through shorter, smoother performances, then efficiency has increased. This increase in efficiency does not alone alter the rate of reinforcement if interresponse time increases concurrently. This is important because more time can be allocated to challenging behavior if the adaptive responses consume less time but do not increase in frequency. Second, when latency of performance-unit initiation decreases, then efficiency increases and, in this case, the rate of reinforcement also increases (under ratio schedules in particular). Third, when both the duration of the performance unit and latency of initiation decrease, then increases in efficiency are maximized. Because supported routines are constructed of existing behavioral sequences and these sequences are bridged where necessary, increased fluency and efficiency can be an immediate result of implementation. Hypotheses regarding increased control over reinforcement, response allocation, and contingency discrimination suggest why increased fluency and efficiency may lead to reduction in challenging behavior in supported routines. Discussion of these hypotheses follows.

## Increased Control

In another view of the concept of competence, White (1959) postulated the existence of an evolutionary adaptive drive, called "effectance motivation," for all organisms to develop mastery or control of the events affecting them. Buyer, Berkson, Winnega, and Morton (1987) concluded that *stereotypy*—one form of challenging behavior—involved two processes: control and stimulation. Berkson, Baranek, and Thompson (1992) further suggested that stereotypy is a function of a desire for "personal control" and becomes a predominant way for some individuals to gain access to or control reinforcers. Recognition of control or increased control as a possible reinforcing function of stereotypy might be applied more broadly to other forms of challenging behavior. For examples, Carr and Durand (1985) and Wacker et al. (1990) have discussed the role of control over reinforcement in the effectiveness of interventions with functional communication training. Thus, if an individual has few effective ways of gaining access to positive reinforcement other than by challenging behavior (Thompson & Berkson, 1985)—as often may be true of people with mental retardation requiring the most extensive supports—then there is little to compete with an increased allocation time to such behavior (Lovaas, Newsom, & Hickman, 1987).

Control or increased control is difficult to conceptualize as a reinforcing *stimulus.* Control is more likely part of what is learned when the consequences of one's behavior are learned. If so, increased control is what is learned when behaving increases the rate of reinforcing consequences. Repeated exposure to reinforcement contingencies should be effective in establishing other stimuli as discriminative for reinforcement for behavior—behavior that can become increasingly efficient in producing reinforcement. In the presence of these discriminative stimuli, the individual allocates less time to challenging behavior because the individual discriminates the differential efficiency of the response alternatives. Increased behavioral efficiency, which can be measured directly, should be an observable indication of increased control. Perhaps supported routines function to create opportunities for responses or behavioral sequences to rapidly become more efficient in the presence of particular contextual stimuli. This seems analogous to an experiment on the matching law with nonhuman animals, in which a new manipulandum is added to the animal's environment, which already contains other manipulanda. In this experiment, the new manipulandum requires less effort than responding on the other manipulanda, and the schedule of reinforcement is at least as rich.

## Response Allocation

The matching law (Herrnstein, 1961, 1970, 1974) was derived from the results of extensive laboratory research dating from the early 1960s (see de Villiers, 1977; Pierce & Epling, 1983, for reviews). Results of some matching law experiments show that, when multiple responses are possible, the relative rate of each response corresponds to the relative rate of reinforcement for each response (Herrnstein, 1961, 1970). Relative proportion of duration of responding often similarly covaries with relative rate of reinforcement (e.g., Baum & Rachlin, 1969; Brownstein & Pliskoff, 1968). More recently, the relationship between the rate of challenging behaviors and the rate of alternative behaviors has been discussed in terms of the rate and quality of reinforcement for the respective behaviors (Horner & Day, 1991; Meyerson & Hale, 1984; Neef, Mace, Shea, & Shade, 1992). Studies of the matching law in applied settings indicate that the distribution of responses across possible alternatives is affected by the respective schedules of reinforcement for the alternatives (e.g., Durand & Crimmins, 1988; Horner, Sprague, O'Brien, & Heathfield, 1990; Sprague & Horner, 1992). Despite critical differences between applied settings and laboratory settings that make extrapolation difficult in both directions (e.g., Fuqua, 1984), McDowell (1982, 1988) suggested that the matching law nevertheless describes the relationship between reinforcement and behavior in natural settings. Meyerson and Hale (1984) suggested that the implications of this relationship are important for designing behavioral interventions. For example, applied studies have shown that when compliance to instructions was increased with reinforcement contingencies, the percentage of intervals with compliance often covaried with the percentage of intervals containing particular targeted challenging behaviors; which challenging behavior covaried with compliance, however, was idiosyncratic across participants (Cataldo, Ward, Russo, Riordan, & Bennett, 1986; Russo, Cataldo, & Cushing, 1981). Halle and Spradlin (1993) and Parrish and Roberts (1993) provided excellent elaboration on the issues in response covariation and response substitution in applied settings, suggested by these and other research reports.

Knowing whether the matching law in any version precisely describes the relationship among reinforcement, socially relevant behavior, and challenging behavior awaits further research. Nevertheless, considering that a matching law equation might generally describe those relationships can be instructive if one attends to some of the procedural components of matching law research. For example, scheduling high-rate reinforcement for the socially valued alternative is only one of the important factors. For any equation of the matching law to apply, an intervention must have the characteristics of a free operant situation; that is, an intervention in which the completion of one response leaves the organism in a position to emit the next response immediately (Catania, 1992). Furthermore, having a reasonable estimate of the upper limits of an individual's fluency in the to-be-reinforced alternative behavior is also critical. Selecting a response that cannot be increased as a function of the reinforcing effects of the scheduled contingency would leave the individual unable to increase the rate of reinforcement. Thus, increased behavioral efficiency would be constrained, and challenging behavior would not be displaced. Finally, the schedule for the reinforcer in the contingency should be selected for its rate enhancement characteristics (see Meyerson & Hale, 1984, for schedule-related considerations; see Binder, 1996, and Lindsley, 1996, for a more thorough discussion of fluency issues).

Thus, potential matching law effects are not dependent solely on the schedules employed and the reinforcers selected because rate of reinforcement is also dependent, in most schedules, on rate of responding. Because supported routines start with identification of existing behavioral sequences, arrange for their enactment at higher rates, arrange reinforcement for their emission, and preclude delays with sequence bridging, a supported routines approach produces higher rates of responding and reinforcement quickly. That is, a supported routine incorporates procedural elements of basic laboratory research. Thus, positive results from the implementation of a supported routines approach are more likely to be a function of matching law effects than many other interventions because supported routines are more procedurally consistent with free operant conditions. Supported routines set the occasion for increases in rate of reinforcement to a therapeutically effective level.

## Contingency Discrimination

Reinforcement for behavioral sequences in supported routines is arranged in two ways. One is briefly described in this introductory paragraph, and the other is discussed shortly. One way is to arrange for the production of naturally occurring reinforcers such as acquisition of food items during a mealtime routine or access to a favorite set of materials used in leisure and recreation to follow a behavioral sequence. In this type of arrangement, each behavioral sequence or series of sequences results in a reinforcing consequence. Thus, the reinforcer has a one-to-one relationship to the overall sequence, and the completion of each intermediate sequence has a one-to-one relationship with the next intermediate sequence (i.e., discriminative stimulus-response). This one-to-one linkage between sequences and reinforcers or continuous behavior–reinforcer covariation may be an important variable in the effectiveness of supported routines.

Lindsley (cited in Rovee-Collier & Gekoski, 1979) suggested that contingencies with continuous covariation between response and consequence may be very common in nature. Williams and Johnston (1992) suggested that such contingencies shape behavior automatically and are involved in the development of skilled perceptual-motor performances such as figure skating or driving. Evidence of the power of direct covariation is most readily found in studies that employed conjugate reinforcement (e.g., Lindsley, Hobika, & Etsten, 1961; Mira, 1968; Rovee & Rovee, 1969). In *conjugate reinforcement procedures*, parameters of the reinforcement, such as duration or rate, vary directly with the same parameters of the response that is reinforced. In the reinforcement arrangement described in this paragraph, the types of consequences that follow behavioral sequences often involve prolonged contact with reinforcing stimuli that appear to be highly preferred by the individual.

Evidence of the power of direct covariation is found also in the functional equivalence literature. Horner et al. (1990) compared the effects of equivalent behaviors in terms of different levels of their efficiency in reinforcer production as replacements for aggression; Horner and Day (1991) evaluated functionally equivalent-response efficiency in terms of physical effort, reinforcement schedule, and delay of reinforcement. Horner and colleagues' experiments demonstrated that the effectiveness of the functional equivalence intervention was lost or greatly reduced when the equivalent response was complex (e.g., signing a sentence, spelling "help please"), required repetitions of the same response (i.e., fixed ratios greater than 1), or created delays in producing the equivalent consequence. That is, although communication responses could be made substitutable for challenging behavior, they were substitutable only when they produced the same reinforcer as the challenging behavior and as efficiently as the challenging behavior.

Because of reports such as Horner and colleagues' and as a function of the results of assessments of discrimination ability on which we depend to create supported routines, in practice we modify the second reinforcement arrangement that we employ to emulate the first. The second arrangement is reinforcement in the form of points, money, food, or brief access to music, as examples, which is scheduled to be delivered by providers or supporters for defined units of performance or sets of behavioral sequences. This latter arrangement is most common to academic and vocational settings, in which particular sequences repeat often but may be invoked in other situations as well. In practice, we use environmental modifications to create a type of one-to-one correspondence between the behavioral sequences in these repetitive situations and the reinforcers delivered. Saunders and Saunders (1997b) demonstrated that without this modification, scheduled contingencies may not become functional contingencies (see Lattal & Poling, 1981) in some individuals with developmental disabilities. This second reinforcement arrangement may not appear to be indicative of what people without developmental disabilities experience—a consideration of some merit—but the differences lie on continua of time and discrimination ability. Therefore, adjusting the temporal parameters and parameters of stimulus presentation to maintain a functional contingency while attempting to reflect a more typical arrangement is an ongoing challenge.

## Summary

When the intervention effectiveness of the practical approach outlined by Saunders and Spradlin (1991) is evaluated in the context of the research literature, the most apparent conclusions are that supported routines may

1. Increase behavioral efficiency (or control over reinforcers)
2. Increase rates of reinforcement by decreasing delays and by permitting increases in fluency
3. Reduce challenging behavior through matching law effects
4. Reduce evokers of challenging behavior by reducing the proportion of time spent in formal training or in tasks for which the individual lacks the prerequisite skills, and by reducing delays in important behavioral sequences
5. Lead to greater discriminative stimulus control by the presence of providers and supporters, a potentially important factor when the individual is exposed subsequently to novel or changing setting conditions

Thus, the supported routines approach is not a package of multiple interventions; rather, it is a unitary intervention informed by multiple facets of empirical behavioral research.

## IMPLEMENTATION

To begin the process of creating one or more supported routines for an individual, all of the results of evaluations and assessments should be assembled into one easy-to-read and easy-to-absorb document. We have referred to this document as an interdisciplinary summary of individual characteristics (Saunders, Saunders, & Hull, 1991). Next, the summary should be made more nearly complete by obtaining assessment results on areas not addressed adequately by the existing assessments. For example, the Auditory Visual Combined test may provide details on discrimination learning ability not ordinarily included in developmental assessments (Kerr, Meyerson, & Flora, 1977; Wacker, Kerr, & Carroll, 1983). The summary should comprehensively address the individual's characteristics in the areas of physical health, physical characteristics, nutritional status, sensorimotor functioning, emotional and social behavior, communication, auditory and visual functioning, cognition, learning characteristics, personal likes and dislikes, and other relevant information. The summary does not need to describe all of an individual's skills such as independent dressing or vocational prowess that compose typical daily routines. The summary should describe all of the individual's abilities such as visual acuity, agility, receptive language, discrimination skills, and so forth. In general, the summary is that information needed to evaluate the *prognosis* for the development of behavioral sequences involved in typical daily routines appropriate to the age and gender of the individual. With sequence-specific prognoses, functional tasks, routines, and activities, or portions thereof, can be selected that match the individual's capabilities more precisely. That is, we can minimize the discrepancy between our expectations and the individual's possible performances. Schalock and Jensen (1986) referred to this as maximizing the "goodness-of-fit." By analogy, the results of examinations, interviews, and letters of reference are material from which the goodness-of-fit between an applicant to graduate school and a department's curriculum and expectations are determined.

To provide a clearer picture of the contents of the summary and its use, a few examples that have arisen previously in designing supported routines may be helpful. Each example is posed as an assessment question or observation followed by a possible outcome.

1. Will the individual be able to discriminate a stainless steel teaspoon from a slightly larger stainless steel serving spoon during family-style dining as the serving dish is passed? If not, substitution of larger colored plastic serving spoons may result in substitution of a discrimination that can be acquired for one that cannot.

2. Is the individual performing at a cognitive level that will result in "forgetting" the location of a napkin when it is placed in the lap and the chair is pushed under the edge of the table or table-

cloth? If not, placing the napkin in the lap would be eliminated from the routine.

3. Will a left-handed person be as efficient in moving assembly-line products from right to left as he or she would be in moving them from left to right? If not, placement of the individual on the opposite side of the assembly line from his or her co-workers would change the direction of flow and would increase fluency and efficiency.

4. A left-handed person prefers to be assisted in tasks from the right side. What will be the consequence of moving this individual into a home in which the bathroom and kitchen sinks have a wall along the right-hand side of the sink? If fluency in routines in these locations would be jeopardized, locate another house with the opposite environmental arrangement.

5. At work, an individual who cannot count is paid (i.e., reinforced) each time she shreds 10 sheets of paper from a large bin of discarded office documents. Will she likely learn the consequences of her work behavior, thereby resulting in higher work rates and more payment? If not, presenting the documents in sets of 10 in a shallow box could create a one-to-one correspondence between an empty box and payment.

6. An individual can put his hands through the sleeves of a coat but does not learn multistep chains easily. Consider having the individual put each hand in a sleeve with the coat in the reverse direction and then flip the coat over the head.

7. An individual is observed to drink independently but is also observed to spill fluid when picking up or putting down the glass. Consider replacing glasses with small bottles with flow limiters (i.e., the mineral water type) or glasses with wide rock-proof bases.

8. At work on an assembly line, an individual is expected to pass items on to the next worker on the line. Does the individual discriminate how far to pass the item so that it is within reach of the co-worker? If not, create a "wicket" hung with plastic strips such that when the item is passed through the wicket, it is out of the individual's sight, but it is passed far enough for the co-worker.

9. An individual has very poor problem-solving, discrimination, and physical manipulation abilities. He has been observed to move items presented on his left to his right by swiping them with the back of his right hand. Place him to the right of the individual described in Item 8 who cannot discriminate how far to pass his completed work units and for whom the wicket was

unsuccessful. Pay this individual at piece-rate based on the degree to which he increases the work rate of the individual to his right who now receives the next unit in a more timely fashion.

10.   At work, an individual is observed to be able to assemble items requiring a few steps but is also observed to periodically pick up assembled items and disassemble them. Consider having the individual place the assembled item into a slot in the table or in a large container from which the assembled item cannot be retrieved.

11.   An individual has a history of learning steps in behavioral sequences when taught in isolation but reacts negatively to multistep training programs based on typical task analyses, particularly when the sequence is lengthy. Consider teaching only one step at a time, beginning with a step adjacent to an already acquired step. Do all of the other steps for the individual without hesitation (bridge) until the new step is acquired, then teach a third step adjacent to the acquired steps. The length of the sequence increases only as the individual acquires more steps.

12.   In nearly all routines, an individual is observed to have difficulty with visual discriminations due to vision impairment, but the problem is most dangerous on stairways, stoops, and so forth. Consider painting the steps in an alternating pattern of a light and dark color. Contrasting colors on stimulus materials in other routines may also improve performance.

13.   A individual who is nonambulatory and who has limited upper body coordination enjoys participation in all activities, particularly social activities, and being involved in choice making; she dislikes being left unattended and unengaged. Consider modifying the individual's wheelchair to be a carryall. Create attachable containers, tool-belt type harnesses, and so forth. Allow this individual to select and transport activity materials, supplies, and clean-up materials for staff.

14.   An individual has few independent, coordinated motor skills, but has good visual and auditory discrimination skills. Consider placing the individual in a situation in which he or she must evaluate the correctness (e.g., quality) of the performance of other co-workers (or other students). Provide a switch-activated alarm for the individual to activate when products of faulty quality pass his or her station.

These examples represent just a few of the problem-solving sequences that go into creating and embellishing supported routines. In applied settings, it is important to create enablement in as many routines as possible and to use consistent approaches to enablement across routines with similar characteristics. Finally, the impact of a supported routines approach is maximized when the routines are enacted consistently across days. A scripting procedure is helpful in producing consistent supports from providers and supporters, particularly when several individuals are supported together. Our clinical interventions have relied on a scripting approach called "scenarios" (Saunders, Rast, & Saunders, 1988) to achieve this consistency. The next section describes some research on the effects of various components of supported routines.

## RESEARCH WITH SUPPORTED ROUTINES

The following section provides evidence that supported routines can be used to reduce challenging behaviors (e.g., rocking, stereotypic facial hitting, self-injury) in academic, home, and vocational settings. The section also discusses the effects of varying reinforcement schedules and facilitating contingency discrimination with supported routines.

### Reducing Rocking and Stereotypic Facial Hitting

Saunders, Saunders, Brewer, and Roach (1996) described an intervention for an 18-year-old male with mental retardation requiring pervasive supports, a seizure disorder, a mild visual acuity loss, and a moderate bilateral hearing loss who engaged in high-rate stereotypic behavior. The stereotypic behavior included body rocking, object mouthing, and repetitive facial hitting that caused continuous bruising around the eyes. These behaviors occurred at high rates during all leisure and instructional classroom activities and at generally lower rates during meals and when walking to and from activities. It was noted that he was generally capable of eating and walking without assistance.

A multiple-baseline design was employed across two instructional activity periods. In baseline, each 1-hour instructional period consisted of roughly 10 minutes of instruction alternating with 10–20 minutes of leisure until the period ended. During baseline of the first period, he received academic instruction on discrimination problems, and in the second period he participated in a group vocational task involving packaging. His teacher used edible reinforcement for correct responses in both periods. The intervention on both baselines was the substitution of a six-step tennis ball packaging task, arranged to permit easy completion, and a change in the distribution of time allocated to work and leisure. This particular intervention was selected because assessments indicated that 1) the student had a poor prognosis for solving the academic discrimination problems but a high prognosis for quickly learning to perform the packaging sequence; and 2) the student had to wait lengthy periods between "turns" in the second-period packaging task, whereas the intervention task would permit continuous work if he so desired. In the intervention, the vocational training sessions were increased to 15 minutes alternating with 5 minutes of leisure until the 1-hour period ended. Each completion of the six-step sequence was followed by token delivery that was exchangeable for a choice of an edible or a drink. The token was delivered regardless of whether body rocking or facial hits occurred and regardless of the number of prompts or error corrections that were required from the teacher for him to complete the sequence. The teachers attempted to block blows to the face and ignored most other responses.

Body rocking ceased almost immediately in both periods on the initiation of the intervention, an effect later determined to be a function of shifting from a molded plastic chair in the baselines to a padded armchair in intervention. Facial hitting did not decrease in the first period until the latency of teacher prompts was decreased, which was done in an attempt to prevent some of the sequencing errors that the student was making (usually following pauses). A reduction in facial hitting followed this change in strategy, and this reduction was replicated in the second baseline. Thereafter, as long as the joint responding of the teacher (prompts) and the student (packaging) produced rates of reinforcement greater than 0.8 per minute, facial hitting was absent from most sessions and at very low rates otherwise. When the student was performing less fluently (often following heavy seizure activity) or in sessions in which the teacher was less quick to prompt steps, the rate of facial hitting was as high as in baseline. Over the course of the study, such sessions became less frequent (even following seizures) as the student became more proficient in packaging, thus rarely requiring prompts from the teacher.

These results provided the first indication that rate of reinforcement for an alternative behavioral sequence and rate of a challenging behavior might covary not in a linear fashion but on either side of a rate-of-reinforcement threshold. That is, the periods with high rates of facial hitting occurred generally in sessions in which rate of packages completed was approximately 0.75 per minute or less; in contrast, sessions with rates of packages completed of 0.8, 0.9, and 1.0 per minute were sessions in which facial hitting did not occur or occurred at very low rates. Threshold shifts have been shown to occur in studies of the matching law when ratio schedules of different values have been contrasted (e.g., Schroeder, 1975) or when the richness of ratio schedule begins to exceed the richness of an interval schedule.

By the end of the formal study, the student's supported routine consisted of exposure to a task in which he was fluent. That is, his packaging had increased to 1.5 packages per minute, sequencing errors were rare, and post-reinforcement pauses were brief. The student had become more efficient in producing reinforcement. It is interesting to also note that his fluency in the packaging task appeared similar to his fluency in eating his meals. Inclusion of a presumably more comfortable chair in the routine precluded body rocking. This relationship was confirmed during a 3-day period in which the padded chair was out of the classroom for repair of a loose arm, during which rocking was observed throughout each vocational session, even as he continued to work at a high rate. Rocking was not observed following return of the padded chair.

## Reducing Self-Injury in a Mealtime Routine

A second student described by Saunders et al. (1996) was an adolescent male with autism and mental retardation requiring extensive supports, who ate quickly and messily and also exhibited hand biting and head hitting. Teacher prompts of appropriate mealtime behavior, interventions to avert potential accidents, and interruptions created by incidental teaching frequently evoked these self-injurious behaviors. Although the adolescent appeared very hungry before breakfast, he often disposed of his meal when the teacher persisted with the various forms of interruption. Moving him away from the dining table or requiring him to continue with the activity following self-injury appeared only to escalate his self-injurious behavior. Observations revealed that many of the errors or accidents in his mealtime routine were a function of discrimination failure and that responding correctly to the teacher's interventions also required making difficult discriminations. Assessments indicated that the individual had a poor prognosis for making these discriminations but exhibited the fine motor and visual discrimination skills required for acquiring many steps in a basic mealtime sequence.

A mealtime supported routine was developed that eliminated many difficult discriminations and permitted the individual to attempt most of the steps in the routine himself. A corresponding routine also was established for the teacher that included bridging at critical points and that minimized making demands that the individual could not meet. The routines were refined further to minimize delays, errors, and arbitrary rules. Cessation of the teacher's interruptions and incidental teaching resulted in almost total elimination of self-injury during the meal. Subsequently, by the end of the formal study, the student had learned to perform nearly 70% of the steps in the new routine independently while continuing to exhibit almost no challenging behavior. Follow-up observations showed that the rates of challenging behavior remained low. Later, a substitute teacher who replaced the teacher during a leave of absence was asked initially to follow the first teacher's earlier instructional program. The re-establishment of these conditions led immediately to an increase in hand biting and facial hitting, but the challenging behavior quickly ceased once the new teacher was instructed how to conduct the supported routine.

The behavior of the teacher in the baseline of this study (in which she performed many of the steps later assigned to the student) may be typical of caregivers' and teachers' attempts to screen people with mental retardation requiring extensive or pervasive supports from interacting with the environment in destructive ways, even in a mild sense (e.g., spilled milk). The delays caused by the teacher's attempts to teach the student subtle but socially important aspects of mealtime behavior—combined with the delays produced by doing steps for him—appeared to be the major evokers of challenging behavior. The results of this study strongly support the suggestion that delays in sequences of responses leading to reinforcement (e.g., eating breakfast) are punishing, particularly when the progression through the routine is under strong motivation.

By the end of the study, in addition to modifications to the teacher's instructional approach, 13 environmental adaptations had been made. These adaptations resulted in the student performing the following: obtaining materials for a place setting from a cart, setting his place, walking to a nearby food cart, pushing the cart near his table, obtaining milk cartons and serving bowls from the cart, seating himself, opening and pouring his milk, serving himself food and condiments, eating (more slowly and with few spills), carrying his dishes and trash to the appropriate locations, washing his hands, and seating himself at another table with leisure materials. It is important to note that the supported routine for this student did not involve introducing additional contingent tangible or social reinforcement for independent steps—*only opportunities to do the steps himself and adaptation of the environment to enable competent performance of the steps*. Thus, the step acquisition effects are from practice—practice presumably reinforced by advancing through the routine to gain access to food to consume or to gain additional servings of food to consume.

## Reducing Stereotypy in a Vocational Activity

Saunders and Saunders (1997a) reported the intervention for a 12-year-old male with mental retardation requiring pervasive supports who engaged in high rates of object "flipping," body rocking, and placing his fingers in his mouth. He sometimes engaged in these behaviors concurrent with on-task behaviors but nearly always engaged in the behaviors when not engaged in another task or routine. A five-step eraser packaging task was being taught by one of his teachers prior to this experiment. The experiment was conducted in an ABAB reversal design. In the initial condition, Condition A (the condition in effect when we began observations), 10 trials or sequences of the task were completed in each session. The student removed one item from each of several containers in sequence (a container base, two erasers, and a container lid) and enclosed the erasers in the container. The teacher prompted a response after a pause between steps or after errors in the packaging sequence, and a reinforcer (an edible) was delivered if the student completed the sequence *without an error in performing the final step of the sequence.* During Condition B, a reinforcer was delivered if the student *completed all steps without error.* Under Condition A, an increase in the rate of packaging and reinforcement occurred and were accompanied by a decrease in all forms of stereotypy. Under Condition B, stereotypy increased to its previously higher level and rate of reinforcement decreased. Reexposure to each condition replicated these effects. Although the contingency in Condition B would appear to be the contingency of choice (between the two) for teaching the student to achieve fewer errors, that would be the case only if the student learned what was involved in the contingency. The results suggest that the discrimination of the elements of the contingency (perhaps either contingency) was too difficult for this student. Thus, the reinforcers probably strengthened packaging but had little differential effect on errors. Condition B had a lower rate of reinforcement, so it was a less effective condition for maintaining packaging and minimizing stereotypy. The reduction of errors across the experiment most likely occurred through negative reinforcement— avoidance of error corrections that slowed the rate of edible reinforcement. The results place an emphasis on selecting contingencies that match the assessed learning characteristics of the individual.

In a second experiment with this student, Saunders and Saunders (1997a) investigated the effects of further environmental modifications to the eraser packaging task. One modification produced low rates of packaging and reinforcement accompanied by a high percentage of training time allocated to stereotypy. A second modification, however, led to a rapid reduction in training time allocated to stereotypy and a doubling of the rate of packaging and reinforcement. Further modifications and extensive practice with the task led to training sessions with little or no time allocated to stereotypy and further increases in rate of packaging. At this point the student had become competent in the task and required virtually no prompting or error correction.

A third experiment with this student examined his behavior at a table with a teacher and another student during two additional packaging routines. Two 15-minute vocational sessions separated by a 5-minute leisure period were observed each day. A toothbrush-packaging task and an audiocassette-packaging task alternated across days as the vocational task. The second student participated in each task such that the two students conducted the packaging in an assembly-line fashion. The experimental design was an ABA reversal design in each vocational task. During Condition A, each student performed the task successively; that is, one student performed his part of the task, and then the other student performed his part of the task. Thus, materials were available to each student approximately half of each session, thereby restricting each student's potential rate of reinforcement. During Condition B, work materials were available to each student throughout the session and both students could work on the task simultaneously. The teacher prompted gesturally whenever errors occurred in each packaging sequence and all instances of stereotypy were ignored. Tokens were delivered on a ratio schedule—determined by the numerical capacity of devices employed to facilitate packaging—to each student. The toothbrush device held five toothbrushes, and the cassette device held three cassette cases. The token was delivered whenever the student completed work on the items in the device and passed the device to the next student or to the teacher.

In general, the rate of onset of stereotypy was lower in sessions in which materials to complete the work required for reinforcement were continuously present than in sessions in which materials were not available continuously. The data also showed that as packaging behaviors gradually increased in rate, as did rate of reinforcement, the rate of onset of stereotypy gradually declined. Comparisons between A and B conditions afforded by the reversal design showed that the individuals' performances were more sensitive to the changes in the toothbrush task. Perhaps this was because the ratio of units to tokens was higher in the toothbrush task (5:1)—a feature that would lead to longer periods of waiting without materials than the smaller ratio in the cassette task (3:1). Comparison of the rates of stereotypy during these vocational tasks (with the period of leisure that occurred between the daily vocational sessions) showed that the rate of onset of stereotypy was highest during leisure and lowest under conditions with materials continuously available. Thus, allocation of time to stereotypic behavior appeared directly related to the availability of vocational materials, ranging from none (leisure), to sometimes (Condition A), to always (Condition B).

## Comparison of Reinforcement Schedules

Saunders, Saunders, and Marquis (in press) measured the rates and durations of stereotypic behaviors in four adolescents with mental retardation requiring pervasive supports during two daily vocational training sessions. Stereotypy also was measured during periods of leisure before, between, and after the vocational sessions. Vocational training was conducted in two different tasks, alternating across days: shredding discarded office documents and placing advertising supplements in a local newspaper. The task requirements for each participant were matched to each participant's learning and performance characteristics as supported routines. In one task, a fixed ratio schedule of tokens exchangeable for food items was employed, and a variable interval schedule for the same consequences was employed in the other task. The experiment was designed as a test of a matching-law based prediction by Meyerson and Hale (1984). Meyerson and Hale predicted that variable interval reinforcement for adaptive behavior would produce less allocation of responding to maladaptive behavior than a ratio schedule for adaptive behavior. When work performances stabilized under these schedules, the schedules of token delivery were reversed across the tasks. The results showed that stereotypy occurred more during leisure than under either schedule during vocational training. The results also showed that reduction of stereotypy during vocational training was less a case of reduced onset frequency and more a case of reduced episode length. Onset of stereotypy in vocational training occurred at higher rates under the interval schedule than under the ratio schedule in both tasks. The results did not disconfirm Meyerson and Hale's prediction, however, because the rates of work (and therefore reinforcement) under fixed ratio had generally increased above the rates under the variable interval schedule; Meyerson and Hale's prediction had assumed equal rates of reinforcement. From an applied perspective, however, the results suggest that a ratio schedule may be superior for increasing the rate of alternative behavior and concurrently reducing challenging behavior.

## Contingency Discrimination Research

Saunders and Saunders (1997a) and Saunders et al. (in press) presented the vocational materials to the students in devices whose capacities matched the size of the ratio in the fixed ratio reinforcement schedules. These devices had been employed as elements of the supported routine from the beginning of training in both studies. Their

inclusion was to create a one-to-one correspondence between reinforcement delivery and a discriminable event that resulted directly
from performing the behavioral sequence (an empty device).

In research nearing completion, Saunders and Saunders (1997b)
investigated whether vocational responding would have come under
schedule control if the devices were not employed. Among seven
adult participants with varying degrees of mental retardation, most
failed to come under schedule control without a presentation device.
That is, rates of work (and challenging behavior) were not affected
when contingent reinforcement and extinction conditions were alternated. Institution of the device-presentation procedure led to increased rates of work and responsiveness to reinforcement-extinction
reversal manipulations in several of these participants. Other participants showed large immediate increases in rates of work, but their
performances were not affected by subsequent extinction conditions.
Empirical evaluation of these two different reactions to the device-
presentation procedure is under way.

## CONCLUSIONS

Consistent with Goldiamond's (1974) constructional approach elements, supported routines can be characterized as focusing attention
on behavioral targets other than the challenging behavior, identifying
current usable repertoires, using implementation procedures suitable
to the new behavioral targets, and creating contingencies that will
maintain the expected behavioral outcome. Supported routines rely
on environmental adaptation, demonstration, skill training, response
bridging, and the provision of new response opportunities in various
combinations. The degree of success obtained with supported routines, however, is directly related to the following: 1) how well the
unique characteristics of individuals can be determined and 2) how
insightfully we can determine how those characteristics interact to facilitate or hinder competent performances. The small, but growing,
research literature on supported routines has begun to validate the
functions of some elements of supported routines during relatively
brief activities and routines. Paradoxically, the greatest effectiveness
of supported routines most likely lies in their pervasive and consistent
implementation—an intervention of such complexity that empirical
validation of the "whole" will be elusive. One intriguing possibility
as an approach to further research is to examine how supported routines affect quality of life (QOL). Heal, Borthwick-Duffy, and Saunders
have suggested that

Scaling QOL along the dimension of the discrepancy between one's needs and the competent fulfillment of those needs has appeal as a parsimonious, universal strategy QOL assessment. Under this conceptualization, QOL is maximized when the control one has over the resources to satisfy one's needs is maximized. This definition is particularly appealing because it can be applied to any setting and any level of ability; it is a definition that is culture-free, episode free, and location-free. It is a definition that can be applied in schools, work settings, homes in any neighborhood, hospitals, or prisons. Given this definition, QOL can be measured with an instrument that objectively compares the disparity, or discrepancy, between an individual's needs and the degree and frequency with which their satisfaction is under the individual's control. (1996, pp. 208–209)

Intuitively, increased personal control, increased reinforcement for socially valued behavior, and increased quality of life are related concepts. Supported routines have emerged as a vehicle for directly affecting, or effecting, these outcomes for people with developmental disabilities. An added bonus appears to be the concomitant reduction in challenging behavior, often without the addition of formal interventions for challenging behavior.

## REFERENCES

Barton, E.S., Guess, D., Garcia, E., & Baer, D.M. (1970). Improvement of retardates' mealtime behaviors by timeout procedures using multiple baseline techniques. *Journal of Applied Behavior Analysis, 3*(1), 77–84.

Baum, W.M., & Rachlin, H.C. (1969). Choice as time allocation. *Journal of the Experimental Analysis of Behavior, 12,* 861–874.

Belfiore, P.J., Lim, L., & Browder, D.M. (1994). The effects of task design remediation and response efficiency on work productivity in adults with moderate and severe mental retardation. *Education and Training in Mental Retardation and Developmental Disabilities, 29,* 202–212.

Belfiore, P.J., & Toro-Zambrana, W. (1995). Programming for efficiency: The effects of motion economy on vocational tasks for adults with severe and profound mental retardation. *Research in Developmental Disabilities, 16,* 205–220.

Berkson, G., Baranek, G., & Thompson, T.J. (1992). Personal control of abnormal stereotyped behaviors [Summary]. *Proceedings of the 25th Annual Gatlinburg Conference on Research and Theory in Mental Retardation and Developmental Disabilities.*

Binder, C. (1996). Behavioral fluency: Evolution of a new paradigm. *The Behavior Analyst, 19,* 163–197.

Bostow, D.E., & Bailey, J.B. (1969). Modification of severe disruptive and aggressive behavior using brief timeout and reinforcement procedures. *Journal of Applied Behavior Analysis, 2*(1), 31–37.

Brownstein, A.J., & Pliskoff, S.S. (1968). Some effects of relative reinforcement rate and changeover delay in response-independent concurrent schedules of reinforcement. *Journal of the Experimental Analysis of Behavior, 11,* 683–688.

Buyer, L.S., Berkson, G., Winnega, M.A., & Morton, L. (1987). Stimulation and control as components of stereotyped body rocking. *American Journal of Mental Deficiency, 91*, 543–547.

Carr, E.G., & Durand, V.M. (1985). The social-communicative basis of severe behavior problems in children. In S. Reiss & R.R. Bootzin (Eds.), *Theoretical issues in behavior therapy* (pp. 219–254). New York: Academic Press.

Carr, E.G., Newsom, C.D., & Binkhoff, J.A. (1976). Stimulus control of self-destructive behavior in a psychotic child. *Journal of Abnormal Child Psychology, 4*, 139–152.

Cataldo, M.F., Ward, E.M., Russo, D.C., Riordan, M., & Bennett, D. (1986). Compliance and correlated problem behavior in children: Effects of contingent and noncontingent reinforcement. *Analysis and Intervention in Developmental Disabilities, 6*, 265–282.

Catania, A.C. (1992). *Learning* (3rd ed.). Englewood Cliffs, NJ: Prentice Hall.

Charlop, M.H., Schreibman, L., & Thibodeau, M.B. (1985). Increasing spontaneous verbal responding in autistic children using a time delay procedure. *Journal of Applied Behavior Analysis, 18*, 155–166.

Charlop, M.H., & Trasowech, J.E. (1991). Increasing autistic children's daily spontaneous speech. *Journal of Applied Behavior Analysis, 24*, 747–761.

Cowdery, G.E., Iwata, B.A., & Pace, G.M. (1990). Effects and side effects of DRO as treatment for self-injurious behavior. *Journal of Applied Behavior Analysis, 23*, 497–506.

de Villiers, P.A. (1977). Choice in concurrent schedules and a quantitative formulation of the law of effect. In W.H. Honig & J.E.R. Staddon (Eds.), *Handbook of operant behavior* (pp. 233–287). Englewood Cliffs, NJ: Prentice Hall.

Durand, V.M., & Carr, E.G. (1987). Social influences on "self-stimulatory" behavior: Analysis and treatment application. *Journal of Applied Behavior Analysis, 20*, 119–132.

Durand, V.M., & Crimmins, D.B. (1988). Identifying the variables maintaining self-injurious behavior. *Journal of Autism and Developmental Disorders, 18*(1), 99–117.

Foxx, R.M., McMorrow, M.J., Fenlon, S., & Bittle, R.G. (1986). The reductive effects of reinforcement on the genital stimulation and stereotypy of a mentally retarded adolescent male. *Analysis and Intervention in Developmental Disabilities, 6*, 239–248.

Foxx, R.M., & Shapiro, S.T. (1978). The timeout ribbon: A nonexclusionary timeout procedure. *Journal of Applied Behavior Analysis, 11*(1), 125–136.

Fuqua, R.W. (1984). Comments on the applied relevance of the matching law. *Journal of Applied Behavior Analysis, 17*, 381–386.

Gilbert, T.F. (1996). *Human competence: Engineering worthy performance.* Amherst, MA: HRD Press.

Goetz, L., Gee, K., & Sailor, W. (1985). Using a behavior chain interruption strategy to teach communication skills to students with severe disabilities. *Journal of The Association for Persons with Severe Handicaps, 10*, 21–30.

Goldiamond, I. (1974). Toward a constructional approach to social problems. *Behaviorism, 2*, 1–84.

Guidubaldi, J., Perry, J.D., & Walker, M. (1989). Assessment strategies for students with disabilities. *Journal of Counseling and Development, 68*, 160–165.

Halle, J.W., Baer, D.M., & Spradlin, J.E. (1982). Teachers' generalized use of delay as a stimulus control procedure to increase language use in handicapped children. *Journal of Applied Behavior Analysis, 14*, 389–409.

Halle, J.W., Marshall, A.M., & Spradlin, J.E. (1979). Time delay: A technique to increase language use and facilitate generalization in retarded children. *Journal of Applied Behavior Analysis, 12,* 95–103.

Halle, J.W., & Spradlin, J.E. (1993). Identifying stimulus control of challenging behavior: Extending the analysis. In J. Reichle & D.P. Wacker (Eds.), *Communication and language intervention series: Vol. 3. Communicative alternatives to challenging behavior: Integrating functional assessment and intervention strategies* (pp. 83–109). Baltimore: Paul H. Brookes Publishing Co.

Halpern, A.S., & Fuhrer, M.J. (Eds.). (1984). *Functional assessment in rehabilitation.* Baltimore: Paul H. Brookes Publishing Co.

Heal, L.W., Borthwick-Duffy, S.A., & Saunders, R.R. (1996). Assessment of quality of life. In J.W. Jacobson & J.A. Mulick (Eds.), *Manual of diagnosis and professional practice in mental retardation* (pp. 199–209). Washington, DC: American Psychological Association.

Herrnstein, R.J. (1961). Relative and absolute strength of response as a function of frequency of reinforcement. *Journal of the Experimental Analysis of Behavior, 4,* 267–272.

Herrnstein, R.J. (1970). On the law of effect. *Journal of the Experimental Analysis of Behavior, 13,* 243–266.

Herrnstein, R.J. (1974). Formal properties of the matching law. *Journal of the Experimental Analysis of Behavior, 21,* 159–164.

Horner, R.H., & Day, H.M. (1991). The effects of response efficiency on functionally equivalent competing behaviors. *Journal of Applied Behavior Analysis, 24,* 719–732.

Horner, R.H., Sprague, J.R., O'Brien, M., & Heathfield, L.T. (1990). The role of response efficiency in the reduction of problem behaviors through functional equivalence training: A case study. *Journal of The Association for Persons with Severe Handicaps, 15,* 91–97.

Iwata, B.A., Dorsey, M.F., Slifer, K.J., Bauman, K.E., & Richman, G.S. (1994). Toward a functional analysis of self-injury. *Journal of Applied Behavior Analysis, 27,* 197–209.

Kerr, N., Meyerson, L., & Flora, J.A. (1977). Mentally retarded children and adults: The measurement of motor, visual and auditory discrimination skills. *Rehabilitation Psychology, 24*(3), 95–112.

Lattal, K.A., & Poling, A.D. (1981). Describing response–event relations: Babel revisited. *The Behavior Analyst, 4,* 143–152.

Lindsley, O.R. (1996). The four free-operant freedoms. *The Behavior Analyst, 19,* 199–210.

Lindsley, O.R., Hobika, J.H., & Etsten, B.E. (1961). Operant behavior during anesthesia recovery: A continuous and objective method. *Anesthesiology, 22,* 937–946.

Lovaas, O.I., Newsom, C., & Hickman, C. (1987). Self-stimulatory behavior and perceptual reinforcement. *Journal of Applied Behavior Analysis, 20,* 45–68.

Mace, F.C., Browder, D.M., & Lin, Y. (1987). Analysis of demand conditions associated with stereotypy. *Journal of Behavior Therapy and Experimental Psychiatry, 18,* 25–31.

Mazaleski, J.L., Iwata, B.A., Vollmer, T.R., Zarcone, J.R., & Smith, R.G. (1993). Analysis of the reinforcement and extinction components in DRO contingencies with self-injury. *Journal of Applied Behavior Analysis, 26,* 143–156.

McDowell, J.J. (1982). The importance of Herrnstein's mathematical law of effect for behavior therapy. *American Psychologist, 37,* 771–779.

McDowell, J.J. (1988). Matching theory in natural human environments. *The Behavior Analyst, 11,* 95–109.

Meyerson, J., & Hale, S. (1984). Practical implications of the matching law. *Journal of Applied Behavior Analysis, 17,* 367–380.

Mira, M. (1968). Individual patterns of looking and listening preferences among learning disabled and normal children. *Exceptional Children, 34,* 649–658.

Neef, N.A., Iwata, B.A., & Page, T.J. (1977). The effects of known-item interspersal on acquisition and retention of spelling and sightreading words. *Journal of Applied Behavior Analysis, 10,* 738.

Neef, N.A., Mace, F.C., Shea, M.C., & Shade, D. (1992). Effects of reinforcer rate and reinforcer quality on time allocation: Extensions of matching theory to educational settings. *Journal of Applied Behavior Analysis, 25,* 691–699.

Parrish, J.M., & Roberts, M.L. (1993). Interventions based on covariation of desired and inappropriate behavior. In J. Reichle & D.P. Wacker (Eds.), *Communication and language intervention series: Vol. 3. Communicative alternatives to challenging behavior: Integrating functional assessment and intervention strategies* (pp. 135–173). Baltimore: Paul H. Brookes Publishing Co.

Pierce, W.D., & Epling, W.F. (1983). Choice, matching, and human behavior: A review of the literature. *The Behavior Analyst, 6,* 57–76.

Rovee, C.K., & Rovee, D.T. (1969). Conjugate reinforcement of infant exploratory behavior. *Journal of Experimental Child Psychology, 8,* 33–39.

Rovee-Collier, C.K., & Gekoski, M.J. (1979). The economics of infancy: A review of conjugate reinforcement. In H.W. Reese & L.P. Lipsitt (Eds.), *Advances in child development and behavior* (Vol. 13, pp. 195–295). New York: Academic Press.

Russo, D.C., Cataldo, M.F., & Cushing, P.J. (1981). Compliance training and behavioral covariation in the treatment of multiple behavior problems. *Journal of Applied Behavior Analysis, 14,* 209–222.

Saunders, M.D. (1998). *Treatment of challenging behavior with differential positive reinforcement: Some questions for future research.* Manuscript submitted for publication.

Saunders, M.D., & Saunders, R.R. (1997a). An analysis of stereotypy during prevocational instruction of an adolescent with severe mental retardation. *Behavioral Interventions, 12,* 1–26.

Saunders, M.D., & Saunders, R.R. (1997b, May). *Analysis of the covariation between work behavior and aberrant behavior in persons with severe retardation.* Poster session at the meeting of the Association for Behavior Analysis, Chicago.

Saunders, M.D., Saunders, R.R., & Marquis, J. (in press). Comparison of reinforcement schedules in the reduction of stereotypy with supported routines. *Research in Developmental Disabilities.*

Saunders, R.R., Butterfield, G., Eiler, J., Lingwood, D., & Tucker, D. (1992, May). *Managing facility improvement with a comprehensive quality assurance system.* Paper presented at the 116th annual meeting of the American Association on Mental Retardation Convention, New Orleans, LA.

Saunders, R.R., O'Meara, P., Fovel, T., Allen, J., & Isley, E. (1994, June). *Continuous improvement in individual lifestyles.* Paper presented at the 118th annual meeting of the American Association on Mental Retardation, Boston.

Saunders, R.R., Rast, J., & Saunders, M.D. (1988). *A handbook for scenario-based active treatment.* Lawrence: University of Kansas.

Saunders, R.R., Saunders, M.D., Brewer, A., & Roach, T. (1996). The reduction of self-injury in two adolescents with profound retardation by the establishment of a supported routine. *Behavioral Interventions, 11,* 59–86.

Saunders, R.R., Saunders, M.D., & Hull, D.D. (1991). *CAPPS: Comprehensive Assessment and Program Planning System.* Parsons: University of Kansas.

Saunders, R.R., & Spradlin, J.E. (1991). A supported routines approach to active treatment for enhancing independence, competence, and self-worth. *Behavioral Residential Treatment, 6,* 11–37.

Schalock, R.L., & Jensen, C.M. (1986). Assessing the goodness-of-fit between persons and their environments. *Journal of The Association for Persons with Severe Handicaps, 11,* 103–109.

Schroeder, S.R. (1975). Perseveration in concurrent performances by the developmentally retarded. *The Psychological Record, 25,* 51–64.

Schussler, N.G., & Spradlin, J.E. (1991). Assessment of stimuli controlling the requests of students with severe mental retardation during a snack routine. *Journal of Applied Behavior Analysis, 24,* 791–797.

Sidman, M. (1960). *Tactics of scientific research.* New York: Basic Books.

Sigafoos, J., Reichle, J., Doss, S., Hall, K., & Pettitt, L. (1990). "Spontaneous" transfer of stimulus control from tact to mand contingencies. *Research in Developmental Disabilities, 11,* 165–176.

Soukhanov, A.H., et al. (Eds.). (1984). *Webster's II New Riverside University Dictionary.* Boston: Riverside.

Sprague, J.R., & Horner, R.H. (1992). Covariation within functional response classes: Implications for treatment of severe problem behavior. *Journal of Applied Behavior Analysis, 25,* 735–745.

Stoddard, L.T. (1982). An investigation of automated methods for teaching severely retarded individuals. In N.R. Ellis (Ed.), *International review of research in mental retardation* (Vol. 11, pp. 163–208). New York: Academic Press.

Thompson, T.J., & Berkson, G. (1985). Stereotyped behavior of severely disabled children in classroom and free-play settings. *American Journal of Mental Deficiency, 89,* 580–586.

Vollmer, T.R., Iwata, B.A., Zarcone, J.R., Smith, R.G., & Mazaleski, J.L. (1993). The role of attention in the treatment of attention-maintained self-injurious behavior: Noncontingent reinforcement and differential reinforcement of other behavior. *Journal of Applied Behavior Analysis, 26,* 9–21.

Wacker, D.P., Kerr, N.J., & Carroll, J.L. (1983). Discrimination skill as a predictor of prevocational performance of institutionalized mentally retarded clients. *Rehabilitation Psychology, 28*(1), 45–59.

Wacker, D.P., Steege, M.W., Northup, J., Sasso, G., Berg, W., Reimers, T., Cooper, J., Cigrand, K., & Donn, L. (1990). A component analysis of functional communication training across three topographies of severe behavior problems. *Journal of Applied Behavior Analysis, 23,* 417–429.

Weeks, M., & Gaylord-Ross, R. (1981). Task difficulty and aberrant behavior in severely handicapped students. *Journal of Applied Behavior Analysis, 14*(4), 449–463.

White, R.W. (1959). Motivation reconsidered: The concept of competence. *Psychological Review, 66,* 297–333.

Williams, D.C., & Johnston, J.M. (1992). Continuous versus discrete dimensions of reinforcement schedules: An integrative analysis. *Journal of the Experimental Analysis of Behavior, 58,* 205–228.

Wolf, M., Risley, T., & Mees, H. (1964). Application of operant conditioning procedures to the behaviour problems of an autistic child. *Behaviour Research and Therapy, 1,* 305–312.

# ～ *12* ～

## *Lifeway Influences on Challenging Behaviors*

Michael J. Cameron,
Russell W. Maguire, and Melissa Maguire

Lucinda does not dance to merengue music anymore. In fact, she has not danced or listened to music at all since Jorge, an accomplished musician, left his position as the supervisor of her group home. Jorge was the person who identified Lucinda's musical interests. He was the person who danced with Lucinda in the living room to the rhythms of plenas and mambos, salsas and aguinaldos; who spent hours with Lucinda listening to different musicians; who took her to concerts on warm autumn afternoons; and who was proud of the fact that she never engaged in life-threatening self-injurious behavior in his presence.

Christopher has not been to his church in more than 6 weeks. He no longer has weekly opportunities to listen to his church's choir, organ music, or the prosody and inflection of his pastor's baritone voice. The staff person who took Christopher to services each week resigned from her position; and because she was the one who functioned as the liaison between Christopher and the congregation, he no longer receives invitations to special events, the weekly church newsletter, or notices about the potluck suppers he liked to attend. The congregation never registered Christopher's home address or telephone number. In fact, no one among the congregation knows Christopher's last name or where he lives.

### DEFINING LIFEWAY

The point of the previous two vignettes is this: In the absence of careful planning, the lifeway of a person with developmental disabilities conforms to the interests of direct services personnel and, consequently, lasts only as long as the term of their employment. *Lifeway* is a neutral term borrowed from cultural psychology; it is an alternative to the word *lifestyle* and is used deliberately throughout this chapter. This term is used as a reminder that there is nothing stylized about the activities of people with developmental disabilities—at least not until their day-to-day lives are based on their strengths and their personal interests and until they are insulated from the overshadowing needs of others.

People with developmental disabilities are often bound to others in a symbiotic fashion. Many people with severe disabilities require support to get through the quotidian routines many individuals take for granted. Their needs, in turn, create employment opportunities for support personnel. Of course, a principal goal of these support personnel is to assist the person with disabilities in activities of the individual's choosing. The person requiring daily support, however, often receives a defined structure in which he or she has little input. More specifically, the individual's living arrangement is often contrived, bears no similarity to the conditions in which a person without disabilities would like to live, and is ultimately arranged to meet the needs of staff—not the needs of the person with disabilities. It should surprise no one that a person with disabilities often faces barriers in terms of ingress to the community; access to preferred social activities; and ability to participate in games and sporting events, to move freely within his or her own home, or to visit with family and friends. Often, these activities are dependent on the individual's demonstration of appropriate behavior. The irony here is that the very people hired to support individuals with disabilities in preferred lifeways are often the same people who prevent them from achieving the same. Certainly, it was an observation of this nature that occasioned the question by Freire: "What is it about the human condition that so readily causes the helper to be transformed into the oppressor" (1993 p. 84)?

The relationship between a person's lifeway and his or her behavior is not obvious to all clinicians. Indeed, if it were, there would be a greater emphasis on the adjustment of lifeways. The professional literature would be replete with discussions of the positive outcomes of designing programs around an individual's personal interests and the negative effects of failing to do so. We would see example after example of how changes in a person's lifeway resulted in an improvement in his or her quality of life and behavioral presentation; but we do not. In fact, with few notable exceptions, it seems that lifeway is rarely a consideration when attempting to change a repertoire of challenging behavior; rather, behavior analysts frequently treat challenging behaviors as if they operated separately and distinctly from the rest of the individual's life. It is fairly common for clinicians to focus on antecedents and consequences that are proximal to a particular behavior; that is, many clinicians look at behavior in a rigorously linear fashion. Although the deficits to such an approach may be readily apparent, managing the behavior of the moment is a widespread practice because it is reinforcing to the practitioner (Cameron & Kimball, 1995).

Given the complexity of human behavior, it is not uncommon to see many behavioral interventions that result in marginal success. Skinner (1953) argued that although human behavior is lawful we cannot always identify the orderly nature of each individual's behavior. In addition, the lawful patterns of human behavior may be further obscured by developmental disabilities and psychiatric disorders. If one takes into account the effects of these variables, then the shortcomings of a strictly linear approach to behavior management become apparent, if not predictable.

Fortunately, there is more to behavior analysis than linear thinking (as evidenced by the many thoughtful chapters in this book). Competent intervention for clinical disorders requires the examination of behavior within its global context. One must determine the interrelatedness of various sources of control (e.g., the actions and effects of parents, peers, teachers, biobehavioral states, and environments on one's behavior). Essentially, a behavior analyst should not only attempt to isolate the conditions under which challenging behavior reliably occurs, but more important, he or she should aim to understand the conditions under which optimal behavior is observed. What is needed is an analysis of an individual's lifeway—a systematic evaluation of a person's living conditions and the impact of these conditions on the person. Simply stated, behavior analysts need to determine those things in a person's life that are preferred and that occasion adaptive behavior; then they need to provide access to those conditions. Concurrently, analysts need to determine the stimulus conditions that are correlated with challenging behaviors and find ways to either avoid them or attenuate their control over behavior. The point is that behavior analysts should conduct a stimulus control analysis of the lifeways of the people whom they serve.

There have been attempts to address lifeway issues within an educational and clinical context. Giangreco, Cloninger, and Iverson (1998), for example, suggested five general areas that may be described as indicators of lifeway: having a safe and stable home, being able to engage in meaningful activities, having meaningful and full relationships, being able to make age-appropriate choices and having control over decisions, and being safe and healthy. Anecdotally, at one time or another, most behavior analysts have heard about the negative impact that occurs when one or more of these five lifeway areas were lacking (i.e., challenging behavior may be described as a function of an "impoverished home life," "boredom," or "the absence of meaningful relationships").

Ford et al. (1989) also identified five nontraditional areas in which educators should focus to improve the quality of life of the people whom they support: community living domains, functional academics, social skills, communication skills, and motor skills. Although Giangreco et al. (1998) and Ford et al. (1989) do not specifically focus on assessing lifeway or modifying challenging behavior, they made the cogent point that instruction (educational or behavioral) must address critical and specific issues in one's life and should not be arbitrarily imposed.

What is necessary is a formal *a priori* stimulus control analysis of the critical variables affecting a person's life. Clinicians should seek to understand a person's preferred and nonpreferred learning, living, working, socializing, and recreating conditions. The remainder of this chapter presents and discusses two case studies in which a person's lifeway was the major focal point of intervention.

## THOMAS

Thomas was a 16-year-old, electively mute boy with a primary diagnosis of autism. Although Thomas had the capacity for speech, he preferred to use pictures to communicate his needs. Prior to this study, Thomas was observed and evaluated at a 24-hour treatment program in which he was receiving educational and residential services. Thomas exhibited pervasive and chronic maladaptive behavior patterns. The behavior of primary concern was aggression. This behavior was recurrent, intense, and ultimately injurious to staff who worked with him. In fact, direct services personnel who provided one-to-one support, which Thomas received during all waking hours, wore protective clothing to mitigate the effect of his assaultive behavior. Despite these protective measures, Thomas routinely injured staff. Thomas's aggressive behavior also strained his relationship with his foster family. At the time of his discharge from the program, it had been 1 year since his foster family had last seen him.

### Method

Pharmacological, contingency-based interventions were used to control Thomas's behavior. Pharmacological intervention included 300 milligrams of Mellaril, which was not adjusted throughout the course of the study. Contingencies included differential reinforcement of other behavior and seclusionary time-out following the occurrence of aggression. Thomas spent an excessive amount of his day in a time-out room. Although the intent of the time-out contingency was to decrease the likelihood of Thomas's aggression, he would often refuse to leave the room when the door was open; or, he would engage in additional aggressive behavior upon egress, which resulted in the re-instatement of the time-out contingency. Thomas's daily activity schedule was driven by his individualized education program (IEP). However, staff could follow Thomas's daily schedule only when he was not in the time-out room.

## Setting

The onset of the study coincided with Thomas's discharge from the 24-hour treatment program to a comparable educational and residential facility for people with severe behavior disorders. Upon admission, Thomas was assigned to a classroom comprising six other students and four teachers—one of whom remained with Thomas on a full-time basis because of his behavior excesses. Beyond the classroom, there was a gymnasium that was available to Thomas without restriction.

With respect to living accommodations, Thomas shared a home with the same students with whom he attended school; moreover, the 1:1 ratio provided in school was carried over into his home. Thomas had a private bedroom with an attached bathroom and an adjoining suite. The suite was used exclusively by Thomas and his staff throughout this study for recreational and leisure activities.

## Target Behaviors, Functional
## Analysis, and Recording Procedures

Thomas's repertoire of challenging behavior included the following: incontinence of bowel and bladder, rectal digging, smearing feces on people and walls, expectorating at others, inserting objects into his ears, property destruction (e.g., overhead lights, his bed, windows), and aggression. Aggression was the predominant behavior in Thomas's repertoire and took the form of closed-fist striking (typically directed toward the most sensitive parts of a person's body), biting, hair pulling, and kicking. In fact, with the exception of inserting objects into his ears, all of these behaviors occurred in the context of an aggressive episode and appeared to be evoked by a person's attempt to manage his assaults.

A scatter plot analysis (Touchette, MacDonald, & Langer, 1985) and a functional assessment (O'Neill et al., 1997) were completed prior to the onset of intervention to determine the functions of his aggressive behavior. The results suggested that aggression was most probable under the following conditions: 1) when peers were present, 2) when demands were imposed, 3) during meals, 4) when preparing to travel to school or home, and 5) when in close proximity to people who made sudden movements or sounds. Fortunately, staff were able to identify several conditions that occasioned low-rate and low-intensity maladaptive behavior. Specifically, Thomas's aggression was minimized along the dimensions of frequency and intensity whenever he was allowed free access to the gymnasium to bounce on a therapy ball, somersault and roll on an air mattress, roller blade, play basketball, and run laps while staff chased him. In addition, Thomas particularly enjoyed performing matching-to-sample activities (e.g., matching a sample photograph of a teacher or a peer to an identical comparison). Thomas's cooperation with performing matching-to-sample tasks, however, could be secured only if he was allowed to work in the gymnasium while sitting on a bolster, which he would rock back and forth while matching pictures. Finally, in the presence of any one of five staff members, there was a high likelihood that Thomas would refrain from aggression. The characteristics that these staff shared were 1) a commitment to giving Thomas control of his environment and activities through choice making (e.g., Thomas could choose the teacher he wanted to work with from one hour to the next, when he ate his meals, and the order in which he would complete activities), 2) the ability to maintain typical conversation and communication with Thomas regardless of the behavior he was exhibiting, 3) the willingness to follow a highly structured and diverse daily routine, 4) extensive training in the management of aggressive behavior, and 5) complete confidence in their ability to protect themselves and Thomas from injury.

The assessments showed that Thomas's aggression served as a means of escaping or avoiding nonpreferred conditions (e.g., being in close proximity to his peers). Moreover, it was clear that a time-out procedure was contraindicated, which was confirmed by the amount of time he spent in seclusion immediately prior to his admission. The time-out procedure employed whenever Thomas became aggressive appeared to serve as a means of protecting his safety and the safety of staff. The procedure did not have a decelerative effect nor was it maintaining low-rate aggressive behavior. Thomas spent a substantial amount of time each day "in treatment" and very little time engaged in meaningful activities. As a consequence, it was determined that the time-out procedure would not be part of any clinical protocol designed for him.

For the purpose of this study, data were recorded for 16 hours per day. The most problematic behavior in Thomas's repertoire, aggression, was targeted for deceleration. Aggression was recorded any time Thomas slapped, punched, kicked, pulled another person's hair, or bit another person. The frequency of aggression was recorded on a standard datasheet. In addition, two quality-of-life indices were documented on a daily basis. According to Meyer and Evans (1993), indicators of a change in quality of life include reduced need for crisis responses and expanded social relationships and networks. Therefore, staff were also required to record the frequency and duration of physical restraint used on an emergency basis and the amount of time that Thomas spent each day integrated with his peers.

### Intervention Formulation

The results of the scatter plot analysis and the functional assessment led to several important decisions about the environment in which Thomas should work and live, the particular people who should initially work with him, and the details of the activity schedule that should be created for him.

*Environmental Selection*  Given that the gymnasium exerted a high degree of stimulus control over Thomas's behavior, this setting was used exclusively as Thomas's activity and work area. Fortunately, the gymnasium was a rather large area and could be divided by an electrically operated curtain. This arrangement allowed Thomas to use half of the gymnasium without compromising the activity schedules of the other students in the school. The home that Thomas moved into upon his arrival was selected, primarily, because of the space that it afforded. Thomas was given his own bedroom with an adjoining suite in an effort to control the proximity of other people in his immediate environment. In general, the environmental arrangements provided a high level of control over the movement of people in relation to Thomas and, to some extent, the level of noise and movement in his immediate environment.

*Interpersonal Stimulus Control*  There were five staff members whose presence occasioned appropriate behavior. More to the point, Thomas would either refrain from maladaptive behavior or exhibit very low rates when these staff worked with him. Therefore, the personal work schedules of these staff members were arranged so that they could provide one-to-one coverage during all of Thomas's awake hours, 7 days per week. No special staffing arrangements were required during the overnight hours, as Thomas was a sound sleeper. At least one of the five staff members, however, was present until Thomas fell asleep at night and when he awoke in the morning. The rationale for limiting Thomas's interactions to a core group of staff was twofold; one, because Thomas refrained from exhibiting maladaptive behavior or exhibited very low rates in their presence, the majority of Thomas's day could be devoted to teaching functional life skills; and two, the staff who worked with Thomas served as role models for the teachers who would provide support services at a later date.

**Individualized Activity Schedule** Thomas's interest in gross motor performances served as the foundation for his activity schedule. It was clear that if staff were going to work effectively with Thomas, they would have to interact with him in the context of the gymnasium. Thomas's schedule also needed to address all of his IEP objectives; therefore, the activities related to his IEP were integrated into his daily routine. In fact, many of his educational lessons were conducted while Thomas was engaged in some gross motor activity (e.g., staff used flash cards for auditory-visual matching-to-sample instruction while they ran around the gymnasium).

Thomas's schedule also included many activities unrelated to his IEP. For example, his schedule included the following: recreation, academics, opportunities for social interactions, communication with his foster family (e.g., staff assisted him in preparing cards to send to his family in an effort to reinstate contact), exercise (e.g., outdoor activities such as running), domestic chores, meal preparation, and community trips. All of these activities occurred independent of Thomas's behavior; that is, they were not made contingent upon appropriate behavior—they simply occurred. Thomas's schedule consisted of a list of activities that he was required to complete each day. Time intervals were deliberately omitted from the schedule because Thomas determined the order of his routines on a daily basis. The schedule was also arranged so that staff could collect data on Thomas's compliance during each phase of the schedule. The activity schedule was predicated on the assumption that both adaptive and maladaptive behavior should be managed within the framework of traditional routines, and the routines should not vary or be canceled due to episodes of maladaptive behavior. In fact, the actual daily routine (i.e., Thomas's new lifeway structure) was regarded as a form of intervention and was the most important independent variable in Thomas's intervention protocol.

## Procedures

There were three phases of this study. During the first phase of the study, staff focused on Thomas's transition into the program. Because interventions were in place at the time of his admission, Phase 1 was considered to be a "treated baseline." Phase 2 of the study focused on the expansion of the number of staff who would work with Thomas, as well as his integration into the environments that his peers used. Finally, in Phase 3, staff focused on the maintenance of appropriate social behavior. Follow-up data were collected 18 months after Thomas's enrollment to evaluate the long-term effects of his intervention protocol. The next sections provide the details of each phase.

**Phase 1**   During the first phase, the gymnasium and Thomas's home were prepared, and Thomas was enrolled in the program. A core group of five staff members worked exclusively with Thomas; the staff-to-student ratio maintained during all awake hours was 1:1. Thomas's daily activity schedule was implemented and staff were instructed to advance through the activity schedule regardless of maladaptive behavior. Finally, Thomas was given the ability to make choices concerning 1) the teachers he worked with from one hour to the next, 2) the sequence in which he performed various activities, and 3) when he wanted to receive his meals. Although Thomas was electively mute, he was able to make choices by pointing to pictures.

**Phase 2**   During the second phase of the study, all of the staff members who would potentially work with Thomas were trained by one of the five core teachers. Thomas's reaction to each of these staff members was evaluated by the trainers, and a second tier of staff who would begin working with Thomas was identified. Thomas also began spending time in his classroom during the second phase of the study. Initially, he was only required to sit in the classroom and could leave anytime he pointed to a picture of the gymnasium. Next, specific IEP programs that Thomas appeared to enjoy performing (e.g., matching-to-sample) were scheduled to be completed in the classroom setting. Thomas could leave the classroom once he completed his academic instruction or whenever he made a request to leave.

**Phase 3**   During the final phase of the study, Thomas's activity schedule was continuously refined based on the data that were collected. For example, some activities were expanded upon because they occasioned highly desirable behavior (e.g., his evening bathing and grooming routine); other activities were modified because they reliably evoked maladaptive behavior (Thomas was initially required to change the sheets on his bed and make his bed each morning; however, the activity reliably produced aggression. As a result, this routine was limited to Thomas' putting the comforter and pillow on his bed after a staff person put the sheets on his mattress); and some activities were added due to the identification of additional interests.

## Results

The results of this case study are shown in Figure 1. The figure shows Thomas's rate of aggression and the amount of time he spent inte-

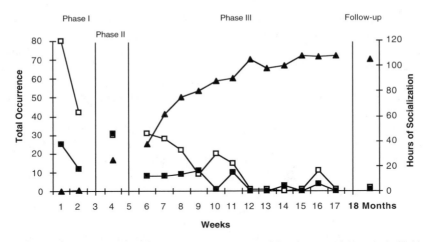

Figure 1. Thomas's rate of aggression and the amount of time he spent integrated with his peers. (Key: Aggression is denoted by an open square, and property destruction is denoted by a filled square; total hours are represented by filled triangles on the figure.)

grated with his peers. The left-hand ordinate shows the total number of episodes of aggression and property destruction. The ordinate on the right side of the figure shows the number of hours per week that Thomas spent integrated with his peers. The abscissa shows the consecutive weeks that data were collected.

Figure 1 shows that during Phase 1 (treated baseline), Thomas engaged in a total of 120 aggressive episodes and 35 episodes of property destruction. Moreover, he spent approximately 1 hour integrated with his peers. During Phase 2 of the study, there was a total of 30 aggressive episodes and 31 episodes of property destruction (see Figure 1). Thomas's integration with his peers increased to a total of 20 hours. Figure 1 shows that in Phase 3 of the study, there was a steady deceleration in maladaptive behavior and an acceleration in Thomas's integration with his peers. Finally, Figure 1 shows that 18 months after the conclusion of the study, Thomas exhibited aggressive behavior on a single occasion, refrained from property destruction, and spent nearly the maximum amount of time possible integrated with his peers.

It should be noted that there were a total of three crisis responses during all three phases of the study (i.e., Thomas had to be physically restrained; the duration per application of restraint was 2 minutes). During the follow-up phase, staff did not need to use a crisis response.

## Discussion

It is worth reiterating that the most important changes made in Thomas's life were along the lines of his environment, the people who were assigned to work with him, and the noncontingent advancement through a daily activity schedule. There was a conspicuous absence of contingencies of reinforcement for appropriate behavior. With respect to the environmental arrangements that were made for Thomas, the initial behavior assessments suggested that appropriate behavior would be optimized if Thomas was given free access to gross motor activity and allowed to work and live in an environment that rendered control over the movements and actions of other people.

## MATTHEW

Matthew was a 60-year-old man with mental retardation requiring extensive supports and a history of significant challenging behaviors. His repertoire included severe aggression, self-injury (e.g., severe head hitting, inserting objects into his nose), and property destruction. Matthew was nonverbal and relied primarily on gestures to express his basic needs. After spending 55 years in a state-operated institution, he moved into a community home with three other men with similar disabilities (most notably, severe challenging behavior). Despite the move to the community, Matthew continued to engage in high-rate maladaptive behaviors, which necessitated one-to-one staffing 24 hours per day. Unfortunately, the one-to-one staffing ratio failed to result in an acceptable degree of behavioral control. In consequence, the staff who worked with Matthew and Matthew's family advocated for a new living arrangement. As a result, a new provider agency was selected to deliver 24-hour supports to Matthew.

### Setting

Prior to Matthew's discharge from his community home, it was determined that his challenging behaviors functioned as a means of communicating his dissatisfaction with his living situation (i.e., living with three other men and the substantial numbers of staff necessary to manage their challenging behavior). This was evidenced by the absence of maladaptive behavior when he was alone with a single staff person in his home. As a result, Matthew was moved into a spacious home that was rented solely for his use. The home served as the base for 24-hour supports.

### Target Behaviors, Functional
### Analysis, and Recording Procedures

The target behaviors of primary concern included aggression and property destruction. Occurrences of maladaptive behavior were recorded throughout the day and evening hours. Matthew's challenging behaviors appeared to be primarily escape motivated. This was determined by observations (i.e., the conditions under which Matthew's target behaviors reliably occurred and did not occur) and the administration of the Motivation Assessment Scale (Durand & Crimmins, 1990). There were several conditions associated with a high probability of maladaptive behavior. As previously noted, Matthew would reliably exhibit his full repertoire of maladaptive behavior in the presence of his peers. Moreover, these behaviors occurred whenever staff imposed demands or unilaterally made changes in his routines, schedule, or environment. During the time that this behavior analysis was being conducted, it was observed that Matthew had little control over his daily schedule; essentially, his schedule was determined by staff. Finally, when Matthew became confused or frustrated due to his inability to communicate his needs, he would become assaultive or would destroy property.

Matthew's challenging behaviors were managed via contingencies, including the frequent use of physical restraint. These interventions did little to change Matthew's behavioral presentation and often resulted in Matthew's incurring serious injuries. Although the staff who supported Matthew genuinely liked him, they viewed his challenging behaviors as aberrant and as requiring a consequence. As a result, aggression and property destruction often had severe implications for Matthew. These behaviors resulted in a loss of activities, immediate physical restraint, and discontinuation of access to his personal property.

Matthew's challenging behaviors resulted in a number of obstacles. Specifically, the occurrence of aggression and property destruction prevented Matthew from being a full and contributing member of his community as staff required him to refrain from these behaviors in order to be allowed into the community.

In the spirit of completing a thorough behavior analysis, conditions under which Matthew refrained from maladaptive behaviors were also identified. The condition that had the greatest impact on Matthew was his immediate environment. That is, if Matthew was allowed to spend time alone with a staff person in his home, he would refrain from all maladaptive behaviors. Matthew also demonstrated the ability to perform daily routines, providing he could initiate them on his own time schedule. When given the liberty to decide the order in which activities would be performed, Matthew would reliably— and appropriately—shower, shave, eat his breakfast, and get ready to go out. Finally, it was determined that Matthew's behavior in the community (once he was allowed ingress), was exemplary; he was quite independent in the community and made friendly overtures to people in stores, restaurants, and banks. Matthew often attempted to communicate with people in the community by extending his hand and making appropriate gestures.

## Intervention Formulation

The analysis of conditions under which Matthew's behavior was likely to occur and prosocial behavior was likely to be optimized proved to be highly beneficial. The following decisions were made based on the findings outlined in the previous discussion:

1. Matthew should live in his own home with his own staff supports.
2. Matthew's support staff should be composed of people flexible enough to not only allow Matthew complete control over his daily schedule but who also understand the critical importance of doing so. Moreover, his support personnel should be people who "listen" to his nonverbal behaviors and accept the fact that his lifeway should comprise those activities that were not correlated with challenging behavior.
3. Matthew required access to the community on a daily basis.
4. Matthew responded optimally when staff used a combination of verbal behavior, pictures, and manual signs when attempting to communicate. Although Matthew had severe impairments with respect to his expressive abilities, receptive skills seemed to be a clear strength (e.g., whenever there was a discussion about going out, Matthew would respond by getting his coat).

### Procedures

The onset of Matthew's program coincided with his move to his own home. The procedures used with Matthew included the following: assignment to a home reserved exclusively for his use; complete control over his daily activity schedule, which included personal hygiene routines, meal preparation, running errands in the community, recreation, and house chores; and unencumbered access to the community. Staff were trained to understand the communicative intent of all of Matthew's unique gestures; moreover, they used a combination of verbal instructions, manual signs, and pictures to communicate with him. The use of multiple communication modalities gave Matthew the ability to understand the communicative efforts of staff.

### Results

The results of Matthew's intervention are presented in Figure 2. It is worth reiterating that the onset of this program coincided with Matthew's move to his new home and the above-mentioned lifeway modifications. The results show that there were 28 occurrences of aggression during the first month of Matthew's program. The total number of episodes of maladaptive behavior increased to 51 during the second month of the program. However, for the following 3 months (May, June, and July) there was a deceleration in the number of episodes of

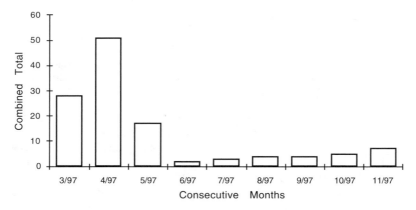

Figure 2. Results of Matthew's intervention. (The ordinate shows the aggregate frequency of aggression and property destruction; the abscissa shows consecutive months.)

challenging behavior. Finally, during the last 3 months of data collection, the aggregate of aggression and property destruction ranged from four to seven occurrences per month.

## Discussion

If data from Matthew's first month of intervention are compared with the data from the last month of intervention, we can conclude that there was a 75% reduction in the aggregate of aggression and property destruction. Although the rate of Matthew's maladaptive behavior was quite high during his first couple of months in his new program, this can be attributed to several factors: 1) the transition from one program to another, 2) the introduction of new staff, and 3) the amount of time it took for staff to learn Matthew's communication system. Once Matthew adjusted to his new lifeway and staff familiarized themselves with Matthew, there was a significant decrease in aggression and property destruction.

### GENERAL DISCUSSION

The two case studies presented in this chapter are linked by their emphasis on lifeway changes as the main source of intervention for high-rate maladaptive behavior. In both cases, there was a deliberate de-emphasis placed on the use of contingencies of reinforcement and punishment for the purpose of changing behavior. The case studies are also united in another important way: Both individuals were chosen for review because of their protracted history of severe maladaptive behavior and their limited ability to communicate. As the results of both case studies suggest, Thomas' and Matthew's lives changed markedly as a result of the changes that were made in their lifeways. Their daily routines were well-documented, and the staff who served both individuals were very clear about their interests and the routines that needed to be maintained on a day-to-day basis. Essentially, the documentation of routines was protection against the needs of staff overshadowing the needs of Thomas and Matthew; moreover, the documentation ensured that the core activities of each daily schedule were associated with a high level of interest and a low rate of challenging behavior.

Once an appropriate lifeway is identified for a person, particular emphasis has to be placed on documentation, staff training, and monitoring by a group of people who are firmly committed to the development and maintenance of individualized lifeways for people with disabilities. In the absence of these three strategies, a person's life is mercurial at best and ultimately inconsistent with his or her needs as a human being.

To summarize, this chapter stresses the importance of developing a lifeway for a person. The lifeway should be driven by a methodical analysis of the stimulus conditions that result in high- and low-rate challenging behavior. Once a person's strengths and interests are entified, daily routines should be developed, documented, and continuously monitored and adjusted by people who are profoundly committed to maintaining individualized lifeways for people with developmental disabilities. The antecedent control of challenging behavior does not necessarily mean that a clinician should search for and change a specific event that reliably precedes a maladaptive behavior; rather, there are times when entire environments need to be changed in order to affect significant change. Behavior is influenced by the context in which it occurs, and lifeway, rather than being marginalized, should be the focus of behavioral intervention.

## REFERENCES

Cameron, M.J., & Kimball, J.W. (1995). Beyond consequences. *Mental Retardation, 33,* 268–270.

Durand, V.M., & Crimmins, D.B. (1990). Assessment. In V.M. Durand (Ed.), *Severe behavior problems: A functional communication training approach* (pp. 31–82). New York: Guilford Press.

Ford, A., Schnorr, R., Meyer, L., Davern, L., Black, J., & Dempsey, P. (1989). *The Syracuse community-referenced curriculum guide for students with moderate and severe disabilities.* Baltimore: Paul H. Brookes Publishing Co.

Freire, P. (1993). *Pedagogy of the oppressed.* New York: Continuum.

Giangreco, M.F., Cloninger, C.J., & Iverson, V.S. (1998). *Choosing outcomes and accommodations for children (COACH): A guide to educational planning for students with disabilities* (2nd ed.). Baltimore: Paul H. Brookes Publishing Co.

Meyer, L.H., & Evans, I.M. (1993). Meaningful outcomes in behavioral intervention: Evaluating positive approaches to the remediation of challenging behaviors. In J. Reichle & D.P. Wacker (Eds.), *Communication and language intervention series: Vol. 3. Communicative alternatives to challenging behavior: Integrating functional assessment and intervention strategies* (pp. 407–428). Baltimore: Paul H. Brookes Publishing Co.

O'Neill, R.E., Horner, R.H., Albin, R.W., Sprague, J.R., Storey, K., & Newton, J.S. (1997). *Functional assessment and program development for problem behavior: A practical handbook.* Pacific Grove, CA: Brooks / Cole.

Skinner, B.F. (1953). *Science and human behavior.* New York: Macmillan.

Touchette, P.E., MacDonald, R.E., & Langer, S.N. (1985). A scatter plot for identifying stimulus control of problem behavior. *Journal of Applied Behavior Analysis, 18,* 343–351.

# ~ *13* ~

# *Curricular Modifications to Promote Desirable Classroom Behavior*

## Lee Kern and Glen Dunlap

As research and practice in behavioral support for people with developmental disabilities have expanded to include a broader range of influential variables, much greater appreciation has been afforded to the influence of various antecedent influences. To a greater extent than ever before, writings in the area of behavioral support since the early 1990s have begun to stress the essential foundation of two basic assumptions regarding our understanding of behavior: 1) behavior is functional in the sense that it serves an identifiable purpose for the individual, and 2) behavior is related to and governed by the context in which it occurs (e.g., Bambara & Knoster, 1995; Koegel, Koegel, & Dunlap, 1996). The emphasis on context is pivotal because it suggests a vast array of potential variables that can be analyzed and mobilized to occasion desirable patterns of responding and to eliminate problematic repertoires. Among the large body of contextual influences is a set of variables that may be considered as intrinsic to the activities in which a person is engaged or the manner with which assignments are prescribed. We have found it useful to refer to these factors as curricular variables (Dunlap & Kern, 1993, 1996).

The term *curricular* can be interpreted as being limited to educational environments; however, we do not mean to imply such a stipulation because, in fact, the kinds of influences that we are referring to can be evident in work settings, domestic routines, and all other circumstances in which a person is engaged in activities with expectations for accomplishment or participation. By *curricular variables*, we are referring to a broad category of antecedent and contextual circumstances including the content and objectives of activities, the materials used to perform them, the behavioral topographies required, their scheduling and sequencing, the ecological and social circumstances in which they are conducted, and the manner with which they are presented. Although the majority of relevant research on these variables has been conducted in school settings, they are present in numerous settings and, thus, can potentially encompass behavioral support components for individuals across contexts and life domains.

The purpose of this chapter is to describe the use of curricular interventions to promote desirable behavior (and reduce problematic responding). Our approach has been one in which individual and idiosyncratic curricular influences are identified through a process of functional assessment and are articulated in the form of hypothesis statements (Dunlap et al., 1993; Repp, Felce, & Barton, 1988). The hypothesis statements then are used to develop assessment-based interventions that involve some modification of one or more curricular components (Dunlap, Kern-Dunlap, Clarke, & Robbins, 1991; Kern, Childs, Dunlap, Clarke, & Falk, 1994). Although we emphasize that curricular interventions are only one aspect of behavioral support, data collected in the 1990s indicate that properly individualized curricular manipulations can be very effective, at least in the specific situations in which they are applied (e.g., Dunlap et al., 1991; Umbreit, 1996).

This chapter begins by addressing some issues of theoretical and practical application, including strategies for selecting appropriate interventions and considerations for classroom utilization. The section that follows discusses the empirical basis that has developed in support of specific curricular interventions, including some of the variety with which the approach can be applied. The final section presents a schema for selecting curricular interventions during task situations based on the patterns of responding that are observed during the assessment phase.

## CONCEPTUAL AND PRACTICAL ISSUES

This section discusses some of the conceptual and practical issues that pertain to curricular interventions for challenging behaviors. The topics addressed include the link between functional assessment information and the design of curricular modifications, factors to consider when selecting a curricular manipulation, and broader concerns of curricular intervention within the context of behavioral support objectives.

## Functional Assessment and Curricular Intervention

*Functional assessment* is a process for acquiring information regarding the relationships between occurrences of a (challenging) behavior and events or circumstances in the environment. The understanding that results from this process is the basis for developing effective, individualized interventions. As we have indicated in previous discussions (e.g., Dunlap & Kern, 1993, 1996; Kern & Dunlap, in press), and as many other authors have asserted (e.g., Carr et al., 1994; Foster-Johnson & Dunlap, 1993; Iwata, Vollmer, & Zarcone, 1990; Lennox & Miltenberger, 1989; O'Neill, Vaughn, & Dunlap, 1998), functional assessment data are necessary for tailoring interventions to the specific characteristics of an individual and his or her target behavior. Functional assessment information provides the guidance to develop a logical connection between the environmental variables that govern the behavior and the intervention components that are designed to transform those connections. An identification of the particular curricular variables that are associated with occurrences and nonoccurrences of the target behavior should be included as an outcome of the functional assessment process. Without such specific information, the selection of an effective curricular intervention from the vast array that are potentially available would be a matter of uninformed happenstance.

The objectives of a functional assessment include the following: 1) a delineation of the operant, communicative, or biological function that is the motivational foundation of the target behavior; and 2) a delineation of the contextual events and circumstances that are associated with high rates of the behavior, as well as those events or circumstances associated with an absence of the behavior (e.g., Dunlap & Kern, 1993; O'Neill, Horner, Albin, Storey, & Sprague, 1990). We have observed that the majority of challenging behaviors exhibited by students with disabilities in instructional contexts are motivated by escape (negative reinforcement); however, whereas it is valuable to conclude that a behavior is "escape motivated," it is insufficient for the purposes of developing effective and contextually relevant interventions (Horner & Carr, 1997). It is necessary to have more precise analyses that permit inferences regarding the specific factors that evoke the escape-motivated responding. Therefore, in our work on curricular interventions, we have found that answers to the latter functional assessment questions—that is, those pertaining to the contextual events or circumstances that are associated with differential rates of behavior—have been the most useful for identifying the curricular features that are relevant for a particular student's support.

The process of information gathering in functional assessment includes direct observation and interview techniques (e.g., Foster-Johnson & Dunlap, 1993; Kern, Dunlap, Clarke, & Childs, 1994; O'Neill et al., 1990), both of which can be useful in identifying curricular variables. In our model of assessment-based curricular intervention (Dunlap & Kern, 1993), we usually begin with fairly broad observational strategies, such as scatter plots (Touchette, MacDonald, & Langer, 1985), and relatively general interview questions (e.g., "Are there particular periods of time during the day that you can predict Jimmy will cry and bang his desk?"). This initial information leads to more focused observations (e.g., Bijou, Peterson, & Ault, 1968; Lalli, Browder, Mace, & Brown, 1993) and more specific interview questions (e.g., "Are there any transitions that are *not* associated with Jimmy's tantrums?" "Is there a specific *type* of transition that is associated most frequently with crying?" "What do you think it *is* about transitions that makes Jimmy so upset?"). As the information gathering becomes more incisive, the purpose becomes more explicitly to identify specific antecedent stimuli or events that control and/or predict occurrences and nonoccurrences of the behavior. In this regard, it is worthwhile to note that the familiarity and sensitivity of intimate informants (e.g., parents, teachers) can be very helpful in guiding the preintervention assessment process to a more rapid conclusion.

Once information has been gathered, functional assessment leads to idiosyncratic hypotheses that reflect an individualized understanding of interactions between curricular variables and the target behavior (Repp et al., 1988). For example, we described three students whose behavior was markedly improved when assignments were modified from traditional analog paradigms such that they included materials and outcomes that were relevant to the individual students' interests and life experiences (Dunlap, Foster-Johnson, Clarke, Kern, & Childs, 1995). The observations that led to these hypotheses were provided by the students' teachers, and the assignments and interests were different across students. Furthermore, it is important to note that these hypotheses would not necessarily be valid for other students.

One feature that we include in the assessment process pertains to the pattern of target behavior production during activity periods. For example, if challenging behavior occurs immediately on the introduction of an activity or stimulus, it is likely that a specific variable can be identified as offensive to the student and that efforts to remove or ameliorate that variable can be effective in reducing or eliminating the behavior. Other patterns can lead to other considerations. In some circumstances, an activity commences with cooperative and desirable behavior but, as the activity continues, the child's behavior deteriorates until highly disruptive or destructive responses occur. In such cases, it is possible that the student has a limited tolerance for the activity and/or boredom develops. What began as an enjoyable or benign activity developed over time into an aversive routine. When such patterns are observed, a logical intervention might be to schedule briefer sessions or to intersperse diverse events within the otherwise predictable routine (e.g., Dunlap & Koegel, 1980). Patterns that indicate inconsistent occurrences of challenging behaviors may suggest the involvement of establishing operations and call for further assessment of distal or physiological influences. The notion of using patterns of responding as one approach for suggesting possible interventions is developed more completely in the section entitled Analyzing within Activity Patterns of Responding.

## Considerations of Effectiveness and Utilization

When a functional assessment has identified behavioral–environmental relationships and has produced applicable hypotheses, it is typical for there to be a variety of alternative manipulations that would be based on the assessment data and would be expected to be effective. For example, if it were determined that a student's aggression was escape-motivated and that it was displayed primarily when assigned tasks were difficult and repetitive, effective options could include removing the difficult tasks from the curriculum, diminishing the level of difficulty, shortening the sessions, interspersing occasional presentations of the difficult task with pleasurable and previously mastered activities, changing the materials or instructional format so that the tasks incorporate more preferred stimuli, increasing the level of reinforcement for task completion, or using any combination of the above possibilities. Similarly, if a child's tantrums were occasioned by anxiety and uncertainty during transitions, alternatives might include developing a picture schedule to enhance comprehension and predictability, assigning a trusted friend as a comforting escort, and/or teaching increased tolerance and self-management strategies. The selection of intervention procedures should be based on the understanding developed through a functional assessment as well as on other considerations.

Some of the issues that should be weighed in the selection of curricular interventions are as follows: 1) the overall goals for the student's education and social and emotional development and how a curricular intervention would contribute to their attainment (i.e., curricular interventions should occupy a compatible place within existing educational and behavioral support plans); 2) the severity, generality, and urgency of the problem that needs to be resolved; 3) the extent to which manipulations would be expected to be effective from short-term and longitudinal perspectives; 4) the extent to which manipulations would be compatible with existing routines and interactions in the target settings; and 5) the recommendations and preferences of those invested in the behavior change endeavor, including teachers, family members, and the student him- or herself. The rest of this section discusses some of these considerations as they pertain to the expected effectiveness and utilization of curricular interventions.

The goals and effectiveness of an intervention can be judged from the perspectives of immediacy, magnitude (rate and intensity), topography, durability, and generality of behavior change. These factors can influence the selection of interventions and the extent to which they will be relied on. On the one hand, if a destructive behavior is severe and has been related to a specific curricular event, it might be appropriate to change the curriculum such that the event is removed from the student's environment. On the other hand, if a problem is not an emergency and if generalization across classrooms and teachers is desired, then an instructional self-monitoring emphasis might be recommended as a principal intervention component. The functional assessment process should offer insights regarding the strength of the stimulus control exerted by curricular variables, the extent to which problems are localized or more general phenomena, and the extent to which intervention options are apt to produce the desired impact. The curricular modifications should be constructed on the basis of that information and then adjusted as ongoing data collection indicates congruence or deviation from anticipated and desired progress.

A set of considerations that has been underappreciated involve the fit among intervention strategies and the characteristics and constraints of the people and settings that will accommodate their utilization (Albin, Lucyshyn, Horner, & Flannery, 1996). A procedure can be demonstrated as having effectiveness but, if it is not used, its effectiveness is a moot potentiality. A number of variables pertain directly to the fit between an intervention and the context of implementation. One issue, for example, relates to the effort that a teacher (or other support provider) must make in order to apply the intervention. If the intervention requires inordinate time, attention, or deviation from an established routine, it is unlikely that the intervention will be used consistently or over time. Similarly, if the procedure compels that instructional time be withdrawn from other students or if the intervention causes a disruption in the environment, utilization will be unlikely. It is important to recognize that a good contextual fit also means that an intervention must be congruent with the values, attitudes, and cultural heritage of the teachers and family members who are invested in the student's performance and involved in the implementation. Some parents, or teachers, may be very uncomfortable with a strategy that temporarily reduces expectations for academic production. In such cases, utilization and support for the effort may be more likely if the intervention consists of alterations in scheduling rather than complete removal of curricular elements. Fortunately, it is usually possible to develop a variety of effective alternatives, and, thus, it is likely that one or more of the options will be consistent with the beliefs and values of the relevant participants.

One way to help ensure that utilization will occur is to engage in a process of program development that is collaborative and that relies on the input and teamwork of teachers and family members (Eno-Hieneman & Dunlap, in press). It is usually the case that people will demonstrate higher levels of commitment to a programmatic effort if they have some responsibility for the program's creation. In addition, the feasibility and contextual fit of an intervention plan can be evaluated most accurately by those who will be responsible for the implementation and who are part of the ecology. A method for promoting utilization is to have classroom teachers actively involved in selecting interventions from a menu of assessment-based alternatives. As an illustration of this strategy, Kern, Childs, et al. (1994) included three teachers in making component selections for implementation in their respective classrooms. Although the components differed to some extent across the classroom settings, the overall program was effective in reducing the challenging behaviors of an elementary school boy with significant behavior challenges. There are many ways to help ensure effectiveness and utilization, and our experience as consultants and researchers is that the legitimate involvement of teachers and parents in the assessment and development phases is probably the most valuable element.

## OVERVIEW OF SUCCESSFUL CURRICULAR INTERVENTIONS

The previous section outlines a strategy of functional assessment and proposed considerations for enhancing the selection of viable interventions. As the previous paragraphs suggest, a growing ensemble of research studies has documented the value of curricular interventions within a plan of behavioral support. These studies have implicated a large number of variables that influence student behavior in the classroom and have likewise described an array of related curricular interventions. This section describes a representative selection of empirically validated curricular interventions.

We have grouped the antecedent curricular interventions described in the literature into three broad categories. The first includes modifications pertaining directly to the task content or to task materials. The second pertains to the manner in which the task is presented. The third focuses on setting events or establishing operations.

## Curricular Interventions that Modify the Task

Many curricular interventions alter the task itself. These interventions either modify the task content or the method by which the task is completed. Conceptually, these types of interventions function to diminish aversive characteristics of the task. For example, task difficulty is a variable that has been demonstrated to influence classroom behavior. In a study by Weeks and Gaylord-Ross (1981), children with severe disabilities were observed to engage in challenging behaviors, including self-injury and aggression, during instructional activities. The difficulty of the task was identified as a potential variable contributing to challenging behavior. The difficulty level then was decreased by simplifying the task or by implementing errorless learning procedures. This modification resulted in significantly reduced rates of challenging behavior.

Instructional media also have been modified to improve student behavior. In a study by Kern, Childs, et al. (1994), Eddie, a 12-year-old boy, engaged in challenging behaviors during tasks requiring writing. Structured interviews identified an impairment in fine motor skills. Appropriate behavior was significantly increased when Eddie was provided with a computer or tape recorder to complete his assignments rather than having to write them by hand. Similarly, fine motor difficulties were identified in a study conducted by Dunlap et al. (1991) with a 13-year-old girl, Jill, who engaged in high rates of disruptive classroom behavior. When Jill was provided gross motor rather than fine motor activities, on-task behavior was significantly increased, and disruptive behavior was reduced to zero levels.

Another task modification, incorporating areas of student interest into instructional activities, has been demonstrated to improve student deportment. In a study by Dunlap et al. (1995), conventional academic activities were modified to reflect individual student interests. For example, with one participant, Jary, challenging behaviors occurred during vocational activities. A task associated with particularly high rates of challenging behavior was pen assembly. An assessment of his interests revealed snack time, including sharing his snacks, was enjoyable to him. Thus, Jary's original task of pen assembly was modified such that, instead, he assembled cracker sandwiches with peanut butter and jelly that, later, he could share with his classmates. This modified assembly task resulted in reduced rates of challenging behavior and increased levels of task engagement.

A related intervention involves ensuring that tasks have functional outcomes. In Jary's case, improved behavior may have occurred because completion of the task was associated with a meaningful outcome. That is, Jary was able to serve snacks to his classmates after assembling the snacks. The potential of this meaningful and reinforcing outcome may have made the task itself less aversive.

## Curricular Interventions that
## Modify the Instructional Presentation

A second broad category of curricular modifications focuses on instructional presentation. In this collection of interventions, the task content remains unchanged; however, variations are made in some aspect of the presentation of the task. One such strategy is choice. Opportunities for choice making can be successful along two dimensions (Bambara, Ager, & Koger, 1994). First, it is assumed that individuals will select preferred tasks. Thus, choice increases the likelihood that the task presented will be a more enjoyable one. Second, choice as a process may be reinforcing for some individuals. Opportunities for choice allow people to exert control during instructional situations, which in itself may have reinforcing effects.

Opportunities for choice making were explored in a study on curricular revision by Dunlap and colleagues (1991). Jill, a 12-year-old girl with multiple disabilities, consistently engaged in challenging behaviors during academic periods. Conditions of choice and no choice were compared. During the no choice condition, Jill's teacher selected which subject (science, social studies, math, or handwriting) Jill would work on during each academic period. During the choice condition, the assignment remained the same, but Jill selected which subject she would work on during each instructional session. When Jill was provided this choice-making option, challenging behaviors were never observed. In addition, her on-task behavior increased twofold.

Task interspersal strategies also have been effective in promoting desirable behavior. Dunlap (1984) and Winterling, Dunlap, and O'Neill (1987) showed that providing a variety of activities, rather than repeating a single activity, can decrease challenging behavior, increase engagement, and improve child affect. A number of other researchers (e.g., Horner, Day, Sprague, O'Brien, & Heathfield, 1991; Mace et al., 1988; Singer, Singer, & Horner, 1987) have demonstrated increased compliance and decreased challenging behaviors by embedding tasks associated with behaviors within a series of tasks with high probabilities of compliance and low probabilities of challenging behavior. For example, Horner and colleagues (1991) reduced the self-injury and aggression in three children by interspersing requests to perform difficult tasks among requests to complete easy tasks.

Modification in the pacing of task presentation is another established strategy for behavior improvement. Dunlap, Dyer, and Koegel (1983) varied the interval of time between students' responses and presentation of the next instruction. When the interval was brief (4 seconds or less), correct responding increased and undesirable behavior decreased. Similar effects were found in a study by West and Sloan (1986). Behavior of students with mental retardation requiring intermittent supports significantly improved when tasks were presented at a fast pace (every 20 seconds) rather than at a slow pace (every 60 seconds) and when tokens were available every 60 seconds rather than every 240 seconds.

Another successful task modification involves manipulations in task size. Task size can be modified by decreasing the overall length of the task or by providing frequent breaks. Sometimes when this type of modification is made, it is also necessary to make the task requirements visually discriminable. Dunlap and colleagues (1991) described a curricular revision with Jill involving shortening the duration of her tasks from 15 minutes to 5 minutes. The task consisted of completing assignments from her textbook. Improvements in behavior were noted only when visual cues were provided indicating the session would be brief. During these sessions, a page was photocopied from her textbook containing only the number of required responses. This resulted in substantial behavior improvements, with regard to both disruptive and on-task behavior. Behavior, however, did not improve during brief assignments that were not accompanied by a clear visual cue. Specifically, when Jill was provided the entire textbook to work from, despite verbal instructions to Jill indicating that a small number of problems needed to be completed, her behavior did not improve.

Presenting partial rather than whole tasks is also a useful antecedent strategy. Weld and Evans (1990) assessed the behavior of adults with mental retardation requiring intermittent to extensive supports during partial tasks and whole tasks. During partial tasks, activities were task analyzed and only one new step was presented during each trial (in addition to previously learned steps). During whole tasks, all steps in the analysis were presented during each trial. Although task acquisition differed within conditions and was related to level of functioning, the partial task procedure resulted in lower rates of challenging behavior for all of the participants.

## Curricular Modifications that
## Alter Setting Events or Establishing Operations

The third broad set of curricular interventions pertains to setting events or establishing operations. This category encompasses temporally distant events that influence a student's immediate behavior. For example, under most circumstances a student may readily complete his or her required classroom tasks; however, an argument ensued on the bus ride to school that day. As a result, under these new circumstances, the student may be noncompliant when given instructions to complete an activity. Likewise, research has shown that variables such as allergy symptoms or sleep deprivation may result in increases in challenging behavior (e.g., Kennedy & Itkonen, 1993; Kennedy & Meyer, 1996). In a study by O'Reilly (1995), aggression in a 31-year-old man described as having mental retardation requiring extensive supports was observed to occur exclusively during demanding situations. The frequency of aggression, however, was highly variable and on some days was absent. A closer analysis showed that aggression occurred during task situations on days when he had slept less than 5 hours the previous night.

When distal events or establishing operations are suspected, it is important to attempt to identify and alter the problematic event. Even when it is possible to identify the event, however, amelioration may not be a simple endeavor. Under these circumstances, immediate curricular accommodations can be made. For example, seating arrangements may need to be modified to separate classmates who fought on the bus. In the case of a student with sleep difficulties, his or her daily schedule can be modified so that more difficult activities occur in the morning when the student is less likely to be fatigued.

## INTERVENTION SELECTION

The purpose of the previous sections is to outline the functional assessment process and related considerations essential for intervention development. The sections also provide an overview of successful curricular interventions reported in the literature. From these sections, it should be apparent that a variety of curricular intervention options may be available for any given situation. The task at hand becomes selecting a curricular intervention that has a reasonable probability of being effective in light of the information available pertaining to the individual and circumstances associated with the target behavior. It is at this juncture that we see a gap in the assessment-intervention process. Specifically, there is a large and growing literature delineating the functional assessment/functional analysis process (e.g., Iwata, Dorsey, Slifer, Bauman, & Richman, 1982; Lalli et al., 1993; Wehby, Symons, & Shores, 1995). In addition, numerous interventions have been catalogued that are matched to particular behavioral functions, such as an escape function (e.g., Mace, Lalli, & Shea, 1992). Far less attention, however, has been granted to connecting the assessment process with intervention selection. In the following paragraphs, we delineate a strategy to assist in bridging this gap.

## Analyzing within Activity Patterns of Responding

As described previously, the process of functional assessment has advanced our understanding of challenging behavior considerably and has resulted in improved interventions. A major outcome of the attention to preintervention assessment is that interventions have become increasingly proactive, with a primary focus being the modification of antecedent variables. There continues to be a gap, however, between information provided through the assessment process and the selection and development of an intervention. For example, as discussed previously, many students engage in challenging behavior when academic demands are placed on them, and several curricular modifications have been suggested in the literature to address such behavior. What may be less clear is how to determine *which* intervention may be most effective in any particular situation. The following paragraphs provide a schema to assist with intervention selection for escape behavior. It should be noted that this is not a comprehensive model, and it has not yet been validated. It was developed primarily as a result of our observations of interventions that have been effective given certain patterns of children's challenging behaviors. The schema also reflects what we view as a logical match between child behavior and antecedent intervention strategies.

Although there are no comprehensive research studies indicating the extent to which challenging behaviors in the classroom occur in response to academic (or other) demands, epidemiologic research in other settings suggests that challenging behaviors occur most frequently in the context of task situations (e.g., Derby et al., 1992; Iwata et al., 1994). In addition, in environments in which learning is an expected outcome, it is likely that task or demand situations characterize a reasonable proportion of events. For this reason, we have focused on task situations for the schema described next.

When difficulties arise during demanding situations, sometimes identifying a logical intervention that is likely to be effective is not difficult. For example, if challenging behaviors occur only when a student is assigned written work, it is reasonable to modify the writing medium. More often, however, the specific attribute of the academic requirement that is associated with challenging behavior is not readily apparent. It is for these cases that we have developed a schema (depicted in Figure 1) to assist with intervention selection.

In this schema, the initial step is to evaluate the pattern of behavior that occurs within an activity period. Consider the following three possible patterns of behavior that may occur. The first is that challenging behavior occurs immediately on presentation of the task. For example, as soon as Mr. Lewis asks the class to get out their math books, Sean begins to engage in disruptive behavior. When Amy's vocational activities are placed at her desk, she immediately throws them on the ground and begins to engage in self-injurious behavior.

The second possible pattern of behavior that students exhibit during demand situations is that they will engage in the activity for a certain period of time, then challenging behavior begins to occur. For example, Jill will generally sort 10 pieces of laundry before beginning to have a tantrum. John will work independently on his science questions for 10–15 minutes before making frequent trips to the pencil sharpener or rummaging through his desk in search of an alternative activity.

The final pattern of challenging behavior that occurs in task situations is that its occurrence is inconsistent across days. Specifically,

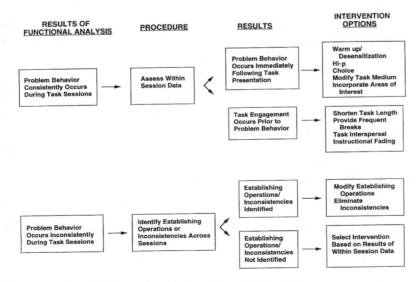

Figure 1. Schema for intervention selection during task situations.

during similar demand situations, on some occasions challenging behaviors occur, and on other occasions they do not. To illustrate, Jacki
generally completes her writing assignment without incident; however, approximately once per week, she rips up the assignment and
refuses to complete further work.

If an individual's challenging behavior is consistent with one of
the patterns described in the previous paragraphs, certain assumptions can be made that may contribute to intervention selection. In the
case of the first pattern—challenging behavior occurs immediately following task presentation—it is likely that some aspect of the task has
become highly aversive. In addition, if this pattern is observed consistently, it is not likely that the child will begin to engage in the task
without significant amounts of challenging behavior occurring. In
these circumstances, interventions can be implemented prior to introducing the task that either focus on desensitizing the child to the task,
increasing initial compliance, modifying the specific aversive feature
of the task, or using instructional fading procedures. For example, a
"warm-up" may be used in which students are exposed to the task
materials in a pleasurable manner prior to the presentation of demands (e.g., Cooper et al., 1995). A high-p (high-probability) sequence
also can be used, in which a series of tasks with a high probability of
compliance are presented before a request to perform a task with a
low probability of compliance. Choice also may be an effective intervention option, whereby individuals are provided the opportunity to
exert some control and/or avoid more aversive activities. Finally, instructional fading procedures can be used, in which the instructional
demands are initially removed and then are gradually reintroduced
at systematically increasing increments.

Another group of interventions congruent with this behavior pattern are those that modify the task itself. These strategies may help to
veil the aversive aspects of the task. Examples include modifying the
instructional medium, incorporating areas of student interest, and providing tasks with functional outcomes.

The second pattern of challenging behavior students exhibit during task situations is that engagement occurs for some period of time
prior to challenging behavior. In these cases, it is reasonable to assume
that challenging behaviors result from boredom, fatigue, difficulty in
sustaining attention, and so forth. Congruent intervention strategies
under these circumstances include shortening the task length, providing frequent breaks, or using task interspersal strategies.

When patterns of behavior fall within the third group—occurrence is inconsistent across days—it is plausible that some type of
distal event is influencing behavior. This is technically referred to as

an *establishing operation*. Specifically, some operation changes the reinforcing or punishing properties of a previously neutral event. For example, although math is a difficult subject for Sammy, he generally completes his classwork without incident; however, he occasionally does not sleep well. Following sleepless nights, he is unable to sustain his concentration adequately and instead engages in challenging behavior. In these cases, it is prudent to attempt to identify and ameliorate the establishing operation. If it is not possible to ameliorate the establishing operation, then demands can be modified accordingly. For example, it may not be possible to regulate Sammy's sleep; instead, he can be given simpler assignments when he has not slept well.

It is also possible that subtle variations are occurring in the task type or style of presentation. For example, the pacing of instructions or the individual presenting the instructions may differ. The type of task also may be inconsistent. That is, on some occasions students may be asked to practice their spelling words by writing them manually, and on other days the assignment may be to practice them orally with a peer. Under these circumstances, it is important to examine variations in the task or presentation. Interventionists can identify then modify the particular stimuli that are associated with challenging behavior.

There is a wide range of events and physiological states that may potentially influence an individual's behavior. As a result, establishing operations or subtle curricular variations may be difficult to identify. When it is not possible to detect establishing operations or subtle variations influencing challenging behavior, we recommend that within activity patterns of behavior be analyzed on days when challenging behaviors occur. Curricular modifications then can be applied consistent with either the first (target behaviors occur immediately) or second (engagement occurs prior to target behavior) pattern described previously.

It also should be noted that the interventions described in this chapter should not necessarily be implemented exclusively. Interventions are sometimes more successful if they are implemented as packages. That is, it may be most effective to simultaneously implement several intervention strategies. For example, task interspersal could be implemented in combination with frequent breaks.

As suggested throughout this chapter, there are typically a variety of intervention options in any given situation. The schema described in this section was designed to identify interventions that are most likely to result in the absence of challenging behaviors. However, many factors need to be considered when selecting an intervention, such as potential risk of injury caused by the challenging behavior, willingness of others to tolerate the challenging behavior, the extent to which the behavior jeopardizes community inclusion, and so forth. Consequently, the intervention schema should not necessarily be considered prohibitive. For example, aggression may occur immediately during task situations; however, it may be very mild and occur during self-care skills that need to be completed for hygiene purposes. Under circumstances such as these, the only option may be to persist with the task, providing frequent breaks.

## SUMMARY

Throughout this chapter we have described a variety of curricular interventions with empirical and pragmatic support. Although curricular intervention has been used primarily in the classroom, its applicability is much broader. The primary focus of these interventions is contextual influences that occasion desirable behavior and abate incompatible behavior. There are few, if any, environments in which contextual features are peripheral to behavior.

We also provided a brief sketch of the functional assessment process, a means integral to implicating specific curricular variables with influential consequences on an individual's behavior. Furthermore, we presented a schema to assist in narrowing the array of intervention options. As indicated previously, this schema addressed behavior problems only during task situations. Additional and alternative models, addressing an expanded array of functions, are needed that provide a more explicit link between assessment and intervention.

As this chapter illustrates, curricular interventions represent a proactive collection of antecedent interventions. We are enthusiastic about the growing interest in antecedent control approaches and believe this direction is critical to an effective plan of behavioral support that considers the growth, well-being, and quality of life of individuals with disabilities and others in their environment.

## REFERENCES

Albin, R.W., Lucyshyn, J.M., Horner, R.H., & Flannery, K.B. (1996). Contextual fit for behavioral support plans: A model for "goodness of fit." In L.K. Koegel, R.L. Koegel, & G. Dunlap (Eds.), *Positive behavioral support: Including people with difficult behavior in the community* (pp. 81–98). Baltimore: Paul H. Brookes Publishing Co.

Bambara, L.M., Ager, C., & Koger, F. (1994). The effects of choice and task preference on the work performance of adults with severe disabilities. *Journal of Applied Behavior Analysis, 27*, 555–556.

Bambara, L.M., & Knoster, T.P. (1995). *Guidelines: Effective behavioral support.* Harrisburg: Pennsylvania Department of Education.

Bijou, S.W., Peterson, R.F., & Ault, M.H. (1968). A method to integrate descriptive and experimental field studies at the level of data and empirical concepts. *Journal of Applied Behavior Analysis, 1,* 175–191.

Carr, E.G., Levin, L., McConnachie, G., Carlson, J.I., Kemp, D.C., & Smith, C.E. (1994). *Communication-based interventions for problem behavior: A user's guide for producing positive change.* Baltimore: Paul H. Brookes Publishing Co.

Cooper, L.J., Wacker, D.P., McComas, J.J., Brown, K.I., Peck, S.M., Richman, D., Drew, J., Frischmeyer, P., & Millard, T. (1995). Use of component analyses to identify active variables in treatment packages for children with feeding disorders. *Journal of Applied Behavior Analysis, 28,* 139–153.

Derby, K.M., Wacker, D.P., Sasso, G., Steege, M., Northup, J., Cigrand, K., & Asmus, J. (1992). Brief functional assessment techniques to evaluate aberrant behavior in an outpatient setting: A summary of 79 cases. *Journal of Applied Behavior Analysis, 25,* 713–721.

Dunlap, G. (1984). The influence of task variation and maintenance tasks on the learning and affect of autistic children. *Journal of Experimental Child Psychology, 37,* 41–64.

Dunlap, G., Dyer, K., & Koegel, R.L. (1983). Autistic self-stimulation and intertrial interval duration. *American Journal of Mental Deficiency, 88,* 194–202.

Dunlap, G., Foster-Johnson, L., Clarke, S., Kern, L., & Childs, K.E. (1995). Modifying activities to produce functional outcomes: Effects on the disruptive behaviors of students with disabilities. *Journal of The Association for Persons with Severe Handicaps, 20,* 248–258.

Dunlap, G., & Kern, L. (1993). Assessment and intervention for children within the instructional curriculum. In J. Reichle & D.P. Wacker (Eds.), *Communication and language intervention series: Vol. 3. Communicative alternatives to challenging behavior: Integrating functional assessment and intervention strategies* (pp. 177–203). Baltimore: Paul H. Brookes Publishing Co.

Dunlap, G., & Kern, L. (1996). Modifying instructional activities to promote desirable behavior: A conceptual and practical framework. *School Psychology Quarterly, 11,* 297–312.

Dunlap, G., Kern, L., dePerczel, M., Clarke, S., Wilson, D., Childs, K.E., White, R., & Falk, G.D. (1993). Functional analysis of classroom variables for students with emotional and behavioral challenges. *Behavioral Disorders, 18,* 275–291.

Dunlap, G., Kern-Dunlap, L., Clarke, S., & Robbins, F.R. (1991). Functional assessment, curricular revision, and severe behavior problems. *Journal of Applied Behavior Analysis, 24,* 387–397.

Dunlap, G., & Koegel, R.L. (1980). Motivating autistic children through stimulus variation. *Journal of Applied Behavior Analysis, 13,* 619–627.

Eno-Hieneman, M., & Dunlap, G. (in press). Some issues and challenges in implementing community-based behavioral support: Two illustrative case studies. In J.R. Scotti & L.H. Meyer (Eds.), *Behavioral intervention: Principles, models, and practices.* Baltimore: Paul H. Brookes Publishing Co.

Foster-Johnson, L., & Dunlap, G. (1993). Using functional assessment to develop effective, individualized interventions. *Teaching Exceptional Children, 25,* 44–50.

Horner, R.H., & Carr, E.G. (1997). Behavioral support for students with severe disabilities: Functional assessment and comprehensive interventions. *Journal of Special Education, 31,* 84–104.

Horner, R.H., Day, H.M., Sprague, J.R., O'Brien, M., & Heathfield, L.T. (1991). Interspersed requests: A nonaversive procedure for reducing aggression and self-injury during instruction. *Journal of Applied Behavior Analysis, 24,* 265–278.

Iwata, B.A., Dorsey, M.F., Slifer, K.J., Bauman, K.E., & Richman, G.S. (1982). Toward a functional analysis of self-injury. *Analysis and Intervention in Developmental Disabilities, 2,* 3–20.

Iwata, B.A., Pace, G.M., Dorsey, M.F., Zarcone, J.R., Vollmer, T.R., Smith, R.G., Rodgers, T.A., Lerman, D.C., Shore, B.A., Mazaleski, J.L., Goh, H., Edwards Cowdery, G., Kalsher, M.J., McCosh, K.C., & Willis, K.D. (1994). The functions of self-injurious behavior: An experimental-epidemiological analysis. *Journal of Applied Behavior Analysis, 27,* 215–240.

Iwata, B.A., Vollmer, T.R., & Zarcone, J.R. (1990). The experimental (functional) analysis of behavior disorders: Methodology, applications, and limitations. In A.C. Repp & N.N. Singh (Eds.), *Perspectives on the use of nonaversive and aversive interventions for persons with developmental disabilities* (pp. 301–330). Sycamore, IL: Sycamore Publishing Co.

Kennedy, C.H., & Itkonen, T. (1993). Effects of setting events on the problem behavior of students with severe disabilities. *Journal of Applied Behavior Analysis, 26,* 32–327.

Kennedy, C.H., & Meyer, K.A. (1996). Sleep deprivation, allergy symptoms and negatively reinforced problem behavior. *Journal of Applied Behavior Analysis, 29,* 133–135.

Kern, L., Childs, K.E., Dunlap, G., Clarke, S., & Falk, G.D. (1994). Using assessment-based curricular intervention to improve the classroom behavior of a student with emotional and behavioral challenges. *Journal of Applied Behavior Analysis, 27,* 7–19.

Kern, L., & Dunlap, G. (in press). Assessment-based interventions for children with emotional and behavioral disorders. In A.C. Repp & R.H. Horner (Eds.), *Functional analysis of problem behavior: From effective assessment to effective support.* Pacific Grove, CA: Brooks/Cole.

Kern, L., Dunlap, G., Clarke, S., & Childs, K.E. (1994). Student-assisted functional assessment interview. *Diagnostique, 19,* 29–39.

Koegel, L.K., Koegel, R.L., & Dunlap, G. (Eds.). (1996). *Positive behavioral support: Including people with difficult behavior in the community.* Baltimore: Paul H. Brookes Publishing Co.

Lalli, J.S., Browder, D.M., Mace, F.C., & Brown, D.K. (1993). Teacher use of descriptive analysis data to implement interventions to decrease students' problem behaviors. *Journal of Applied Behavior Analysis, 26,* 227–238.

Lennox, D.B., & Miltenberger, R.G. (1989). Conducting a functional assessment of problem behavior in applied settings. *Journal of The Association for Persons with Severe Handicaps, 14,* 304–311.

Mace, F.C., Hock, M.L., Lalli, J.S., West, B.J., Belfiore, P., Pinter, E., & Brown, D.F. (1988). Behavioral momentum in the treatment of noncompliance. *Journal of Applied Behavior Analysis, 21,* 123–141.

Mace, F.C., Lalli, J.S., & Shea, M.C. (1992). Functional analysis and treatment of self-injury. In J.K. Luiselli, J.L. Matson, & N.N. Singh (Eds.), *Self-injurious behavior: Analysis, assessment and treatment* (pp. 122–152). New York: Springer-Verlag.

O'Neill, R., Vaughn, B.J., & Dunlap, G. (1998). Comprehensive behavioral support: Assessment issues and strategies. In A.M. Wetherby, S.F. Warren, & J. Reichle (Eds.), *Communication and language intervention series: Vol. 7. Transitions in prelinguistic communication* (pp. 313–342). Baltimore: Paul H. Brookes Publishing Co.

O'Neill, R.E., Horner, R.H., Albin, R.W., Storey, K., & Sprague, J.R. (1990). *Functional analysis of problem behavior: A practical assessment guide.* Sycamore, IL: Sycamore Publishing Co.

O'Reilly, M.F. (1995). Functional analysis and treatment of escape-maintained aggression correlated with sleep deprivation. *Journal of Applied Behavior Analysis, 28,* 225–226.

Repp, A., Felce, D., & Barton, L. (1988). Basing the treatment of stereotypic and self-injurious behaviors on hypotheses of their causes. *Journal of Applied Behavior Analysis, 21,* 281–289.

Singer, G.H., Singer, J., & Horner, R.H. (1987). Using pretask requests to increase the probability of compliance for students with severe disabilities. *Journal of The Association for Persons with Severe Handicaps, 12,* 287–291.

Touchette, P.E., MacDonald, R.F., & Langer, S.N. (1985). A scatter plot for identifying stimulus control of problem behavior. *Journal of Applied Behavior Analysis, 18,* 343–351.

Umbreit, J. (1996). Assessment and intervention for the problem behaviors of an adult at home. *Journal of The Association for Persons with Severe Handicaps, 21,* 31–38.

Weeks, M., & Gaylord-Ross, R. (1981). Task difficulty and aberrant behavior in severely handicapped students. *Journal of Applied Behavior Analysis, 14,* 449–463.

Wehby, J.H., Symons, F.J., & Shores, R.E. (1995). A descriptive analysis of aggressive behavior in classrooms for children with emotional and behavioral disorders. *Behavioral Disorders, 20,* 87–105.

Weld, E.M., & Evans, I.M. (1990). Effects of part versus whole instructional strategies on skill acquisition and excess behavior. *Journal of Applied Behavior Analysis, 14,* 449–463.

West, R.P., & Sloan, H.N. (1986). Teacher presentation rate and point delivery rate. *Behavior Modification, 10,* 267–286.

Winterling, V., Dunlap, G., & O'Neill, R.E. (1987). The influence of task variation on the aberrant behaviors of autistic children. *Education and Treatment of Children, 10,* 105–119.

# ~ *14* ~

## Interventions for Noncompliance Based on Instructional Control

### Jennifer J. McComas and Patrick R. Progar

*Noncompliance* has been defined as a failure to perform requests presented by others or to perform as expected by general or local standards of acceptable conduct, or both (Mace, 1992). The term *noncompliance* has been applied to children and adults with multiple disabilities and developmental disabilities such as mental retardation, autism, and neurological impairment who do not perform as expected in a variety of settings such as school, home, and community. As a result of continued or severe noncompliance, teachers and other professionals often modify instructional content, which results in a restriction of the types and number of skills that an individual learns (Horner, Day, Sprague, O'Brien, & Tuesday Heathfield, 1991). Procedures that reduce noncompliance, or more specifically that increase compliance, are needed. The form of noncompliance may vary from passive inaction to behavior that is contrary to a request or standard of conduct. For example, in response to a request to fold laundry, an individual may passively refuse to respond or may be excessively slow to respond. Alternatively, the individual may exhibit other behavior (e.g., aggression, self-injury, stereotypy, disruptive outbursts) in response to a request to perform a particular task. When this is the case, noncompliance and the covarying behavior may be treated individually or as two elements of the same response class, depending on the results of an experimental analysis of the operant mechanisms responsible for the responses (see previous chapters for descriptions

The authors wish to express their deepest appreciation to Bud Mace for his early input and to Jennifer Asmus and Tim Vollmer for their feedback on an earlier draft of this chapter.

of these types of experimental analyses). Antecedent interventions that focus on increasing compliance and reducing the occurrence of challenging behavior have been successful in many cases and appear promising (e.g., Davis, Brady, Williams, & Hamilton, 1992; Horner et al., 1991; Kennedy, 1994; Mace & Belfiore, 1990; Mace et al., 1988). This chapter discusses the operant basis for noncompliance and focuses on two ways in which compliance can be obtained: via instruction in rule-governed or contingency-shaped behaviors. The chapter also discusses the basic elements of operant behavior, some hypothesized reasons for why instruction may fail, and specific intervention options for rule-governed and contingency-shaped behaviors.

The operant basis for noncompliance can be viewed as a lack of instructional or stimulus control. One way to examine stimulus control is to consider two types of operant behavior: 1) rule-governed and 2) contingency-shaped. *Rule-governed behavior* is defined as a response to a contingency-specifying stimulus (Skinner, 1969) or as the specification of a relationship among two or more events to a listener by a speaker (Chase & Danforth, 1991). For example, many people adhere to the rule, *Speak quietly in the museum.* It may be that we follow the rule because the museum serves as a stimulus that occasions particular behavior or because following similar rules (e.g., *Speak quietly in the library*) in the past has been reinforced even if we have never been in a museum before. Alternately, *contingency-shaped behavior* may be defined as a response that corresponds to a specific instruction, which is reinforced, at least on an intermittent basis. For example, when an instructor says, "Sit down," and the response of sitting is at least intermittently reinforced (e.g., with praise or the commencement of a lesson), the response is said to have been reinforced and maintained by contingencies.

Skinner argued that behavior under discriminative control of rules is distinct from behavior controlled directly by the contingencies that the rules specify (Skinner, 1969) and that an individual whose behavior is shaped by contingencies behaves more skillfully than one who is following instructions (Skinner, 1971). To illustrate, rules are often provided to children learning a new sport: *Keep your left arm straight, Catch a fly ball with two hands, Keep your eye on the ball, Use your hips when you swing.* The behavior of children exposed to these rules versus those who have experienced the actual contingencies is clearly different. The behavior of those children exclusively exposed to rules might be slow and inefficient in the context of the game, whereas the behavior of those who have experienced the actual contingencies is likely to be more efficient in response to the action of the game.

The distinction between rule-governed and contingency-shaped behavior may arise from distinct sources of instructional control, but each can be examined on three levels: 1) basic elements, 2) hypothesized reasons for failure to respond, and 3) potential interventions for increasing compliance. Rule-governed and contingency-shaped behavior are considered separately in terms of these three levels.

## CONTINGENCY-SHAPED BEHAVIOR

Contingency-shaped responses occur as a function of the reinforcing contingencies. A member of a response class must contact the contingencies of reinforcement in the presence of an antecedent stimulus for the stimulus to exert any discriminative control. When a response occurs more often in the presence of a particular discriminative stimulus than in its absence, that response is said to be under stimulus control. A common example of stimulus control can be found while driving; stopping at busy intersections is under the stimulus control of red traffic lights.

### Basic Elements

There are two basic elements surrounding the contingency-shaped response: the antecedent stimulus and the consequent stimulus. The left side of Figure 1 contains the basic elements of contingency-shaped responses. For the purposes of this chapter, we assume that the antecedent stimulus is discriminative for a schedule of reinforcement but that due to some feature of the discriminated operant, it fails to evoke the desired response. A discriminative stimulus ($S^D$) for a task might specify a single-step response. An example might consist of a verbal instruction, "Pick up the shirt." Conversely, a stimulus might require multiple responses to complete. For example, a stimulus for a task might consist of a verbal instruction, "Do the laundry." Stimulus control might be exerted by a single stimulus or a class of stimuli in the immediate environment. In the case in which multiple stimuli are present, any one stimulus or class of stimuli may be controlling the response, whereas other stimuli may signal competing schedules of reinforcement.

Any discussion of stimulus control would be incomplete without consideration of the role of reinforcement. A stimulus may fail to evoke a response because of an insufficient schedule of reinforcement. An abundant body of applied literature has demonstrated that at least four factors related to the response-reinforcer contingency influence the probability of compliance, including the quantity, quality, immediacy, and the response requirements (i.e., response effort). Although

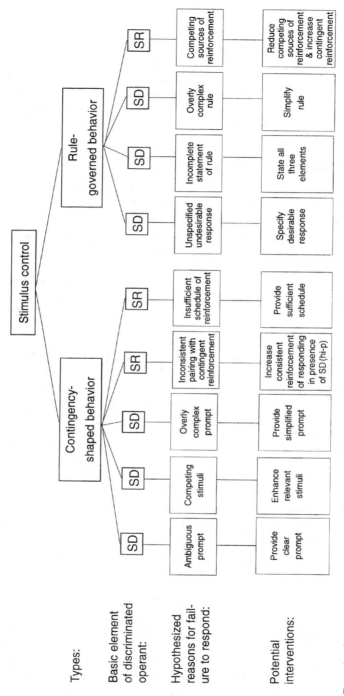

Figure 1. Conceptualization of instructional control.

the effects of reinforcement are predictable, these factors can have idiosyncratic effects and interactions and, therefore, should not be overlooked (Neef, Shade, & Miller, 1994). Consider first the quantity and quality of reinforcement. Schedules of highly preferred (quality) reinforcers tend to reinforce a higher rate of responding than schedules of reinforcement that involve a lower rate or quality of reinforcement (e.g., Neef, Mace, Shea, & Shade, 1992). As a result, if an individual is engaged in a densely reinforced response (e.g., playing a video game) and is then instructed to complete a task (e.g., brushing her teeth), the probability of complying with the instruction is low unless the schedule of reinforcement (quantity or quality) is increased to effectively compete with the alternative source of reinforcement (playing the video game).

Immediacy, or delay to reinforcement, is also an important factor that influences responding. When an individual is instructed to complete a task, if the reinforcer for completing the task is delayed and there is a more immediate source of reinforcement available, the individual is more likely to engage in the response that produces the more immediate reinforcer than to comply with the task that will result in delayed reinforcement (e.g., Neef, Mace, & Shade, 1993). For example, if a child is instructed to practice the piano, which will result in social approval during a recital scheduled for the following week, but he can gain immediate access to social approval simply by telephoning a grandparent, he may be less likely to practice the piano.

Another factor involves the response effort involved in the task demand. If the response effort is too great in comparison with the arranged consequences, the likelihood of compliance will be low. For example, if an agreement is made with a teen to mow a 1-acre yard for $10 per week, then the likelihood is low that she will comply with a request to mow a 10-acre yard for the same fee.

The possibility that noncompliance itself is reinforced either negatively or through the physical interaction that occurs during contingent-guided compliance should always be considered. To increase the likelihood that a consequence will reinforce compliance, relevant stimuli should be arranged to increase the schedule of reinforcement for compliance and to reduce the schedule for noncompliance. Finally, discussion of the effects of consequences would be incomplete without a note regarding establishing operations. Generally speaking, establishing operations are those stimuli or events that establish particular stimuli as reinforcing. Thus, efforts should be directed at arranging stimuli or events to maximize the reinforcing effectiveness of the consequent stimuli. Consider again the example of the child who is engaged in a densely reinforcing activity (playing a video game). To increase the likelihood that she will comply with an instruction that is less reinforced (e.g., brushing her teeth), establishing operations may be manipulated to increase the effects of the lower-quality reinforcer. Specifically, if listening to a bedtime story is the reinforcer for brushing her teeth, a favorite story that involves props and that is rarely available could be offered as the contingency.

## Hypothesized Reasons for Failure to Respond

There are several hypothesized reasons to explain why someone would fail to respond to an $S^D$. Although in the context of a discriminated operant consequent stimuli are inextricably tied to discriminative stimuli and, therefore, are a critical component of contingency-shaped behavior, the discussion in this chapter focuses on the $S^D$s. The left side of Figure 1 depicts just a few. To begin, the stimulus may have been ambiguous. For example, a request may have been delivered that consisted of the verbal instruction "Do your chores." This verbal instruction is ambiguous in terms of the precise response requirement, and, thus, it may fail to evoke the desired response. Similarly, the stimulus may be overly complex. For example, the instruction "Do the laundry" involves multiple steps. If the individual has difficulty completing any one of the component steps or has trouble making the transition from step to step, the verbal instruction "Do the laundry" will not evoke the desired response.

Another reason why the desired response is not evoked may be that the individual attends to competing stimuli. If the verbal instruction "Do the laundry" is delivered in the individual's home rather than in the vocational training setting, the individual may attend to competing stimuli that are irrelevant to the task demand such as different features of the appliances, family photographs on display, or preferred activities that are available. Alternately, an individual may fail to respond to a stimulus because there has been an inconsistent relationship between the instructional stimulus and contingent reinforcement. For example, if picking up shirts in response to the verbal instruction "Pick up the shirt" is not consistently or differentially reinforced, the stimulus may be less likely to evoke the desired (or any) response. Finally, a stimulus may fail to evoke a desired response because there is an insufficient schedule of reinforcement (involving any or all of the factors discussed previously).

## Potential Interventions for Lack of Stimulus Control

A number of different types of antecedent-based interventions are available for increasing instructional control. In general, an intervention to increase the likelihood of a behavioral response can be directed toward any element of the discriminated operant. Interventions may include, but certainly are not limited to, the following: 1) clarifying the prompt, 2) enhancing relevant stimuli, 3) simplifying the prompt, 4) implementing a high-probability (high-p) request procedure, or 5) providing a sufficient schedule of reinforcement. To illustrate, if prompts seem ambiguous, they can be made distinct or more clear. Returning to the example, "Do your chores," it may be necessary to clearly state the response requirements. The ambiguous prompt "Do your chores" might be more clearly restated as "Make your bed, vacuum the living room, and take out the garbage." Similarly, overly complex stimuli may be simplified to increase the likelihood of compliance. The request "Do the laundry" may be too complex. The task could be broken down into its constituent parts; thus, a simplified request might be "Put all of the white clothes into the washing machine." In addition, relevant stimuli could be enhanced if it appeared as though there are competing stimuli that precluded compliance. If during a laundry task the individual attends to competing stimuli (e.g., the box of fabric softener sheets), the relevant stimuli on the washing machine could be highlighted by colors or some other cues to increase attention to the relevant stimuli.

An intervention for making the relationship between the instructional stimulus and contingent reinforcement consistent involves the use of high-p requests. High-p requests are those instructions that have a high probability of being completed, whereas low-probability (low-p) requests are those that have a low probability of being completed. Several studies on compliance have focused on the use of high-p requests to facilitate compliance to subsequent low-p requests. For example, interspersing maintenance tasks with novel tasks has been shown to improve acquisition of new spelling words (Neef, Iwata, & Page, 1980). Horner and his colleagues (1991) interspersed three to five short, simple requests with difficult tasks for individuals with severe cognitive disabilities who engaged in aggressive and self-injurious behavior. The results indicated that interspersing simple requests (high-p) was effective at increasing compliance with difficult tasks (low-p) and in decreasing challenging behavior. In a five-experiment study involving four adult males with moderate to severe disabilities, Mace et al. (1988) demonstrated an increased likelihood of compliance with low-p requests that were delivered immediately after a series of high-p requests. Results from all five experiments demonstrated that the high-p procedure consistently resulted in enhanced responding to low-p requests. In a subsequent investigation, Mace and Belfiore (1990) implemented a high-p procedure immediately prior to delivery of the low-p request with an adult woman with mental retardation requiring extensive supports who exhibited stereotypic behavior. Results indicated that compliance to low-p demands such as "Please hang up your coat" increased, and stereotypic responding decreased. As a final example, Davis and her colleagues (1992) studied the effects of a high-p treatment on children with severe disabilities and behavior disorders. The target low-p request involved single-step requests such as "Sit in your chair." Results of this investigation were similar to those of Mace et al. (1988) and Mace and Belfiore (1990) in that compliance with low-p requests occurred more often when the requests were preceded by a high-p procedure than when the requests were delivered in isolation.

Other investigators, however, have identified situations in which the high-p treatment alone is ineffective at increasing compliance with low-p requests. Results of an investigation by Rortvedt and Miltenberger (1994) demonstrated a failure of a high-p procedure to increase compliance with a low-p request such as "Put your glass in the sink" for two developmentally typical 4-year-old girls. When a time-out procedure was added, however, compliance increased to acceptable levels. Zarcone, Iwata, Hughes, and Vollmer (1993) attempted to increase compliance with low-p requests with a woman with profound disabilities. Results suggested that a sequence of high-p requests did not function to increase compliance; rather, compliance increased when escape extinction was implemented. These failures of the high-p procedure to increase compliance with low-p requests are indicative of the need to more closely examine how interventions for contingency-shaped behavior are selected.

## RULE-GOVERNED BEHAVIOR

Similarities exist between the instructional stimuli involved in contingency-shaped behavior and their rule-governed counterparts. Rules facilitate appropriate behavior in situations in which a contingency has not been experienced. Consider again the example of *Speak quietly in the museum.* The same rule can be applied to other comparable situations (e.g., hospitals, book stores) without the listener having to experience the consequences associated with each situation.

### Basic Elements

The contingency-specifying stimulus, or rule, may be referred to as an $S^D$. The right side of Figure 1 provides examples of the basic elements of stimulus control involved in rule-governed behavior. Rules might consist of a one-component instruction. For example, the rules, *Don't run in the halls* and *Don't smoke* address single, specific actions; yet, a rule may be more complex, consisting of several discrete components. An example might be, *Avoid sweets, floss, and brush your teeth after every meal*, which comprises multiple instructions. Consequences also affect rule-governed behavior. Rules may involve immediate, delayed, intermittent, or uncertain consequences, stated either explicitly or implicitly. For example, *Don't get too close to the fire* implies an immediate consequence, whereas *Avoid sweets, floss, and brush your teeth after every meal* implies delayed consequences (i.e., tooth decay). *Don't run in the halls* implies a rather intermittent consequence (i.e., sustaining an injury), and *Don't smoke* implies an uncertain consequence (i.e., cancer).

## Hypothesized Reasons for Failure to Respond

The work of Malott and Garcia (1991) suggested several reasons why an individual may fail to comply with rules and why rules sometimes produce less than optimal response patterns. Figure 1 includes a sample of the hypothesized reasons for the failure of a rule to guide behavior. First of all, the rule may provide an instruction regarding what *not* to do but may not specify what *to do*. Consider the examples *Don't play with matches* and *Don't go anywhere with a stranger*. The undesirable behavior is specified, but a more appropriate alternative response is not. A second reason may be that the rule is incomplete—that is, it does not specify the antecedent, response, and consequence. For example, the rule *Just say no* fails to specify the stimulus conditions or the reinforcer. A third reason may be that the rule is overly complex. In the example, *Avoiding sweets, flossing, and brushing your teeth after every meal will help prevent tooth decay*, three response requirements are specified: 1) avoiding sweets, 2) flossing, and 3) brushing teeth. An individual might follow only some components of such a rule or disregard the rule altogether.

When considering the reasons why rules may fail to control behavior, the role of consequences cannot be ignored. The consequences for rules may be unclear, delayed, intermittent, or uncertain, or the individual may never experience the contingency at all. The rule *Don't throw rocks on the playground* does not explicitly state a contingency. In this case, the individual may be less likely to obey a rule whose consequences are unclear. Delayed consequences also may result in a failure of a rule to control behavior. For example, tooth decay is a delayed consequence for failure to follow the rules of good oral hygiene. In the case of intermittent consequences, such as *Don't run in the halls or you'll get hurt*, a child may run in the halls for several weeks or months before sustaining an injury; thus, she may fail to obey the rule. Another reason may be the uncertainty of the consequences. In the example, *Don't smoke or you may get cancer*, some may never experience the contingency.

## Potential Interventions for Failure of Rules to Govern Behavior

There are numerous potential interventions available when a rule fails to guide behavior. These include but are not limited to 1) explicitly stating the desired response; 2) specifying the complete rule including the antecedent conditions, the target behavior, and the consequence; 3) simplifying an overly complex rule; and 4) manipulating the consequences for following the rule. Rules that are stated in terms of "Don't" could be altered to explicitly state what to do. As an example, *Don't play with matches* could be restated as *Always give matches to an adult*. Reese (1992) argued an alternative solution: Rules that specify *each* element of the discriminated operant (i.e., the antecedent stimulus, response, and reinforcer) are more likely to be followed than those that specify only one or two components. Thus, in the example, *Always give matches to an adult*—in which only the response is specified—it may be unlikely that the rule is followed rigidly. One way to increase compliance to this rule might be to state the conditions under which the rule applies. For example, *If you find matches, give them to an adult* indicates the stimulus conditions under which someone should engage in the stated response. In addition, the reinforcer could be specified (e.g., *If you find matches, give them to an adult so you won't get burned*). In the case of the overly complex rule, providing a simplified rule may function to increase compliance with the rule. For example, the rule for dental care could be simplified to *Brush your teeth carefully after every meal*.

Discussion of interventions to increase the likelihood that rule-governed behavior evokes desired responses should not be limited to the $S^D$s. The consequences also should be considered. Several aspects of the consequences may be relevant, including making the consequences more clear, more immediate, less intermittent, or less uncertain. Making the consequences more clear might involve stating or even demonstrating the contingency. The instructor might follow the rule *Don't throw rocks on the playground* with *or someone might get hurt*, or the instructor could show a videotape of a simulation of an injury as a result of a child throwing rocks. Similarly, if the consequences are implicit, one intervention option is to make the consequences explicit, as in *If your clothes catch on fire and you stop, drop, and roll, you will be able to put out the fire. If you run instead, you will be badly burned*. In the case in which the consequences are delayed, the instructor might consider ways to make the consequences more immediate. Tooth decay may be a delayed consequence of failure to follow rules of good oral hygiene; however, chewable tablets that turn dental plaque red may serve as a more immediate consequence and visible warning of the delayed consequence of poor oral hygiene. If the consequences are intermittent, one intervention option is to make the consequences less intermittent. For example, with the *Stop, drop, and roll* rule, a dense schedule of consistent praise or tangible reinforcers (e.g., fire safety stickers, magnets, other fire safety paraphernalia) could be provided contingent on practicing the rule. Finally, consequences that seem im-probable could be made more probable. Consider the smoking ex-ample again. One consequence of smoking is getting cancer, yet this consequence may be uncertain to a teen experimenting with smoking. Thus, public service announcements in the 1990s have focused on the decline in peer acceptance of smoking (e.g., no one likes to kiss an ashtray), which may be more certain than getting cancer.

Although a list of potential interventions may be a good place to start, the question remains, under what conditions will rules guide behavior? Reese (1992) suggested that "strong" rules are those that have a short delay to reinforcement, a large reinforcer, and a high rate of reinforcement. Similarly, research on concurrent operants (two or more classes of alternative responses that may be compatible or in-compatible) suggests that factors such as the quality, magnitude, rate, and delay to reinforcement in competing sources of reinforcement are critical determinants of operant behavior (e.g., Mace, Neef, Shade, & Mauro, 1994; Neef et al., 1994). In concurrent operant paradigms in which the response options involve contingency-shaped and rule-governed responses, contingency-shaped behavior may affect the probability of rule following. To illustrate, often a rule such as *Look left, right, left before crossing the street* will efficiently control behavior. If a concurrent operant is present, however, such as when children are playing ball and the ball goes in the street, the rule may no longer control behavior. The child may dash into the street to immediately gain access to the ball because following the rule (looking left, right, left) would create a delay to reinforcement (i.e., getting the ball). Other relevant factors would include the amount of vehicle traffic on the road. That is, on very busy city streets, looking left, right, left would receive a high rate of negative reinforcement (i.e., avoiding being hit by a car), whereas the same behavior on a quiet cul-de-sac would receive a lower rate of reinforcement. Similarly, considering the smok-ing example again, for many people, there are powerful, immediate reinforcers for smoking that outweigh the relatively delayed and un-certain aversive consequences. To the extent that differences exist in the rate, magnitude, and delay to reinforcement between rules and contingencies, different allocations of behavior will result. The probability that a rule or contingency will guide behavior depends on many factors, all of which need to be considered when selecting an intervention.

## FACTORS TO CONSIDER FOR INTERVENTION SELECTION

There are numerous interventions available for improving compliance, yet each intervention will not always be effective, as demonstrated by the results of the Rortvedt and Miltenberger (1994) and Zarcone et al. (1993) studies. Thus, the selection of effective interventions should depend on the results of an experimental analysis (Iwata, Vollmer, & Zarcone, 1990; Iwata, Vollmer, Zarcone, & Rodgers, 1993). Iwata, Pace, Cowdery, and Miltenberger (1994) expanded on the considerations for appropriate selection of functional interventions by specifying the types of extinction that should be implemented based on the operant function of a response. The results of analyses with three individuals indicated the types of extinction-based interventions that are therapeutic, irrelevant, and contraindicated for responses that are attention-maintained, escape-maintained, and maintained by sensory reinforcement. The same type of conceptualization could be applied to antecedent stimuli delivered to occasion responding. That is, the selection of interventions should be based on the environmental variables that are responsible for noncompliance. Instructional stimuli could be evaluated based on the hypothesized reason for noncompliance, and intervention selection could be based on the results of the analysis.

Figure 2 displays the expected outcomes of interventions applied to different hypothesized reasons for noncompliance. Across the top of the figure are some hypothesized reasons for failure to comply, and listed vertically on the left side of the figure are potential interventions for increasing compliance. Each cell indicates the effects of the match between a particular hypothesized reason for noncompliance and a specified intervention. An intervention may be either irrelevant (i.e., have no functional effect on the desired response) or therapeutic (i.e., be functionally matched and therefore affect meaningful change on the desired response), depending on the appropriateness of the match. Specific examples for contingency-shaped and rule-governed behavior follow.

The top panel of Figure 2 pertains to intervention selection for contingency-shaped behavior. If the hypothesized reason for noncompliance involves an ambiguous prompt, the therapeutic intervention would be to clarify rather than to simplify the prompt or implement

| Potential interventions | Hypothesized reason for failure to respond to contingencies | | | | |
| --- | --- | --- | --- | --- | --- |
| | Ambiguous prompt | Competing stimuli | Overly complex prompt | Inconsistent R-S$^R$ pairing |
| Clarify prompts | Therapeutic | Irrelevant | Irrelevant | Irrelevant |
| Enhance relevant stimuli | Irrelevant | Therapeutic | Irrelevant | Irrelevant |
| Simplify | Irrelevant | Irrelevant | Therapeutic | Irrelevant |
| High-p treatment | Irrelevant | Irrelevant | Irrelevant | Therapeutic |

Figure 2. Expected outcomes of interventions based on hypothesized reasons for noncompliance.

(continued)

Figure 2. (continued)

| Potential interventions | Hypothesized reason for failure to respond to rules | | | |
|---|---|---|---|---|
| | Unspecified desirable response | Incomplete statement of rule | Overly complex rule | Competing sources of reinforcement |
| Specify desirable response | Therapeutic | Irrelevant | Irrelevant | Irrelevant |
| State all three elements of discriminated operant | Irrelevant | Therapeutic | Irrelevant | Irrelevant |
| Simplify rule | Irrelevant | Irrelevant | Therapeutic | Irrelevant |
| Reduce competing sources of reinforcement/ increase contingent reinforcement | Irrelevant | Irrelevant | Irrelevant | Therapeutic |

a high-p treatment. Similarly, if the hypothesized reason for noncompliance is that there is an inconsistent response-reinforcer pairing, the intervention of choice would be a high-p procedure rather than simplifying prompts or interventions that are specific to other aspects of the discriminated operant such as decreasing the response requirements or providing a higher rate of reinforcement.

The bottom panel of Figure 2 pertains to intervention selection for rule-governed behavior. If the rule is stated in terms of what *not* to do (i.e., *Don't* rules), the therapeutic intervention would involve restating the rule to specify the desired response rather than specifying the contingencies or simplifying the rule. Similarly, if the hypothesized reason for noncompliance involves an overly complex rule, simplifying the rule would be the therapeutic intervention, whereas making changes in the way the consequences are arranged or specifying the response would be expected to be irrelevant changes. By selecting interventions based on the hypothesized function of noncompliance, it may be possible to increase the likelihood that an effective intervention will be identified.

One final issue regarding contingency-shaped and rule-governed behavior should be considered. Much overlap exists between contingency-shaped and rule-governed behavior, and, ultimately, even rule-governed behavior is maintained by consequences. Perhaps one of the most widely cited weaknesses of rule-governed behavior, however, is the general insensitivity of rule-governed behavior to changes in programmed contingencies (e.g., Hayes, Brownstein, Zettle, Rosenfarb, & Korn, 1986; Kaufman, Baron, & Kopp, 1966). Returning to the example *Don't run in the halls or you will get hurt,* one would predict that if the child were strictly obeying the rule, the child would continue to obey the rule regardless of changes in contingencies (e.g., an emergency). This presents a clear problem for which at least two solutions exist. First, the teacher could provide a reinforcement history for compliance under a wide variety of conditions. LeFrancois, Chase, and Joyce (1988) found that exposing individuals to a wide variety of instructions specifying an array of response patterns produced heightened sensitivity to changing contingencies. Thus, explicit instructions regarding when running is allowed and when it is not allowed (identification of the appropriate discriminative stimuli) would help guide appropriate responses in particular stimulus situations. Behavior skills training procedures that involve modeling, instructions, rehearsal, and feedback have been employed to increase the likelihood that an individual will engage in a particular response in the presence of a specified set of stimuli. For example, Poche, Brouwer, and Swearingin (1981) used behavior skills training procedures to teach abduction prevention skills to three preschool children. Role-play situations were arranged in which unfamiliar adults approached children on the playground and encouraged the children to leave with them. The desired response (saying "No, I have to ask my teacher" and returning to school) was first modeled. Then the children rehearsed the desired response during additional role-play situations, and the desired response was praised. The results of skill training procedures such as this may serve to build a history of reinforcement for responding in a desirable manner in the presence of particular stimuli and, thus, increase the likelihood of appropriate compliance with rules (e.g., obeying adults but not strangers).

The second solution to address the insensitivity of rule-governed behavior to programmed contingencies is to determine the relative rates of reinforcement for rule following versus responding to the actual contingencies. The more consistently rule following is reinforced (positively or negatively), the less likely it is that the response will be influenced by actual contingencies. For example, consider the rule *Don't put anything smaller than your elbow into your ear*. Consistently following this rule is negatively reinforced (avoidance of injuring the inner ear); however, an individual who follows this rule strictly may fail to take the steps necessary to remove a foreign object from the ear and, in turn, suffer a hearing loss. Chase and Danforth (1991) further hypothesized that as rule following is reinforced less often relative to responding to the actual contingencies, behavior that is maintained by rules would become more sensitive to changing contingencies. Consider the concurrent operant research, which is relevant in cases in which the individual may either follow a stated rule or respond to the actual contingencies. That is, if the rate of reinforcement for responding to contingencies is greater than that for rigidly responding to a rule, the concurrent operant literature predicts that responding to changing contingencies would be more likely to occur than continuing to respond to a rule. A common occurrence in urban areas might illustrate this point. Consider the preteen whose parents instruct him to avoid interactions with the gang members (*Stay away from the gang*). The gang members, however, threaten to hurt the adolescent if he refuses to deliver a package for them. The negative reinforcement for compliance with the gang members is more immediate and more likely to guide the adolescent's behavior than the rule provided by his parents.

## CONCLUSIONS

This chapter discusses specific aspects of contingency-shaped and rule-governed behavior. At some point, the question arises, under what conditions is rule-governed behavior preferred over contingency-shaped behavior? Skinner (1974) and Vaughan (1985) argued that rule-governed behavior has several advantages over contingency-shaped behavior. Often, behavior can be more quickly shaped by rules than by directly contacting the contingencies. For example, if a teacher were instructing a child on the use of a microwave oven, the teacher could provide him with some rules such as *Do not use aluminum foil in the microwave, Do not microwave eggs in their shells,* or the teacher could allow the child to cook a variety of items in the microwave. Eventually, the student might attempt to use foil in the microwave or cook an egg in its shell, but the consequences of these types of errors combined with the time it might take to contact those consequences make contingency-shaped behavior less efficient than teaching a rule.

Lowe and colleagues (e.g., Bentall, Lowe, & Beasty, 1985; Lowe, Beasty, & Bentall, 1983) found that schedule performance of young preverbal children is similar to that of other non-human animals, suggesting that contingency-shaped behavior develops before rule-governed behavior. As children grow, rule-governed behavior begins to exert some control. At almost any time, then, an individual's behavior may be partially under the control of both rules and the actual contingencies operating in the environment. Indeed, rule-governed behavior is only truly rule-governed until the response actually contacts the contingencies specified by the rule (Adronis, 1991). For example, given the rule, *No throwing rocks on the playground,* the rule itself may control the child's behavior exclusively until the child actually throws rocks. At that point, presumably, the natural consequences or those specified by the child's teacher will follow the behavior. Subsequently, an individual's behavior will be governed both by the rule and the contingencies in effect.

This chapter distinguished between two types of instructional control, one maintained by a history of reinforcement for following rules and the other maintained by the actual contingencies. In many situations, both rule-governed and contingency-shaped behavior operate concurrently. The question then becomes "In what situations should each type of instructional stimuli be used?" Several suggestions have been offered. For example, if one wants children to behave in a particular manner very quickly, stating a strong rule may be the most effective technique. If one is more concerned with children's acquiring a high level of expertise in a particular response class, however, whether it be academic, athletic, or musical in nature, substantial contact with the contingencies is necessary.

Noncompliance may be the result of one or more problems, including an inconsistent relationship between the response and reinforcement in rule-governed or contingency-shaped behavior. Explicitly stating the contingencies or implementing an intervention such as a series of high-p instructions, among other interventions, may be used to increase compliance. Interventions should be selected based on an experimental analysis of the hypothesized reasons for noncompliance or the concomitant challenging behavior. Figures 1 and 2 and the discussion contained in this chapter are designed to assist in the consideration of instructional control and development of hypotheses that could be further validated via use of experimental analyses. In this way, the probability of identifying therapeutic interventions to increase compliance will be maximized.

## REFERENCES

Adronis, P. (1991). Rule governance: Enough to make a term mean. In L.J. Hayes & P.N. Chase (Eds.), *Dialogues on verbal behavior* (pp. 226–235). Reno, NV: Context Press.

Bentall, R.P., Lowe, C.F., & Beasty, A. (1985). The role of verbal behavior in human learning: II. Developmental differences. *Journal of the Experimental Analysis of Behavior, 43,* 165–181.

Chase, P.N., & Danforth, J.S. (1991). The role of rules in concept learning. In L.J. Hayes & P.N. Chase (Eds.), *Dialogues on verbal behavior* (pp. 205–225). Reno, NV: Context Press.

Davis, C.A., Brady, M.P., Williams, R.E., & Hamilton, R. (1992). Effects of high probability requests on the acquisition and generalization of responses to requests in young children with behavior disorders. *Journal of Applied Behavior Analysis, 25,* 905–916.

Hayes, S.C., Brownstein, A.J., Zettle, R.D., Rosenfarb, I., & Korn, Z. (1986). Rule-governed behavior and sensitivity to changing consequences of responding. *Journal of the Experimental Analysis of Behavior, 45,* 237–256.

Horner, R.H., Day, H.M., Sprague, J.R., O'Brien, M., & Tuesday Heathfield, L. (1991). Intersperse requests: A nonaversive procedure for reducing aggression and self-injury during instruction. *Journal of Applied Behavior Analysis, 24,* 265–278.

Iwata, B.A., Pace, G.M., Cowdery, G.E., & Miltenberger, R.G. (1994). What makes extinction work: Analysis and extinction of self-injurious escape behavior. *Journal of Applied Behavior Analysis, 27,* 131–144.

Iwata, B.A., Vollmer, T.R., & Zarcone, J.R. (1990). The experimental (functional) analysis of behavior disorders: Methodology, applications, and limitations. In A.C. Repp & N.N. Singh (Eds.), *Perspectives on the use of nonaversive and aversive interventions for persons with developmental disabilities* (pp. 301–330). Sycamore, IL: Sycamore.

Iwata, B.A., Vollmer, T.R., Zarcone, J.R., & Rodgers, T.A. (1993). Treatment classification and selection based on behavioral function. In R. Van Houten & S. Axelrod (Eds.), *Behavior analysis and treatment* (pp. 101–125). New York: Plenum.

Kaufman, A., Baron, A., & Kopp, R.E. (1966). Some effects of instructions on human operant behavior. *Psychonomic Monograph Supplements, 1,* 243–250.

Kennedy, C. (1994). Manipulating antecedent conditions to alter the stimulus control of problem behavior. *Journal of Applied Behavior Analysis, 27,* 161–170.

LeFrancois, J.R., Chase, P.N., & Joyce, J.H. (1988). The effects of a wide variety of instructions on human fixed interval performance. *Journal of the Experimental Analysis of Behavior, 49,* 383–393.

Lowe, C.F., Beasty, A., & Bentall, R.P. (1983). The role of verbal behavior in human learning: Infant performance on fixed-interval schedules. *Journal of the Experimental Analysis of Behavior, 39,* 157–164.

Mace, F.C. (1992). Noncompliance. In E.A. Konarski, J.E. Favell, & J.E. Favell (Eds.), *Manual for the assessment and treatment of the behavior disorders of people with mental retardation* (Tab BD12, pp. 1–6). Morgantown, NC: Western Carolina Center Foundation.

Mace, F.C., & Belfiore, P. (1990). Behavioral momentum in the treatment of escape-motivated stereotypy. *Journal of Applied Behavior Analysis, 23,* 507–514.

Mace, F.C., Hock, M.L., Lalli, J.S., West, B.J., Belfiore, P., Pinter, E., & Brown, D.F. (1988). Behavioral momentum in the treatment of noncompliance. *Journal of Applied Behavior Analysis, 21,* 123–141.

Mace, F.C., Neef, J.A., Shade, D., & Mauro, B.C. (1994). Limited matching on concurrent-schedule reinforcement of academic behavior. *Journal of Applied Behavior Analysis, 27,* 585–596.

Malott, R.W., & Garcia, M.E. (1991). Role of private events in rule-governed behavior. In L.J. Hayes & P.N. Chase (Eds.), *Dialogues on verbal behavior* (pp. 237–254). Reno, NV: Context Press.

Neef, N.A., Iwata, B.A., & Page, T.J. (1980). The effects of interspersal training versus high density reinforcement on spelling acquisition and retention. *Journal of Applied Behavior Analysis, 13,* 153–58.

Neef, N.A., Mace, F.C., & Shade, D. (1993). Impulsivity in students with serious emotional disturbance: The interactive effects of reinforcer rate, delay, and quality. *Journal of Applied Behavior Analysis, 26,* 37–52.

Neef, N.A., Mace, F.C., Shea, M.C., & Shade, D. (1992). Effects of reinforcer rate and reinforcer quality on time allocation: Extensions of matching theory to educational settings. *Journal of Applied Behavior Analysis, 25,* 691–699.

Neef, N.A., Shade, D., & Miller, M.S. (1994). Assessing influential dimensions of reinforcers on choice in students with serious emotional disturbance. *Journal of Applied Behavior Analysis, 27,* 575–583.

Poche, C., Brouwer, R., & Swearingin, M. (1981). Teaching self-protection to young children. *Journal of Applied Behavior Analysis, 14,* 169–176.

Reese, H.W. (1992). Rules as nonverbal entities. In S.C. Hayes & L.J. Hayes (Eds.), *Understanding verbal relations* (pp. 121–134). Reno, NV: Context Press.

Rortvedt, A.K., & Miltenberger, R.G. (1994). Analysis of a high probability instructional sequence and time-out in the treatment of child noncompliance. *Journal of Applied Behavior Analysis, 27,* 327–330.

Skinner, B.F. (1969). *Contingencies of reinforcement: A theoretical analysis.* Englewood Cliffs, NJ: Prentice Hall.

Skinner, B.F. (1971). *Beyond freedom and dignity.* New York: Alfred A. Knopf.

Skinner, B.F. (1974). *About behaviorism.* New York: Alfred A. Knopf.

Vaughan, M.E. (1985). Repeated acquisition in the analysis of rule-governed behavior. *Journal of the Experimental Analysis of Behavior, 44,* 175–184.

Zarcone, J.R., Iwata, B.A., Hughes, C.E., & Vollmer, T.R. (1993). Momentum versus extinction effects in the treatment of self-injurious escape behavior. *Journal of Applied Behavior Analysis, 26,* 135–136.

# ~ *15* ~

## *Establishing Operations and the Motivation of Challenging Behavior*

Craig H. Kennedy and Kim A. Meyer

The consequences of responding select the behaviors that we observe in the future. When a person emits a particular response that occasions an event functioning as a positive reinforcer, we are more likely to see that response in similar situations. For example, a young man whose screaming causes his peers to interact with him learns that when he emits "challenging behavior," it is followed by peer attention—in this case, a positive reinforcer. Obversely, when a person emits a response that terminates or avoids a negative reinforcer, the response will increase in probability on future occasions. For example, a student who has learned to hit her teacher when instructional demands are presented does so because this action terminates a noxious situation and is negatively reinforced. Working in relation to each other, positive and negative reinforcers are the consequent events that select and maintain behavior (Skinner, 1981).

However, there is more to the cause of behavior than what follows a response. As behavior unfolds into the psychological present, a multitude of events have predated the behavior that we see—the antecedents of responding. The similarities and differences between the physical characteristics of the environment—the stimulus control of behavior—that have, and have not, in the past occasioned a response being reinforced alter the momentary probability of responding. Not unlike stimulus control, motivational variables are antecedents to responding that make behavior more, or less, likely to occur. Motivation,

The authors thank Lisa Cushing and Margaret Werts for their comments on an earlier version of this chapter.

however, affects response probability by altering the reinforcing value of maintaining consequent events. As a domain for experimental analysis, the antecedents of responding have a long and rich scientific history (see Chapter 1). And, although the analysis of antecedents has at times been controversial, no credible behavior analyst denies their importance. Disagreements about the antecedents of behavior are analogous to the blind sages who, each encountering a different part of an elephant, arrive at different observations. One sage says the animal is like a snake, another says it is like a tree, and so forth. The state of affairs in the analysis of antecedent events in the late 1990s is similar; the parts are not clearly defined and do not yet appear to add up to the sum of the natural phenomenon being studied. This confusion, however, does not diminish the importance of these events in a scientific account of human conduct.

We can demonstrate that the presence versus the absence of different people affects the occurrence of challenging behavior, just as we can show that sleep deprivation, the rate of instructional demands, or the period of time since a person's last social interaction alters the probability of a response. Parsing out these various antecedent events and understanding their *motivational significance* is the focus of this chapter. As will become clear, not all antecedent events have direct motivational effects, whereas other antecedents directly affect motivation. Our thesis is that a clearer conceptual analysis of antecedent events having direct motivational effects on challenging behavior will help researchers understand their role in the occurrence of behavior and, by illation, how we intervene to reduce significant behavior problems.

## DEFINING MOTIVATION

"Motivation" has a long history in experimental psychology, a history fraught with disagreements and competing theories but little actual data (Fantino, 1973). Perhaps the problem with adequately defining *motivation* is that, like many other psychological constructs (e.g., "love," "friendship," "self-esteem"), there are as many definitions as definers (Goldiamond, 1962). It is our perspective that any psychological construct either can be debated at the level of discourse or defined and experimentally analyzed. Our preference is to explicitly state our theoretical perspective, define our terms in relation to motivation, and then use that conceptual vantage to review the relevant data.

The theoretical perspective taken in this chapter, as in most of the other chapters, is an operant system (e.g., Baum, 1994; Chiesa, 1994;

Keller & Schoenfeld, 1950; Michael, 1993b; Skinner, 1938). Other perspectives are represented in the motivation literature (e.g., interbehaviorism, neurophysiology, humanistic approaches). Because the primary innovations in assessing and treating challenging behavior have come from operant theory, however, it seems judicious to stay within a demonstrably effective theoretical system. In brief, we view *operant theory* as an event-based science that studies the interrelationship between behavior and environment (cf. Skinner, 1953).

That observation has important implications for how we do, and do not, define the motivation of challenging behavior, as well as how we integrate that conceptualization into a broader theoretical framework. Therefore, before reviewing the literature on how motivation functions as an antecedent influence affecting challenging behavior, a few definitions and clarifications are necessary.

## Defining Motivation as Establishing Operations

As noted previously, behavior is a function of the positive and negative reinforcers that maintain responding. These reinforcing stimuli, however, are not static entities that are functionally constant; instead, they are dynamic. To illustrate, for a long-distance runner, water has an identifiable positively reinforcing value prior to exercising (for convenience, we will call this the baseline level), and that value changes after the person exercises (the reinforcing value of water increases—she is deprived of water). The value changes again after the person has consumed a large quantity of liquid (the reinforcing value of water decreases and, in fact, can become a form of punishment—she is sated of water) (see Figure 1). This dynamic effect on reinforcement is referred to as an *establishing operation* (EO). These stimulus functions are the changes in the effectiveness of positive and negative reinforcers from one moment to the next. Formally, EOs are defined as events that alter the value of a reinforcer without altering the schedule of reinforcement or discriminative stimuli associated with reinforcer availability (Keller & Schoenfeld, 1950; Michael, 1982, 1993a). Put another way, what changes is the "power" of the consequence to function as a reinforcer.

Informally, we talk about a person's becoming more motivated because the reinforcer value increases (deprivation) or less motivated because the reinforcer value decreases (satiation). The net effect is to increase or decrease the probability that a particular behavior, or class of responses, will be exhibited. As a collection, each class of reinforcers that maintains each class of behaviors is constantly in flux between baseline levels of reinforcer value and deprivation/satiation. When an EO becomes extreme, for example, a person is very deprived of food,

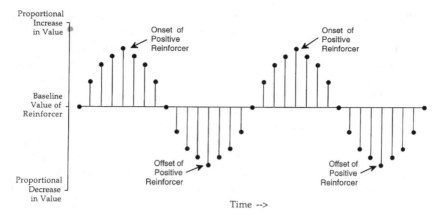

Figure 1. An example of how establishing operations affect the value of positive reinforcement. Unit time is displayed along the x-axis; the proportional change in the value of positive reinforcement relative to baseline value is arrayed along the y-axis. Reinforcer value begins at time-1 (t) at baseline levels. As time since the last occurrence of the reinforcer elapses, deprivation for the positive reinforcer increases (an establishing operation) and the reinforcer value increases. At t-5, positive reinforcement value is at its peak. As responding is reinforced (t-5 through t-13), the value of the reinforcer diminishes to the point where it no longer functions as a positive reinforcer. This process is an ongoing cyclical pattern among responding, establishing operations, and reinforcement.

dramatic changes in the probability of responding can be observed even though no other aspect of the situation has changed. Now that a basic definition of EOs has been offered, two points of clarification are necessary in relation to other antecedent terms.

**Establishing Operations versus Discriminative Stimuli** The first clarification distinguishes two stimulus functions that occur prior to responding. In particular, an accurate understanding of motivation cannot be arrived at without distinguishing between EOs and discriminative stimuli ($S^D$) (see Figure 2). $S^D$s are events that are differentially associated with the availability of reinforcement contingent on responding. As stimuli that allow a person to discriminate when responding will be reinforced (in the presence of the stimulus) and responding will not be reinforced (in the absence of the stimulus), $S^D$s can occasion abrupt changes in the rate of behavior (Ray & Sidman, 1970; Terrace, 1966).

This rapid change in responding, however, is often confused with changes in reinforcer value associated with EOs. $S^D$s "signal" a change in the availability of reinforcers, whereas EOs alter the value of reinforcers. For example, the presentation of a dessert tray at the end of a meal serves as an $S^D$ for a mand for a particular selection; whether the person is hungry is the EO. In the absence of the $S^D$, responding

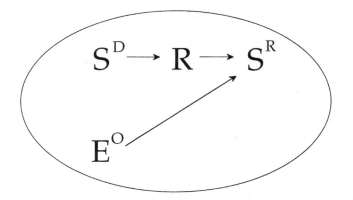

Figure 2. A conceptual unit showing the functional interrelations among discriminative stimuli ($S^D$s), responding (R), reinforcing stimuli ($S^R$s), and establishing operations (EOs). Discriminative stimuli differentially predict the availability of reinforcement for responding, whereas establishing operations alter the value of reinforcement.

should not occur (e.g., when offered the wine list, a diner does not ask for dessert). When the $S^D$ is present, however, the EO affecting the value of dessert as a reinforcer can alter the probability of making a selection versus declining.

When analyzing the antecedents of challenging behavior, it is important to note what types of stimulus changes are occurring prior to responding. If a person enters the room, or a particular item is made visible, and challenging behavior occurs, the probability that those events are functioning as $S^D$s is high. However, if challenging behavior begins to occur in the absence of any discernible change in the environment, then EOs may be a potential causal source. This distinction is important because, as is demonstrated in this chapter, interventions focusing on EOs can be substantially different from interventions focusing on $S^D$s.

**Establishing Operations versus Setting Events**  The second clarification deals with two motivational terms from related, but distinct, behavioral perspectives (i.e., the operant nature of EOs versus the interbehavioral nature of setting events). Both EOs and setting events have long histories in the conceptual analysis of behavior (both terms were first used in the 1950s). The two terms, however, are elements in different theoretical systems (Morris, 1982). On the one hand, EOs, as discussed previously, have emerged from an operant analysis of behavior (Michael, 1993a). Setting events, on the other hand, are part of an interbehavioral account of human behavior (Kantor, 1959). The two terms have often been used interchangeably because both focus on antecedent events that influence response probability by altering the value of reinforcement. This interchangeability, however, has led to confusion (Leigland, 1984).

Two observations may be prescient. First, when operant theorists use the setting event concept or interbehaviorists use the EO concept, researchers are mixing "apples and oranges." That is, one should expect some conceptual incompatibility when borrowing a term from another theoretical system. A second observation is that the two concepts, coming from different systems, are not isomorphic. It appears as if the setting event concept (with a largely structural definition) is more inclusive than the EO concept (with a largely functional definition). However, operant theorists have often employed the setting event concept within an operant framework. The reasons for this are largely historical. Setting events have long been discussed in the literature (e.g., Bijou & Baer, 1965); whereas EOs have emerged only since the 1960s as a viable theoretical concept. As a result, the concept of "setting events" was used in many cases in which contemporary researchers would use EOs. Whether there are experimentally identifiable differences between EOs and setting events awaits empirical demonstration. However, in this chapter and in the research we discuss, EOs are used instead of setting events because the framework from which our analyses are conducted is an operant, rather than an interbehavioral, system.

## HOW ESTABLISHING OPERATIONS AFFECT CHALLENGING BEHAVIOR

Since the beginning of the 1990s, the functional assessment of behavior problems has demonstrated that self-injury and aggression often are maintained by positive reinforcers (e.g., social attention, preferred activities, sensory changes) and/or negative reinforcers (e.g., termination of demands or nonpreferred activities) (Carr, 1977; Iwata, Dorsey, Slifer, Bauman, & Richman, 1982; Mace & Lalli, 1991; O'Neill, Horner, Albin, Sprague, & Storey, 1995). It is suggested, however, that some of the less-robust data from the literature may be due to the effects of establishing operations inducing variability through the strengthening or weakening of reinforcers. Although the effects of some EOs are well documented in the experimental literature (e.g., deprivation and satiation of food reinforcers), research regarding the influence of EOs in applied settings is still nascent.

Previous investigations have examined the influence of EOs on self-injury in highly controlled settings (e.g., Corte, Wolf, & Locke, 1971). In general, however, research in this area either has emphasized the observed relationships between EOs and changes in rates of challenging behavior without actually manipulating the EO (e.g., Kennedy & Itkonen, 1993; Kennedy & Meyer, 1996) or has experimentally manipulated an EO and examined changes in the rate of arbitrary responses (e.g., Vollmer & Iwata, 1991). The focus of this section is to review the existing literature regarding EOs and to provide examples of how EOs affect challenging behavior. It should be noted that careful assessment and measurement are a prerequisite to identifying relationships between EOs and challenging behavior.

## Establishing Operations and Attention

Gewirtz and Baer (1958a, 1958b) demonstrated that the reinforcing strength of praise changed as a function of prior social interactions. Praise maintained higher rates of behavior on a task if children's access to social attention was limited prior to the experimental sessions. However, lower rates of behavior were observed when the participants had social interactions prior to the experimental sessions. In a related study, when access to social interaction was manipulated prior to experimental sessions, adults with developmental disabilities exhibited higher rates of responding following periods of no interaction compared with frequent interaction (Vollmer & Iwata, 1991).

These findings have direct relevance for practitioners who suspect attention may play a role in causing challenging behavior. If a functional assessment indicates that self-injury is maintained by social attention, the manipulation of EOs may serve to reduce the reinforcing function of attention. This may be done through periodically programming interactions between self-injury and attention throughout the school day or prior to those times when self-injury is most likely to occur. If assessments suggest that self-injury is likely to occur 1–2 hours after school begins, an intervention may target the EO by having the teacher and student interact for 10–15 minutes shortly after school begins. Providing attention to the student in this way may reduce the strength of attention as a reinforcer later in the day.

## Establishing Operations and
## Gaining Access to Preferred Activities

Corte et al. (1971) found that a snack functioned as a positive reinforcer for behaviors other than self-injury only after several hours had elapsed since the last meal. If the individual ate lunch prior to experimental sessions, the snack ceased to function as a positive reinforcer. Vollmer and Iwata (1991) also demonstrated that access to certain foods (e.g., raisins) maintained an arbitrary response at a higher rate when sessions were run prior to lunch, rather than following lunch.

In addition, they also found that listening to music for short periods of time was more reinforcing if access to such activities was limited prior to the sessions.

The implications of these studies seem quite clear for personnel working with individuals who exhibit challenging behaviors. Any intervention that utilizes positive reinforcement needs to consider the effect EOs have on the value of that reinforcer, particularly when previously effective interventions appear to be ineffectual. Although the reoccurrence of challenging behavior does not necessarily suggest the diminishing strength of a reinforcing event, it should certainly occasion the examination of such possibilities.

## Establishing Operations and Demands

Researchers have also demonstrated a relationship between establishing operations and increased rates of behavior that terminate a noxious situation (Smith, Iwata, Goh, & Shore, 1995). Smith et al. (1995) demonstrated that, among other events, increases in the rate of instructional demands can function as EOs making escape from instruction contingent on challenging behavior negatively reinforcing. In addition, sleep deprivation and the presence of allergy symptoms have been correlated with increases in behavior problems during settings in which demands were frequently placed on students whose challenging behavior was negatively reinforced by escape from demands (Kennedy & Itkonen, 1993; Kennedy & Meyer, 1996; O'Reilly, 1995). It appears that certain EOs may increase the "noxiousness" of certain events and result in increased rates of challenging behavior functioning to escape from those situations.

A practitioner may be more likely to encounter the effects of EOs and negative reinforcement when a significant amount of variability is observed in a student's behavior across various instructional/demand situations that otherwise appear similar. For example, a student may work appropriately on the majority of days but exhibit intense self-injurious behavior on occasional days. A thorough assessment may reveal that, because of arguing between his parents, the student had little sleep the night preceding the occurrence of self-injury; conversely, when the student had his usual amount of sleep, he exhibited few if any problems during instructional periods. A situation such as this would indicate that an intervention targeting his lack of sleep, or more directly those events prohibiting him from sleeping (i.e., his parents' disputes), should be a primary focus of intervention.

## Establishing Operations and Sensory Consequences

Although the literature is mixed, certain studies have suggested a relationship between activity levels and frequencies of stereotypical behavior that may be maintained by sensory consequences. For example, vigorous jogging prior to instructional periods may reduce stereotypical responses (e.g., Bachman & Fuqua, 1983). Similarly, Kern, Koegel, Dyer, Blew, and Fenton (1982) reported fewer disruptions and noncompliance on days when individuals with stereotypical behavior exercised as opposed to days when they did not exercise. In these cases, one interpretation may be that an EO (increased exercise) reduces the value of whatever internal mechanisms might be maintaining the stereotypical behavior. It should also be noted, however, that stereotypical behaviors are so labeled by a default process. That is, because as of this writing it is not possible to identify a maintaining variable, it is assumed that an internal event may be maintaining the behavior (see Kennedy, 1994; Kennedy & Souza, 1995; for further discussion).

## QUANTITATIVE DIMENSIONS
## AFFECTING ESTABLISHING OPERATIONS

Any specific reinforcer that maintains responding has an associated EO, and, more important, how those various EOs effect reinforcer value can be summarized along a few basic quantitative dimensions. In a paper that elaborated on Herrnstein's (1961, 1970, 1974) quantitative summary of the "law of effect," Killeen further developed the motivational component of reinforcement (i.e., EOs). In that paper, Killeen arrived at the following formula to summarize the mechanics of motivation (1995, p. 410):

$$EO_t = d_o + (M - mR) \, t$$

Where $d_o$ is the initial deficit in reinforcer value, $M$ is the deprivation component (output), $mR$ is the satiation component (input), and $t$ is unit time.

This equation illustrates how deprivation and satiation affect the value of reinforcement. In essence, this is a quantitative summary of the cyclical pattern displayed in Figure 1. For example, as responding is continually positively reinforced, the value of that reinforcer diminishes over time. Of particular interest are the M and mR components of the equation; that is, how does the value of a reinforcer increase or decrease? It is important to note that EOs do not have their affect on reinforcer value simply as a matter of the passage of time, but instead are affected by patterns of contact with the reinforcing event. This observation requires that basic dimensions of the contact be defined (Johnston & Pennypacker, 1992).

At least four different dimensional quantities—frequency or rate, magnitude, duration, and inter-reinforcement time (IRT)—can be used to describe patterns of stimulation with reinforcing events. That is, as responses are emitted, contact with reinforcing events occurs. That pattern of contact is what alters the extent to which the value of reinforcers increases or decreases (Skinner, 1938). *Frequency*, or *rate*, with which the event occurs is one means of summarizing contact with reinforcers. For example, how many times per hour does a particular response occasion a reinforcer (or class of reinforcers)? A second way of summarizing reinforcer contact is the *magnitude* of the reinforcer, that is, the "amount" of the reinforcer presented after responding. A third characteristic to reinforcing stimulation is the *duration* of the event, that is, how long the reinforcer is presented. The fourth dimensional quantity is *IRT*, which summarizes the average amount of time between exposures to a reinforcing event. For example, if 5 minutes occurred between exposure at Time 1 and Time 2 and 10 minutes occurred between exposure at Time 2 and Time 3, then an IRT of 7.5 minutes could be used to describe the events. As a collection, these dimensions of reinforcing stimulation summarize how positive and negative reinforcers occur in relation to behavior.

All other variables being equal, the greater the frequency, magnitude, or duration of reinforcing event, the more rapidly satiation occurs. Working in an opposite manner, the greater the IRT, the less rapidly satiation occurs. As a set of dimensions describing the effect of reinforcing stimulation on reinforcer value, they can provide researchers with an objective means of describing how different patterns of stimulation influence EOs (i.e., via M and mR of the original equation).

## SPECIFIC VERSUS GENERAL ESTABLISHING OPERATIONS

Now that we have an outline of the mechanism for how EOs affect reinforcer value and have specifics regarding dimensions of stimulation, a distinction should be made about how EOs affect various reinforcers. In some instances, events functioning as EOs alter the value of a particular reinforcer. For example, when a person ingests salt, there is an increase in the positively reinforcing value of drinking water. In contrast, there are also EOs that cause a change in value across a range of reinforcers. For example, sleep deprivation may reduce the value of positive reinforcers such as eating while increasing the value of negative reinforcers such as completing a work assignment.

### Specific Establishing Operations

The longer that a person is deprived of access to a preferred event (e.g., playing basketball) the greater is the EO effect on the value of the positively reinforcing event. That is, as the time since a person last played basketball increases (i.e., he or she is increasingly deprived, or M increases in value), the more powerful access to basketball becomes as a positive reinforcer. However, that deprivation may not affect the reinforcing value of eating, playing music, or watching television. There is a demonstrable effect on a specific response-reinforcer class related to a particular type of EO. Similarly, as the frequency of demands is increased, there may be an increase in the negatively reinforcing value of escape from instruction (Smith et al., 1985). The increase in demand rate as an EO, however, may not affect the value of other reinforcers such as eating or completing another work assignment.

In each example, the effect of particular EOs is largely focused on a specific class of maintaining events. It is important to note that the types of interventions developed for specific EOs will focus on the specific response-reinforcer relationships being affected. For instance, decreasing the rate or frequency of demands may reduce the noxiousness of an instructional context, making escape less negatively reinforcing. Or, in the example of positive reinforcement, increasing the IRT for playing basketball will increase its salience as a reinforcing event.

## General Establishing Operations

Unlike specific EOs, some events function to alter a broader array of reinforcer classes associated with various response classes. As indicated by the example of sleep deprivation provided previously, not only are events that typically function as positive reinforcers diminished, but other events such as escaping from instruction are increased in value. Whether these effects are due to a general increase in the value of sleep, or whether sleep deprivation has a broader functional effect on behavior, remain unanswered questions (see Kennedy & Meyer, 1996; O'Reilly, 1995). Similar effects on reinforcer classes appear to occur for allergies (Kennedy & Meyer, 1996), menses (Bailey & Pyles, 1989; Carr, Reeve, & Magito-McLaughlin, 1996; Horner, Vaughn, Day, & Ard, 1996), migraines (Carr et al., 1996), otitis media (O'Reilly, in press), and other biobehavioral events. The implications for intervention for these types of events, however, are different than specific EOs. For instances of biobehavioral interactions (cf. Cataldo & Harris, 1982; Horner et al., 1996) such as sleep deprivation or menses, interventions may need to target the EO for elimination or a reduction in the symptomatology associated with the EO, respectively. The implications for both specific and general EOs are further addressed in the next section.

## PRACTICAL EXAMPLES: ASSESSMENT AND INTERVENTION

In this section, the implications for both specific and general EOs are addressed using a series of case studies. The case studies illustrate complex interactions among different types of reinforcers and EO effects.

### Challenging Behavior
### Maintained by Access to Preferred Activities

Luke was a 7-year-old boy with autism who exhibited a variety of challenging behaviors including aggression, self-injury, property destruction, and elopement. Interviews with Luke's mother suggested that his delay was related to at least two factors: a severe seizure at age 2 years that required medical personnel to induce coma and possible neglect during a long-term abduction (approximately 30 months) by his paternal grandparents. Although his mother had no information regarding the time he was gone, when he was returned, he was covered with sores, grossly overweight (110 pounds at 5 years), and using little language.

Although Luke had made significant gains by age 7 years, both his parents and school personnel indicated that his challenging behaviors were causing significant disruptions. A functional assessment of his challenging behaviors indicated that they were maintained by a number of variables. That is, attention from adults was related to his aggression against peers and siblings, access to preferred activities was related to temper tantrums (which often included property destruction and elopement), and escape from instructional settings at both home and school were frequently preceded by any, or all, of the other challenging behaviors.

As a result of the assessment data, a multicomponent intervention was developed. First, teachers and staff were asked to differentially reinforce Luke for appropriate play with his peers. In addition, his speech-language therapist agreed to improve Luke's communication skills when interacting with his peers (previously, the focus of communication was with adults). The second part of Luke's intervention was aimed at curricular revisions. It appeared that much of Luke's schoolwork was too difficult for him so revisions included simplifying the work and gradually increasing demands. In addition, interspersed requests (Horner, Day, Sprague, O'Brien, & Heathfield, 1991; Mace et al., 1988) were incorporated into his curriculum.

As a result of these interventions, Luke's frequency of appropriate behavior increased dramatically (with corresponding decreases in challenging behavior). However, his mother reported that he would still occasionally exhibit severe tantrums at home. She stated that they occurred less frequently than before but were still problematic. Over the course of the next several weeks, further assessment indicated that temper tantrums occurred on Wednesday or Thursday evenings. On such occasions, Luke's mother found that the most effective way to end the tantrum was to take him to dinner at a fast-food restaurant. She also reported that Luke had no problems during a week in which he attended the party of a classmate at another fast-food restaurant. She also noted that the family would typically go out for food once or twice each weekend.

The information suggested that length of time since a visit to a fast-food restaurant functioned as an EO for eating certain types of food. Luke's mother was instructed to take the family out to eat on Wednesday for the next 2 weeks and also to continue to collect information regarding Luke's behavior. Two weeks later, she reported that Luke's behavior had been excellent. She then was instructed to skip a week; she later reported that Luke again had exhibited a tantrum on Thursday evening. As a result, it was suggested that she attempt to incorporate this activity into the family schedule on a regular basis.

## Challenging Behavior Maintained by Escape from Demands

Marcello was a 15-year-old boy diagnosed as having mental retardation requiring pervasive supports, and he communicated only through facial expressions and gestures. He had an extensive history (12 years) of self-injury and aggression, which included head banging and hitting himself or others with his fists. The intensity was such that protective equipment (e.g., helmet, arm splints) had occasionally been used in the past to protect him from re-opening wounds. Although he wore no protective equipment at the time of the consultation, Marcello did frequently "self-restrain" by wrapping his arms in an oversized basketball jersey that he wore on a daily basis.

Information obtained from Marcello's parents and teacher indicated that the amount of sleep he had each night affected his school performance the next day, suggesting that sleep may have served as an EO. As a result, his parents were asked to record his sleep habits for his teacher on a regular basis. In addition, his parents reported that, as a result of limited sleep, his behavior in the mornings prior to school was much worse than following normal nights of sleep. When the challenging behaviors occurred, they would dress him in an oversized coat with the sleeves tied behind his back (this served as a restraint to reduce self-hitting). Marcello's teacher also noted which days he arrived at school wearing the oversized jacket.

A series of different tasks was then programmed for Marcello to assess any relationships between his sleep and his challenging behavior. A block of four 10-minute sessions was used each day to assess his challenging behavior when 1) social attention was contingent on challenging behavior; 2) escape from demands occurred following self-injury; 3) preferred activities were programmed and attention was provided on a regular basis; and 4) he sat alone, receiving no attention, and no activities were programmed.

Results of Marcello's functional analysis indicated that his challenging behavior was maintained by negative reinforcement (see Figure 3). It was also clear, however, that rates of challenging behavior were higher during demand conditions on days following little sleep than on days when he presumably was less tired. It is interesting to note that rates of challenging behavior in the other conditions showed little change across days, regardless of the amount of sleep.

These findings indicated that sleep deprivation might function as an establishing operation, serving to "strengthen" escape as a negative reinforcer from a presumably aversive situation (demands). In this case, a multicomponent intervention was developed. First, a family-based intervention was developed to increase the amount of sleep Marcello gained each evening. Prior to intervention, his family had Marcello go to bed directly after dinner. The result was that he often slept a few hours and then was awake most of the night, sleeping later at school. The intervention—having him go to bed at 10 P.M.

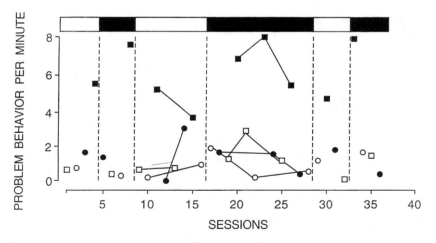

Figure 3.   An example of how an establishing operation can alter the frequency of challenging behavior across days. Marcello's data are presented as the frequency per minute of challenging behavior per 10-minute session. One block of four sessions was conducted each day (i.e., attention, demand, no attention, and recreation). The shaded area above the graph parallel to the horizontal axis indicates sessions when Marcello was sleep deprived. (Key: ●, Attention; ■, Demand; ○, No Attention; □, Recreation.) (Source: Kennedy & Meyer, 1996.)

—resulted in stable and typical sleep patterns with associated decreases in negatively reinforced challenging behavior. Second, a combination of functional communication training (Carr & Durand, 1985) and curricular revision (Dunlap, Kern-Dunlap, Clarke, & Robbins, 1991) were introduced throughout his day to provide for an alternative escape-response and to minimize EOs that might make instruction unpleasant, respectively.

## SUMMARY

The function of challenging behavior is its logic. The environmental basis of behavior, as has been made explicit by functional assessment techniques, selects behavior (Sidman, 1960). As is noted in the introduction, the consequences of responding provide the direct causal link between environment and behavior. However, events that occur prior to responding—the antecedents of behavior—also influence the likelihood that behavior will occur (Goldiamond, 1962; Ray & Sidman, 1970; Skinner, 1938). Our charge in this chapter has been to explicate the role of motivation as an antecedent influence on challenging behavior. An operant analysis of motivation leads to their conceptualization as establishing operations. EOs influence response rate by altering the value of available reinforcement. Unlike other antecedent events (e.g., discriminative stimuli), however, EOs do not differentially predict the availability of reinforcement contingent on responding; EOs only make that reinforcement more, or less, effective.

What we have tried to demonstrate in this chapter is that EOs 1) are real events that occur in space and time, 2) can account for variability—increases or decreases in rate—in challenging behavior that was previously unidentified, 3) can be modeled quantitatively to illuminate basic dimensions along which such events affect reinforcer value, 4) fall into two general classes based on their affects or effects on reinforcer value, and 5) are important in the assessment of challenging behavior and need to be considered prior to developing interventions. There appear to be three different approaches to developing interventions based on the direct manipulation of EOs. It is the nature of EOs that dictate which approach is taken (see also Horner et al., 1996). One approach is to remove or prevent the occurrence of the event functioning as an EO (e.g., sleep deprivation). If the EO event can be altered, this may be the preferred approach to EO-based intervention. Second, if a reinforcer is serving to maintain responding, then satiating the behavior with the reinforcer (the reciprocal of extinction) can reduce challenging behavior. Not all events functioning as EOs can be eliminated (e.g., menses, headaches), however. In these cases it appears as if marginalizing the physiological effects of EOs may be a preferred approach to intervention (e.g., taking a medication to reduce premenstrual or headache symptomatology).

Practitioners should note that the motivation of challenging behavior is an important issue to be addressed in assessment and intervention. For researchers, it is clear that any comprehensive account of the causes of challenging behavior needs to explicitly take into account motivational properties of events occurring prior to responding. Our goal in this chapter has been to summarize the conceptual and experimental literature related to the motivation of challenging behavior. We have attempted to synthesize a clear conceptualization of establishing operations to demonstrate how such events influence challenging behavior. It is hoped that this analysis and synthesis will contribute to the continuing expansion of research and theory related to the motivation of challenging behavior—an expansion that should result in a better understanding of why people engage in challenging behavior.

## REFERENCES

Bachman, J.E., & Fuqua, R.W. (1983). Management of inappropriate behaviors of trainable mentally impaired students using antecedent exercise. *Journal of Applied Behavior Analysis, 16,* 477–484.

Bailey, J.S., & Pyles, D.A.M. (1989). Behavioral diagnostics. In E. Cipani (Ed.), *The treatment of severe behavior disorders* (pp. 85–107). Washington, DC: Monographs of the American Association on Mental Retardation.

Baum, W.M. (1994). *Understanding behaviorism: Science, behavior, and culture.* New York: HarperCollins.

Bijou, S.W., & Baer, D.M. (1965). *Child development: The universal stage of infancy* (Vol. 2). Englewood Cliffs, NJ: Prentice Hall.

Carr, E.G. (1977). The motivation for self-injurious behavior: A review of some hypotheses. *Psychological Bulletin, 84,* 800–816.

Carr, E.G., & Durand, V.M. (1985). Reducing behavior problems through functional communication training. *Journal of Applied Behavior Analysis, 18,* 111–126.

Carr, E.G., Reeve, C.E., & Magito-McLaughlin, D. (1996). Contextual influences on problem behavior in people with developmental disabilities. In L.K. Koegel, R.L. Koegel, & G. Dunlap (Eds.), *Positive behavioral support: Including people with difficult behavior in the community* (pp. 403–424). Baltimore: Paul H. Brookes Publishing Co.

Cataldo, M.J., & Harris, J.C. (1982). The biological basis for self-injury in the mentally retarded. *Analysis and Intervention in Developmental Disabilities, 2,* 21–39.

Chiesa, M. (1994). *Radical behaviorism: The philosophy and the science.* Boston: Authors Cooperative.

Corte, H.E., Wolf M., & Locke, B.J. (1971). A comparison of procedures for eliminating self-injurious behavior of retarded adolescents. *Journal of Applied Behavior Analysis, 4,* 201–213.

Dunlap, G., Kern-Dunlap, L., Clarke, S., & Robbins, F.R. (1991). Functional assessment, curricular revision, and severe problem behavior problems. *Journal of Applied Behavior Analysis, 24,* 387–397.

Fantino, E. (1973). Emotion. In J.A. Nevin (Ed.), *The study of behavior* (pp. 281–320). Glenview, IL: Scott, Foresman and Company.

Gewirtz, J.L., & Baer, D.M. (1958a). Deprivation and satiation of social reinforcers as drive conditions. *Journal of Abnormal and Social Psychology, 57,* 165–172.

Gewirtz, J.L., & Baer, D.M. (1958b). The effect of brief social deprivation on behaviors for a social reinforcer. *Journal of Abnormal and Social Psychology, 56,* 49–56.

Goldiamond, I. (1962). Perception. In A.J. Bachrach (Ed.), *Experimental foundations of clinical psychology* (pp. 280–340). New York: Basic Books.

Herrnstein, R.J. (1961). Relative and absolute strength of response as a function of frequency of reinforcement. *Journal of the Experimental Analysis of Behavior, 4,* 267–272.

Herrnstein, R.J. (1970). On the law of effect. *Journal of the Experimental Analysis of Behavior, 13,* 243–266.

Herrnstein, R.J. (1974). Formal properties of the matching law. *Journal of the Experimental Analysis of Behavior, 21,* 159–164.

Horner, R.H., Day, H.M., Sprague, J.R., O'Brien, M., & Heathfield, L.T. (1991). Interspersed requests: A nonaversive procedure for decreasing aggression and self-injury during instruction. *Journal of Applied Behavior Analysis, 24,* 265–278.

Horner, R.H., Vaughn, B.J., Day H.M., & Ard, W.R. (1996). The relationship between setting events and problem behavior: Expanding our understanding of behavioral support. In L.K. Koegel, R.L. Koegel, & G. Dunlap (Eds.), *Positive behavioral support: Including people with difficult behavior in the community* (pp. 381–402). Baltimore: Paul H. Brookes Publishing Co.

Iwata, B.A., Dorsey, M.F., Slifer, K.J., Bauman, K.E., & Richman, G.S. (1982). Toward a functional analysis of self-injury. *Analysis and Intervention in Developmental Disabilities, 2,* 3–20.

Johnston, J.M., & Pennypacker, H.S. (1992). *Strategies and tactics of behavioral research* (2nd ed.). Hillsdale, NJ: Lawrence Erlbaum Associates.

Kantor, J.R. (1959). *Interbehavioral psychology* (2nd ed., rev.). Bloomington, IN: Principia Press.

Keller, F.S., & Schoenfeld, W.N. (1950). *Principles of psychology.* New York: Appleton-Century-Crofts.

Kennedy, C.H. (1994). Automatic reinforcement: Oxymoron or hypothetical construct? *Journal of Behavioral Education, 4,* 387–395.

Kennedy, C.H., & Itkonen, T. (1993). Effects of setting events on the problem behavior of students with severe disabilities. *Journal of Applied Behavior Analysis, 26,* 321–327.

Kennedy, C.H., & Meyer, K.A. (1996). Sleep deprivation, allergy symptoms, and negatively reinforced problem behavior. *Journal of Applied Behavior Analysis, 29,* 133–135.

Kennedy, C.H., & Souza, G. (1995). Functional analysis and treatment of eye-poking. *Journal of Applied Behavior Analysis, 28,* 27–37.

Kern, L., Koegel, R.L., Dyer, K., Blew, P.A., & Fenton, L.R. (1982). The effects of physical exercise on self-stimulation and appropriate responding in autistic children. *Journal of Autism and Developmental Disorders, 12,* 399–419.

Killeen, P.R. (1995). Economics, ecologics, and mechanics: The dynamics of responding under conditions of varying motivation. *Journal of the Experimental Analysis of Behavior, 64,* 405–431.

Leigland, S. (1984). On "setting events" and related concepts. *The Behavior Analyst, 7,* 41–45.

Mace, F.C., Hock, M.L., Lalli, J.S., West, B.J., Belfiore, P., Pinter, E., & Brown, D.K. (1988). Behavioral momentum in the treatment of noncompliance. *Journal of Applied Behavior Analysis, 21,* 123–141.

Mace, F.C., & Lalli, J.S. (1991). Linking descriptive and experimental analyses in the treatment of bizarre speech. *Journal of Applied Behavior Analysis, 24,* 553–562.

Michael, J.L. (1982). Distinguishing between discriminative and motivational functions of stimuli. *Journal of the Experimental Analysis of Behavior, 37,* 149–155.

Michael, J. (1993a). *Concepts and principles of behavior analysis.* Kalamazoo, MI: Society for the Advancement of Behavior Analysis.

Michael, J. (1993b). Establishing operations. *The Behavior Analyst, 16,* 191–206.

Morris, E.K. (1982). Some relationships between interbehavioral psychology and radical behaviorism. *Behaviorism, 10,* 187–216.

O'Neill, R.E., Horner, R.H., Albin, R., Sprague, J., & Storey, K. (1995). *Functional analysis and assessment: A guide for practitioners* (2nd ed.). Pacific Grove, CA: Brooks/Cole.

O'Reilly, M.F. (1995). Functional analysis and treatment of escape-maintained aggression correlated with sleep deprivation. *Journal of Applied Behavior Analysis, 28,* 225–226.

O'Reilly, M.F. (in press). Sequential analogue analysis of episodic self-injury correlated with recurrent otitis media. *Journal of Applied Behavior Analysis.*

Ray, B.A., & Sidman, M. (1970). Reinforcement schedules and stimulus control. In W.N. Schoenfeld (Ed.), *The theory of reinforcement schedules* (pp. 187–214). New York: Appleton-Century-Crofts.

Sidman, M. (1960). Normal sources of pathological behavior. *Science, 132,* 61–68.

Skinner, B.F. (1938). *The behavior of organisms: An experimental analysis.* New York: Appleton-Century-Crofts.

Skinner, B.F. (1953). *Science and human behavior.* New York: Macmillan.

Skinner, B.F. (1981). Selection by consequences. *Science, 213,* 501–504.

Smith, R.G., Iwata, B.A., Goh, H.L., & Shore, B.A. (1995). Analysis of establishing operations for self-injury maintained by escape. *Journal of Applied Behavior Analysis, 28,* 515–536.

Terrace, H.S. (1966). Stimulus control. In W.K. Honig (Ed.), *Operant behavior: Areas of research and application* (pp. 271–344). New York: Appleton-Century-Crofts.

Vollmer, T.R., & Iwata, B.A. (1991). Establishing operations and reinforcement effects. *Journal of Applied Behavior Analysis, 24,* 279–291.

# ~ 16 ~

## Establishing and Transferring Stimulus Control
### Teaching People with Developmental Disabilities

Anthony J. Cuvo and Paula K. Davis

Historically, procedures for reducing the challenging behaviors of people with developmental disabilities have focused on delivering consequences contingent upon the emission of the undesired behavior. More recently, antecedent control strategies such as those described in the other chapters have been recognized as critical elements of any behavioral support plan. One final integral part of any program designed to address challenging behaviors is the inclusion of a skill acquisition component. Any plan designed to reduce inappropriate behavior also should focus on the development of age-appropriate, functional skills for several reasons. First, new skills may provide the person with behavioral alternatives to the challenging behaviors. Second, new behaviors may provide access to additional reinforcers. Third, new skills may permit the person more independence and access to the community. Fourth, increased independence and decreased challenging behavior may permit the person to achieve a more desirable lifestyle.

Since the 1970s, there has been increasing effort devoted to conducting applied behavioral research on the acquisition, maintenance, and generalization of functional skills by children and adults with developmental and other disabilities. These functional skills have been derived from academic and daily living domains (e.g., vocational, leisure, community, social), and their instructional environments include both school and community settings. Comprehensive behavior models for conducting that applied research have been presented elsewhere (e.g., Cuvo & Davis, 1983; Sulzer-Azaroff & Mayer, 1991). Procedures for promoting and transferring stimulus control are central to these training models and any behavioral intervention program. This chapter focuses on the critical antecedent issue of how to prompt desirable responses so that meaningful skills can be taught and acquired. Specifically, the chapter addresses the role of prompts and consequences for promoting stimulus control. In addition, the transfer of control from artificial to more natural discriminative stimuli as well as problems in promoting and transferring stimulus control are discussed.

## STIMULUS CONTROL

Some stimuli set the occasion (i.e., are discriminative) for responding to achieve certain functional outcomes. Responding to these discriminative stimuli leads to positive consequences. Other stimuli in the environment do not produce positive consequences and should be ignored. For example, one door to a fast-food restaurant may be located to the right of another door. The former may say "enter" on the outside, and the latter may be labeled "exit" on the inside. The stimulus cues that identify it as a door—such as its shape, location, opening mechanism, and printed words—are discriminative to make a certain response (e.g., push) to enter. If a person responds appropriately to these discriminative stimuli, he or she will receive a positive consequence (e.g., enter the door) and his or her door-opening behavior will be reinforced. When the individual encounters those discriminative stimuli in the future, the probability of a push response should be increased. If one were to attempt to push open the door on the left, however, it very well might not open. Push behavior, therefore, would not be reinforced but would be extinguished over time because the stimulus properties of the door on the left are not associated with positive consequences.

One characteristic of some people with developmental disabilities is that the natural discriminative stimuli do not reliably occasion responding. This is because the responses are not in the behavioral repertoires of these individuals and not because of inadequate contingencies. For example, individuals may not be able to make important discriminations that are correlated with reinforcement. They may not be able to discriminate a square from a circle, a fork from a spoon, or the word "bed" from the word "bad." They may not be able to discriminate the "men's room" from the "women's room" in public facilities. They may not be able to discriminate the various visual and auditory cues that control when and where to cross streets safely. They may not be able to discriminate tomato soup from chicken noodle soup on the grocery store shelf.

Because they cannot make these discriminations does not necessarily mean that individuals cannot emit the appropriate response chains that would be occasioned by the discriminations. Some individuals, for example, could emit the appropriate behavior chain of using the rest room if someone told them which rest room to use (i.e., made the discrimination for them). In other cases, people with developmental disabilities require instruction on making the necessary discriminations as well as on emitting the appropriate behavior chains. For example, adolescents and adults with limited behavioral repertoires may need instruction, not only on discriminating tomato soup from chicken noodle soup but also on how to cook the soup and perhaps even on how to eat it in a socially acceptable manner in public. School-age children may need instruction on discriminating addition problems from subtraction problems and on how to perform the steps for completing the problems.

The process of instruction involves using procedures to bring the learner, ultimately, under the stimulus control of natural discriminative stimuli and consequences. Because these stimuli are neutral prior to instruction, training involves conditioning responses using stimulus control procedures engineered by the instructor. Stimulus control is accomplished by the instructor's using various prompts to occasion the target responses and then providing reinforcing stimuli subsequent to those responses. Over training trials, the learner comes to emit reliably the responses evoked by the prompts and strengthened by the consequences. Because the ultimate goal is for learners to perform in the presence of the natural stimuli rather than in the presence of instructor-delivered prompts, however, the prompts need to be transferred in a systematic fashion. A good instructional program, therefore, would include instructional prompts, consequences for performance, and strategies for transferring stimulus control from instructor-delivered to naturally occurring prompts and consequences.

## INSTRUCTIONAL PROMPTS

Four types of instructional prompts are used frequently in programs to teach skills to people with developmental disabilities. They are 1) verbal instructions, 2) visual cues, 3) modeling, and 4) physical prompts.

### Verbal Instruction

Verbal instructions are part of virtually every training package. They have been implemented along a continuum from less to more explicit response specification. Providing the least response specificity, and perhaps the least control over behavior, are nonspecific verbal prompts such as asking questions about the response that should be emitted. For example, in a program to teach laundry skills, when adolescents with mental retardation requiring limited supports hesitated 5 seconds in emitting a response, the instructor asked, "What is next?" (Cuvo, Jacobi, & Sipko, 1981). In a janitorial skills program, if adolescents with mental retardation omitted one of the subtasks when cleaning a rest room, the participants were asked, for example, "What about the toilet?" (Cuvo, Leaf, & Borakove, 1978). In a classroom, a teacher who is instructing a student how to use punctuation marks might ask, "What do you put at the end of a sentence?" When teaching students to discriminate a noun from words that are not nouns, a teacher might prompt the correct response by asking "Is the word a person, place, or thing?" These questions may serve to occasion the appropriate behavior to be performed.

A more controlling discriminative stimulus along the verbal prompting continuum is a statement that describes the response to be performed (e.g., the next step of a task analysis). The statement may describe the step in general terms or instead may be more detailed and describe the action to be performed. For example, to teach one step of a multistep task such as doing laundry, a verbal instruction to prompt the step of wiping down the top of the washing machine could be a brief statement such as "clean the washing machine" or a more descriptive statement such as, "Wipe the edges and lid of the detergent dispenser (of the washing machine) with the sponge until all dirt is removed" (Cuvo et al., 1981). Similarly, verbal prompts that describe the response to be performed can be delivered for academic tasks as either general statements or instructions that describe the specific action. For example, to teach subtraction with regrouping, a verbal instruction for one step could be "borrow one 10." A more descriptive prompt for that step might be "Borrow one 10 by crossing out the top number in the 10s column and reducing the crossed out number by 1."

When the desired response is verbal, the verbal instruction often provides a partial or complete model of the correct response. For example, in a study to teach fast-food restaurant usage, if participants did not respond appropriately to the question, "Where do we eat?," the instructor would provide prompts such as "We go to Mc . . ." (Marholin, O'Toole, Touchette, Berger, & Doyle, 1979). Similar verbal prompts are often given when teaching students how to read words or label signs (e.g., "st . . ." in the presence of a picture of a stop sign).

Although verbal instructions typically have been provided in person by an instructor, they also can be delivered by an audiotape in a

Walkman-type cassette tape recorder. For example, high school students with severe disabilities were taught to operate a washing machine, prepare a sandwich and a cup of soup, and assemble a multi-piece pipe unit with verbal prompts delivered on audiotapes (Alberto, Sharpton, Briggs, & Stright, 1986). After performing a number of links in a response chain, the audiotape directed the student to stop the activity, survey the materials, and determine whether the responses had been completed correctly (i.e., self-evaluate his or her performance). In a similar fashion, an audiotape could be used to direct a student to perform the steps of academic tasks such as completing arithmetic problems.

Verbal instruction is advantageous because it generally requires little instructor effort, is easy to fade in or out, is economical because it does not require additional materials or expense, and can be administered with a reasonable distance between the instructor and learner. Verbal instructions may be less stigmatizing than other prompts because they also are used to teach people without disabilities in a variety of settings.

A disadvantage of verbal instruction is that it generally is an "extra" (i.e., extraneous) stimulus prompt rather than a within-stimulus prompt. For example, community living skills often involve complex visual discriminations required in activities such as boarding a bus, entering the correct rest room, and using a washing machine; therefore, verbal prompting is presented along a verbal dimension rather than a visual one. Extra stimulus prompts may not be as effective as within-stimulus prompts to promote acquisition of discriminations by people who have mental retardation (Wolfe & Cuvo, 1978) or autism (Schreibman, 1975).

## Visual Cues

Another kind of instructional prompt that has been used to teach skills to people with developmental disabilities is visual cues. One of the most frequently employed forms of the visual cue is the picture prompt, which can take the form of a line drawing or a photograph. In a program to teach cooking skills, recipes to teach boiling, baking, and broiling foods were presented on paper, with written instructions on the left and corresponding hand drawings on the right (Johnson & Cuvo, 1981). Instructional books composed of sequentially arranged photographs that depict each step of task analyses also have been used to teach vocational skills such as conduit assembly (Wacker, Berg, Berrie, & Swatta, 1985), food service tasks (Wilson, Schepis, & Mason-Main, 1987), valve assembly set-up (Wacker & Berg, 1983), and other jobs. For people who can read, written rather than pictorial task analyses can serve as visual cues to prompt step performance as illustrated in a study to teach adults in rehabilitative services to perform home cleaning tasks (McAdam & Cuvo, 1994).

Pointing (gestural) prompts and match-to-sample cues also are common visual prompts used in instructional programs for learners with developmental disabilities. In a study to teach cooking to adults with mental retardation requiring intermittent to limited supports, the instructor used a pointing prompt to teach the specific position to set a kitchen timer and stove dials and to show the level to which liquids should be poured in a saucepan or a measuring cup (Johnson & Cuvo, 1981). She used a match-to-sample procedure by pointing to sample broiled food (e.g., hot dog, muffin) and verbally describing the stimulus properties and appropriate responses. For example, she would say, "See how my muffin is brown on top. Your muffin is not brown." In another illustration, gestures or match-to-sample visual prompts could be used to teach students to use money by pointing to the correct coin combination to select or by presenting a sample of the correct coin combination and requesting that the student select coins that match the sample.

Other visual cues also have been used to teach new skills to people with developmental disabilities. In a study to teach bus-riding skills to a young woman who had severe disabilities, pocket-size bus route cards were constructed to contain the following information: 1) bus route name, 2) intended bus stop, and 3) picture cues that permitted the participant to choose the route card for a specific destination (Coon, Vogelsberg, & Williams, 1981). These cards served to prompt appropriate public transportation responses. To increase the learner's attention to the relevant aspects of the stimuli during training, color and size cues on the bus route names were highlighted.

Similar use of visual cues have been used to teach academic tasks. For example, children working on addition problems may be presented problems in numeric and pictorial form simultaneously. A child might see the problem 4 + 1 along with four dogs under the "4" and one dog under the "1." The pictures supply a visual prompt to assist the child in solving the problem. To teach reading of new words, students may be presented with a picture of a word along with the written word (e.g., a picture of a cat is provided along with the word "cat"). To teach the correspondence between written numerals and number of objects, visual cues also could be used. The child could, for example, be presented with a card showing the numeral 3. She would also be presented with three cards showing a differing number of circles on each card (e.g., 1, 3, 7). The circles on the card containing three circles would be larger (or of a different color) than the circles presented on the other two cards. In all three of these examples, cues that prompt through the visual medium are used to set the occasion for the correct response.

Visual cues can be highly effective discriminative stimuli because they may 1) be salient and hold participants' attention, 2) serve a match-to-sample function (i.e., a permanent product to which participants can match their responses), and 3) be economically and efficiently administered in a wide variety of settings. Research, however, suggests a caveat in their implementation. The use of pictures assumes that learners have formed a stimulus equivalence between a two-dimensional representation and its corresponding three-dimensional object. Research has demonstrated that nonverbal adolescents who have mental retardation requiring extensive supports have failed to demonstrate photo–object matching (Dixon, 1981). Further analyses in Dixon's study revealed that photo–object matching may be facilitated by using cut-out figures of the objects rather than complete rectangular photographs. Also, there may be some time and monetary cost to develop visual cues. Despite these potential disadvantages, visual cues can be powerful tools in the hands of behavior analysts.

## Modeling

Modeling, which can be employed to teach virtually every skill, provides a demonstration of the response to be performed. Instructors can verbally describe their motor responses as they perform them. Typically the model is a service provider (e.g., residential facility employee, graduate student experimenter, school teacher) or a peer. Modeling prompts have been used to teach verbal as well as nonverbal behavior including naming coins (Miller, Cuvo, & Borakove, 1977), ordering food at a restaurant (Marholin et al., 1979), talking on the telephone (Matson, 1982), engaging in self-advocacy (Sievert, Cuvo, & Davis, 1988), making photocopies (Wacker & Berg, 1984), completing janitorial (Cuvo et al., 1978) and apartment upkeep tasks (Williams & Cuvo, 1986), planning meals, planning and shopping for groceries (Wilson, Cuvo, & Davis, 1986), and doing the laundry (Cuvo et al., 1981), among other community living skills. In addition, modeling frequently is used to teach traditional academic tasks. For example, teachers model how to print letters of the alphabet, complete division problems, and measure using a ruler.

Response demonstrations can be provided live or by videotape. When using videotaped modeling, instructors typically provide verbal instructions that correspond to the videotaped model's behavior while the tape plays as well as after the tape is shown (Kelly, Wildman, & Berler, 1980). Instructors also have used a modeling videotape that is played uninterrupted or is stopped periodically to permit learners to imitate the model and receive feedback (Gibson, Lawrence, & Nelson, 1976). An alternative to live or videotaped human models has been the use of dolls or figures as models. On a poster board simulation of four square city blocks, rubber dolls were moved to model appropriate pedestrian (Page, Iwata, & Neef, 1976) and bus-riding (Neef, Iwata, & Page, 1978) behavior in response to discriminative stimuli presented on the simulation.

Modeling has several advantages as an instructional procedure. It typically provides strong control as a discriminative stimulus because it is essentially an exact visual representation of the response to be performed. Learners can observe directly the response to be performed rather than listen to a verbal description or view a two-dimensional pictorial representation of the response. Modeling, therefore, provides topographical similarity with the target behavior compared to verbal and some other visual cues; thus, with contingent positive reinforcement, it can exert good stimulus control over behavior.

There are, however, disadvantages to modeling. Modeling may be 1) obtrusive and stigmatizing in public if it draws attention to learners' impairments, 2) not as efficient as verbal instruction or picture cues that could be delivered more rapidly, and 3) difficult to implement in some artificial or simulated environments.

## Physical Prompts

Physical prompts have been employed as instructional discriminative stimuli to promote the acquisition of behavior, especially by people with severe disabilities or young children learning motor tasks. The most controlling type of physical prompting involves the instructor's grasping the participant's relevant body part and manipulating it to occasion the appropriate response. Physical prompts can be on a continuum that ranges from the full prompting just described to light touches. Physical prompts have been used to teach basic skills such as greeting with a hand wave (Stokes, Baer, & Jackson, 1974), using a spoon to eat (O'Brien & Azrin, 1972), and brushing teeth (Horner & Keilitz, 1975). They also are used to teach traditional school-related tasks such as holding a pencil or throwing a ball, and physical prompts have been incorporated in instructional programs to teach complex behavior such as janitorial (Cuvo et al., 1978), laundry (Cuvo et al., 1981), bus-riding (Sowers, Rusch, & Hudson, 1979), monetary (Smeets, 1978), cooking (Johnson & Cuvo, 1981), and telephone (Risley & Cuvo, 1980) skills, among others.

The typical format has been to combine physical prompting and verbal instruction as the final error correction procedure in a hierarchy that includes several less-controlling prior prompts (e.g., verbal instruction, modeling). Physical prompting typically has been used contingent on participants not responding to the previously administered less-controlling prompts.

The primary advantage of physical prompting is the relatively high probability that learners will respond appropriately and will be reinforced. Physical prompting exerts strong stimulus control over behavior. The major disadvantages of physical prompting are 1) the necessity for close physical proximity between the instructor and the learner; 2) the possible stigma that physical prompting can cause when administered in public; and 3) philosophical, ethical, and legal opposition to intrusive procedures.

## CONSEQUENCES

For the antecedent conditions described in the previous section to become discriminative for responding, it is necessary that the responses emitted be followed by differential reinforcement. *Differential reinforcement* refers, on the one hand, to providing consequences that will increase the future probability of the desired response being emitted to the neutral stimulus and, on the other hand, to not providing reinforcing consequences to the same behavior emitted in response to other stimulus conditions (Sulzer-Azaroff & Mayer, 1991). Although a wide variety of consequences have been used to positively reinforce responses being conditioned, verbal and social consequences predominate. Participants typically are told that their performance is correct, and they may be praised as well.

A wide variety of reinforcers have been provided contingently on correct performance, including edibles such as M&Ms, apple slices, and candy bars (e.g., Lowe & Cuvo, 1976). Other reinforcers that have been used successfully with people with developmental disabilities include the following: 1) pennies exchangeable for edible or activity reinforcers (Snell, 1982), 2) graphic feedback (Davis, Bates, & Cuvo, 1983), 3) self-recording (Smeets & Kleinloog, 1980), 4) self-evaluation (Matson, Marchetti, & Adkins, 1980), and 5) tokens (Weitz & Roll, 1977).

## TRANSFER OF STIMULUS CONTROL

During the process of instruction, responses taught initially come under the stimulus control of an instructor's prompts. One of the major challenges facing behavior analysts is to transfer stimulus control from these instructor-delivered prompts to naturally occurring discriminative stimuli. Various strategies for transferring stimulus control have been used successfully with people with developmental disabilities.

## Fading Across Prompt Type

Fading, particularly prompt fading, has been used most frequently as a transfer of stimulus control procedure. Qualitatively different prompts have been sequenced in various ways to bring responses under stimulus control. The sequence frequently cited in the literature, termed "system of least prompts," orders instructional prompts from lesser to greater control (Snell & Brown, 1993). Initially, the learner is allowed to perform with no help. Contingent on an error, prompts are faded in to gain stimulus control of a response. Verbal instruction typically is attempted first, followed by a visual cue (often a gesture), then by a modeling prompt, and finally by physical guidance. On subsequent trials, participants are given the opportunity to perform without assistance, and instructional prompts may be faded in, once again, as required. Each new trial, therefore, represents a test for generalization to natural discriminative stimuli. This prompt fading procedure has been employed to teach pedestrian (Vogelsberg & Rusch, 1979), fire escape (Haney & Jones, 1982), cleaning (Cuvo et al., 1978), and bus-riding (Coon et al., 1981) skills.

In contrast to the system of least prompts in which prompts are transferred to the natural stimulus by fading in prompts, a decreasing prompt hierarchy also could be used. In this system, the prompt hierarchy would commence with a highly controlling prompt, which would fade to less controlling prompts to transfer stimulus control to natural discriminative stimuli. For example, to teach a student to insert coins into the coin slot of a vending machine, the instructor might begin with a physical prompt. Following a predetermined number of trials with that level of assistance, the teacher might use a gestural prompt on the next three trials by pointing to the coin slot, followed by a verbal instruction for three trials, and finally no assistance.

The specific prompts used in the hierarchy would be determined by the nature of the task and the needs of the student. For example, not all students would need to begin with physical assistance. The decreasing hierarchy of some students might begin with a gestural prompt, fade to a specific verbal instruction followed by a nonspecific verbal instruction such as a question, and finally end in a no-prompt condition. Unlike the system of least prompts in which the prompt is delivered contingent on the student either making an error or not responding, prompts in the decreasing hierarchy are usually delivered prior to the participant's response. If the student does not respond correctly at a particular prompt level on a preselected number of trials, the instructor typically delivers a more controlling prompt on the subsequent trial and proceeds to fade out the prompts again.

Behavior analysts who adopt either of the two prompt-fading procedures (i.e., fade in versus fade out) described in this section subjectively determine that their qualitatively different prompts are, in fact, ordered in a faded sequence. It is possible, however, that some detailed verbal instructions may be more controlling discriminative stimuli than some types of modeling. It is not possible, therefore, to establish, a priori, a universal sequence of fading qualitatively different prompts. The specific nature of the prompt must be considered when evaluating its degree of control over responding.

## Fading within a Prompt Type

In addition to fading across qualitatively different types of prompts, some studies have reported fading within a prompt type. Fading across physical prompts, often referred to as "graduated guidance," involves slowly reducing the amount of physical assistance provided to the learner. For example, when using physical prompts to teach a student to use a spoon, the instructor would place his or her hand over the student's hand and exert sufficient pressure to assist the student in using the spoon. As the student responds appropriately, the instructor exerts progressively less pressure until the student is using the spoon without any physical assistance from the teacher. At that point, the teacher might use "shadowing" in which the instructor's hand remains near but not touching the student's hand unless the student makes an error. As an alternative to shadowing, the teacher might move the locus of the physical assistance as hand-over-hand guidance is eliminated. In the example of holding a spoon, when the student no longer needs full physical guidance, the teacher gradually could move the location of the physical touch to the wrist, then the elbow, and finally the shoulder.

Fading within a prompt type also is used frequently with verbal prompts. For example, three verbal prompts providing differing levels of textual stimuli could be faded in or out when teaching someone to complete the motor task of signing a check. For example, the student could be told the following: 1) "What do you do after you write the amount of the check in words?" 2) "Sign your name," or 3) "Sign your whole name on the line at the bottom right hand corner of the check." Verbal prompts used to occasion verbal behavior could be faded in a different fashion. In the study to teach restaurant usage skills, the instructor faded the verbal prompt by providing progressively more information such as "We go to Mm . . .," "We go to Mc . . .," "We go to McDon . . ." (Marholin et al., 1979).

This type of fading can be used with modeling prompts as well. For example, in a study evaluating a program to teach laundry skills, participants were taught to sort clothes prior to washing them (Cuvo et al., 1981). Initially, full modeling was used in which sorting a basket of 21 garments into three color categories was demonstrated by the instructor. After the response was brought under the stimulus control of the full model prompt, modeling was faded out using a rather large stimulus change. Only one garment of each of the three color categories was sorted to provide partial modeling.

Fading within a prompt type also has been done with pictures, color, and size cues. In the math and reading examples described previously, the visual cues that are used initially to prompt correct performance are gradually faded until they are no longer necessary. For example, the darkness of the pictures of the dogs used to cue the correct answer to the addition problem of 4 + 1 is lightened over a series of trials until the pictures are no longer visible to the student. In a similar manner, pictures used to cue correct reading or labeling would be faded in a series of steps until students responded without the visual prompt. When color or size cues are used to prompt correct performance, they, too, are slowly and systematically removed.

Within-stimulus fading of color and size also has been used to teach nonacademic skills. For example, when the color and size cues of the printed names of bus routes were used to prompt student selection of the appropriate bus, those prompts were gradually faded out until the student could read the name without the extra cues (Coon et al., 1981).

## Prompt Delay

Prompt delay, also termed "time delay," is another strategy that has been used to transfer stimulus control. The initial step in this procedure is to pair the training discriminative stimulus (i.e., prompt) simultaneously with the natural discriminative stimulus to which control is to be transferred. Transfer is accomplished by programming either a constant or an increasing delay between presentation of the natural discriminative stimulus first and then the instructor's prompt (Snell & Gast, 1981; Striefel & Owens, 1980).

A constant prompt delay procedure was used to teach community-referenced sight words to students with mental retardation (Cuvo & Klatt, 1992). On the first training trial, the instructor said, "What does this sign say?" while presenting the initially neutral stimulus (word on the flash card). With no delay, he immediately provided the verbal model of the correct response. During all subsequent training trials, the instructor waited for 4 seconds before providing the verbal model.

If the participant made errors on three consecutive training trials, the instructor returned to the 0-second prompt delay for one trial.

In one of the first studies to use prompt delay relevant to community living skills, bedmaking was taught using progressive rather than constant prompt delay (Snell, 1982). During the initial trials, prompts were given immediately after the request to make a bed. This brought responding under the stimulus control of the instructor's prompts. Subsequently, a prompt delay of 2 seconds was instituted and increased gradually to 8 seconds following the bedmaking directive. Over trials, learners began to respond to the natural discriminative stimuli and transfer of stimulus control took place.

Prompt delay also has been used to teach a variety of other skills to people with developmental disabilities. These skills have included following recipes (Schuster & Griffen, 1991), using vending machines (Browder, Snell, & Wildonger, 1988), and performing math skills (Mattingly & Bott, 1990).

## STIMULUS CONTROL AND TRANSFER PROBLEMS

The previous sections of this chapter present principles and illustrations for promoting and transferring stimulus control during instruction of people with disabilities. Although there is a considerable body of research demonstrating the efficacy of the procedures discussed in the previous sections, instruction using these methods does not always proceed smoothly and without difficulty. Sometimes there are problems implementing the prompting and transfer procedures, either because of the learner's behavior during instruction or because the teacher has not analyzed the learning context adequately prior to implementing instruction. As a consequence, problems may arise in promoting and transferring stimulus control in learners with disabilities. At times, these problems may be attributable to the manner in which the prompts are used or the mechanisms employed for promoting stimulus control. On other occasions, however, performance problems may lie in other variables affecting learning that are discussed in other chapters. The next section provides a comprehensive overview of problems in instruction, with a special focus on issues of stimulus control and its transfer.

### Attentional Control Problems

For learning to occur, the student must attend to instructional stimuli presented by the teacher. Teacher-delivered prompts will not evoke control over responding without prior instructional control. For learners with severe disabilities, in particular, it may be necessary to train

instructional control prior to proceeding with teaching the discriminations or behavior chains, such as those discussed in the previous
sections. Students may have to be taught to orient toward and attend
to the instructor and to respond to stimuli presented. Learners who
have never received systematic instruction, including learners with
autism and mental retardation requiring extensive to pervasive supports, may require extensive instructional control training. Others who
have been recipients of instruction may just need to be taught to generalize their attention to new teachers. All learners, however, may
need to be reinforced for their attention to the teacher throughout
instruction. This issue is discussed in greater detail in Chapter 14.

## Behavior Not in Learner's Repertoire

An obvious first question to ask is whether the learner has any physical or sensory limitations that interfere with learning. Does the learner
have adequate visual and hearing acuity, manual dexterity, locomo-
tion, eye–hand coordination, and so forth to respond to instructional
stimuli?

*Reflexivity* Other stimulus control problems may arise because
learners lack certain prerequisite discriminations or stimulus relations
that an instructor has not adequately evaluated prior to instruction.
To illustrate, this section provides some examples of problems students may experience with stimulus equivalence. The most basic relationship between stimuli—matching identical stimuli with each
other—is termed *reflexivity*. Suppose learners in a supported work position in a restaurant are required to wash, sort, and store silverware.
Sorting requires workers to match spoons with spoons, forks with
forks, and knives with knives. Learners must have acquired the reflexive relation among identical pieces of cutlery to sort properly. That
reflexive relation should be tested prior to instruction and should not
be just assumed. An instructor who merely develops a task analysis
and considers the problem one of response chaining may encounter
learner discrimination errors. Incorrect responses may occur when
prompts are used because the learner has not previously acquired the
reflexive relations that are required to perform the behavior chain. In
some cases, the first step in promoting stimulus control, therefore, may
be to teach the basic reflexive discriminations involved in the task.

*Symmetry* Another common equivalence relation, termed symmetry, also may create problems if assumed to be in but is not in
learners' repertoires. This relationship is at the next level of complexity
compared with reflexivity. For example, there is a substantial literature
on using visual prompts to teach functional skills. Photographs of
steps of a task analysis have been used to teach learners with mental

retardation requiring limited or extensive supports to assemble valves and circuit boards (Wacker & Berg, 1983). The acquisition of stimulus control assumes that learners have the visual-visual symmetry relationship between two-dimensional photographic stimuli such as pictures of valve parts and their counterparts, the actual three-dimensional stimuli on the job. Research has examined the comparative control of various pictorial stimuli and the variables that control their effectiveness (Lignugaris/Kraft, McCuller, Exum, & Salzberg, 1988).

The symmetry relation is also inherent in promoting stimulus control using verbal instruction. Verbal prompts often involve an auditory–visual relationship in which the teacher verbally prompts the learner to respond to an object in the environment. The teacher may prompt the learner by saying, for example, "Put the spoon next to the dish" or "Pick up the mop." For these verbal prompts to control learners' responding, learners must have acquired the symmetrical relationship between the auditory stimulus emitted by the instructor (e.g., the word "spoon") and its visual referent (the actual spoon). Modeling prompts also may require relationships between stimuli manipulated by the instructor and those available to the learner. The instructor may model how six crayons of different colors should be packaged in a plastic envelope, and the learner is required to imitate with a different but equivalent set of materials.

## Contextual Variables

Performance problems may occur because stimulus control is more complex than the three-term contingency discussed in the previous sections (i.e., antecedents or instructional prompts, behavior, consequences). Stimulus control and its transfer may have been successful for teaching a task in a given situation; however, a fourth term, the context in which behavior occurs, may need to enter the contingency. In many situations, it is necessary for learners to form conditional discriminations and emit a response under certain environmental conditions and not others. A stimulus control problem may arise if learners have not been conditioned to respond differentially based on the prevailing setting events (i.e., contextual discriminative stimuli that alter the function of other discriminative stimuli).

For example, a restaurant busperson who has mental retardation requiring limited supports may have been taught successfully to clean tables using stimulus control and transfer procedures. Performance problems may arise, however, because the three-term contingency used to establish the original stimulus control did not require the learner to form the conditional discrimination that the table should be washed and the floor around it swept only after diners have left the table and not when they are still seated. The worker will have to be taught when to emit and when not to emit the cleaning behavior based on contextual variables. Understanding relevant setting events, such as this, should be an important item on instructors' stimulus control agenda.

Another type of contextual variable, establishing operations (EOs), more commonly identified as motivational variables, plays an indirect role in the success of stimulus control procedures. EOs are setting events that alter the function of a stimulus's reinforcing or punishing function. A learner may be inattentive or not respond to prompts because of the role that EOs play. Problems in stimulus control may arise because the reinforcer is momentarily ineffective because the student is satiated. Although EOs are not stimulus control procedures themselves, they can affect the probability that prompts will occasion responses. Instructors, therefore, are advised to consider the role that contextual variables, including setting events and EOs, will play in their efforts to promote and transfer stimulus control. These issues are discussed more fully in Chapter 15.

## Antecedent Stimulus Problems

Antecedent stimulus problems may occur in both the establishment of stimulus control using prompting procedures and the transfer of control from those prompts to natural discriminative stimuli. In the establishment of stimulus control, a particular problem has been noted with respect to the use of physical prompts with students with severe disabilities, such as autism. The term *tactile defensive* refers to learners who attempt to avoid or escape physical contact such as that which might be provided in a manual guidance procedure. Physical contact functions as an aversive stimulus, and these students attempt to avoid or escape from close proximity and actual physical touch by a teacher.

After stimulus control has been obtained by the instructor's prompts, additional concerns pertain to whether control by artificial discriminative stimuli should be transferred to natural discriminative stimuli, and, if they should, the procedures that should be used for facilitating that transfer. Sometimes it may not be cost efficient to attempt to transfer stimulus control from artificial prompts to natural discriminative stimuli. This is especially true of a number of the visual cues described previously that could be left in place as permanent prompts after training. Permanent prompts may be especially useful when learners with limited behavioral repertoires are acquiring complex skills or when learners have severe physical or sensory disabilities. The principle of partial participation endorses the use of various environmental modifications, such as permanent prompts, on a continuing basis to allow learners with disabilities to participate to the extent feasible in normalizing activities (Baumgart et al., 1982).

Many examples of permanent prompts or prosthetic devices exist in the community living skills literature. Also, participants have been taught to make emergency telephone calls with their own three-page modified telephone directory (Risley & Cuvo, 1980). Each page had a picture of one emergency service person (e.g., firefighter, police officer, doctor), that person's printed occupation, and that person's telephone number. Picture recipe cookbooks have been provided as permanent prompts to teach people with mental retardation to prepare simple meals (Johnson & Cuvo, 1981; Robinson-Wilson, 1977). Color and shape cues have been used as permanent prompts to teach several different community living skills, such as burner and oven use and measuring in cooking skills programs (Matson, 1979; Robinson-Wilson, 1977). Permanent prompts also have been used in other experiments to teach bus-riding (Coon et al., 1981), grocery shopping (Matson, 1981; Wheeler, Ford, Nietupski, Loomis, & Brown, 1980), and money (Smeets & Kleinloog, 1980) skills.

Despite the many advantages of permanent prompts, care should be taken in their selection and use (Wheeler et al., 1980). They should not be programmed indiscriminately, especially in a stigmatizing manner. Learners should be given the opportunity, at first, to learn a skill that they might be able to acquire without the permanent prompt.

If the decision is made to transfer stimulus control from artificial prompts rather than leaving them in place as permanent prompts, problems can arise in the transfer process. One generic problem that cuts across different transfer techniques is the speed of programming transfer. One variable affecting speed is the size of the increment when using a transfer procedure. If the progressive prompt delay procedure is used, for example, one could increase too rapidly the delay between the presentation of the natural discriminative stimulus and the instructor's prompt. The same problem of speed of transfer can occur for the increment of modifying the stimulus when using fading or shaping to transfer stimulus control. These procedures involve gradually changing an artificial or noncriterion stimulus to the natural criterion stimulus. For example, when a picture cue is used to prompt correct reading of a functional sign, a problem in transfer can occur if the picture cue is faded out too rapidly.

A second variable affecting speed of transfer is the performance criterion designated for response mastery at a given increment. For example, when using a more-to-less assistance prompt hierarchy, the stringency of the performance criterion at each prompt level before fading to the next level can affect performance. If the criterion is not stringent enough, learner errors may occur when less controlling prompts are provided.

## Response Problems

Problems in promoting stimulus control may occur because of task difficulty or the response effort required. Task effort can be conceptualized as functioning as punishment, and tasks that are difficult may occasion escape or avoidance behavior. Students may refuse to engage in the task, make repeated errors, or physically attempt to remove themselves from the instructional setting. This behavior may be negatively reinforced if students successfully escape the task. Instructional control may be difficult to maintain in this situation and learners may not respond to prompts when the task is aversive. Less controlling prompts, such as verbal instructions, visual cues, and even modeling, may not occasion responding. Instead, instructors may have to resort to physical prompts, and, even then, there is the possibility that learners will attempt to escape the physical contact as suggested previously. In some instructional instances, a possible solution to a task difficulty problem is to do more shaping and to break a more complex task down into successive approximations so that less effort is required to receive reinforcement. Other solutions are to provide the students with frequent breaks and to teach students to request assistance. This issue is discussed more fully in Chapter 13.

## Response Consequence Problems

To promote stimulus control, neutral stimuli are conditioned to become discriminative stimuli by using differential reinforcement. Problems in stimulus control, such as prompts not occasioning responses, may arise because of the ineffectiveness of the consequences used to reinforce performance. Arbitrarily selected teacher-manipulated consequences may not, in fact, serve as positive reinforcers. A reinforcement assessment procedure can be implemented to increase the probability of identifying effective reinforcing stimuli, and their quantity and schedule can be modified over time to achieve effective levels. In addition, the natural reinforcement for performing a task may change over time, and adjustment will be needed with respect to the reinforcing stimuli. It is also possible that the inherent reinforcement in performing the task itself may not be reinforcing to individual students, perhaps because of the difficulty level or aversiveness of the task (see Chapter 13 for suggestions). In fact, as task difficulty level increases, corresponding adjustments can be made on the reinforcing variables such as making the schedule richer.

Another response consequence problem in stimulus control may arise among students for whom teacher attention is a powerful reinforcer. Student errors to verbal and modeling prompts, for example, may be inadvertently reinforced by the teacher's continuing to provide those prompts or manual guidance. The term "prompt dependent" has been used to refer to learners whose failure to respond at all, or to make errors, is reinforced by additional teacher prompts and attention. When learner errors are reinforced by teacher attention and physical contact, transfer of stimulus control will be more difficult. The teacher should work on differentially reinforcing the student's successful task performance. Instructors, therefore, should continually ascertain the reinforcing variables for each learner as they may change during the course of intervention.

## Generalization Problems

Problems in stimulus control also may occur when students who have acquired a new skill in one training situation do not perform the new skill outside of the training environment (e.g., in the natural environment). For example, a student with mental retardation requiring limited supports may have learned the steps of completing a load of laundry using a washer and dryer in a classroom but may not perform the newly acquired behavior in a Laundromat in the community. In instances such as this, the problem may arise because the discriminative stimuli in the natural environment are not similar enough to those in the training environment, and the responses also may be different. For example, in the training environment, the discriminative stimulus to activate the washing machine may be a button requiring a push response. In contrast, in the community laundry, the discriminative stimulus to activate the machine may be a knob requiring a turn response.

Transfer of stimulus control problems also may arise if the materials used in the training environment are not similar to those used in the natural environment. For example, if students are taught to count change using pictures of coins or cardboard coins, then they may not generalize their money-counting skills to actual coins.

In general, the more dissimilar the training environment (i.e., setting and materials) and required response topographies are from those encountered in the natural environment, the greater the challenge to promote transfer of stimulus control. Problems with transfer may be addressed by training in the natural environment using actual materials. For situations in which such training is not feasible, it will be necessary to test for transfer of stimulus control to natural conditions and, if appropriate, to provide training in that environment.

## SUMMARY

People with developmental disabilities frequently need instruction in the variety of tasks necessary to function in their daily lives at school, in the community, and at work. Stimulus control is the central issue around which such training programs are developed. Critical elements in these instructional programs are prompts (verbal instruction, visual cues, modeling, and physical guidance), reinforcing consequences for performance, and procedures for transferring stimulus control from instructor-delivered to naturally occurring discriminative stimuli. Commonly used transfer techniques include fading across prompt types, fading within prompt types, and prompt delay. Although programs using these critical elements have been successful in teaching a wide variety of skills to people with developmental disabilities, instructional problems may arise. Sources of those problems may include lack of attentional control, prerequisite behavior not in a learner's repertoire, contextual variables, antecedent stimulus problems in both the establishment and transfer of stimulus control, response problems, and response consequence problems. Behavior analysts may need to examine these potential problem areas when their students are having difficulty learning new tasks.

## REFERENCES

Alberto, P.A., Sharpton, W.R., Briggs, A., & Stright, M.H. (1986). Facilitating task acquisition through the use of a self-operated auditory prompting system. *Journal of The Association for Persons with Severe Handicaps, 11*, 85–91.

Baumgart, D., Brown, L., Pumpian, I., Nisbet, J., Ford, A., Sweet, M., Messina, R., & Schroeder, J. (1982). Principle of partial participation and individual adaptations in educational programs for severely handicapped students. *Journal of The Association for Persons with Severe Handicaps, 7*, 17–27.

Browder, D.M., Snell, M.E., & Wildonger, B.A. (1988). Simulation and community-based instruction of vending machines with time delay. *Education and Training in Mental Retardation, 23*, 175–185.

Coon, M.E., Vogelsberg, R.T., & Williams, W. (1981). Effects of classroom public transportation instruction on generalization to the natural environment. *Journal of The Association for Persons with Severe Handicaps, 6*, 23–29.

Cuvo, A.J., & Davis, P.K. (1983). Behavior therapy and community living skills. In M. Hersen, R.M. Eisler, & P.M. Miller (Eds.), *Progress in behavior modification* (Vol. 14, pp. 125–172). New York: Academic Press.

Cuvo, A.J., Jacobi, L., & Sipko, R. (1981). Teaching laundry skills to mentally retarded students. *Education and Training of the Mentally Retarded, 16*, 54–64.

Cuvo, A.J., & Klatt, K.P. (1992). The effects of in vivo, videotape, and flashcard instruction of community referenced sight words on students with mental retardation. *Journal of Applied Behavior Analysis, 25*, 499–512.

Cuvo, A.J., Leaf, R.B., & Borakove, L.S. (1978). Teaching janitorial skills to the mentally retarded: Acquisition, generalization, and maintenance. *Journal of Applied Behavior Analysis, 11*, 345–355.

Davis, P.K., Bates, P., & Cuvo, A.J. (1983). Training a mentally retarded client to work competitively: Effect of graphic feedback and a changing criterion design. *Education and Training of the Mentally Retarded, 18,* 158–163.

Dixon, L. (1981). A functional analysis of photo-object matching skills of severely retarded adolescents. *Journal of Applied Behavior Analysis, 14,* 465–478.

Gibson, F.W., Lawrence, P.S., & Nelson, R.O. (1976). Comparison of three training procedures for teaching social responses to developmentally disabled adults. *American Journal of Mental Deficiency, 81,* 379–387.

Haney, J.I., & Jones, R.T. (1982). Programming maintenance as a major component of a community-centered preventive effort: Escape from fire. *Behavior Therapy, 13,* 47–62.

Horner, R.D., & Keilitz, I. (1975). Training mentally retarded adolescents to brush their teeth. *Journal of Applied Behavior Analysis, 8,* 301–309.

Johnson, B.F., & Cuvo, A.J. (1981). Teaching mentally retarded adults to cook. *Behavior Modification, 5,* 187–202.

Kelly, J.A., Wildman, B.G., & Berler, E.S. (1980). Small group behavioral training to improve the job interview skills repertoire of mildly retarded adolescents. *Journal of Applied Behavior Analysis, 13,* 461–471.

Lignugaris/Kraft, B., McCuller, G.L., Exum, M., & Salzberg, C.L. (1988). A review of research on picture reading skills of developmentally disabled individuals. *Journal of Special Education, 22,* 297–329.

Lowe, M., & Cuvo, A.J. (1976). Teaching coin summation to the mentally retarded. *Journal of Applied Behavior Analysis, 9,* 483–489.

Marholin, D., O'Toole, K.M., Touchette, P.E., Berger, P.L., & Doyle, D.A. (1979). "I'll have a Big Mac, large fries, large Coke, and apple pie," . . . or teaching adaptive community skills. *Behavior Therapy, 40,* 236–248.

Matson, J.L. (1979). A field tested system of training meal preparation skills to the retarded. *British Journal of Mental Subnormality, 25,* 14–18.

Matson, J.L. (1981). Use of independence training to teach shopping skills to mildly retarded adults. *American Journal of Mental Deficiency, 86,* 178–183.

Matson, J.L. (1982). Independence training vs. modeling procedures for teaching phone conversation skills to the mentally retarded. *Behavior Research and Therapy, 20,* 505–511.

Matson, J.L., Marchetti, A., & Adkins, J.A. (1980). Comparison of operant- and independence-training procedures for mentally retarded adults. *American Journal of Mental Deficiency, 84,* 487–494.

Mattingly, J.C., & Bott, D.A. (1990). Teaching multiplication facts to students with learning problems. *Exceptional Children, 56,* 438–449.

McAdam, D.B., & Cuvo, A.J. (1994). Textual prompts as an antecedent cue self-management strategy for persons with mild disabilities. *Behavior Modification, 18,* 47–65.

Miller, M.A., Cuvo, A.J., & Borakove, L.S. (1977). Teaching naming of coin values: Comprehension before production versus production alone. *Journal of Applied Behavior Analysis, 10,* 735–736.

Neef, N.A., Iwata, B.A., & Page, T. J. (1978). Public transportation training: In vivo versus classroom instruction. *Journal of Applied Behavior Analysis, 11,* 331–344.

O'Brien, F., & Azrin, N.H. (1972). Developing proper mealtime behaviors of the institutionalized retarded. *Journal of Applied Behavior Analysis, 5,* 389–399.

Page, T.J., Iwata, B.A., & Neef, N.A. (1976). Teaching pedestrian skills to retarded persons: Generalization from the classroom to the natural environment. *Journal of Applied Behavior Analysis, 9,* 433–444.

Risley, R., & Cuvo, A.J. (1980). Training mentally retarded adults to make emergency telephone calls. *Behavior Modification, 4,* 513–525.

Robinson-Wilson, M.A. (1977). Picture recipe cards as an approach to teaching severely and profoundly retarded adults to cook. *Education and Training of the Mentally Retarded, 12,* 69–73.

Schreibman, L. (1975). Effects of within-stimulus and extra-stimulus prompting on discrimination learning in autistic children. *Journal of Applied Behavior Analysis, 8,* 91–112.

Schuster, J.W., & Griffen, A.K. (1991). Using constant time delay to teach recipe following skills. *Education and Training in Mental Retardation, 26,* 411–419.

Sievert, A.L., Cuvo, A.J., & Davis, P.K. (1988). Training self-advocacy skills to adults with mild handicaps. *Journal of Applied Behavior Analysis, 21,* 299–309.

Smeets, P.M. (1978). Teaching coin summation and purchasing power to retarded adults using a slide rule procedure. *British Journal of Mental Subnormality, 47,* 90–99.

Smeets, P.M., & Kleinloog, D. (1980). Teaching retarded women to use an experimental pocket calculator for making financial transactions. *Behavior Research of Severe Developmental Disabilities, 1,* 1–20.

Snell, M.E. (1982). Analysis of time delay procedures in teaching daily living skills to retarded adults. *Analysis and Intervention in Developmental Disabilities, 2,* 139–155.

Snell, M.E., & Brown, F. (1993). Instructional planning and implementation. In M.E. Snell (Ed.), *Instruction of students with severe disabilities* (4th ed., pp. 99–151). New York: Merrill.

Snell, M.E., & Gast, D.L. (1981). Applying the time delay procedure to the instruction of the severely handicapped. *Journal of The Association for Persons with Severe Handicaps, 6,* 3–14.

Sowers, J., Rusch, F.R., & Hudson, C. (1979). Training a severely retarded young adult to ride the city bus to and from work. *AAESPH Review, 4,* 15–23.

Stokes, T.F., Baer, D.M., & Jackson, R.L. (1974). Programming the generalization of a greeting response in four retarded children. *Journal of Applied Behavior Analysis, 7,* 599–610.

Striefel, S., & Owens, C.R. (1980). Transfer of stimulus control procedures: Applications to language acquisition training with the developmentally handicapped. *Behavior Research of Severe Developmental Disabilities, 1,* 307–331.

Sulzer-Azaroff, B., & Mayer, G.R. (1991). *Behavior analysis for lasting change.* Fort Worth, TX: Holt, Rinehart, & Winston.

Vogelsberg, R.T., & Rusch, F.R. (1979). Training severely handicapped students to cross partially controlled intersections. *AAESPH Review, 4,* 264–273.

Wacker, D.P., & Berg, W. (1983). Effects of picture prompts on the acquisition of complex vocational tasks by mentally retarded adolescents. *Journal of Applied Behavior Analysis, 16,* 417–433.

Wacker, D.P., & Berg, W. (1984). Use of peer instruction to train a complex photocopying task to moderately and severely retarded adolescents. *Analysis and Intervention in Developmental Disabilities, 4,* 219–234.

Wacker, D.P., Berg, W.K., Berrie, P., & Swatta, P. (1985). Generalization and maintenance of complex skills by severely handicapped adolescents following picture prompt training. *Journal of Applied Behavior Analysis, 18,* 329–336.

Weitz, S.E., & Roll, D.L. (1977). Survival skills for community-bound retarded youths. *Journal of Clinical Child Psychology, 6,* 41–44.

Wheeler, J., Ford, A., Nietupski, J., Loomis R., & Brown, L. (1980). Teaching moderately and severely handicapped adolescents to shop in supermarkets using pocket calculators. *Education and Training in Mental Retardation, 15,* 105–112.

Williams, G.E., & Cuvo, A.J. (1986). Training apartment upkeep skills to rehabilitation clients: A comparison of task analytic strategies. *Journal of Applied Behavior Analysis, 19,* 39–51.

Wilson, P.G., Cuvo, A.J., & Davis, P.K. (1986). Training a functional skill cluster: Nutritious meal planning within a budget, grocery list writing, and shopping. *Analysis and Intervention in Developmental Disabilities, 6,* 179–201.

Wilson, P.G., Schepis, M.M., & Mason-Main, M. (1987). In vivo use of picture prompt training to increase independent work at a restaurant. *Journal of The Association for Persons with Severe Handicaps, 12,* 145–150.

Wolfe, V.F., & Cuvo, A.J. (1978). Effects of within-stimulus and extra-stimulus prompting on letter discrimination by mentally retarded persons. *American Journal of Mental Deficiency, 83,* 297–303.

# ~ VI ~

## Conclusions

# ~ *17* ~

## *Conclusions and Future Directions*

### James K. Luiselli and Michael J. Cameron

There have been many developments in our understanding of antecedent control for the behavioral support of people with developmental disabilities. This book captures the evolution of knowledge concerning antecedent control from both theoretical and applied perspectives. Although many of the chapter authors state that antecedent influences on human behavior have been recognized for some time, it is apparent that this orientation has not been embraced as commonly as consequence-based methods. As demonstrated by increased publications, conference presentations, and discussions within the professional community, however, the critical role of antecedent stimuli in the etiology and maintenance of challenging behaviors has begun to be more widely accepted in the late 1990s. Furthermore, behavioral support plans are more likely to incorporate antecedent manipulations, and, in many instances, they are a primary feature of intervention. This concluding chapter summarizes some of the factors responsible for these trends and highlights future directions in practice and research.

## EVOLUTIONARY TRENDS

It is instructive to consider the forces that have shaped professional opinions about the relevance of antecedent control approaches to behavioral support. Changes in philosophies of how to intervene with people who have developmental disabilities and challenging behaviors certainly seem to be influential in this regard. For example, the majority of people with mental retardation and autism receive community-based habilitation and typically reside in neighborhood homes (with parents or "live-in" care providers) instead of in state institutions (Koegel, Koegel, & Dunlap, 1996). One impact from the "normalization" movement and related developments such as person-centered planning (Mount, 1992) has been the critical need to adapt intervention procedures that include natural sources of support (Horner et al., 1990). Thus, behavioral intervention should be evaluated not only by its reductive effects but also by the contexts in which it is applied, how it compares with what is experienced by people who do not have disabilities, and how it is accepted by individuals who are responsible for implementation. Highly restrictive, punitive, and procedurally complex interventions are not compatible with the exigencies of community support. It should also be noted that changes in "treatment" philosophy emphasize that efforts at behavior reduction should decrease rather than increase distress and discomfort in the lives of people with developmental disabilities. Such discussions fuel the heated and continuing debates concerning "aversive versus non-aversive" procedures and the "right to effective treatment" (Repp & Singh, 1990; Van Houten et al., 1988).

As illustrated in the chapters of this book, antecedent control interventions address the topic of challenging behaviors with reference to many sources of natural support. Factors such as a person's physical condition, daily activity schedule, stimulus preferences, lifestyle, and language abilities, to name a few, are critical targets for the design of behavioral support plans. Challenging behaviors are viewed in light of the method in which instructions are presented, the individual's choice-making opportunities, the demands of training, and the co-variation with functional abilities. It is understandable, then, that methods of antecedent control would gain popularity as sequelae to the evolution of improved standards of care, emphasis on positive behavioral support, and community-referenced intervention for people with developmental disabilities.

Another source that seems to have hastened the contemporary focus on antecedent control is the increasing alliance between basic and applied learning theory research (Mace & Wacker, 1994). This confluence is most evident for the concept of establishing operations (EOs). Virtually every chapter in this book included a discussion of EOs as a central topic that guides both a theoretical and pragmatic understanding of antecedent control. Michael (1982, 1988, 1993), in particular, has contributed significantly to the integration of basic learning principles that define EOs and the functional properties that govern their use in educational and clinical applications. Recall that EOs relate to the motivational aspects of reinforcing stimuli—namely, increasing or decreasing the potency of consequence events by manipulating otherwise neutral variables. The ability to alter the evocative functions of antecedent stimuli so that an individual is more likely to behave desirably and is less likely to engage in challenging behaviors is, of course, of great value in formulating intervention plans.

Finally, many professionals have remarked about the importance of programming for and routinely assessing the long-term effects of behavioral interventions (Foxx, 1996). Maintenance of behavior change is essential to evaluate because it informs us of whether initial supports are sufficient to ensure durability or whether additional procedures are required to sustain positive outcomes. Indeed, a frequent criticism of behavioral therapeutic approaches is that intervention effects are short lived and diminish rapidly when contingencies are removed or altered. The appeal of antecedent control procedures is that by attending to variables such as the physical environment, personal lifestyle, and instructional strategies, lasting change is possible. The desire for better clinical efficacy from behavioral interventions has prompted interest in antecedent control.

## ASSESSMENT AND ANALYSIS

We are encouraged by the increasing focus on the assessment of antecedent conditions for the purpose of formulating behavioral support plans. The identification of possible antecedent–behavior relationships, however, does not demonstrate conclusive evidence of the sources of functional control. Rather, a two-phase process of assessment and analysis is required. First, assessment procedures should address antecedent conditions within which challenging behaviors occur. If sources of antecedent control become evident, then the second phase of assessment would be to perform more fine-grained analyses that are directed at isolating the function(s) of the antecedent–behavior relationship.

The preceding recommendation perhaps is illustrated best by the example of escape-motivated challenging behavior. Systematic assessment might reveal that the "tantrum" behavior of a child with autism occurs most frequently when he participates in instructional activities as opposed to less demanding events such as play, outdoor recess, or listening to music. The conclusion is that instruction is an aversive interaction for the student and provokes tantrum behavior that has been reinforced previously by termination of (i.e., escape from) demands. The aversive features of instruction, however, may be a function of one or more variables, such as the materials that are used, the amount of time devoted to certain tasks, the manner in which verbal requests are given, or the learner's response requirements. It also could be that the tantrum behavior that occurs during instruction is actually affected by contingent social attention and not by escape. Smith and Iwata (1997), for example, noted that the relative absence of attention (in this example, perhaps by the instructor interacting with other students) could function as an EO that increases the probability of socially reinforced challenging behaviors during demand situations. In effect, the student who has a tantrum might do so not to escape instruction but, instead, to elicit attention. As revealed in research done in the 1990s, the association between antecedent conditions and challenging behaviors can be influenced by highly idiosyncratic sources of stimulus control (Carr, Yarbrough, & Langdon, 1997) and the complex interaction of EOs with discriminative stimuli (Horner, Day, & Day, 1997). Our educational and clinical efforts, therefore, likely will require and benefit from more molecular analyses of antecedent control functions. A better understanding of the controlling functions of distal EOs and biological setting events also should be integral to a complete technology of behavioral assessment (Carr & Smith, 1995).

Several investigators have suggested guidelines to improve and refine functional assessment and analysis procedures related to antecedent control. One recommendation is that when assessments are conducted, it is desirable to maintain the reinforcement contingency that is maintaining the challenging behavior so as not to confound controlling variables (Smith & Iwata, 1997). Keeping behavior-contingent consequences in place also is advisable when antecedent manipulations are made for the purpose of therapeutic control (Smith, Iwata, Goh, & Shore, 1995). Carr et al. (1997) proposed that detailed analyses of antecedent conditions should be considered when 1) there is a discrepancy between informant-generated information and data-based functional assessments, 2) different results are found for identical assessment methodologies that occur in different settings, or 3) results are disparate across days under the same assessment conditions. To reiterate a point made by several authors in this book, the direction of functional assessment and analysis procedures in the area of antecedent control clearly points to the emergence of a more sophisticated and comprehensive methodology. To this observation we would add the need to tailor these approaches to the practical constraints inherent within applied settings.

## TEACHING, INSTRUCTION, AND TRAINING

Several chapters in this book discuss antecedent control interventions for challenging behaviors encountered during academic instruction, skills training, and similar demand conditions. The objective in these cases is to reduce and perhaps eliminate behaviors that compete with learning, disrupt performance, and place others at risk. The overriding characteristic of intervention, then, is one of behavior reduction. Two essential points should be realized, however. First, many programs of skill acquisition can be used to decrease challenging behaviors by teaching alternative and compensatory responses. In effect, behavior difficulties are overcome when people learn how to perform more efficiently within their surroundings. Second, antecedent control approaches can contribute significantly to the composition of skill building and instructional protocols. That is, outside the role of antecedent-based techniques for the purpose of behavior reduction, antecedent control approaches are useful in improving both the manner in which teaching and training activities are implemented and the responsiveness of learners.

Providing instruction within the context of preferred routines is one way to enhance motivation and learning. Thus, many children with developmental disabilities may be more responsive to instruction when it is delivered during activities that feature active movement and sensorimotor tasks versus sedentary, discrete trial conditions. Poor performance in response to novel task presentation can be overcome by embedding familiar and mastered tasks within the curriculum. In addition, identifying an individual's stimulus preferences and learning style can improve the methods and outcome of instruction. As an illustration, an adult with mental retardation who exhibits a poor response to daily living skills training but appears to enjoy movement activities and vibration might perform more favorably if he were taught a domestic skill such as using an electric vacuum cleaner. The pleasurable stimulation from gross-motor activity and vibration are contained within the training task.

## TECHNOLOGICAL DISSEMINATION

In a critical appraisal of consequence-based interventions for challenging behaviors, Luiselli (1995) posited that the apparent reliance on such methods is based, for many reasons, on the fact that practitioners frequently are not aware of alternative strategies. Antecedent control assessment and behavioral support methodologies represent approaches that have not reached applied settings with sufficient regularity. One limiting factor is that college and university coursework in applied behavior analysis and behavioral psychology has de-emphasized theoretical, conceptual, and clinical discussions of antecedent control. The outcome is that many educators, psychologists, and service providers are poorly informed about the full array of available procedures. Notwithstanding the increased numbers of publications on antecedent control that have appeared since the early 1990s, professionals who provide consultation and clinical decision making in public schools, residential care facilities, vocational training sites, and other community settings have had very few archival references to guide their work, suggest options, and serve as a source of continuing education.

The dissemination of antecedent control procedures to service settings, combined with relevant staff training, is a priority for behavioral clinicians and others responsible for education and habilitation programming. For many practitioners, the rationale for and implementation of antecedent control interventions are immediately appealing and reflect common-sense thinking about how to induce behavior change and enhance the therapeutic effects of other procedures. Making alterations in physical environments, activity schedules, and the presence or absence of certain triggering stimuli, in particular, are seen intuitively as useful approaches. Therefore, providing hands-on demonstrations of antecedent control techniques, giving staff interesting case studies that describe successful applications (e.g., reprints of publications), and conducting seminars on the topic should be encouraged as a component of personnel training in human services organizations.

## SUMMARY

Refining assessment methodologies, conducting detailed functional analyses, discovering additional ways to manipulate EOs, addressing skill acquisition programming, and increasing comprehensive dissemination efforts are just some of the topics worthy of attention as antecedent control approaches to behavioral support continue to expand and evolve. In addition to highlighting these areas, this concluding chapter also has considered some of the influences that have shaped contemporary thinking about antecedent control and that certainly will guide future directions. There are many impressive findings and possibilities that have emerged from applied research on antecedent control, and, more than ever, these inquiries are being linked to basic learning principles. Such integration will help to clarify the theoretical and conceptual foundations of antecedent control, define a richer technology of behavioral support, and lead to truly innovative ways to enhance the lives of people with developmental disabilities.

# REFERENCES

Carr, E.G., & Smith, C.E. (1995). Biological setting events for self-injury. *Mental Retardation and Developmental Disabilities Research Reviews, 1,* 94–98.

Carr, E.G., Yarbrough, S.C., & Langdon, N.A. (1997). Effects of idiosyncratic stimulus variables on functional analysis outcomes. *Journal of Applied Behavior Analysis, 30,* 673–686.

Foxx, R.M. (1996). Twenty years of applied behavior analysis in treating the most severe problem behavior: Lessons learned. *Behavior Analyst, 19,* 225–235.

Horner, R.H., Day, M.H., & Day, J.R. (1997). Using neutralizing routines to reduce problem behaviors. *Journal of Applied Behavior Analysis, 30,* 601–614.

Horner, R.H., Dunlap, G., Koegel, R.L., Carr, E.G., Sailor, W., Anderson, J., Albin, R.W., & O'Neill, R.E. (1990). Toward a technology of "nonaversive" behavioral support. *Journal of The Association for Persons with Severe Handicaps, 15,* 125–132.

Koegel, L.K., Koegel, R.L., & Dunlap, G. (1996). (Eds.). *Positive behavioral support: Including people with difficult behavior in the community.* Baltimore: Paul H. Brookes Publishing Co.

Luiselli, J.K. (1995). A critical appraisal of consequence control treatments in applied behavior analysis. *The Habilitative Mental Healthcare Newsletter, 14,* 106–110.

Mace, F.C., & Wacker, D.P. (1994). Toward greater integration of basic and applied behavioral research: An introduction. *Journal of Applied Behavior Analysis, 27,* 569–574.

Michael, J. (1982). Distinguishing between the discriminative and motivational functions of stimuli. *Journal of the Experimental Analysis of Behavior, 37,* 149–155.

Michael, J. (1988). Establishing operations and the mand. *Analysis of Verbal Behavior, 6,* 3–9.

Michael, J. (1993). Establishing operations. *Behavior Analyst, 16,* 191–206.

Mount, B. (1992). *Person-centered planning: Finding directions for change using personal futures planning.* New York: Graphic Futures, Inc.

Repp, A.C., & Singh, N.N. (1990). (Eds.). *Perspectives on the use of nonaversive and aversive interventions for persons with developmental disabilities.* Sycamore, IL: Sycamore.

Smith, R.G., & Iwata, B.A. (1997). Antecedent influences on behavior disorders. *Journal of Applied Behavior Analysis, 30,* 343–375.

Smith, R.G., Iwata, B.A., Goh, H.L., & Shore, B.A. (1995). Analysis of establishing operations for self-injury maintained by escape. *Journal of Applied Behavior Analysis, 28,* 433–445.

Van Houten, R., Axelrod, S., Bailey, J.S., Favell, J.E., Foxx, R.M., Iwata, B.A., & Lovaas, O.I. (1988). The right to effective behavioral treatment. *Journal of Applied Behavior Analysis, 21,* 381–384.

# ~ *Subject Index* ~

Page numbers followed by *t* or *f* indicate tables or figures, respectively.

381

Quality of life
  change, indicators of, 279
  choice making and, 187–188
  lifeway influences and, 276, 279
  molar intervention and, 7, 19–20
  psychopharmacology and, 142, 144
  supported routines and, 267–268
Question asking, antecedent, 175–176
Questionnaires, 51–53

Race/ethnicity, and drug response, 147–148, 159
Rate enhancement, 254
Rate of reinforcement, 337–338
Rating scales, 51–53
  reliability and validity, 55
Real-time analysis, 128, 129f
Receptor mechanism, 147
Reciprocal interactions, 156
Recycling, in assessment, 133, 133t
Reflexivity, 360
Reinforcement
  altering effectiveness of, 42
  antecedents and, 69f, 69–71
  automatic, 53
  of challenging behavior, 198
    classes of, 53
    contingencies of, 48–50
  choice making and, 193
    personal selection strategies, 196–197
  conjugate, 255
  in contingency-shaped behavior, 311–315
  in correspondence training, 224, 226–237
  differential, 75, 247, 355, 364
  dimensions of, 80–81, 311–313, 319–320, 337–338
  establishing operations (EOs) and, 33–34, 331–339, 332f–333f, 342–343, 374–375
  during experimental analysis, 71f, 71–73, 97, 110f
  in functional equivalence training, 248
  immediacy of, 311–313
  in language intervention
    natural and direct, 172–173

  reinforcing attempts, 170–171
  needs as, 13–14
  negative, 49–50, 248, 291
    establishing operations (EOs) and, 331–332, 334, 336, 338–339, 342–343
  noncontingent, 21, 40
  positive, 49–50, 248
    establishing operations (EOs) and, 331–332, 332f, 334–336, 338–339
    limitations and restrictions, 31–32
  responses and, 67–69, 311–313, 325–326
  in rule-governed behavior, 319–320, 324
  schedule of, 337–338
    in contingency-shaped behavior, 311–313
    in supported routines, 266
    variable interval, 80
  and stimulus control, 355, 364–365
  in supported routines, 246–268
Reinforcement of Do-Report Correspondence, 224, 226–230, 236
Reinforcement of Report-Do Correspondence, 224, 230–231, 236–238
Reinforcement Set-up on Intermediate Behaviors, 224, 235–237
Reinforcement Set-up on Reports, 224, 231–233
Reinforcers, see Reinforcement
Relaxation techniques, 23, 127
Repeated measurement, 89, 102f
Replacement skills, 40
Replication, 60–61, 89–90
Report-Intermediate Behavior-Do, 225, 233
Reports, in correspondence training, 224–237
Reprimands, 15–16
Residential facilities, psychopharmacology in, 142–143
Responding, patterns of, 292–293, 300–304
Response allocation, 253–254

# ∼ *Author Index* ∼